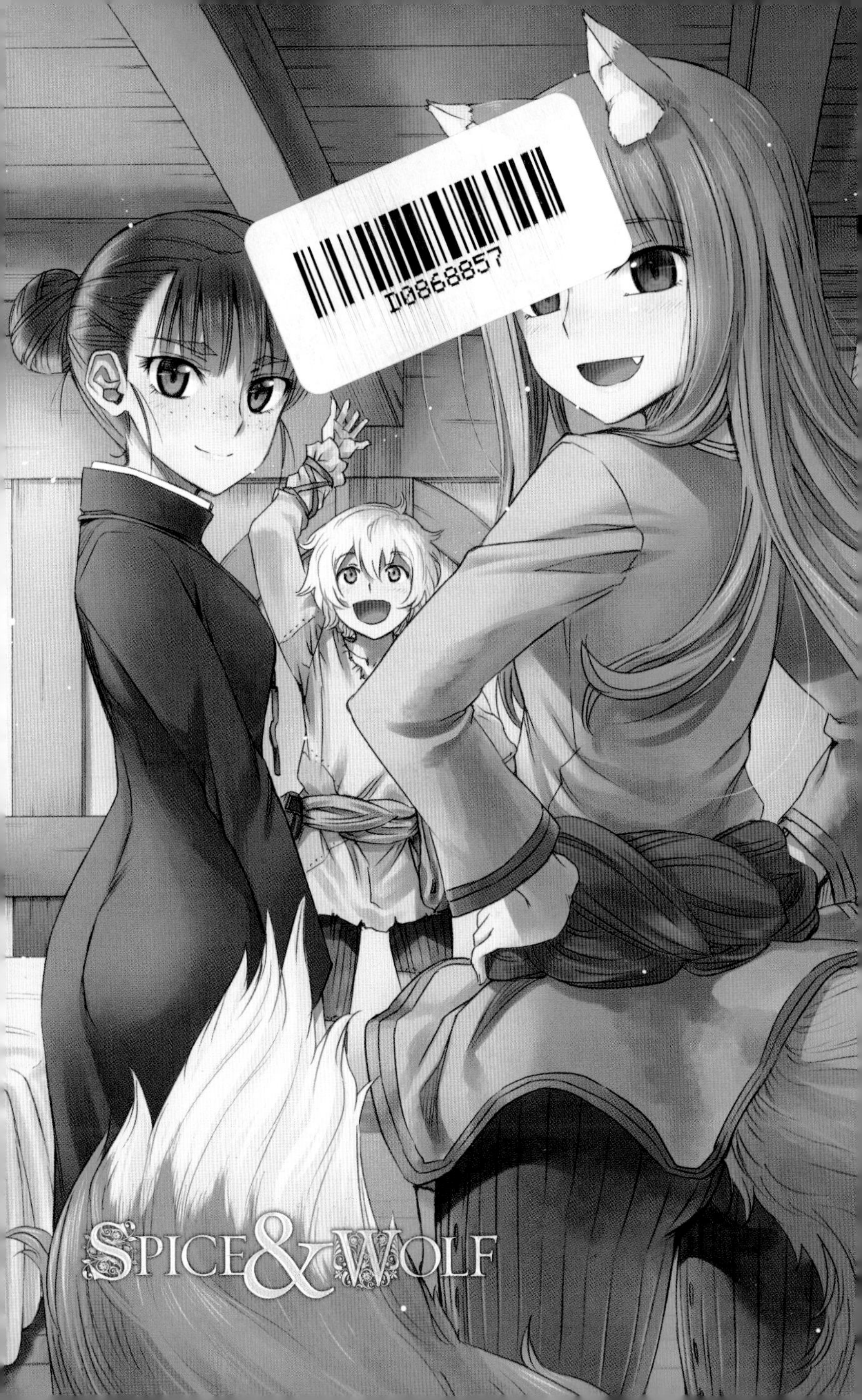
SPICE & WOLF

SPICE & WOLF
CONTENTS

Chapter 68 •••••••••••••••••••••• 3

Chapter 69 •••••••••••••••••••• 27

Chapter 70 ••••••••••••••••••••• 45

Chapter 71 •••••• ••••••••••••••• 71

Chapter 72 ••••••••••••••••••••• 93

Chapter 73 ••••••••••••••••••••• 123

Chapter 74 •••••••••••••••••••• 145

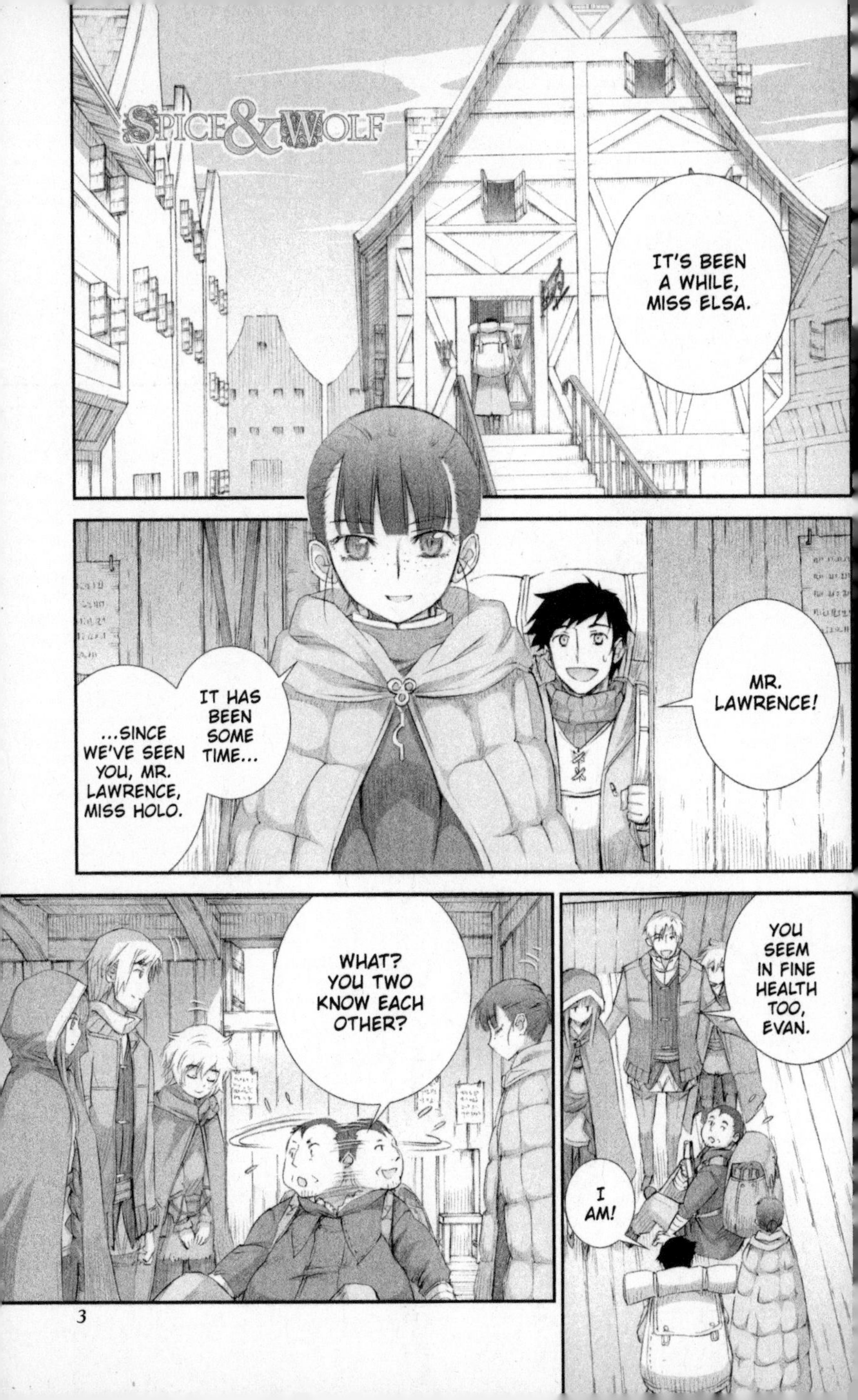
SPICE & WOLF
IT'S BEEN A WHILE, MISS ELSA.
MR. LAWRENCE!
IT HAS BEEN SOME TIME...
...SINCE WE'VE SEEN YOU, MR. LAWRENCE, MISS HOLO.
YOU SEEM IN FINE HEALTH TOO, EVAN.
I AM!
WHAT? YOU TWO KNOW EACH OTHER?

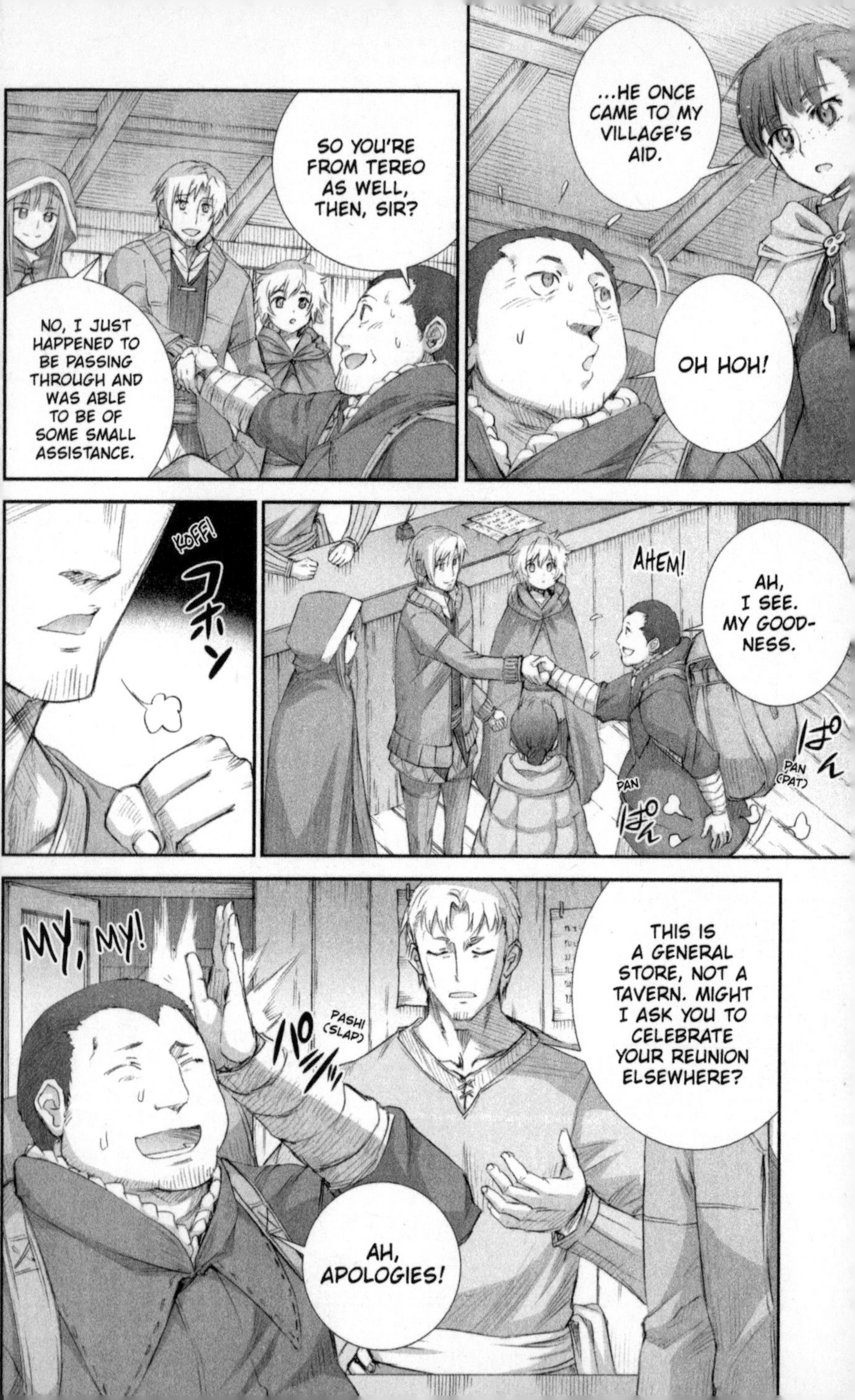
...HE ONCE CAME TO MY VILLAGE'S AID.
OH HOH!
SO YOU'RE FROM TEREO AS WELL, THEN, SIR?
NO, I JUST HAPPENED TO BE PASSING THROUGH AND WAS ABLE TO BE OF SOME SMALL ASSISTANCE.
AH, I SEE. MY GOOD-NESS.
AHEM!
ぱん
PAN (PAT)
ぱん
PAN
KOFF!
コホン
THIS IS A GENERAL STORE, NOT A TAVERN. MIGHT I ASK YOU TO CELEBRATE YOUR REUNION ELSEWHERE?
パ
PASHI (SLAP)
MY, MY!
AH, APOLOGIES!

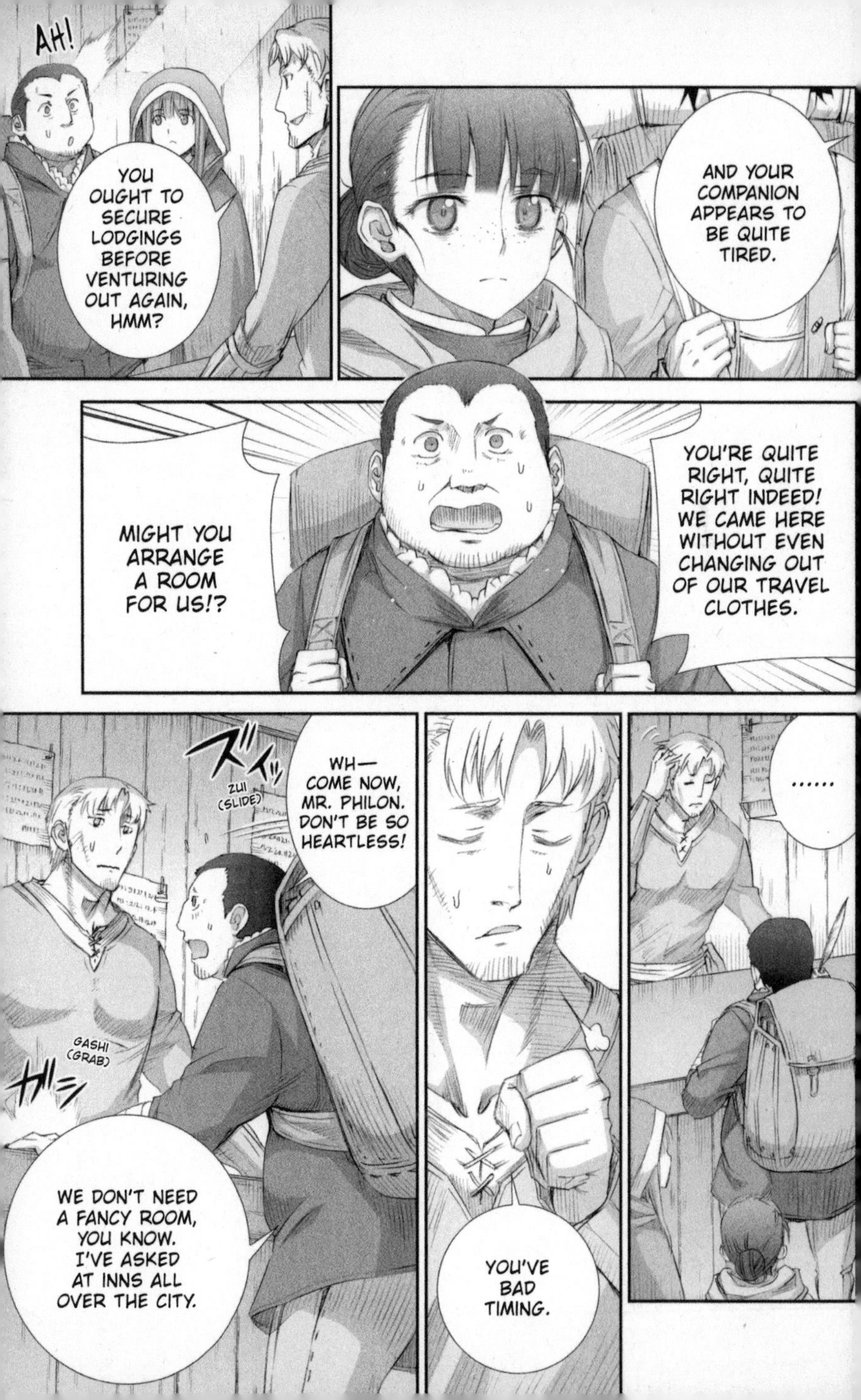
AND YOUR COMPANION APPEARS TO BE QUITE TIRED.
AH!
YOU OUGHT TO SECURE LODGINGS BEFORE VENTURING OUT AGAIN, HMM?
YOU'RE QUITE RIGHT, QUITE RIGHT INDEED! WE CAME HERE WITHOUT EVEN CHANGING OUT OF OUR TRAVEL CLOTHES.
MIGHT YOU ARRANGE A ROOM FOR US!?
......
YOU'VE BAD TIMING.
WH— COME NOW, MR. PHILON. DON'T BE SO HEARTLESS!
ZUI (SLIDE)
GASHI (GRAB)
WE DON'T NEED A FANCY ROOM, YOU KNOW. I'VE ASKED AT INNS ALL OVER THE CITY.

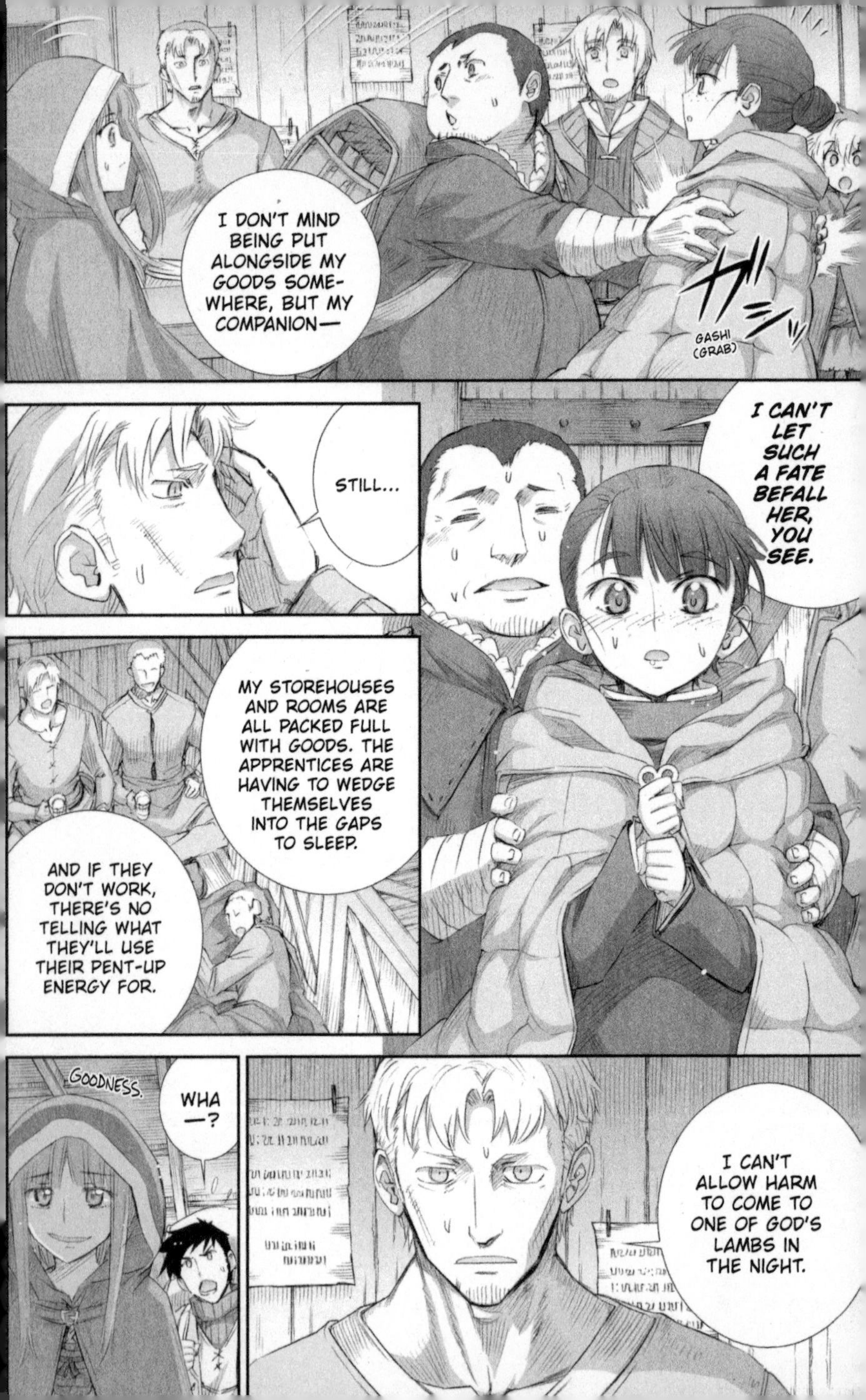
I DON'T MIND BEING PUT ALONGSIDE MY GOODS SOME-WHERE, BUT MY COMPANION—
GASHI (GRAB)
I CAN'T LET SUCH A FATE BEFALL HER, YOU SEE.
STILL...
MY STOREHOUSES AND ROOMS ARE ALL PACKED FULL WITH GOODS. THE APPRENTICES ARE HAVING TO WEDGE THEMSELVES INTO THE GAPS TO SLEEP.
AND IF THEY DON'T WORK, THERE'S NO TELLING WHAT THEY'LL USE THEIR PENT-UP ENERGY FOR.
I CAN'T ALLOW HARM TO COME TO ONE OF GOD'S LAMBS IN THE NIGHT.
GOODNESS.
WHA—?

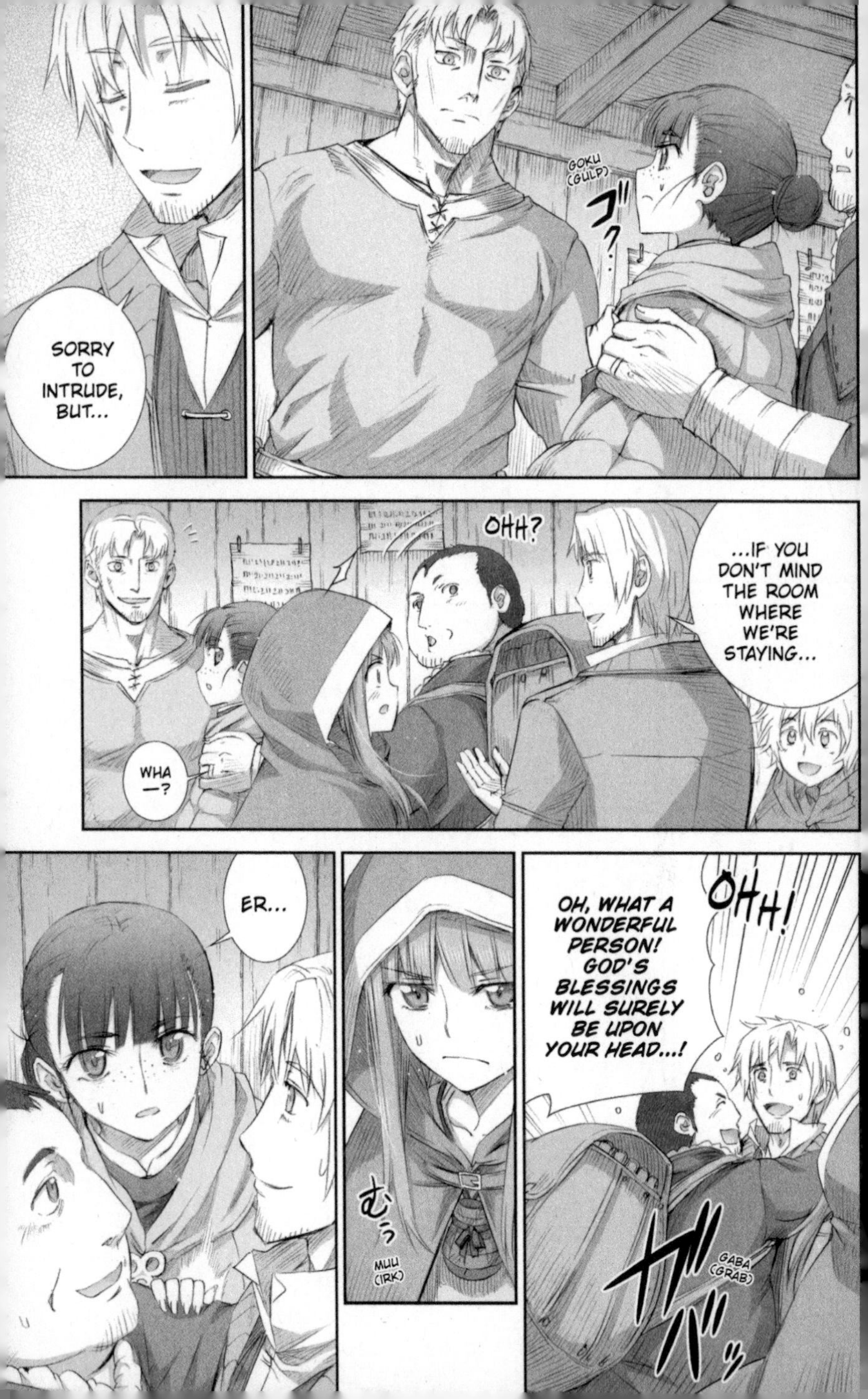
GOKU (GULP)
SORRY TO INTRUDE, BUT...
...IF YOU DON'T MIND THE ROOM WHERE WE'RE STAYING...
OHH?
WHA—?
OHH!
OH, WHAT A WONDERFUL PERSON! GOD'S BLESSINGS WILL SURELY BE UPON YOUR HEAD...!
GABA (GRAB)
MUU (IRK)
ER...

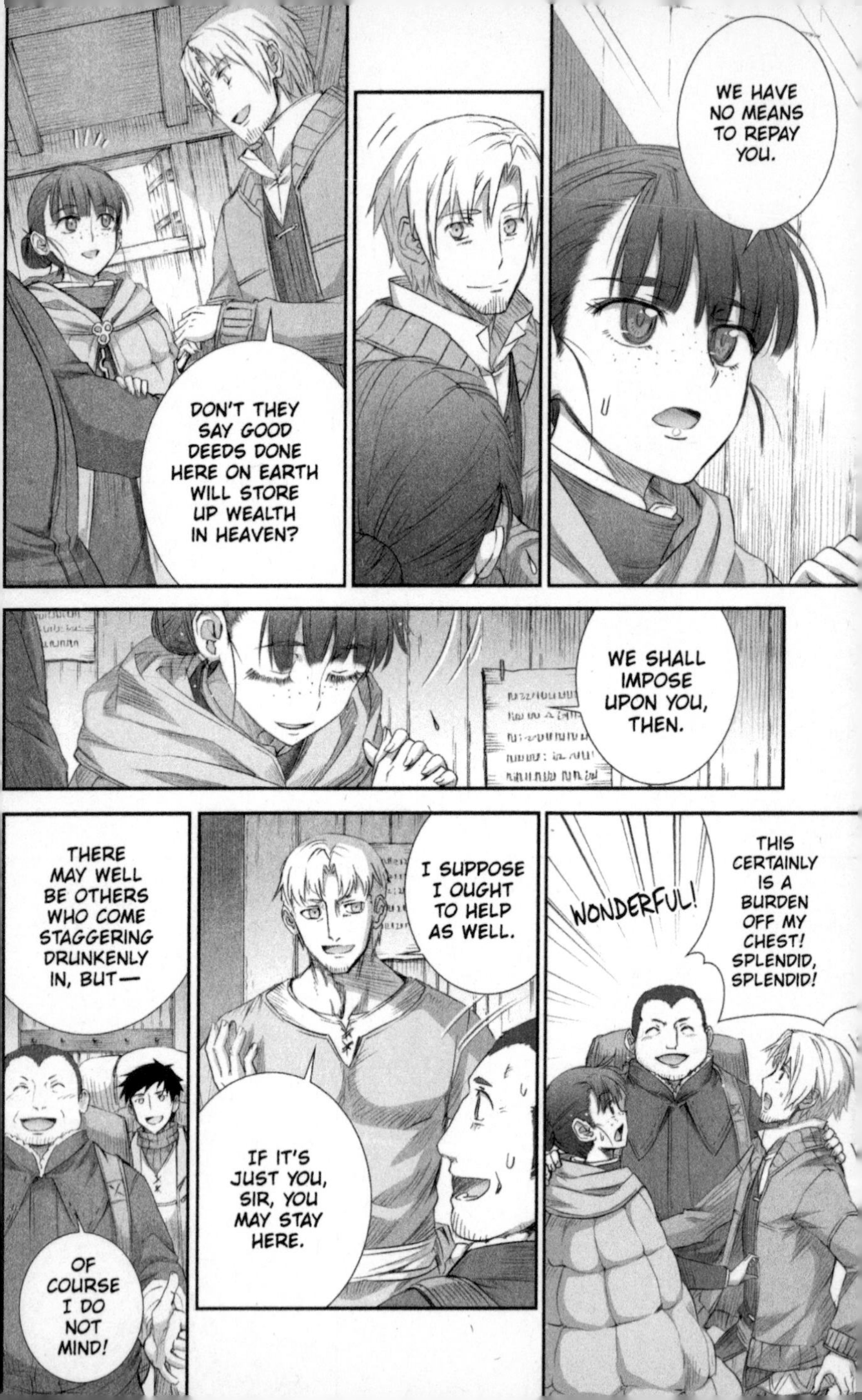
WE HAVE NO MEANS TO REPAY YOU.
DON'T THEY SAY GOOD DEEDS DONE HERE ON EARTH WILL STORE UP WEALTH IN HEAVEN?
WE SHALL IMPOSE UPON YOU, THEN.
THIS CERTAINLY IS A BURDEN OFF MY CHEST! SPLENDID, SPLENDID!
WONDERFUL!
I SUPPOSE I OUGHT TO HELP AS WELL.
IF IT'S JUST YOU, SIR, YOU MAY STAY HERE.
THERE MAY WELL BE OTHERS WHO COME STAGGERING DRUNKENLY IN, BUT—
OF COURSE I DO NOT MIND!

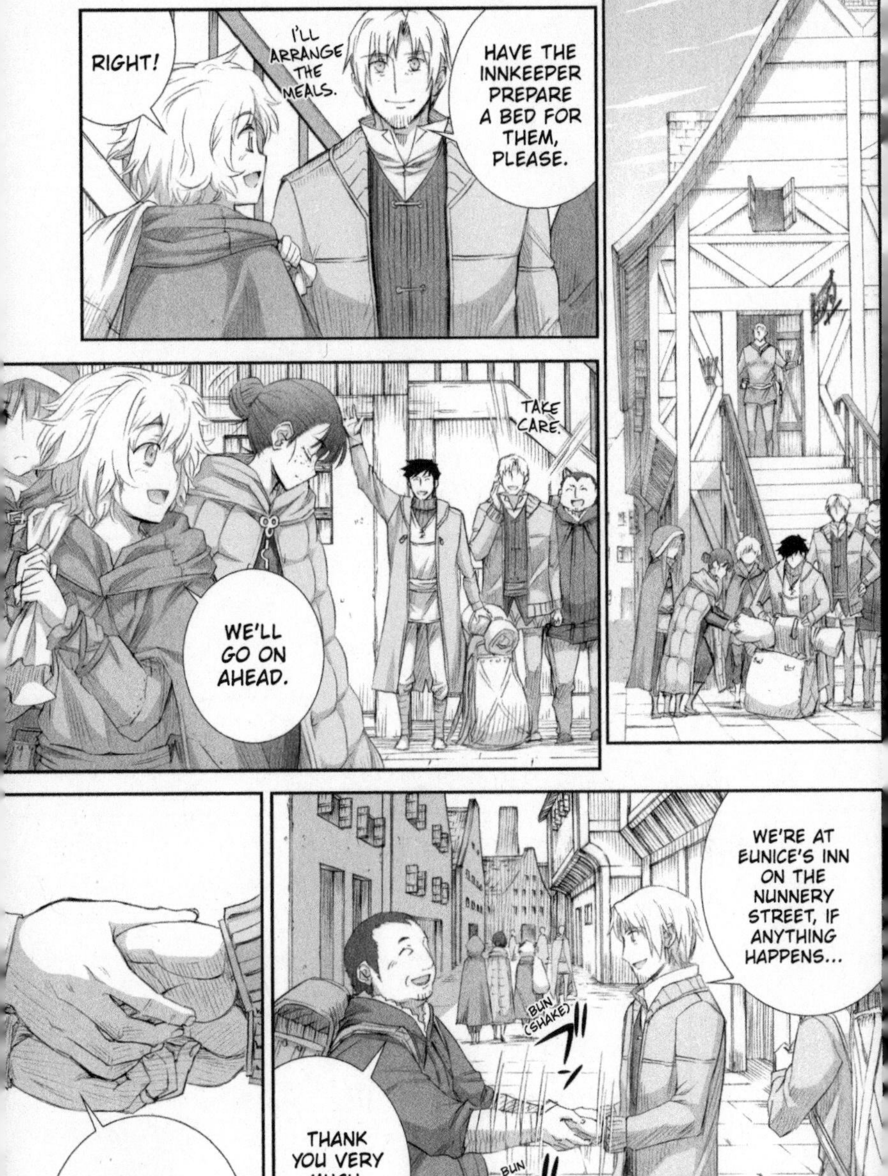
HAVE THE INNKEEPER PREPARE A BED FOR THEM, PLEASE.
I'LL ARRANGE THE MEALS.
RIGHT!
TAKE CARE.
WE'LL GO ON AHEAD.
WE'RE AT EUNICE'S INN ON THE NUNNERY STREET, IF ANYTHING HAPPENS...
BUN (SHAKE)
THANK YOU VERY MUCH.
BUN
OH, I'M BEING RUDE TO MY SAVIOR—

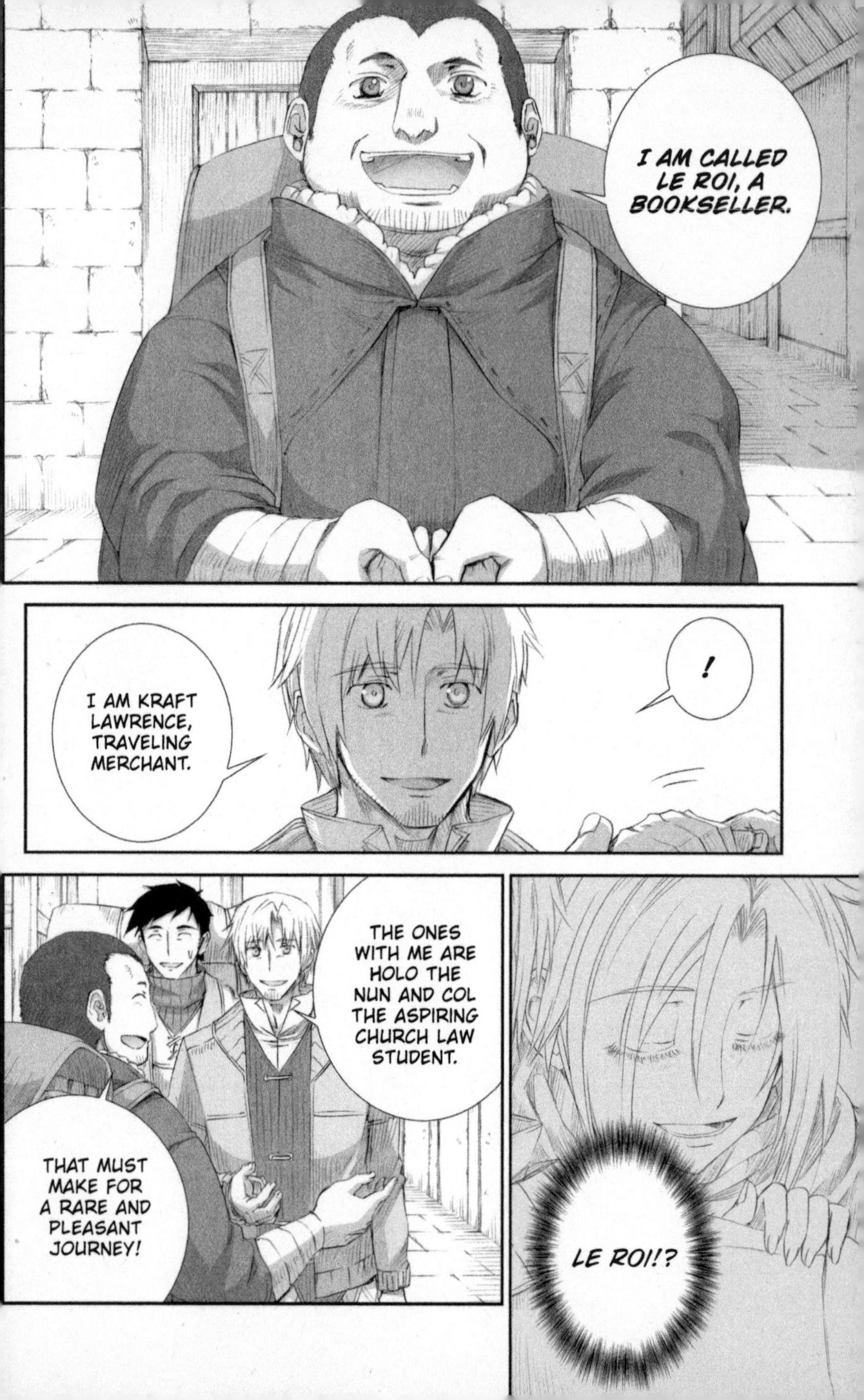
I AM CALLED LE ROI, A BOOKSELLER.
!
I AM KRAFT LAWRENCE, TRAVELING MERCHANT.
LE ROI!?
THE ONES WITH ME ARE HOLO THE NUN AND COL THE ASPIRING CHURCH LAW STUDENT.
THAT MUST MAKE FOR A RARE AND PLEASANT JOURNEY!

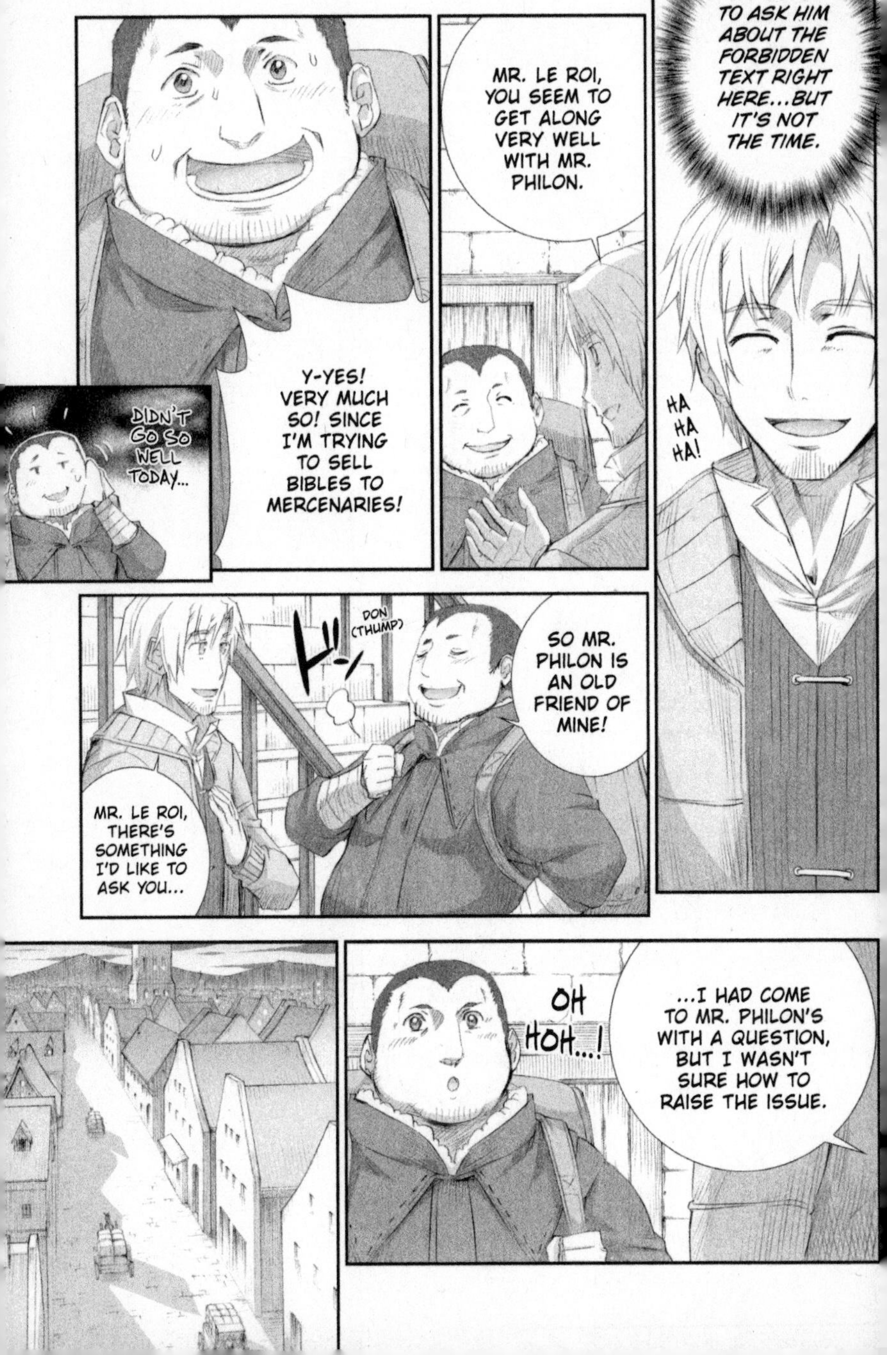
I'D LOVE TO ASK HIM ABOUT THE FORBIDDEN TEXT RIGHT HERE...BUT IT'S NOT THE TIME.
HA HA HA!
MR. LE ROI, YOU SEEM TO GET ALONG VERY WELL WITH MR. PHILON.
Y-YES! VERY MUCH SO! SINCE I'M TRYING TO SELL BIBLES TO MERCENARIES!
DIDN'T GO SO WELL TODAY...
SO MR. PHILON IS AN OLD FRIEND OF MINE!
DON (THUMP)
MR. LE ROI, THERE'S SOMETHING I'D LIKE TO ASK YOU...
...I HAD COME TO MR. PHILON'S WITH A QUESTION, BUT I WASN'T SURE HOW TO RAISE THE ISSUE.
OH HOH...!

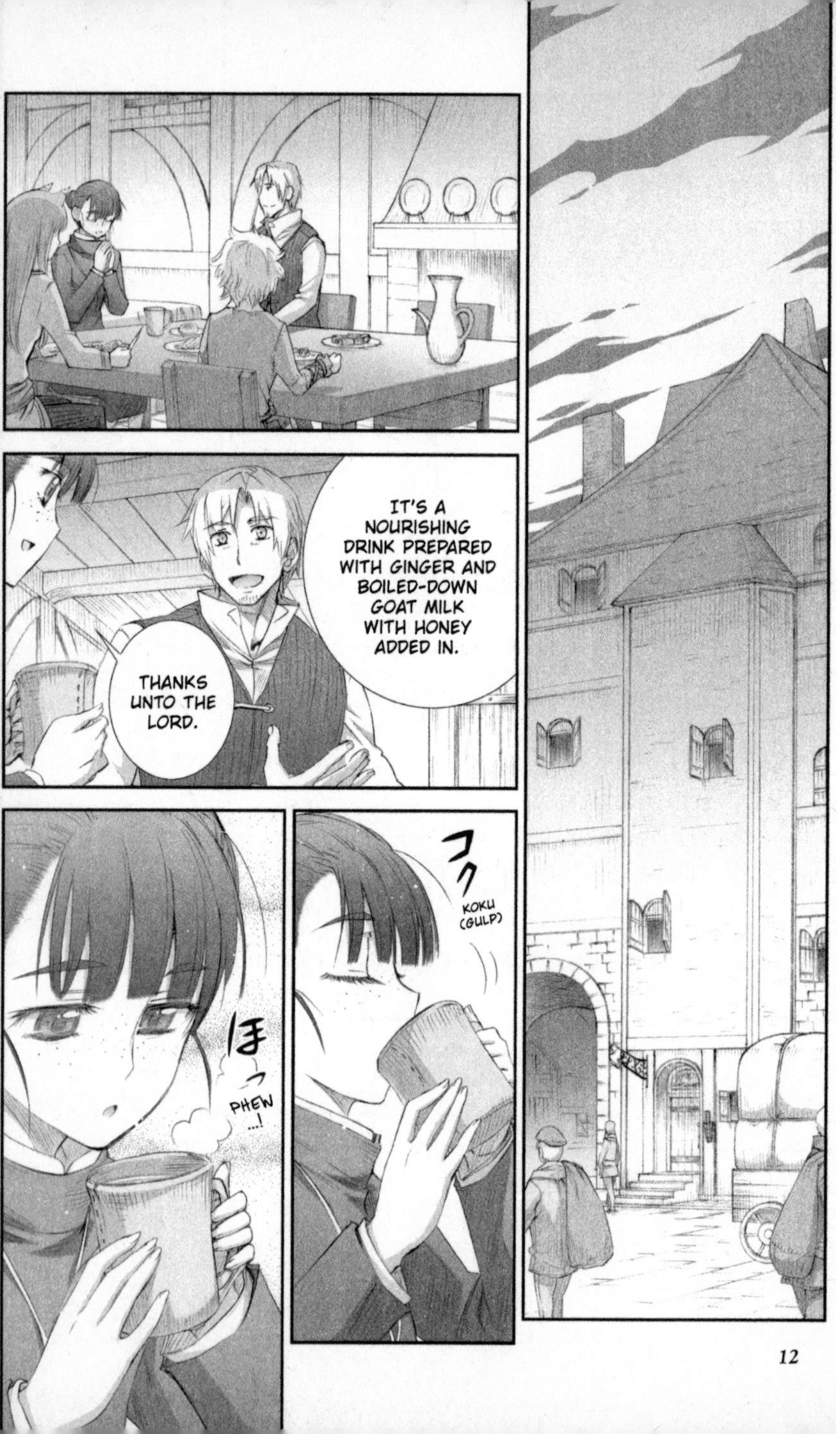
IT'S A NOURISHING DRINK PREPARED WITH GINGER AND BOILED-DOWN GOAT MILK WITH HONEY ADDED IN.
THANKS UNTO THE LORD.
コク
KOKU (GULP)
ほっ
PHEW ...!

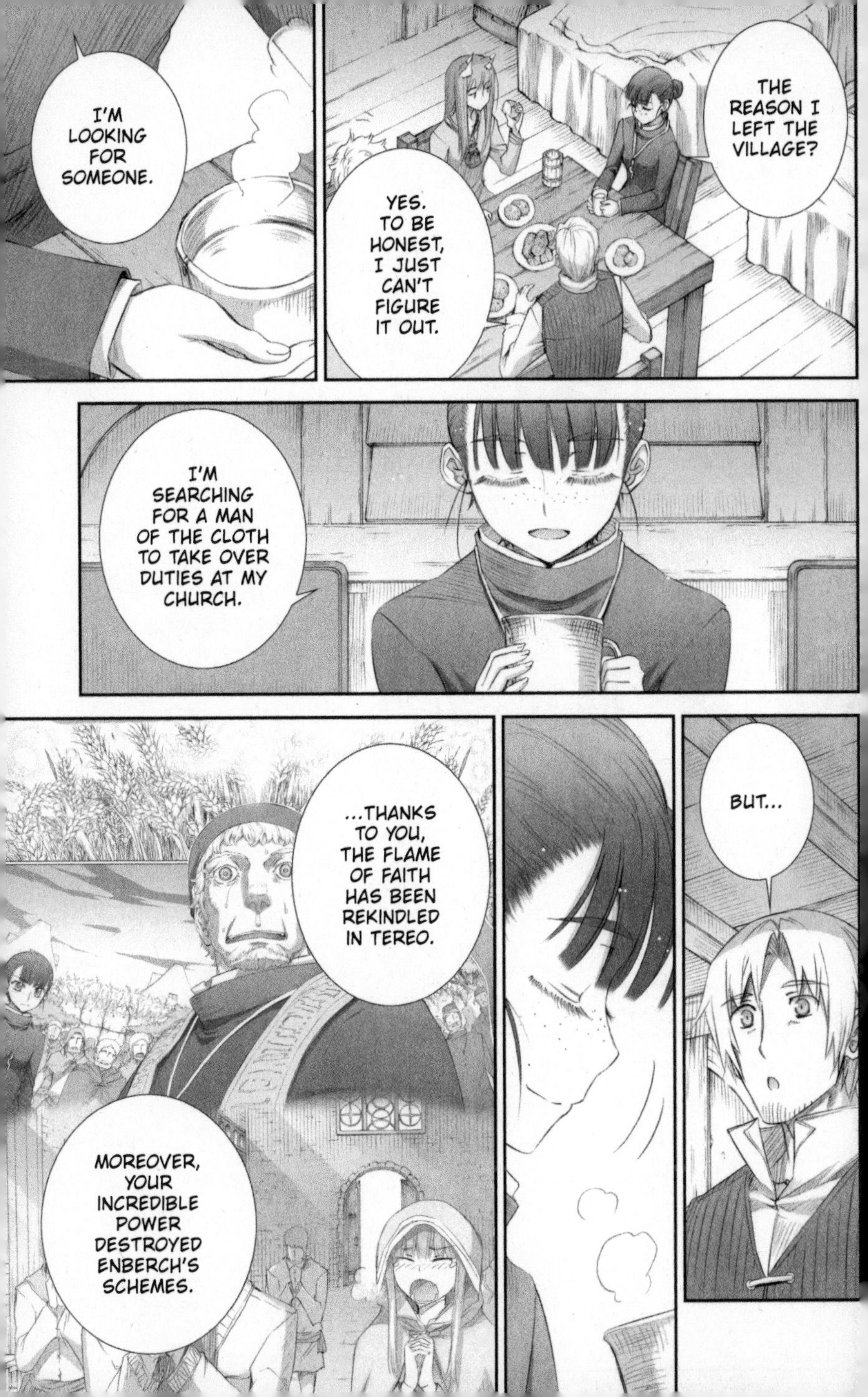
THE REASON I LEFT THE VILLAGE?
YES. TO BE HONEST, I JUST CAN'T FIGURE IT OUT.
I'M LOOKING FOR SOMEONE.
I'M SEARCHING FOR A MAN OF THE CLOTH TO TAKE OVER DUTIES AT MY CHURCH.
BUT...
...THANKS TO YOU, THE FLAME OF FAITH HAS BEEN REKINDLED IN TEREO.
MOREOVER, YOUR INCREDIBLE POWER DESTROYED ENBERCH'S SCHEMES.

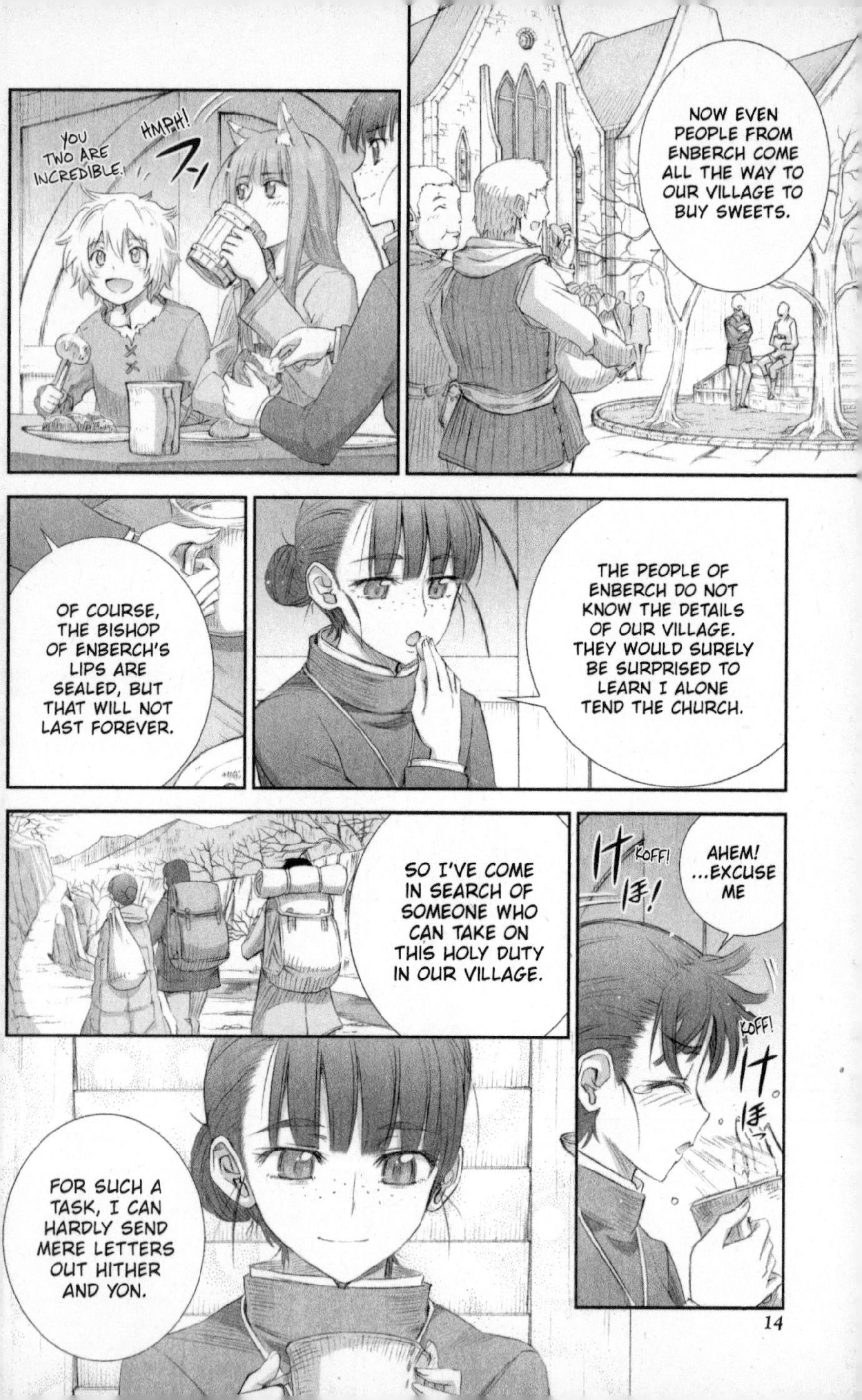
NOW EVEN PEOPLE FROM ENBERCH COME ALL THE WAY TO OUR VILLAGE TO BUY SWEETS.
HMPH!
YOU TWO ARE INCREDIBLE.
THE PEOPLE OF ENBERCH DO NOT KNOW THE DETAILS OF OUR VILLAGE. THEY WOULD SURELY BE SURPRISED TO LEARN I ALONE TEND THE CHURCH.
OF COURSE, THE BISHOP OF ENBERCH'S LIPS ARE SEALED, BUT THAT WILL NOT LAST FOREVER.
AHEM! ...EXCUSE ME
けほ!
KOFF!
KOFF!
けほっ
SO I'VE COME IN SEARCH OF SOMEONE WHO CAN TAKE ON THIS HOLY DUTY IN OUR VILLAGE.
FOR SUCH A TASK, I CAN HARDLY SEND MERE LETTERS OUT HITHER AND YON.

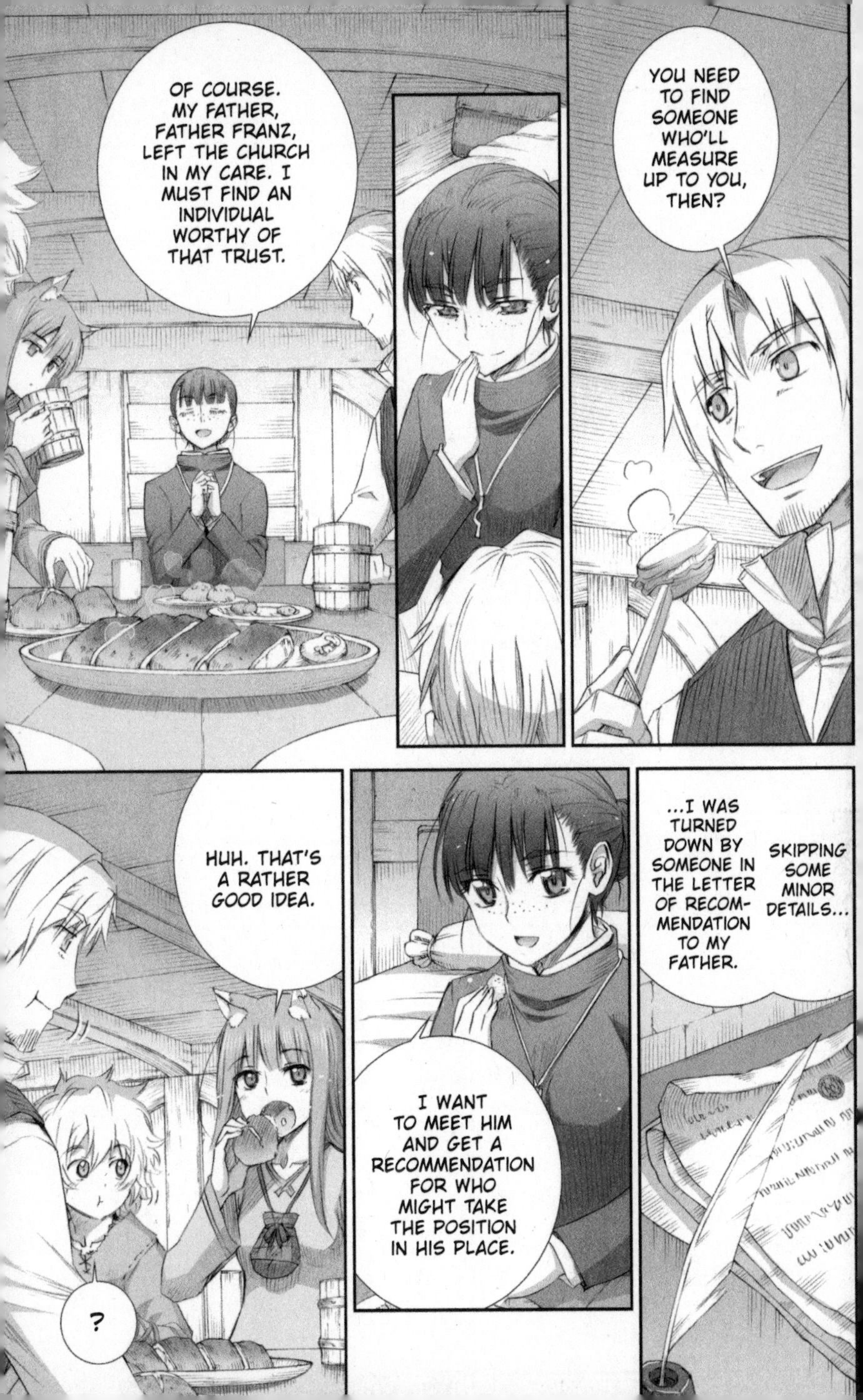
YOU NEED TO FIND SOMEONE WHO'LL MEASURE UP TO YOU, THEN?
OF COURSE. MY FATHER, FATHER FRANZ, LEFT THE CHURCH IN MY CARE. I MUST FIND AN INDIVIDUAL WORTHY OF THAT TRUST.
SKIPPING SOME MINOR DETAILS...
...I WAS TURNED DOWN BY SOMEONE IN THE LETTER OF RECOM-MENDATION TO MY FATHER.
I WANT TO MEET HIM AND GET A RECOMMENDATION FOR WHO MIGHT TAKE THE POSITION IN HIS PLACE.
HUH. THAT'S A RATHER GOOD IDEA.
?

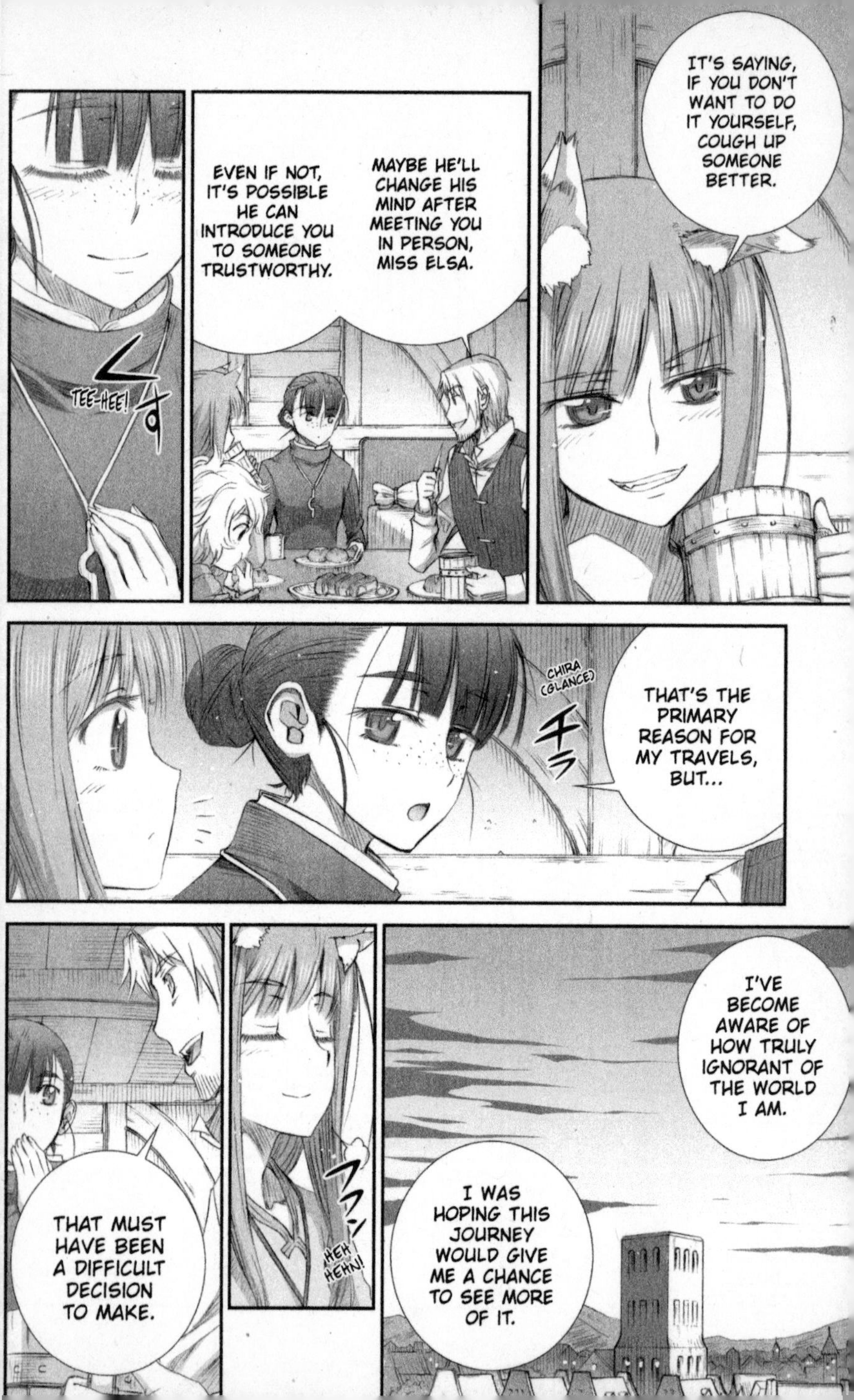
IT'S SAYING, IF YOU DON'T WANT TO DO IT YOURSELF, COUGH UP SOMEONE BETTER.
MAYBE HE'LL CHANGE HIS MIND AFTER MEETING YOU IN PERSON, MISS ELSA.
EVEN IF NOT, IT'S POSSIBLE HE CAN INTRODUCE YOU TO SOMEONE TRUSTWORTHY.
くす
TEE-HEE!
チラ
CHIRA (GLANCE)
THAT'S THE PRIMARY REASON FOR MY TRAVELS, BUT...
I'VE BECOME AWARE OF HOW TRULY IGNORANT OF THE WORLD I AM.
I WAS HOPING THIS JOURNEY WOULD GIVE ME A CHANCE TO SEE MORE OF IT.
フフン
HEH HEHN!
THAT MUST HAVE BEEN A DIFFICULT DECISION TO MAKE.

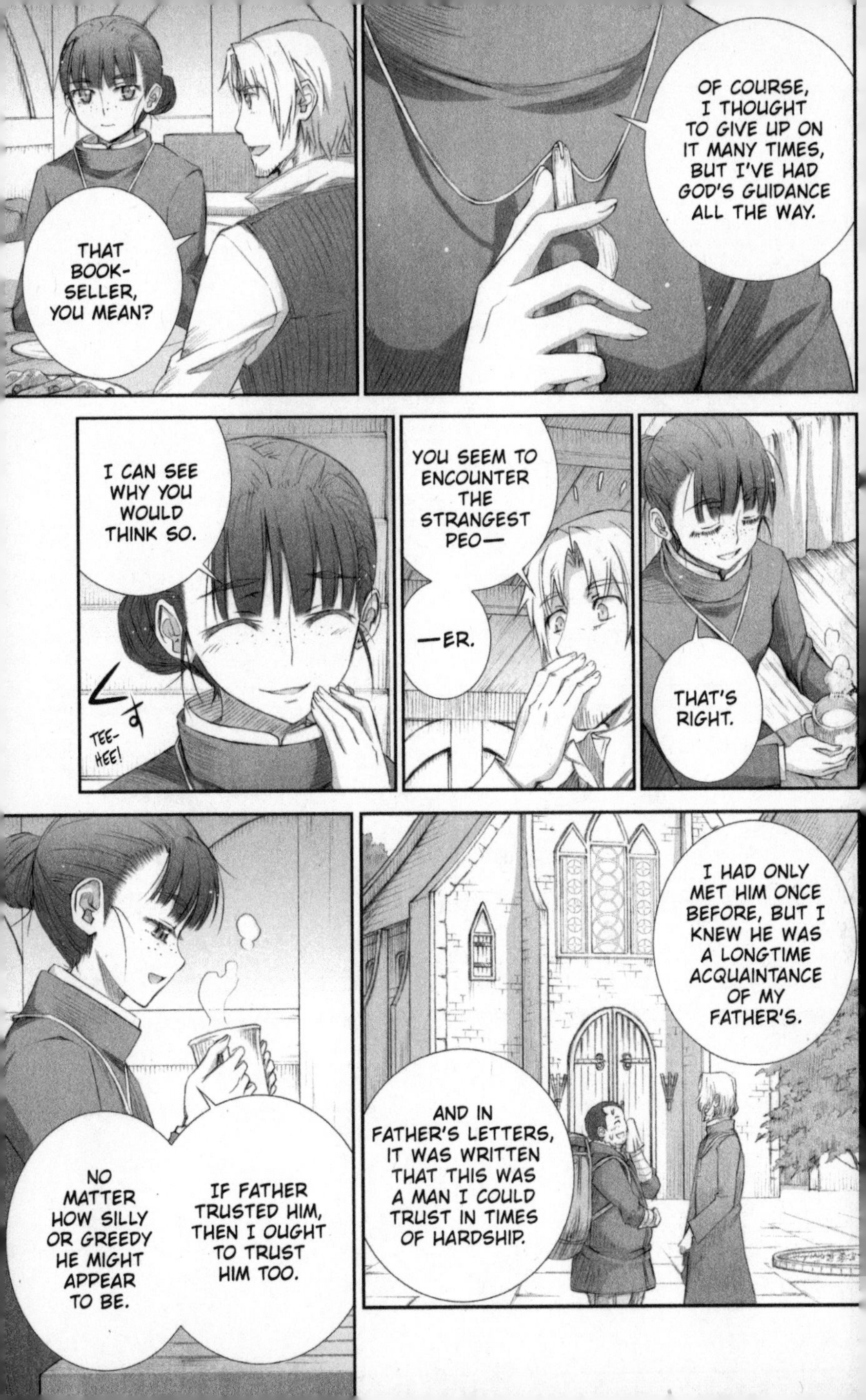
OF COURSE, I THOUGHT TO GIVE UP ON IT MANY TIMES, BUT I'VE HAD GOD'S GUIDANCE ALL THE WAY.
THAT BOOK-SELLER, YOU MEAN?
THAT'S RIGHT.
YOU SEEM TO ENCOUNTER THE STRANGEST PEO—
—ER.
I CAN SEE WHY YOU WOULD THINK SO.
くす
TEE-HEE!
I HAD ONLY MET HIM ONCE BEFORE, BUT I KNEW HE WAS A LONGTIME ACQUAINTANCE OF MY FATHER'S.
AND IN FATHER'S LETTERS, IT WAS WRITTEN THAT THIS WAS A MAN I COULD TRUST IN TIMES OF HARDSHIP.
IF FATHER TRUSTED HIM, THEN I OUGHT TO TRUST HIM TOO.
NO MATTER HOW SILLY OR GREEDY HE MIGHT APPEAR TO BE.

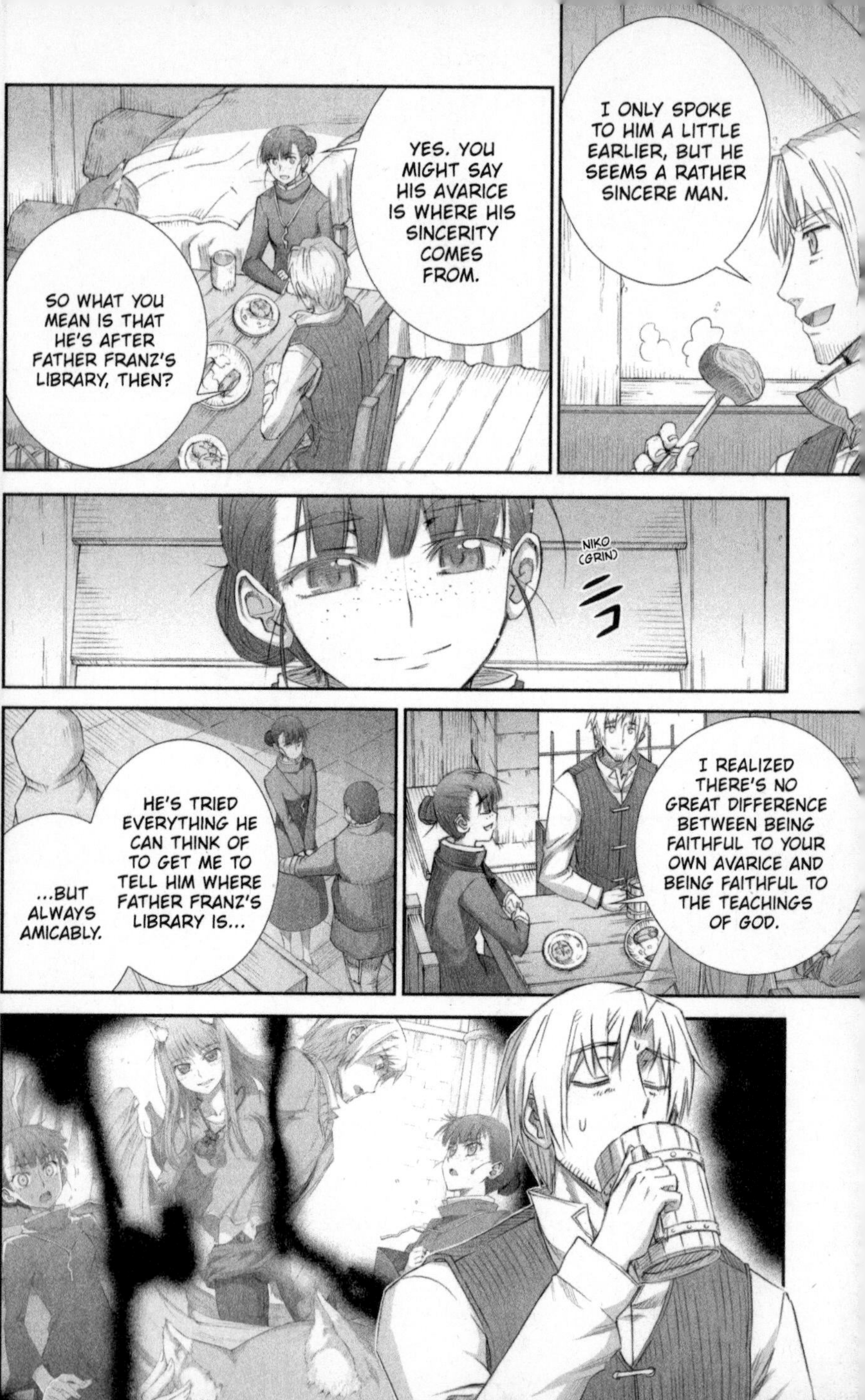

I ONLY SPOKE TO HIM A LITTLE EARLIER, BUT HE SEEMS A RATHER SINCERE MAN.
YES. YOU MIGHT SAY HIS AVARICE IS WHERE HIS SINCERITY COMES FROM.
SO WHAT YOU MEAN IS THAT HE'S AFTER FATHER FRANZ'S LIBRARY, THEN?
NIKO (GRIN)
I REALIZED THERE'S NO GREAT DIFFERENCE BETWEEN BEING FAITHFUL TO YOUR OWN AVARICE AND BEING FAITHFUL TO THE TEACHINGS OF GOD.
HE'S TRIED EVERYTHING HE CAN THINK OF TO GET ME TO TELL HIM WHERE FATHER FRANZ'S LIBRARY IS...
...BUT ALWAYS AMICABLY.

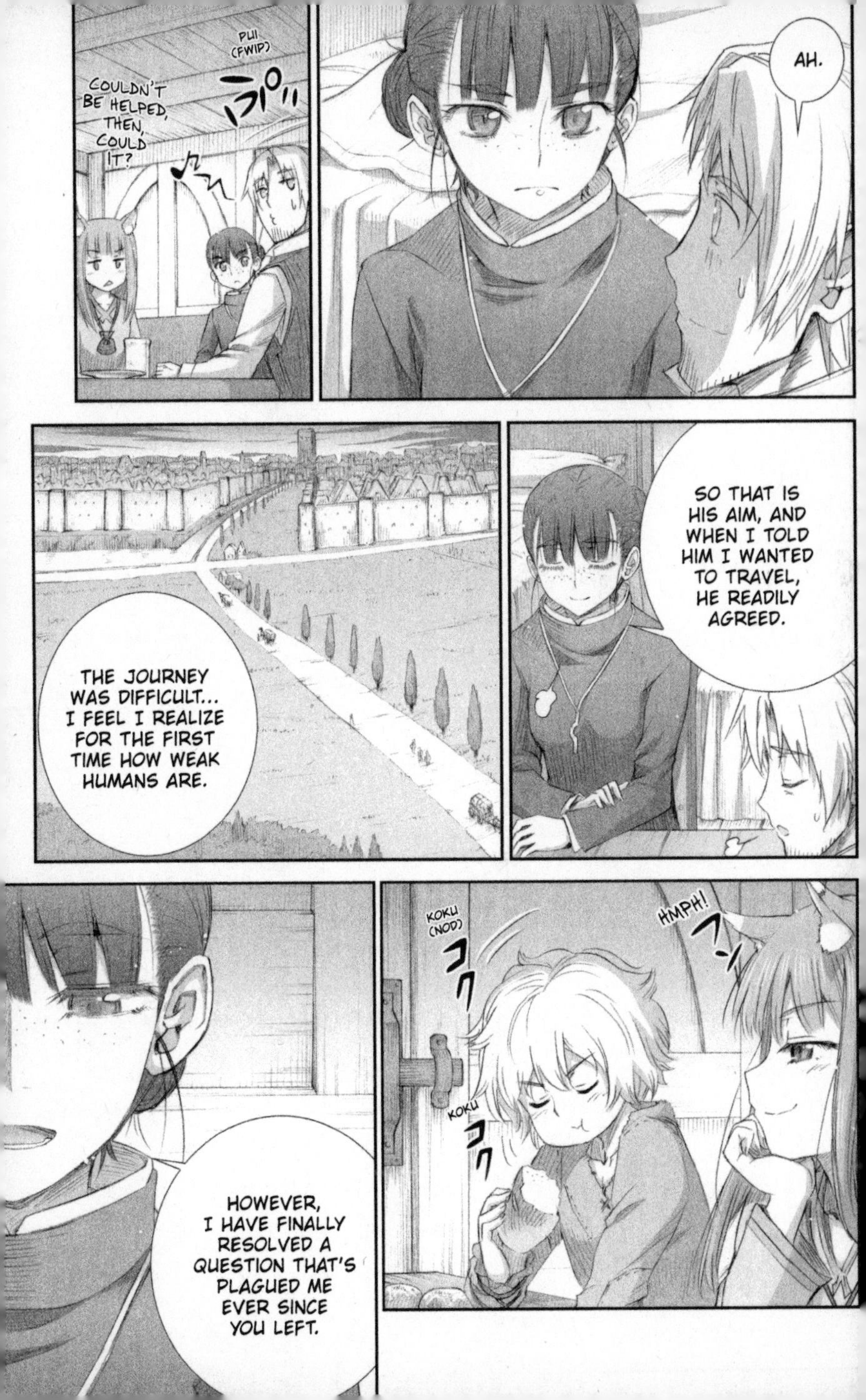
AH.
PUI (FWIP)
COULDN'T BE HELPED, THEN, COULD IT?
SO THAT IS HIS AIM, AND WHEN I TOLD HIM I WANTED TO TRAVEL, HE READILY AGREED.
THE JOURNEY WAS DIFFICULT... I FEEL I REALIZE FOR THE FIRST TIME HOW WEAK HUMANS ARE.
HMPH!
KOKU (NOD)
KOKU
HOWEVER, I HAVE FINALLY RESOLVED A QUESTION THAT'S PLAGUED ME EVER SINCE YOU LEFT.

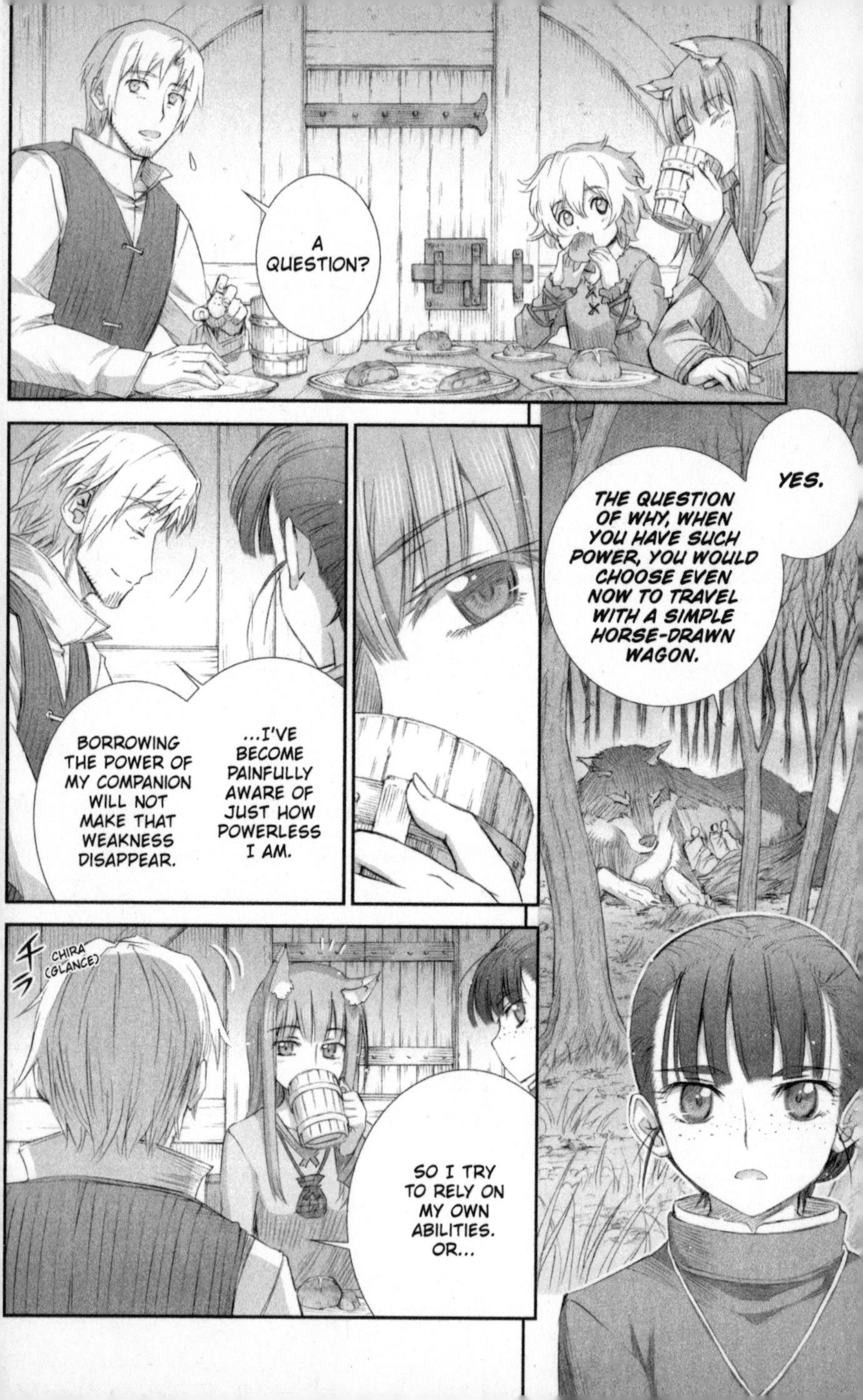
A QUESTION?
YES.
THE QUESTION OF WHY, WHEN YOU HAVE SUCH POWER, YOU WOULD CHOOSE EVEN NOW TO TRAVEL WITH A SIMPLE HORSE-DRAWN WAGON.
...I'VE BECOME PAINFULLY AWARE OF JUST HOW POWERLESS I AM.
BORROWING THE POWER OF MY COMPANION WILL NOT MAKE THAT WEAKNESS DISAPPEAR.
チラ
CHIRA (GLANCE)
SO I TRY TO RELY ON MY OWN ABILITIES. OR...

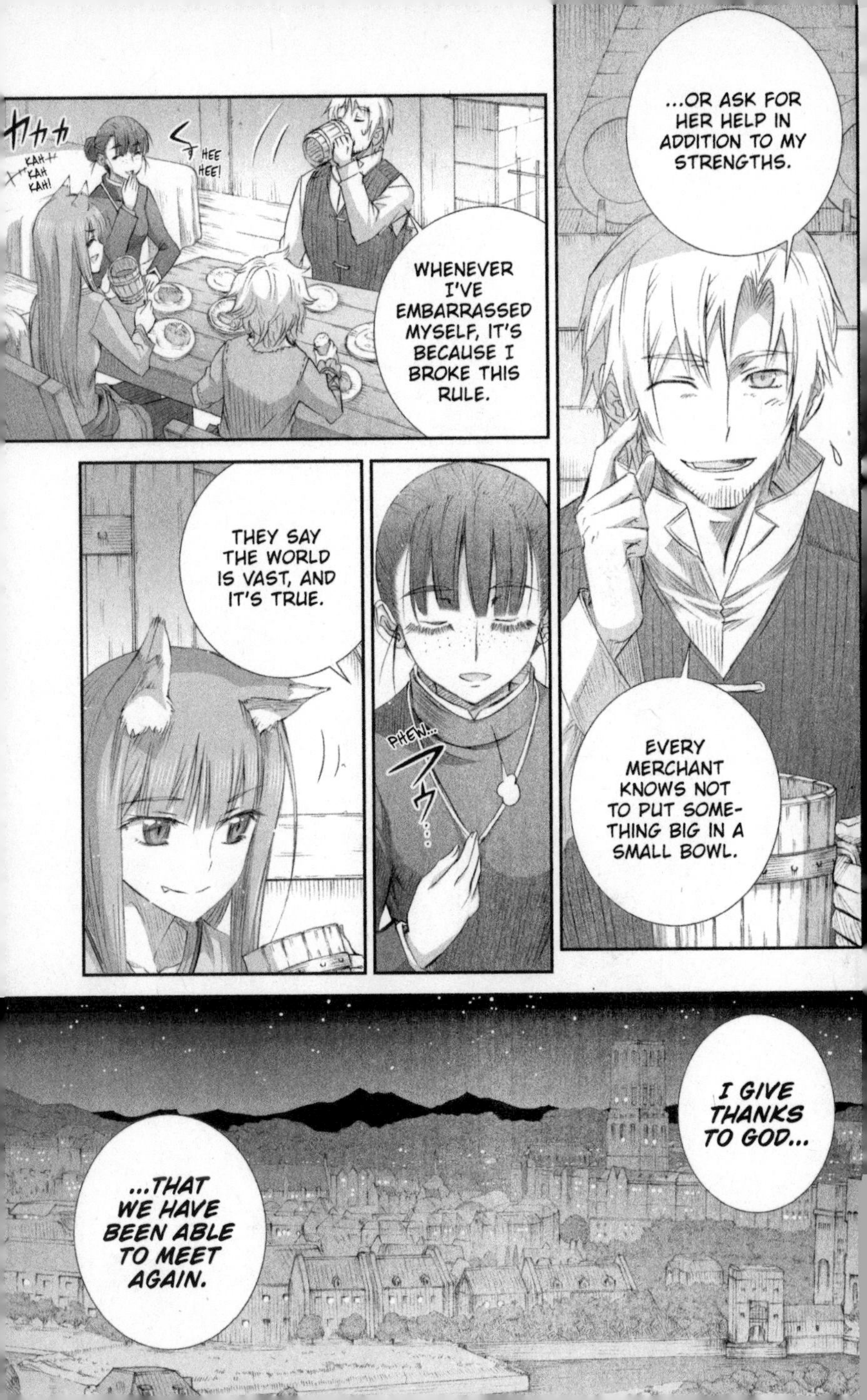
...OR ASK FOR HER HELP IN ADDITION TO MY STRENGTHS.
EVERY MERCHANT KNOWS NOT TO PUT SOME-THING BIG IN A SMALL BOWL.
HEE HEE!
KAH KAH KAH!
WHENEVER I'VE EMBARRASSED MYSELF, IT'S BECAUSE I BROKE THIS RULE.
PHEW...
THEY SAY THE WORLD IS VAST, AND IT'S TRUE.
I GIVE THANKS TO GOD...
...THAT WE HAVE BEEN ABLE TO MEET AGAIN.

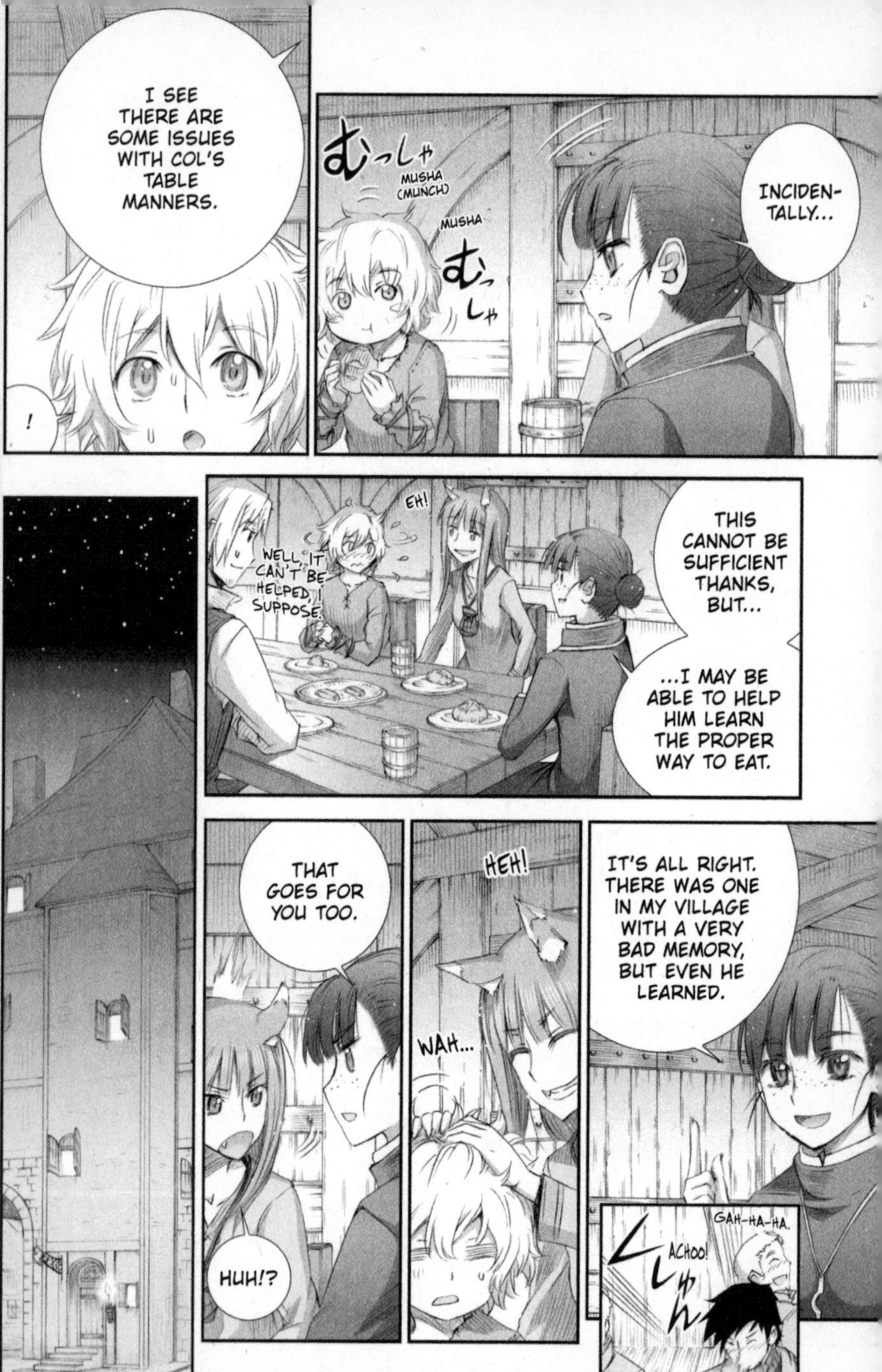
INCIDEN-TALLY...
むっしゃ
MUSHA (MUNCH)
MUSHA
むっしゃ
I SEE THERE ARE SOME ISSUES WITH COL'S TABLE MANNERS.
!
THIS CANNOT BE SUFFICIENT THANKS, BUT...
...I MAY BE ABLE TO HELP HIM LEARN THE PROPER WAY TO EAT.
EH!
WELL, IT CAN'T BE HELPED, I SUPPOSE.
IT'S ALL RIGHT. THERE WAS ONE IN MY VILLAGE WITH A VERY BAD MEMORY, BUT EVEN HE LEARNED.
GAH-HA-HA.
ACHOO!
くしゅん
HEH!
WAH...
THAT GOES FOR YOU TOO.
HUH!?

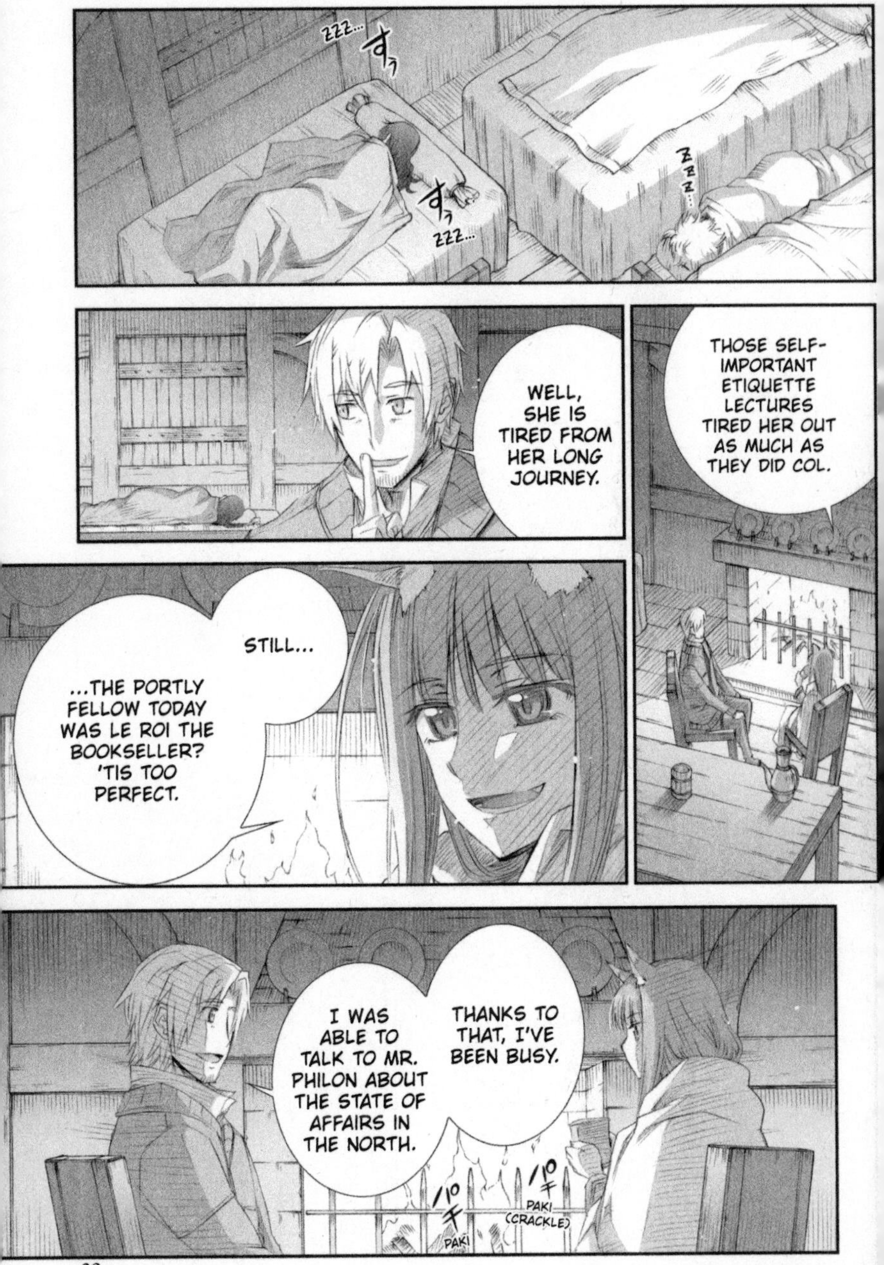
ZZZ...
ZZZ...
ZZZ...
THOSE SELF-IMPORTANT ETIQUETTE LECTURES TIRED HER OUT AS MUCH AS THEY DID COL.
WELL, SHE IS TIRED FROM HER LONG JOURNEY.
STILL...
...THE PORTLY FELLOW TODAY WAS LE ROI THE BOOKSELLER? 'TIS TOO PERFECT.
THANKS TO THAT, I'VE BEEN BUSY.
I WAS ABLE TO TALK TO MR. PHILON ABOUT THE STATE OF AFFAIRS IN THE NORTH.
PAKI (CRACKLE)
PAKI

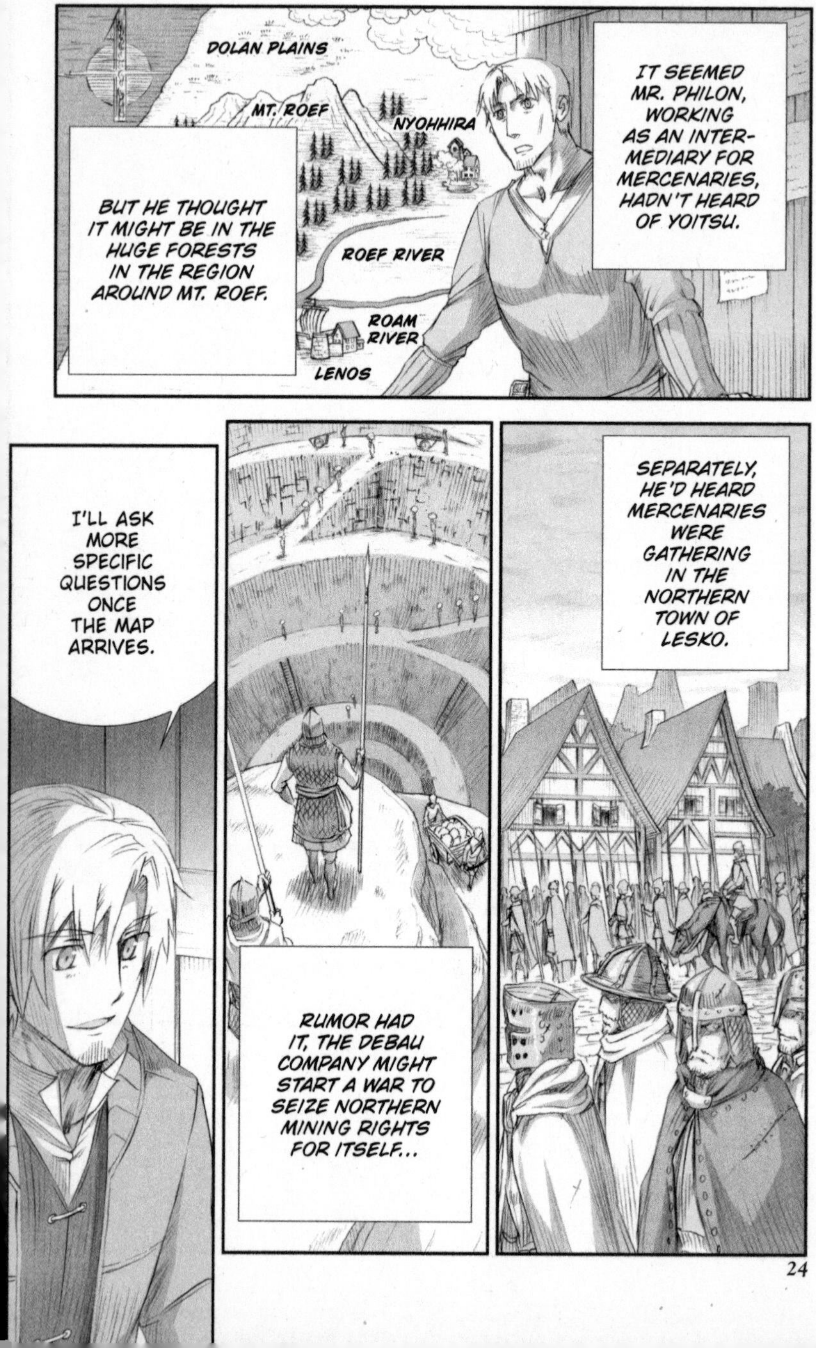
IT SEEMED MR. PHILON, WORKING AS AN INTER-MEDIARY FOR MERCENARIES, HADN'T HEARD OF YOITSU.
DOLAN PLAINS
MT. ROEF
NYOHHIRA
ROEF RIVER
ROAM RIVER
LENOS
BUT HE THOUGHT IT MIGHT BE IN THE HUGE FORESTS IN THE REGION AROUND MT. ROEF.
SEPARATELY, HE'D HEARD MERCENARIES WERE GATHERING IN THE NORTHERN TOWN OF LESKO.
RUMOR HAD IT, THE DEBAU COMPANY MIGHT START A WAR TO SEIZE NORTHERN MINING RIGHTS FOR ITSELF...
I'LL ASK MORE SPECIFIC QUESTIONS ONCE THE MAP ARRIVES.

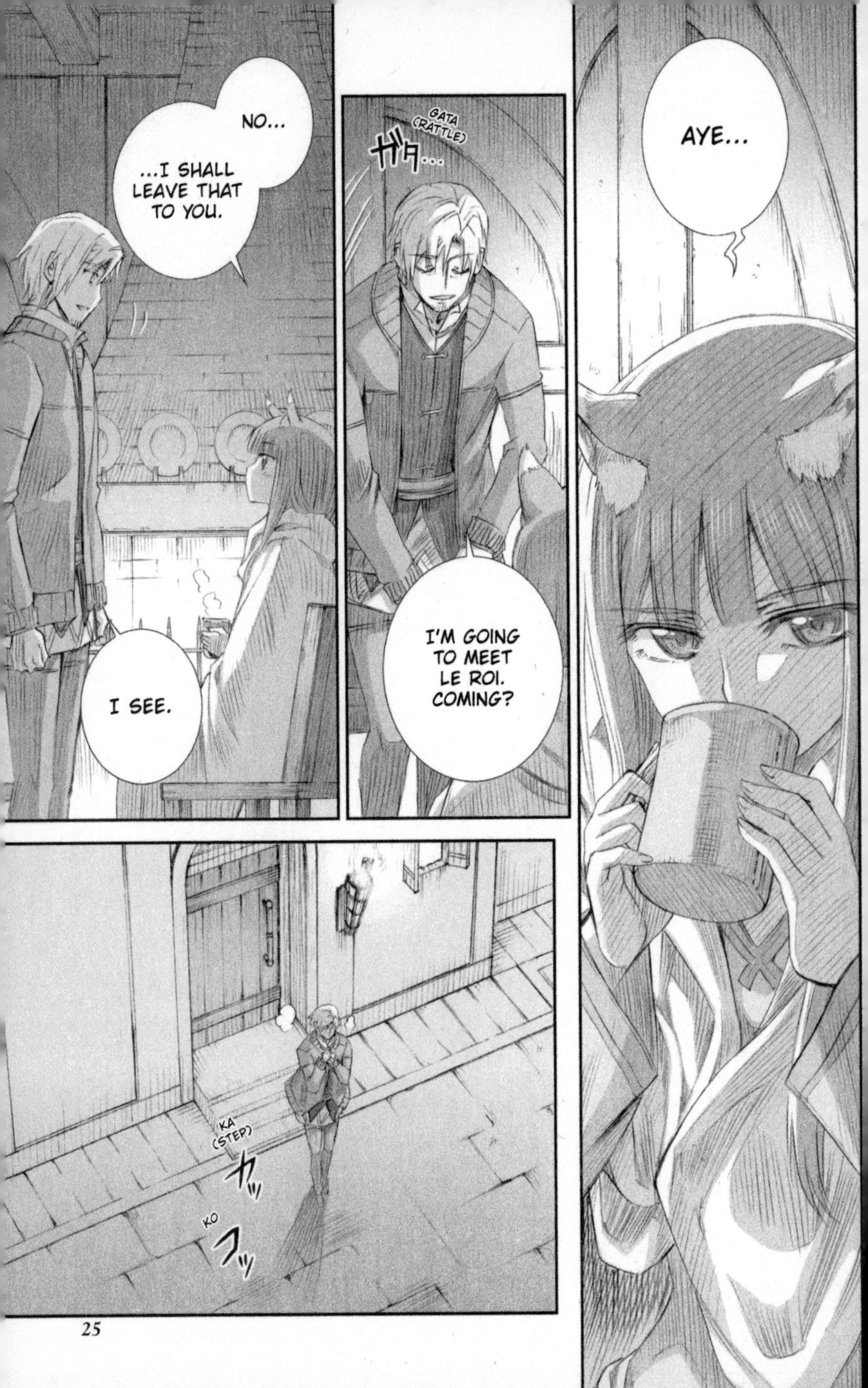
AYE...
GATA (RATTLE)
ガタ...
I'M GOING TO MEET LE ROI. COMING?
NO...
...I SHALL LEAVE THAT TO YOU.
I SEE.
KA (STEP)
カッ
KO
コッ

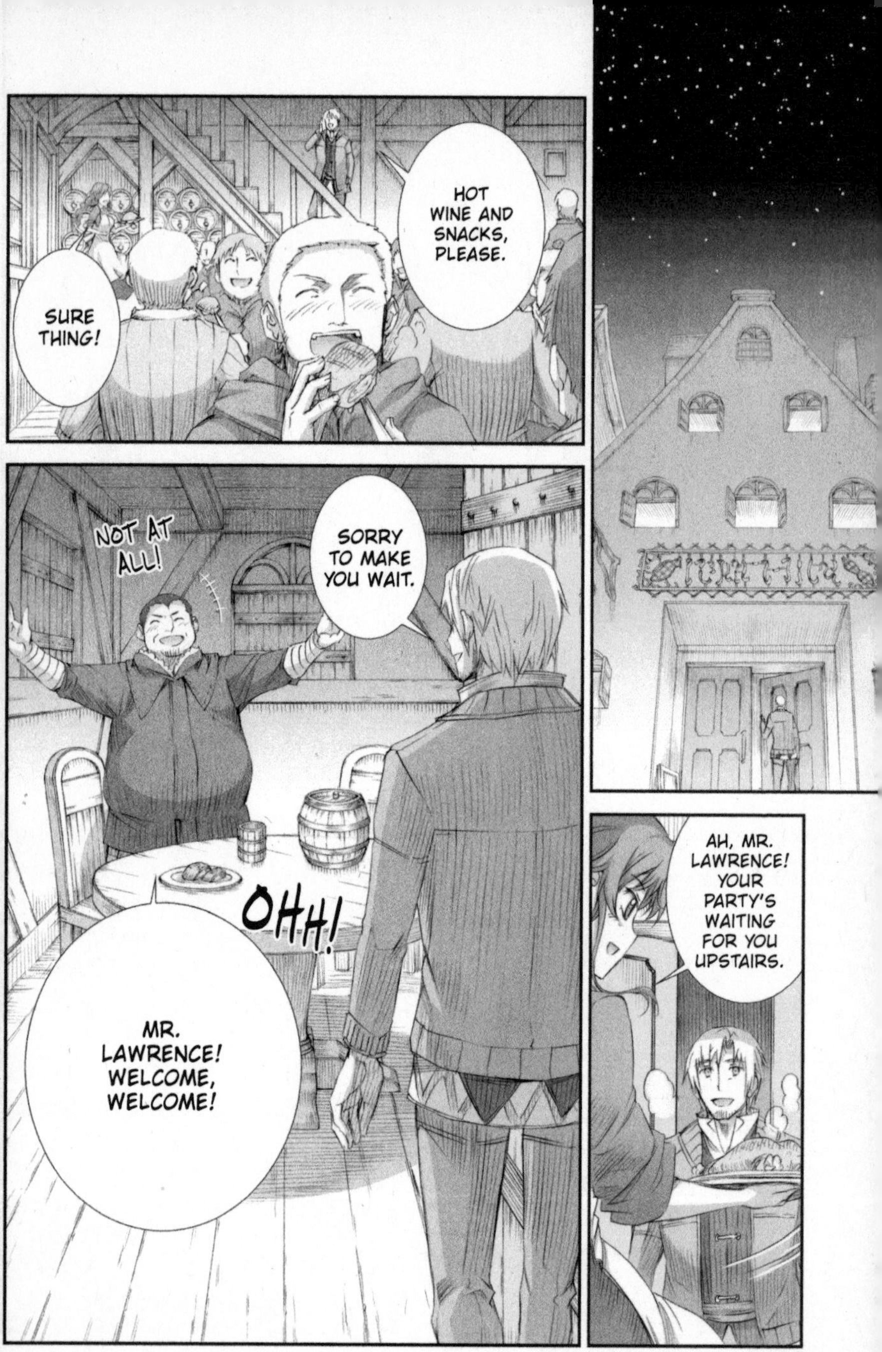
AH, MR. LAWRENCE! YOUR PARTY'S WAITING FOR YOU UPSTAIRS.
HOT WINE AND SNACKS, PLEASE.
SURE THING!
SORRY TO MAKE YOU WAIT.
NOT AT ALL!
OHH!
MR. LAWRENCE! WELCOME, WELCOME!

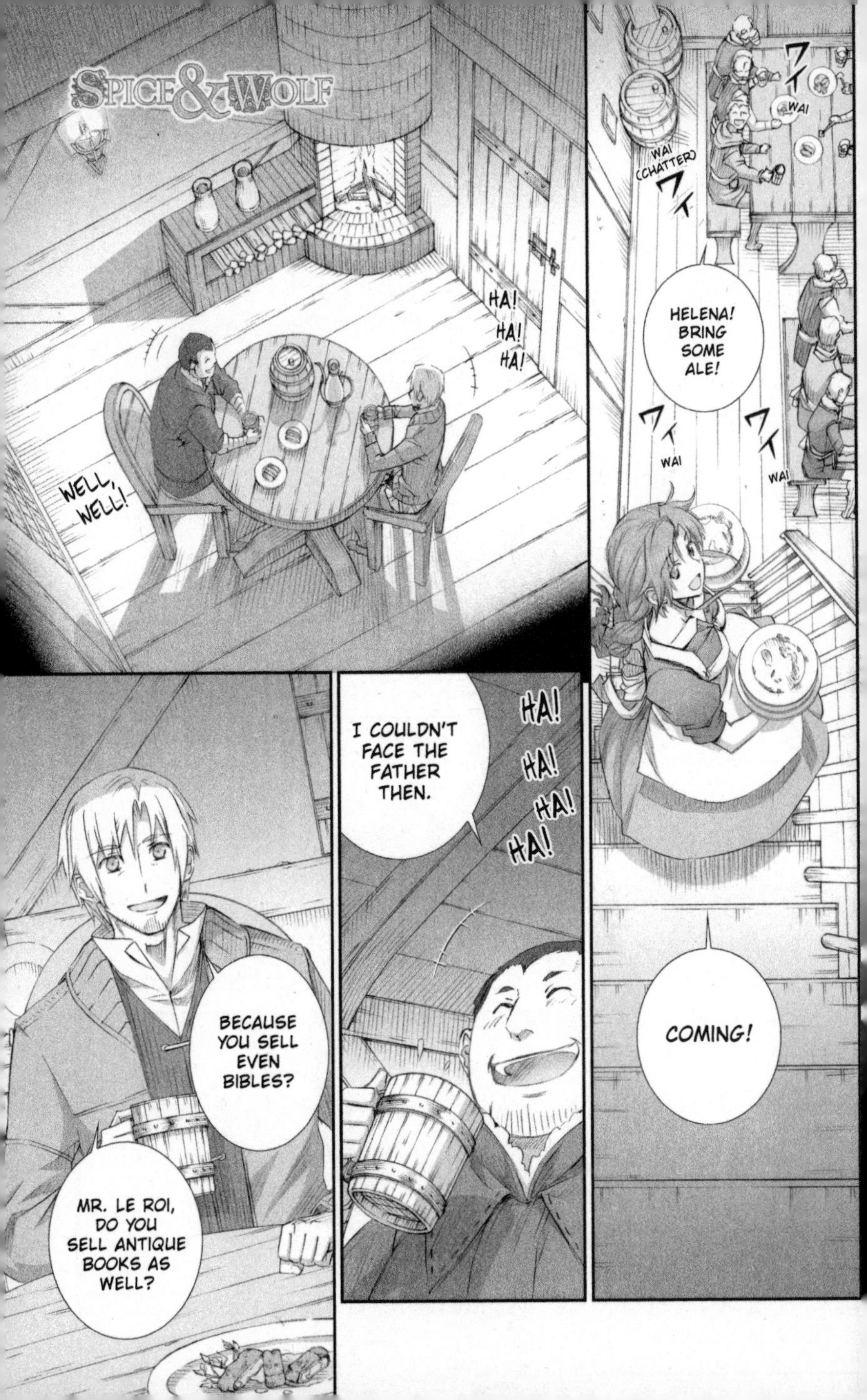
ワイ
WAI
WAI (CHATTER)
ワイ
HELENA! BRING SOME ALE!
ワイ
WAI
ワイ
WAI
COMING!
SPICE & WOLF
HA! HA! HA!
WELL, WELL!
HA! HA! HA! HA!
I COULDN'T FACE THE FATHER THEN.
BECAUSE YOU SELL EVEN BIBLES?
MR. LE ROI, DO YOU SELL ANTIQUE BOOKS AS WELL?

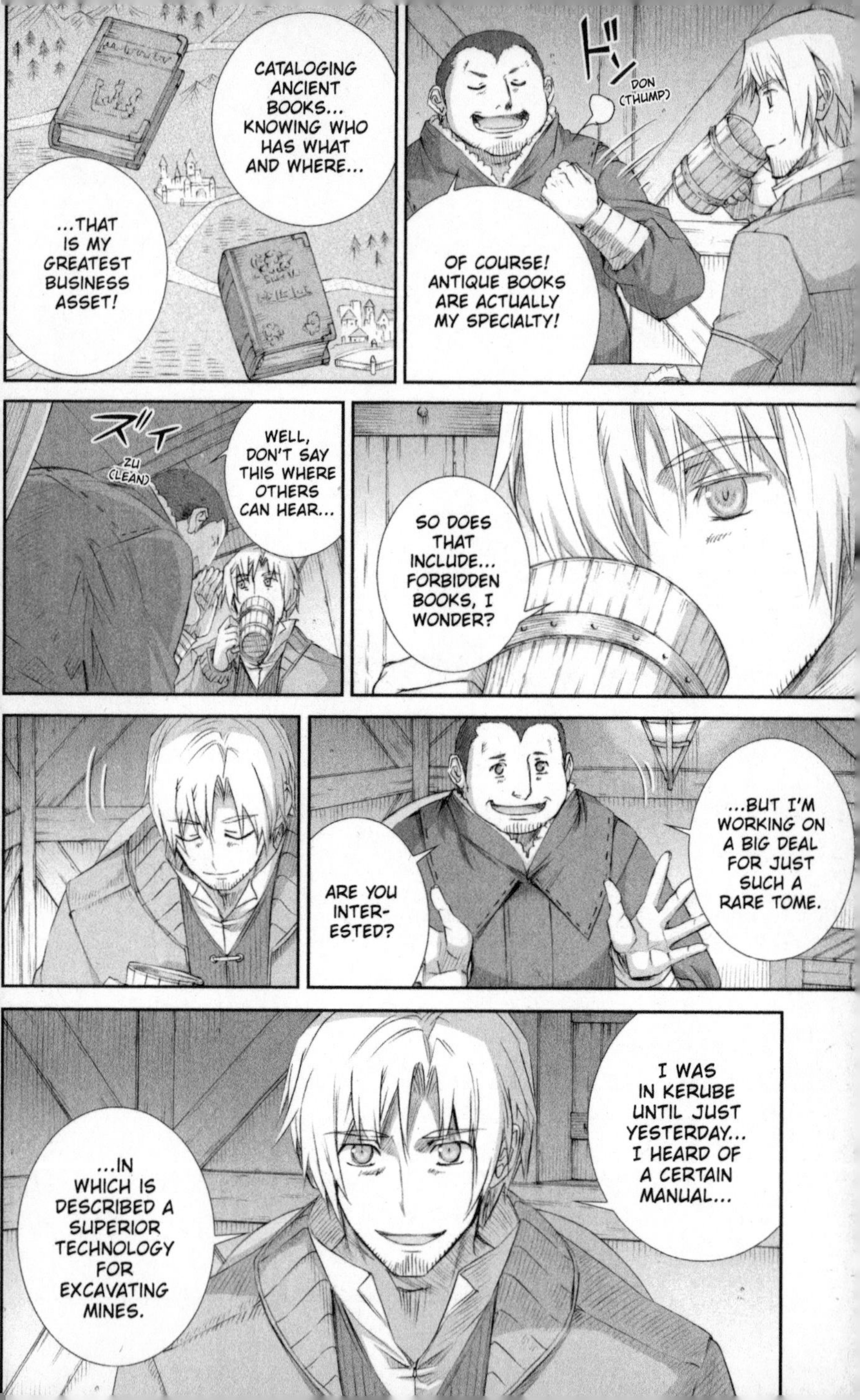
ドン
DON (THUMP)
OF COURSE! ANTIQUE BOOKS ARE ACTUALLY MY SPECIALTY!
CATALOGING ANCIENT BOOKS... KNOWING WHO HAS WHAT AND WHERE...
...THAT IS MY GREATEST BUSINESS ASSET!
SO DOES THAT INCLUDE... FORBIDDEN BOOKS, I WONDER?
ズイ
ZU (LEAN)
WELL, DON'T SAY THIS WHERE OTHERS CAN HEAR...
...BUT I'M WORKING ON A BIG DEAL FOR JUST SUCH A RARE TOME.
ARE YOU INTER-ESTED?
I WAS IN KERUBE UNTIL JUST YESTERDAY... I HEARD OF A CERTAIN MANUAL...
...IN WHICH IS DESCRIBED A SUPERIOR TECHNOLOGY FOR EXCAVATING MINES.

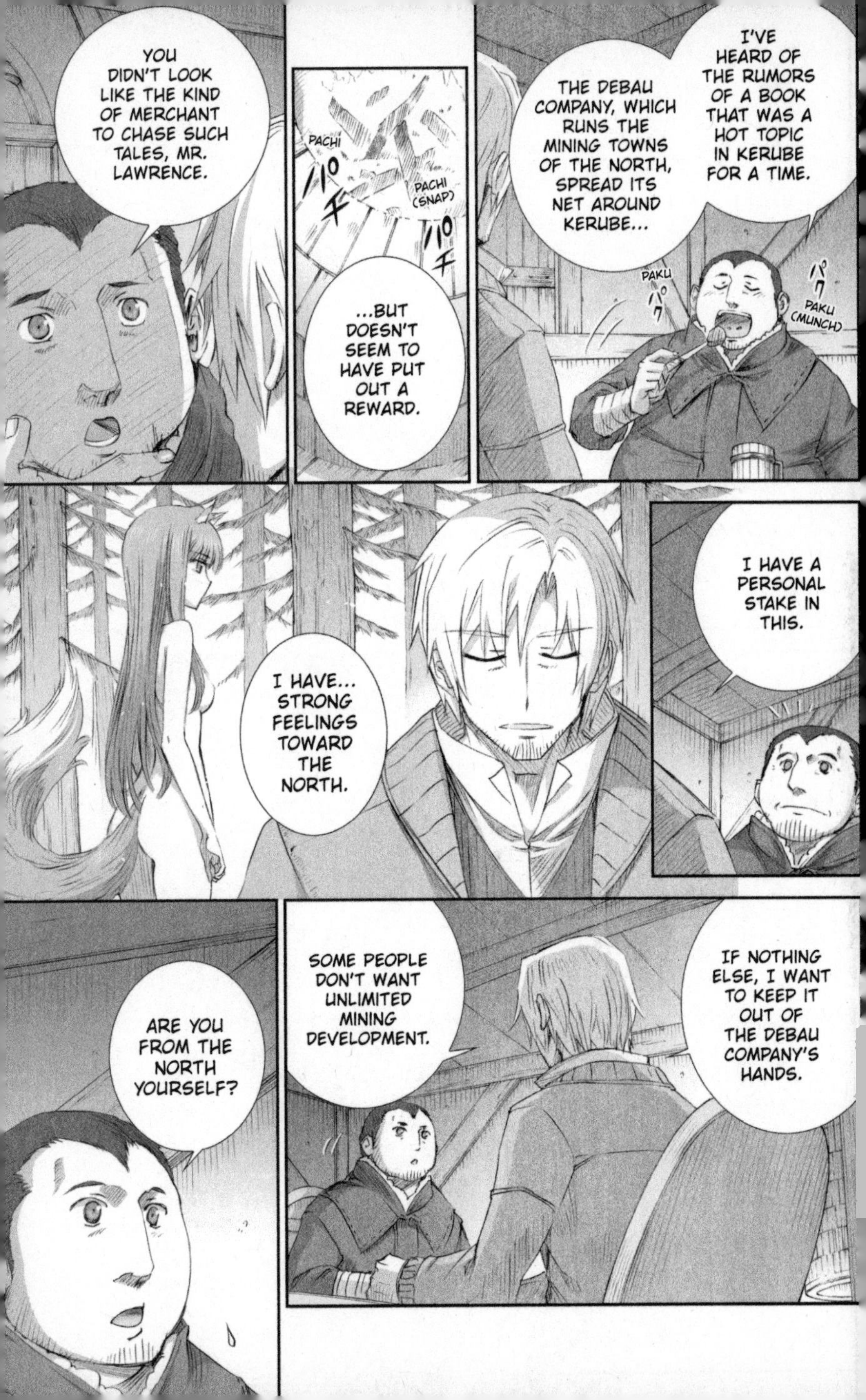
I'VE HEARD OF THE RUMORS OF A BOOK THAT WAS A HOT TOPIC IN KERUBE FOR A TIME.
THE DEBAU COMPANY, WHICH RUNS THE MINING TOWNS OF THE NORTH, SPREAD ITS NET AROUND KERUBE...
PAKU
PAKU (MUNCH)
PACHI
PACHI (SNAP)
...BUT DOESN'T SEEM TO HAVE PUT OUT A REWARD.
YOU DIDN'T LOOK LIKE THE KIND OF MERCHANT TO CHASE SUCH TALES, MR. LAWRENCE.
I HAVE A PERSONAL STAKE IN THIS.
I HAVE... STRONG FEELINGS TOWARD THE NORTH.
IF NOTHING ELSE, I WANT TO KEEP IT OUT OF THE DEBAU COMPANY'S HANDS.
SOME PEOPLE DON'T WANT UNLIMITED MINING DEVELOPMENT.
ARE YOU FROM THE NORTH YOURSELF?

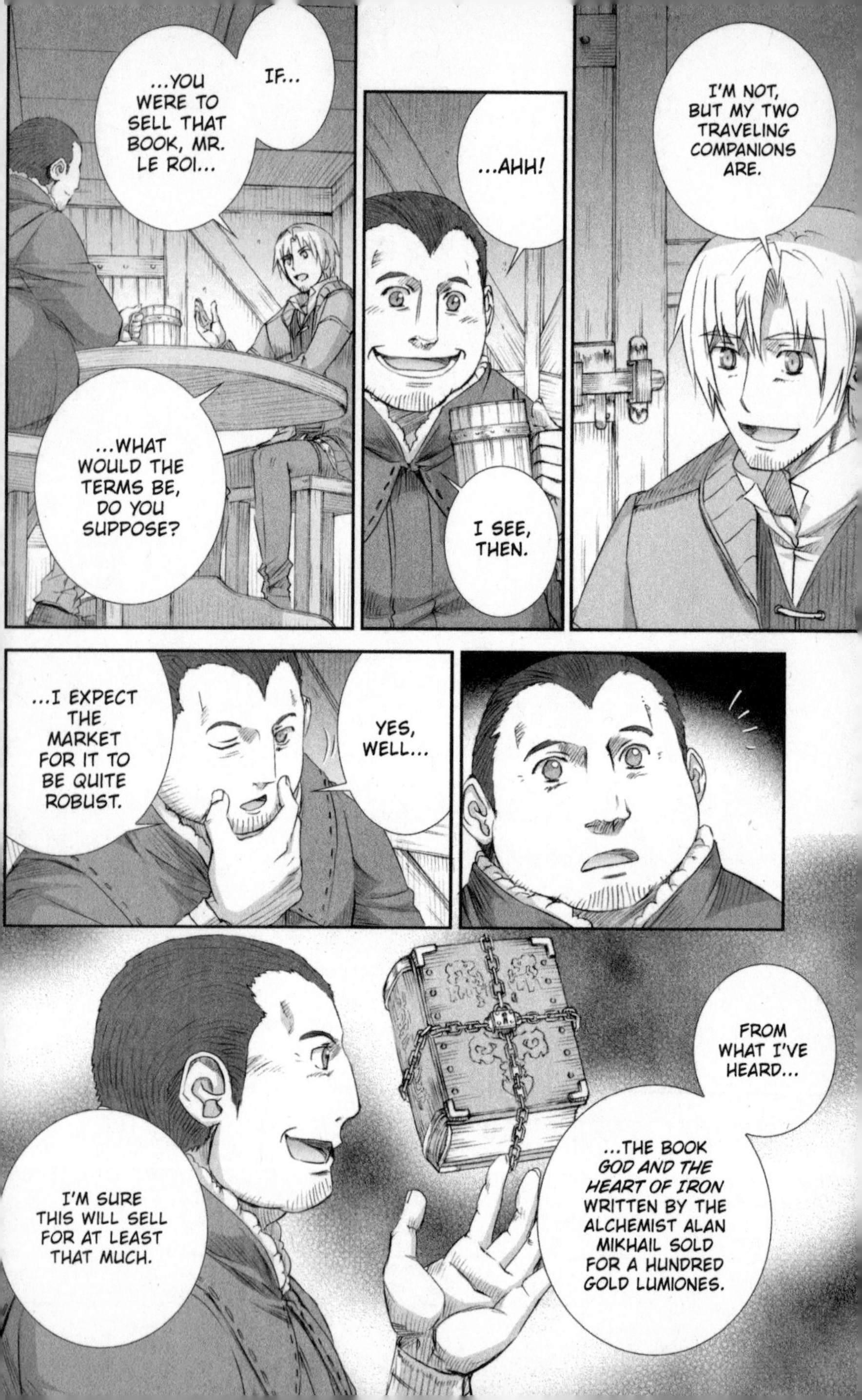
I'M NOT, BUT MY TWO TRAVELING COMPANIONS ARE.
...AHH!
I SEE, THEN.
IF...
...YOU WERE TO SELL THAT BOOK, MR. LE ROI...
...WHAT WOULD THE TERMS BE, DO YOU SUPPOSE?
YES, WELL...
...I EXPECT THE MARKET FOR IT TO BE QUITE ROBUST.
FROM WHAT I'VE HEARD...
...THE BOOK *GOD AND THE HEART OF IRON* WRITTEN BY THE ALCHEMIST ALAN MIKHAIL SOLD FOR A HUNDRED GOLD LUMIONES.
I'M SURE THIS WILL SELL FOR AT LEAST THAT MUCH.

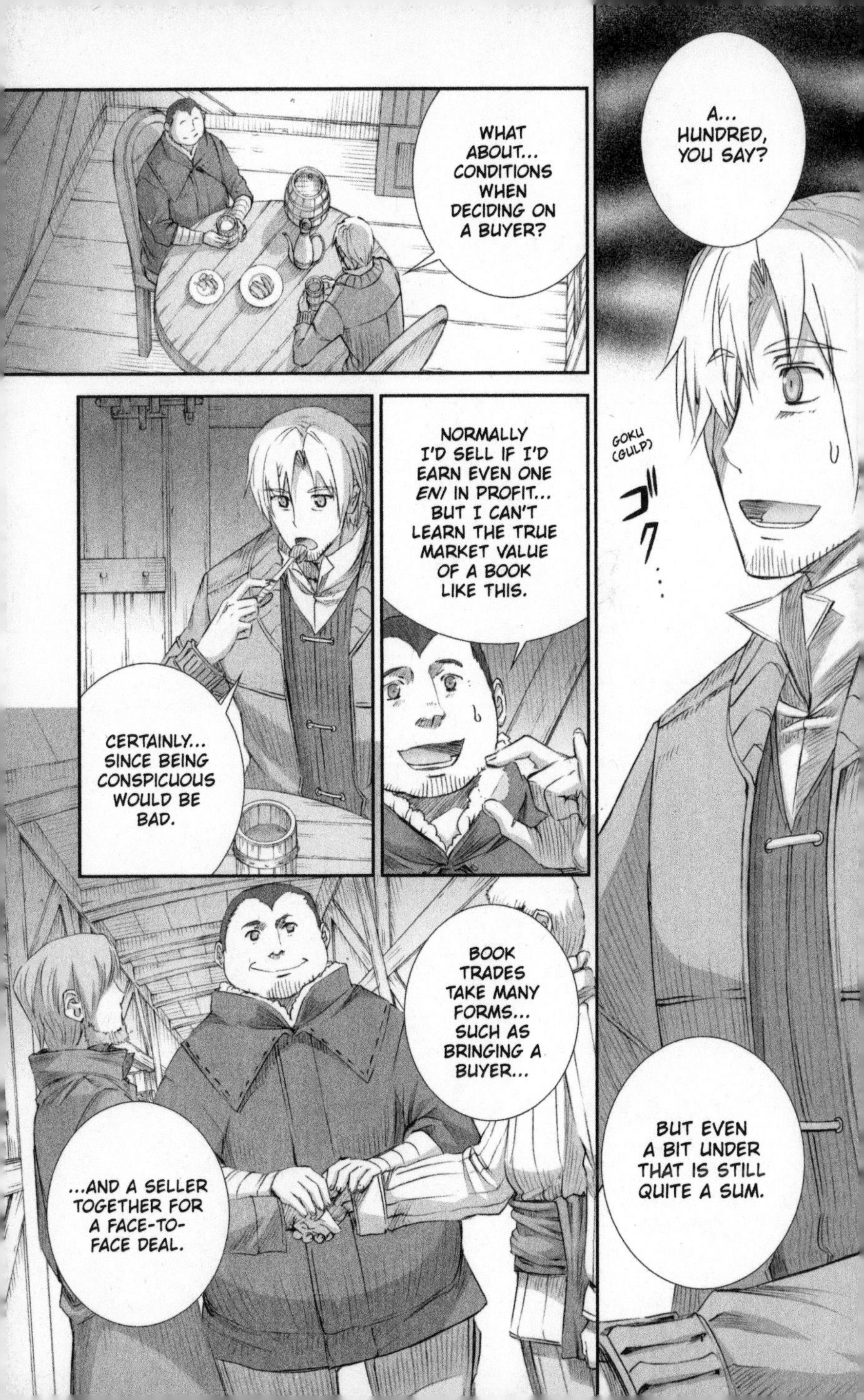
A... HUNDRED, YOU SAY?
GOKU (GULP)
ゴク...
BUT EVEN A BIT UNDER THAT IS STILL QUITE A SUM.
WHAT ABOUT... CONDITIONS WHEN DECIDING ON A BUYER?
NORMALLY I'D SELL IF I'D EARN EVEN ONE *ENI* IN PROFIT... BUT I CAN'T LEARN THE TRUE MARKET VALUE OF A BOOK LIKE THIS.
CERTAINLY... SINCE BEING CONSPICUOUS WOULD BE BAD.
BOOK TRADES TAKE MANY FORMS... SUCH AS BRINGING A BUYER...
...AND A SELLER TOGETHER FOR A FACE-TO-FACE DEAL.

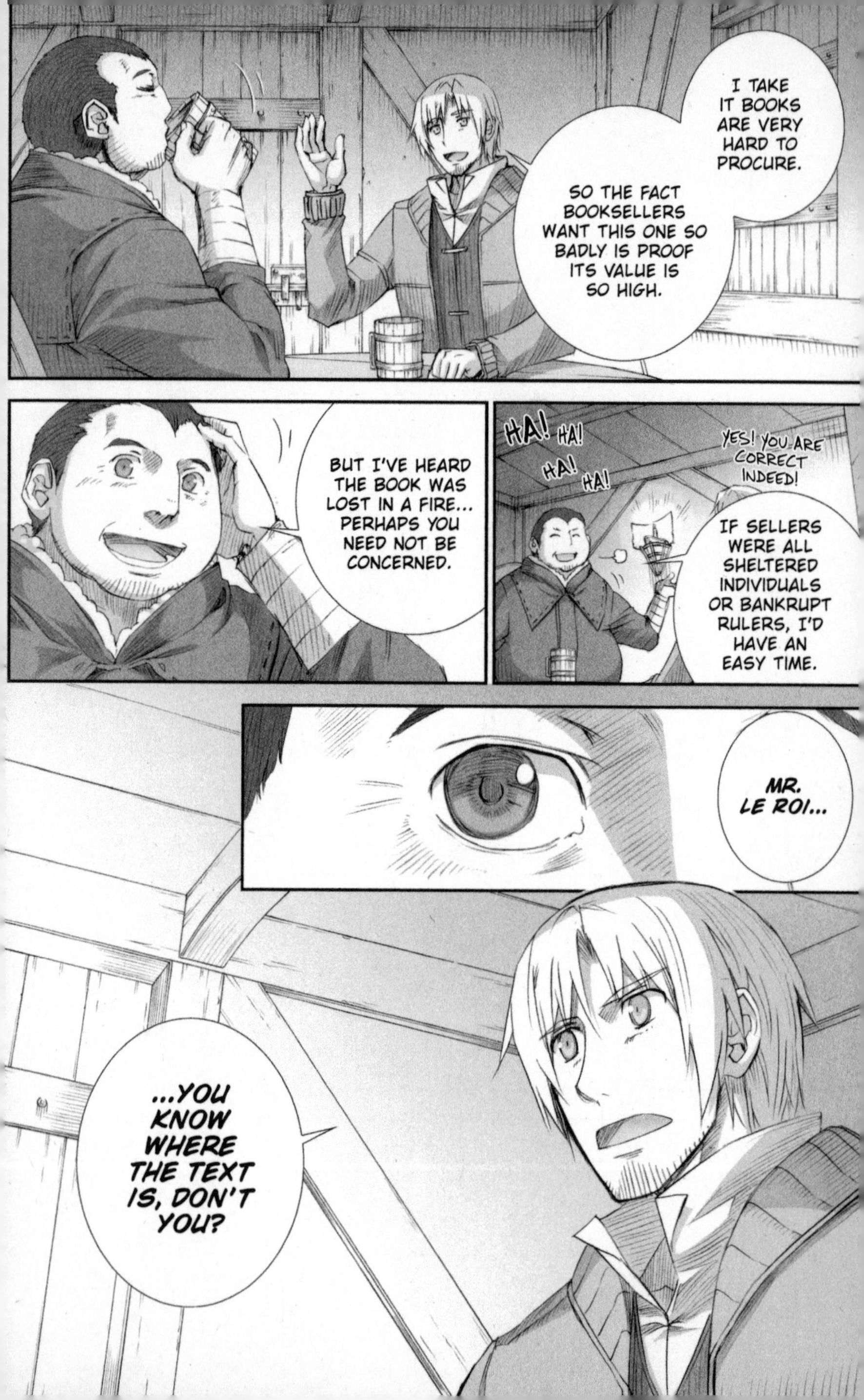
I TAKE IT BOOKS ARE VERY HARD TO PROCURE.
SO THE FACT BOOKSELLERS WANT THIS ONE SO BADLY IS PROOF ITS VALUE IS SO HIGH.
HA! HA! HA! HA!
YES! YOU ARE CORRECT INDEED!
IF SELLERS WERE ALL SHELTERED INDIVIDUALS OR BANKRUPT RULERS, I'D HAVE AN EASY TIME.
BUT I'VE HEARD THE BOOK WAS LOST IN A FIRE... PERHAPS YOU NEED NOT BE CONCERNED.
MR. LE ROI...
...YOU KNOW WHERE THE TEXT IS, DON'T YOU?

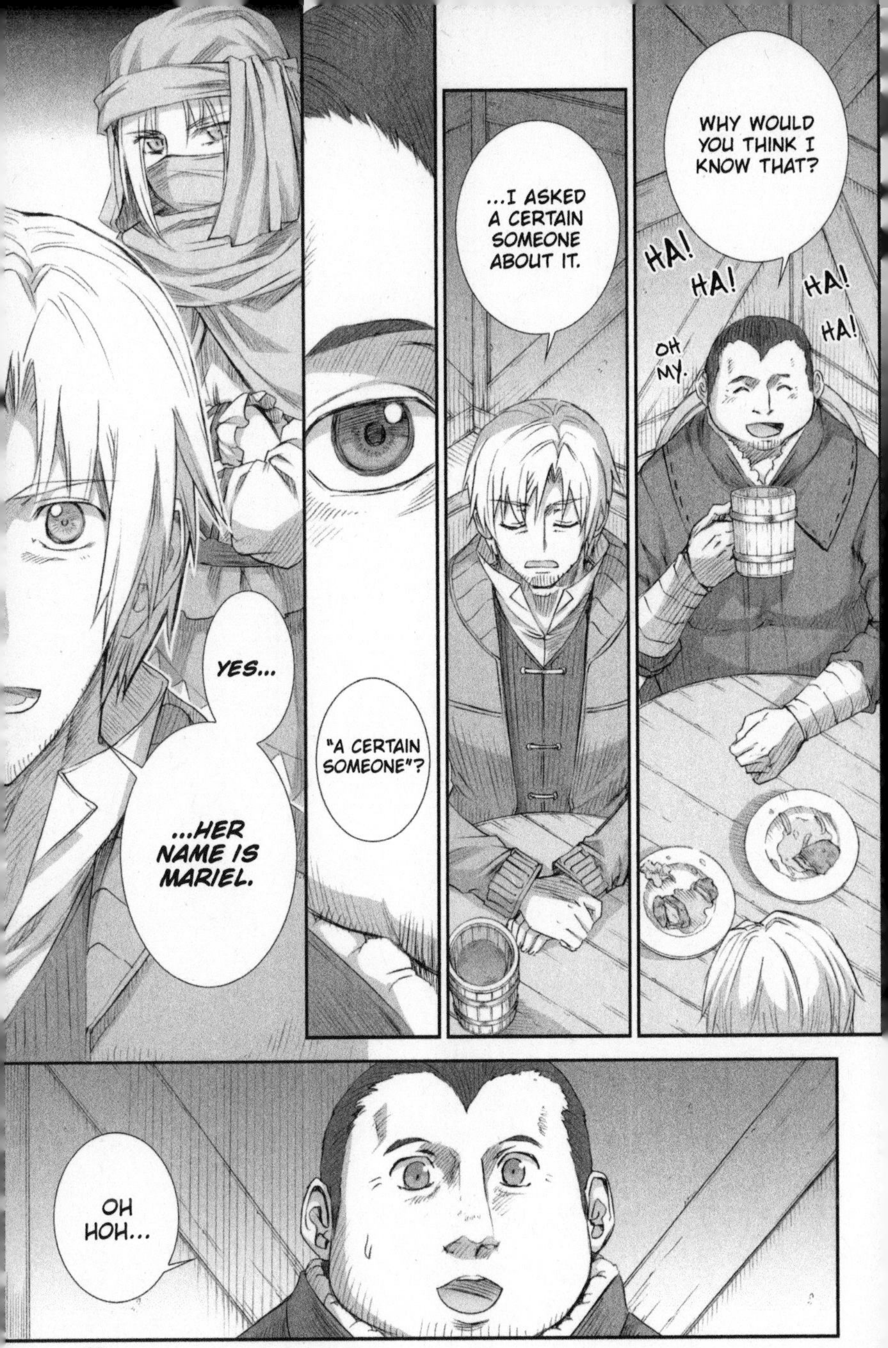
WHY WOULD YOU THINK I KNOW THAT?
HA! HA! HA! HA!
OH MY.
...I ASKED A CERTAIN SOMEONE ABOUT IT.
"A CERTAIN SOMEONE"?
YES...
...HER NAME IS MARIEL.
OH HOH...

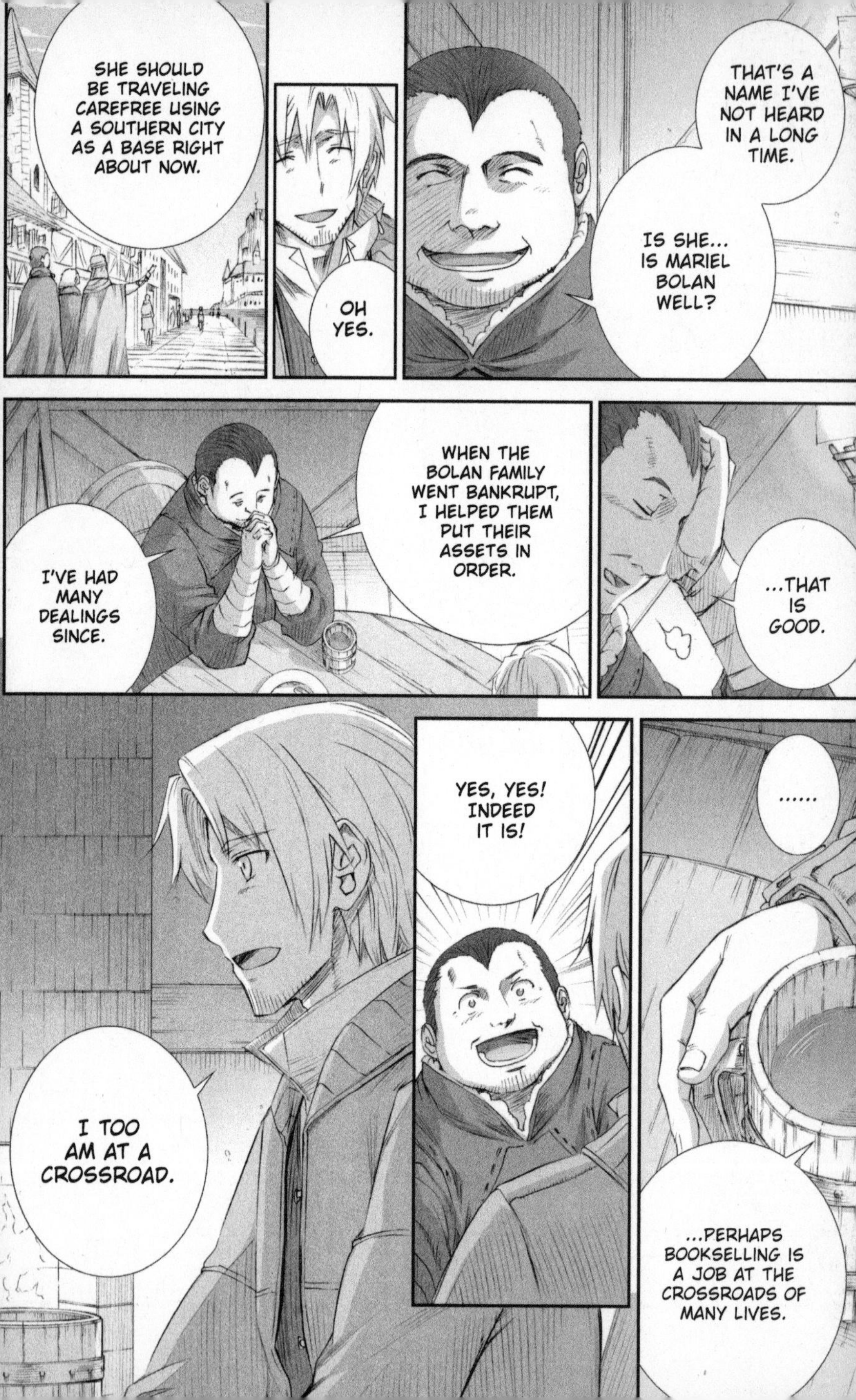
THAT'S A NAME I'VE NOT HEARD IN A LONG TIME.
IS SHE... IS MARIEL BOLAN WELL?
OH YES.
SHE SHOULD BE TRAVELING CAREFREE USING A SOUTHERN CITY AS A BASE RIGHT ABOUT NOW.
...THAT IS GOOD.
WHEN THE BOLAN FAMILY WENT BANKRUPT, I HELPED THEM PUT THEIR ASSETS IN ORDER.
I'VE HAD MANY DEALINGS SINCE.
......
...PERHAPS BOOKSELLING IS A JOB AT THE CROSSROADS OF MANY LIVES.
YES, YES! INDEED IT IS!
I TOO AM AT A CROSSROAD.

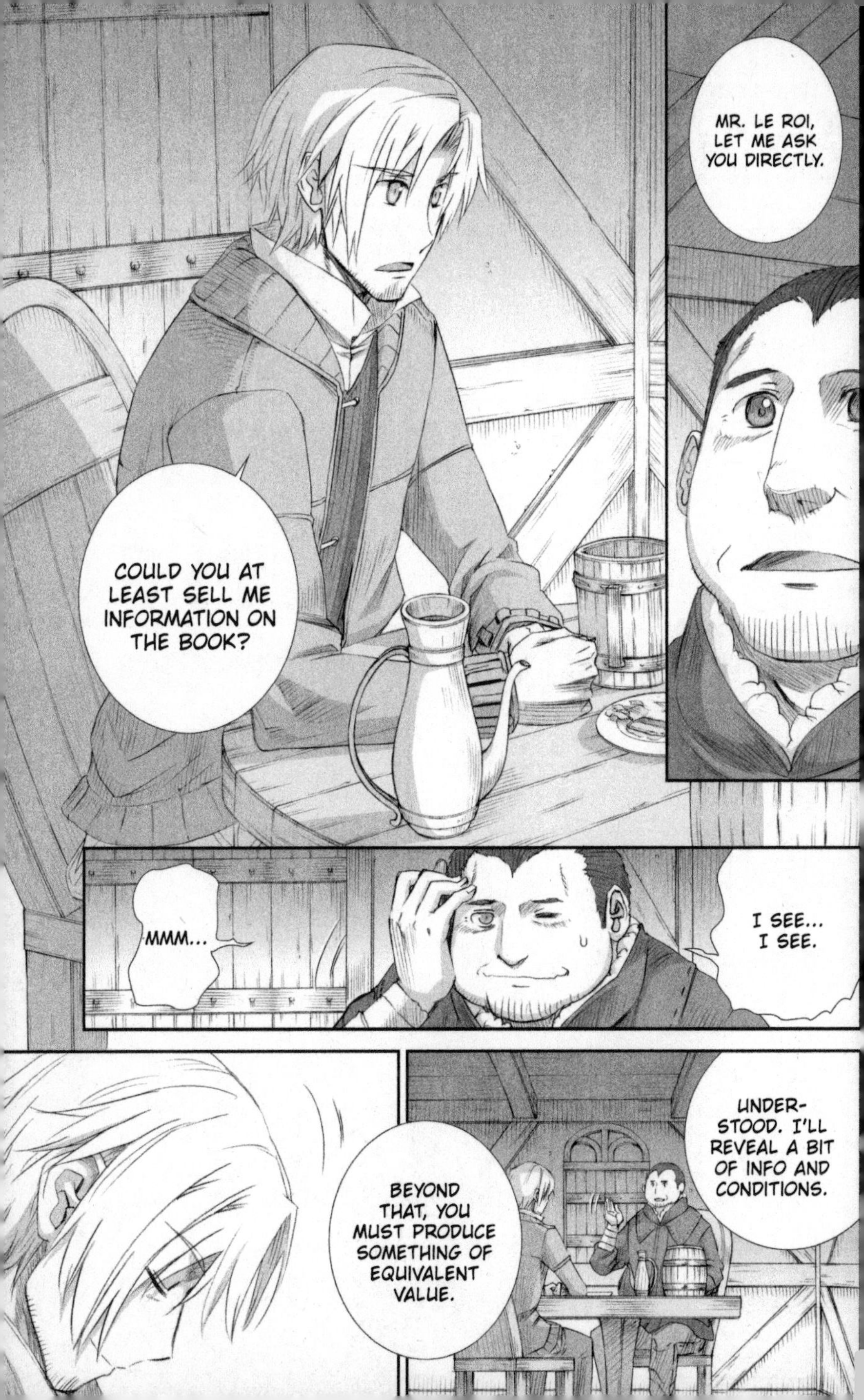
MR. LE ROI, LET ME ASK YOU DIRECTLY.
COULD YOU AT LEAST SELL ME INFORMATION ON THE BOOK?
I SEE... I SEE.
MMM...
UNDERSTOOD. I'LL REVEAL A BIT OF INFO AND CONDITIONS.
BEYOND THAT, YOU MUST PRODUCE SOMETHING OF EQUIVALENT VALUE.

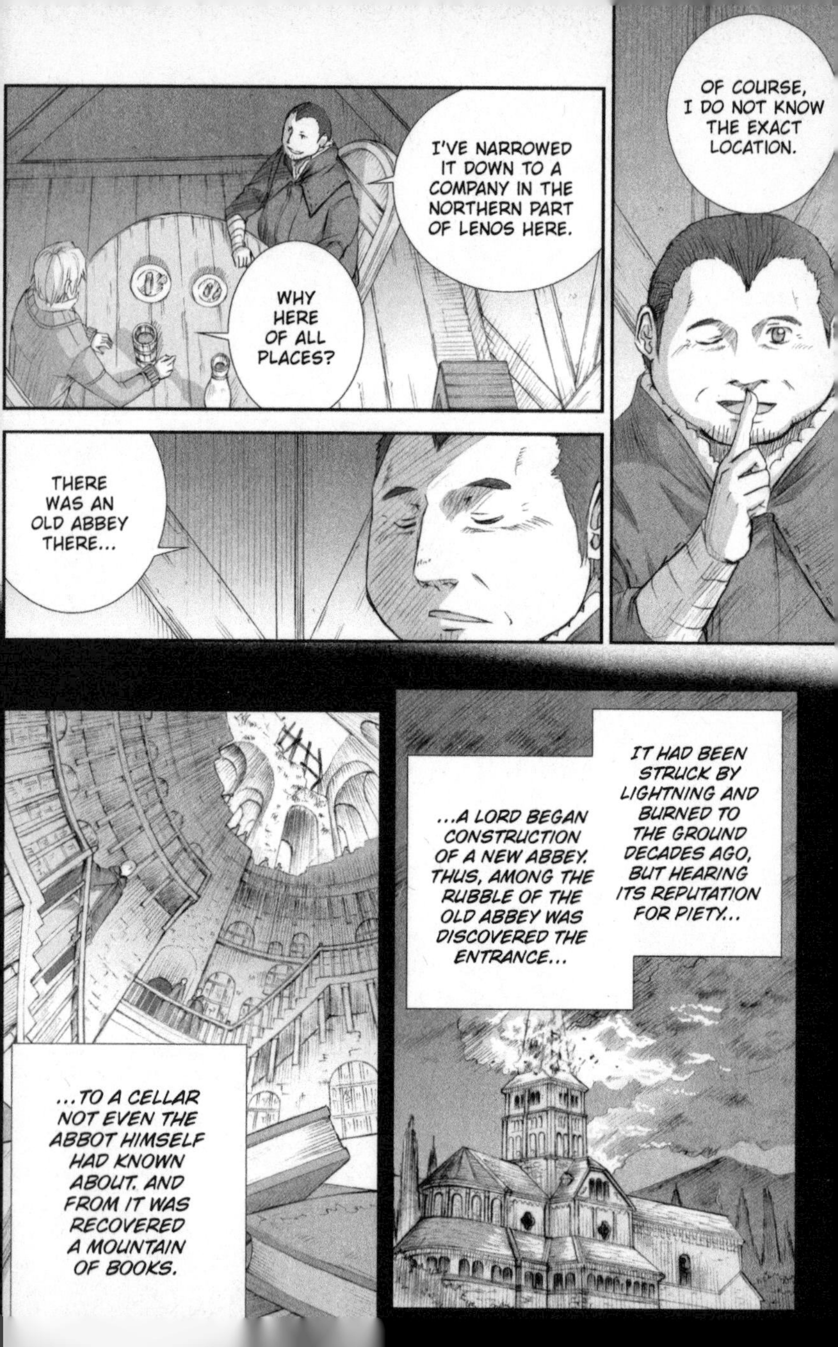
OF COURSE, I DO NOT KNOW THE EXACT LOCATION.
I'VE NARROWED IT DOWN TO A COMPANY IN THE NORTHERN PART OF LENOS HERE.
WHY HERE OF ALL PLACES?
THERE WAS AN OLD ABBEY THERE...
IT HAD BEEN STRUCK BY LIGHTNING AND BURNED TO THE GROUND DECADES AGO, BUT HEARING ITS REPUTATION FOR PIETY...
...A LORD BEGAN CONSTRUCTION OF A NEW ABBEY. THUS, AMONG THE RUBBLE OF THE OLD ABBEY WAS DISCOVERED THE ENTRANCE...
...TO A CELLAR NOT EVEN THE ABBOT HIMSELF HAD KNOWN ABOUT. AND FROM IT WAS RECOVERED A MOUNTAIN OF BOOKS.

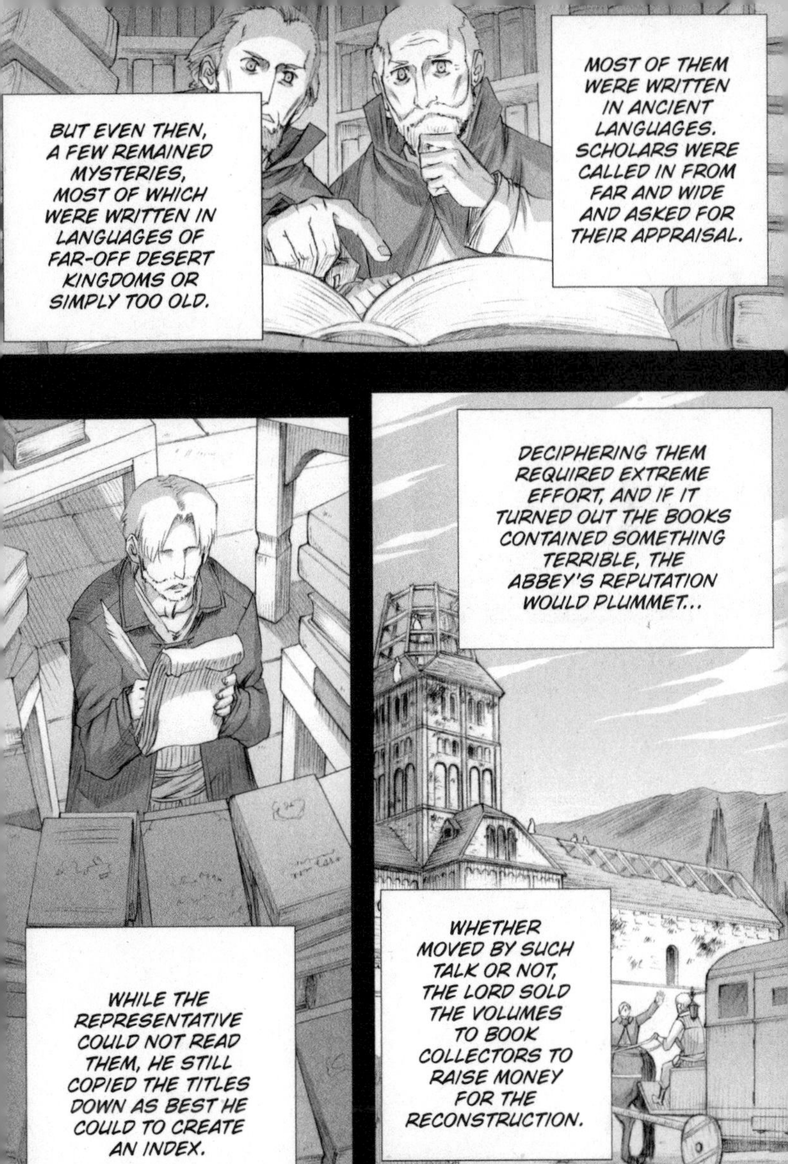
MOST OF THEM WERE WRITTEN IN ANCIENT LANGUAGES. SCHOLARS WERE CALLED IN FROM FAR AND WIDE AND ASKED FOR THEIR APPRAISAL.
BUT EVEN THEN, A FEW REMAINED MYSTERIES, MOST OF WHICH WERE WRITTEN IN LANGUAGES OF FAR-OFF DESERT KINGDOMS OR SIMPLY TOO OLD.
DECIPHERING THEM REQUIRED EXTREME EFFORT, AND IF IT TURNED OUT THE BOOKS CONTAINED SOMETHING TERRIBLE, THE ABBEY'S REPUTATION WOULD PLUMMET...
WHETHER MOVED BY SUCH TALK OR NOT, THE LORD SOLD THE VOLUMES TO BOOK COLLECTORS TO RAISE MONEY FOR THE RECONSTRUCTION.
WHILE THE REPRESENTATIVE COULD NOT READ THEM, HE STILL COPIED THE TITLES DOWN AS BEST HE COULD TO CREATE AN INDEX.

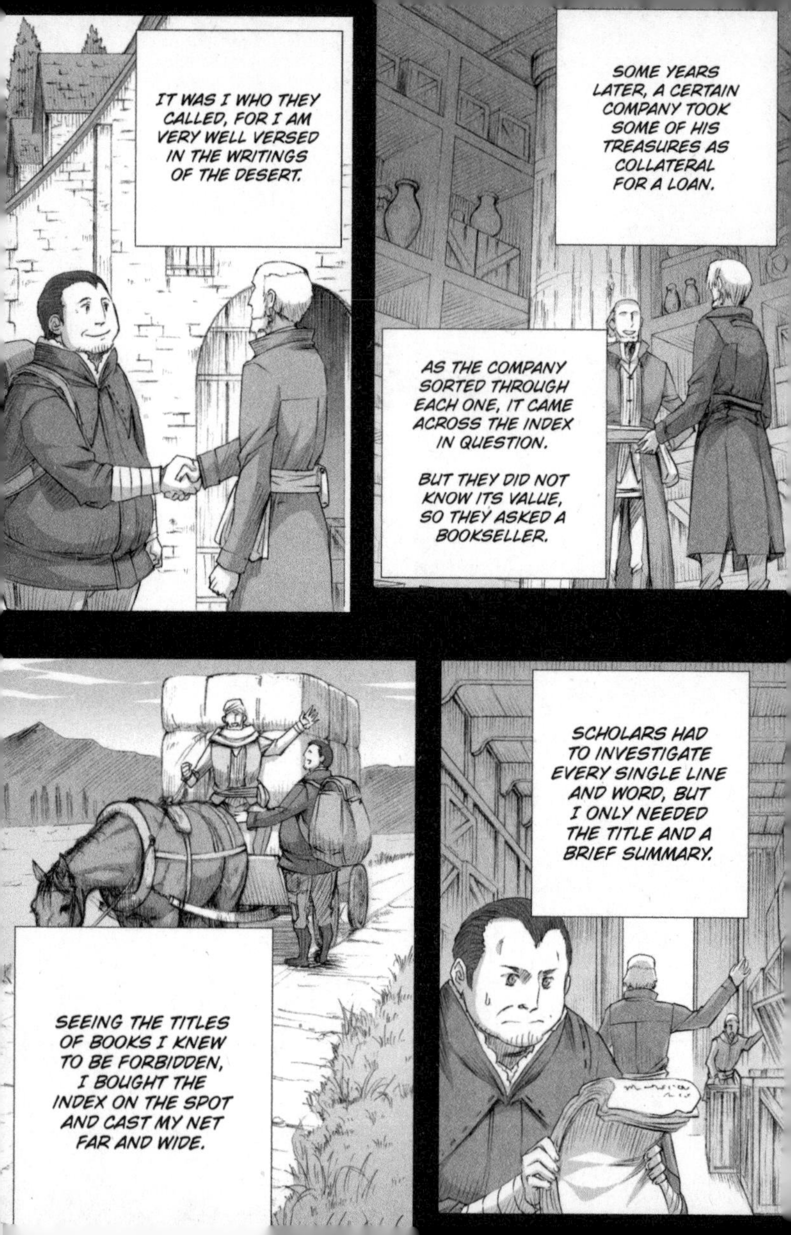
SOME YEARS LATER, A CERTAIN COMPANY TOOK SOME OF HIS TREASURES AS COLLATERAL FOR A LOAN.
AS THE COMPANY SORTED THROUGH EACH ONE, IT CAME ACROSS THE INDEX IN QUESTION.
BUT THEY DID NOT KNOW ITS VALUE, SO THEY ASKED A BOOKSELLER.
IT WAS I WHO THEY CALLED, FOR I AM VERY WELL VERSED IN THE WRITINGS OF THE DESERT.
SCHOLARS HAD TO INVESTIGATE EVERY SINGLE LINE AND WORD, BUT I ONLY NEEDED THE TITLE AND A BRIEF SUMMARY.
SEEING THE TITLES OF BOOKS I KNEW TO BE FORBIDDEN, I BOUGHT THE INDEX ON THE SPOT AND CAST MY NET FAR AND WIDE.

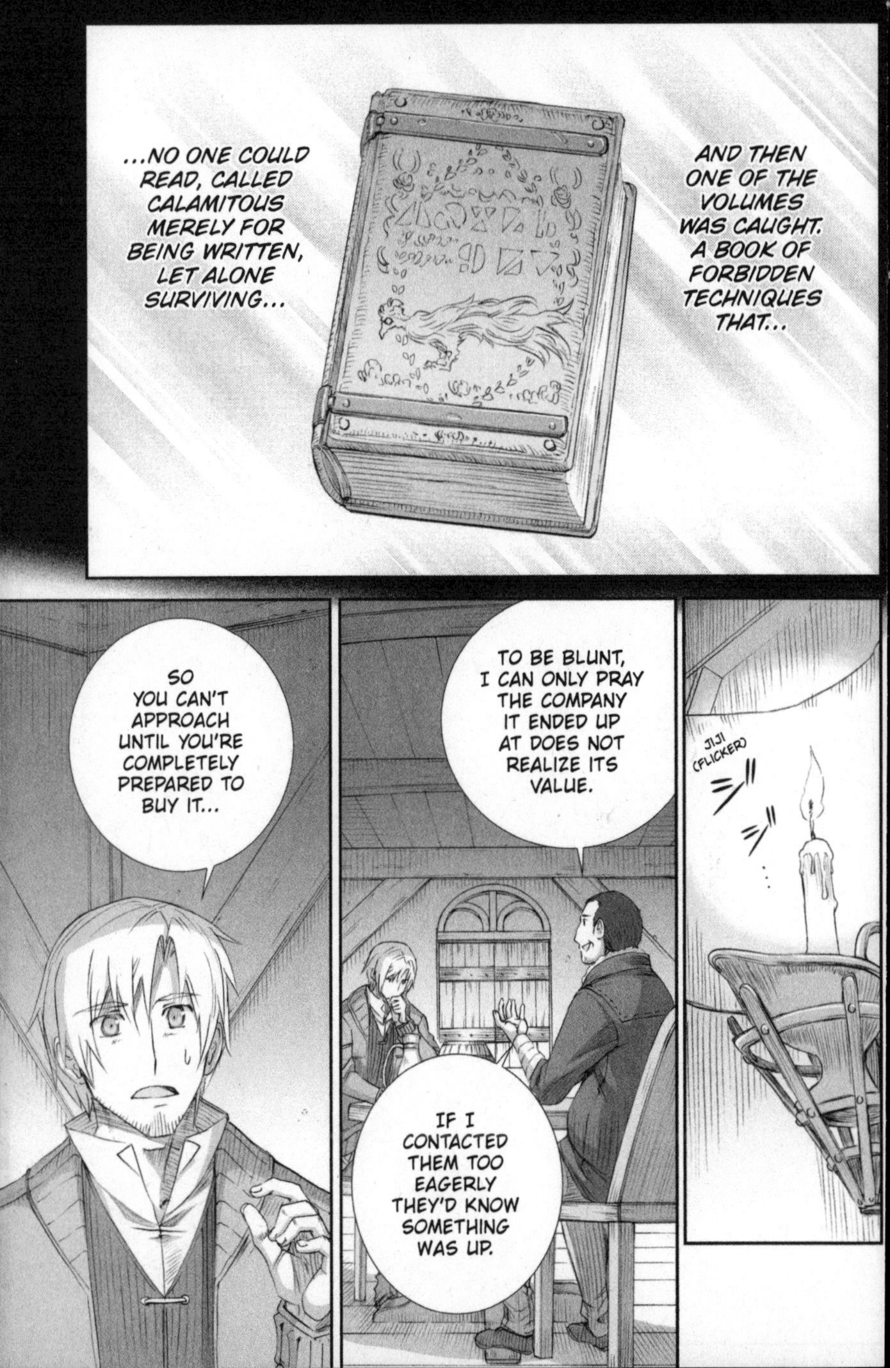
AND THEN ONE OF THE VOLUMES WAS CAUGHT. A BOOK OF FORBIDDEN TECHNIQUES THAT...
...NO ONE COULD READ, CALLED CALAMITOUS MERELY FOR BEING WRITTEN, LET ALONE SURVIVING...
JIJI (FLICKER)
TO BE BLUNT, I CAN ONLY PRAY THE COMPANY IT ENDED UP AT DOES NOT REALIZE ITS VALUE.
IF I CONTACTED THEM TOO EAGERLY THEY'D KNOW SOMETHING WAS UP.
SO YOU CAN'T APPROACH UNTIL YOU'RE COMPLETELY PREPARED TO BUY IT...

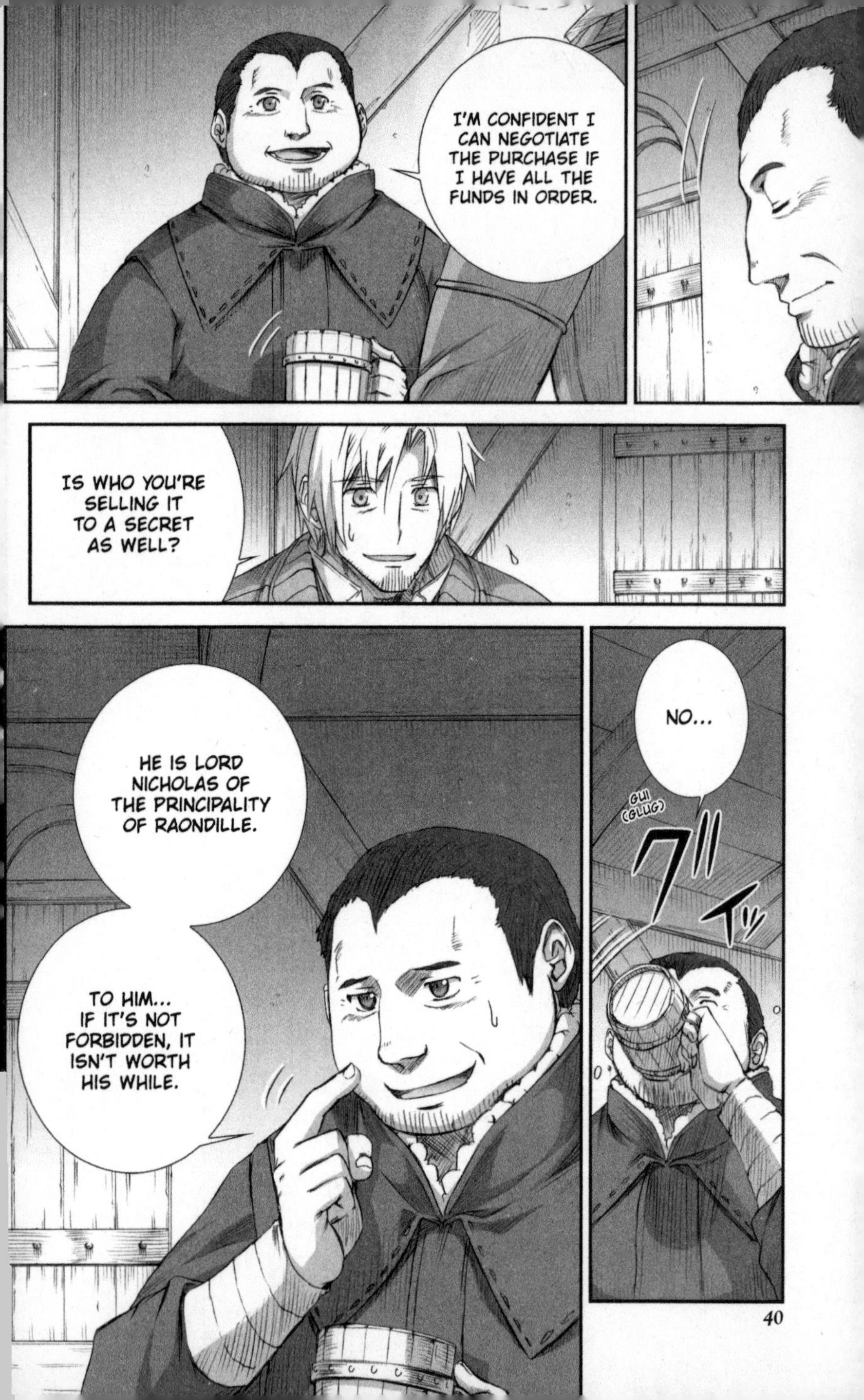
I'M CONFIDENT I CAN NEGOTIATE THE PURCHASE IF I HAVE ALL THE FUNDS IN ORDER.
IS WHO YOU'RE SELLING IT TO A SECRET AS WELL?
NO...
GUI (GLUG)
HE IS LORD NICHOLAS OF THE PRINCIPALITY OF RAONDILLE.
TO HIM... IF IT'S NOT FORBIDDEN, IT ISN'T WORTH HIS WHILE.

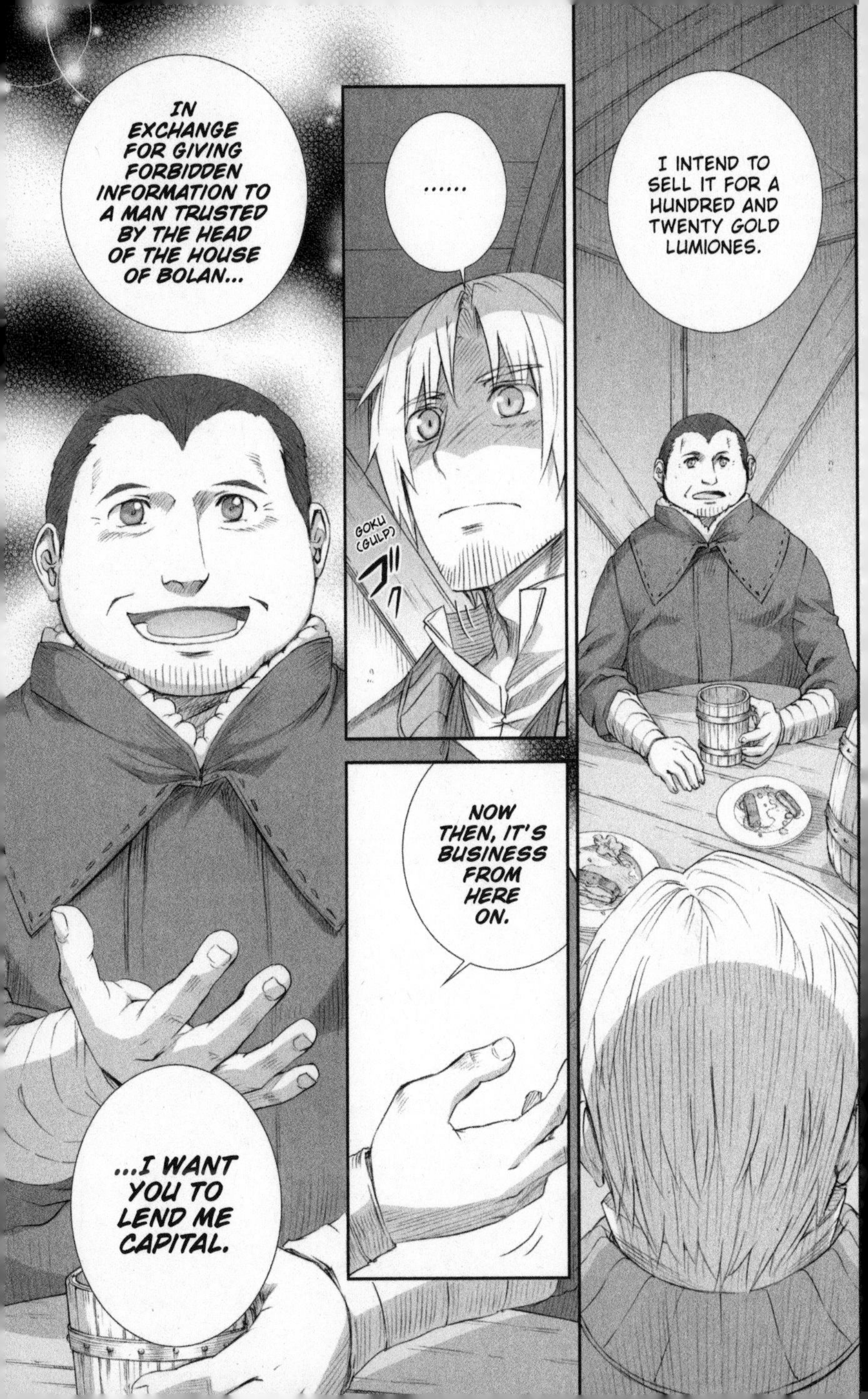
I INTEND TO SELL IT FOR A HUNDRED AND TWENTY GOLD LUMIONES.
......
GOKU (GULP)
ゴク
NOW THEN, IT'S BUSINESS FROM HERE ON.
IN EXCHANGE FOR GIVING FORBIDDEN INFORMATION TO A MAN TRUSTED BY THE HEAD OF THE HOUSE OF BOLAN...
...I WANT YOU TO LEND ME CAPITAL.

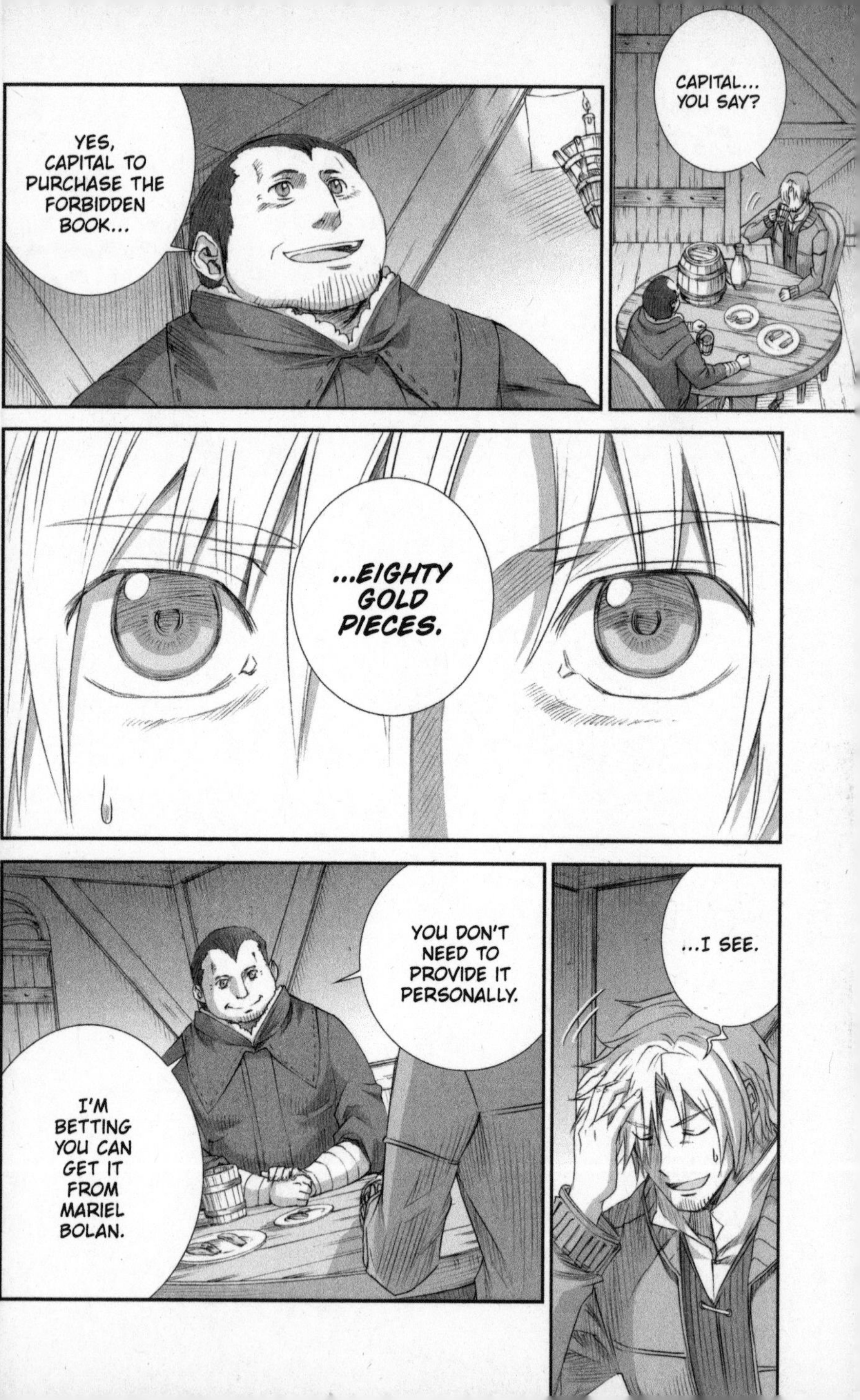
CAPITAL... YOU SAY?
YES, CAPITAL TO PURCHASE THE FORBIDDEN BOOK...
...EIGHTY GOLD PIECES.
...I SEE.
YOU DON'T NEED TO PROVIDE IT PERSONALLY.
I'M BETTING YOU CAN GET IT FROM MARIEL BOLAN.

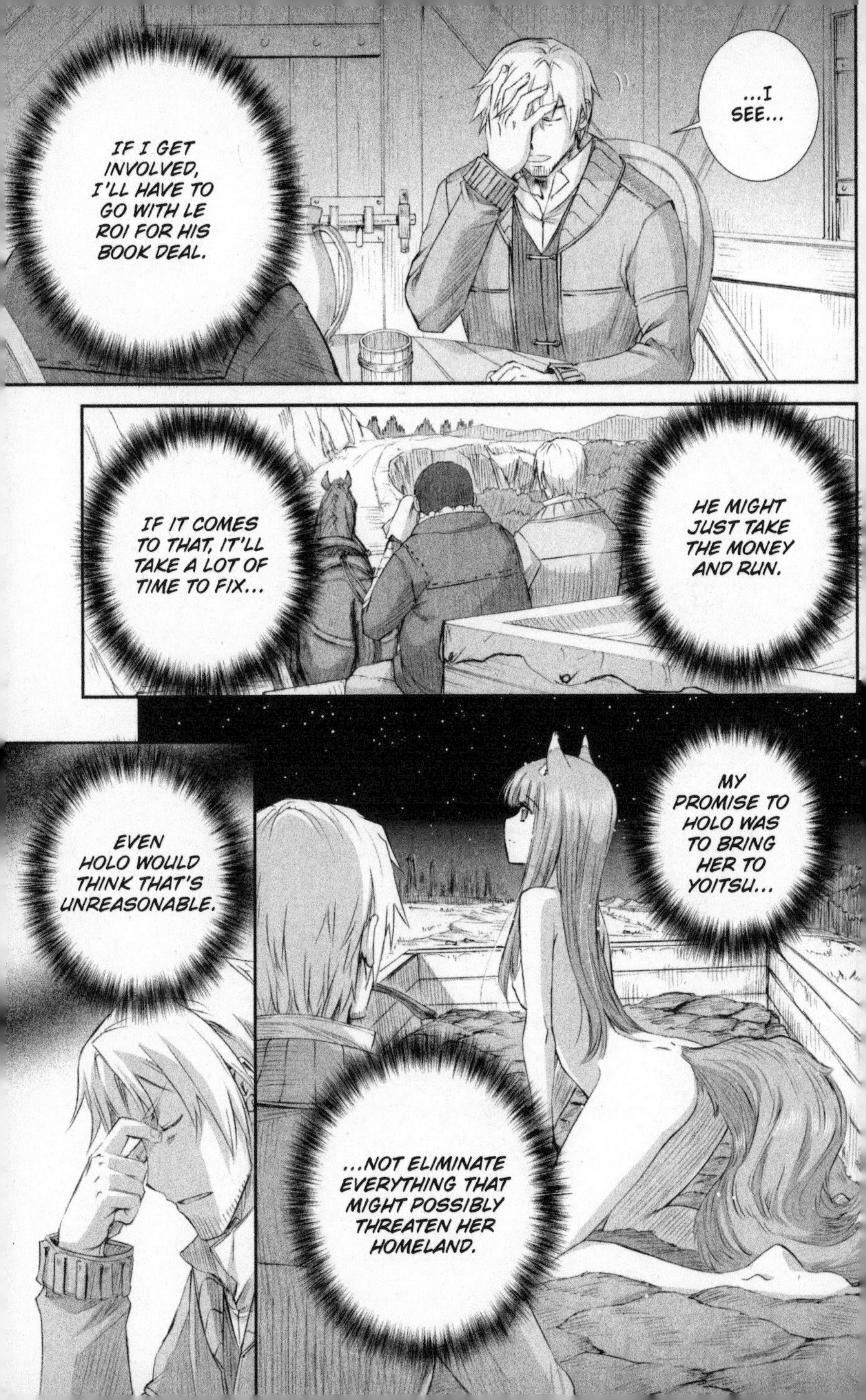
...I SEE...
IF I GET INVOLVED, I'LL HAVE TO GO WITH LE ROI FOR HIS BOOK DEAL.
HE MIGHT JUST TAKE THE MONEY AND RUN.
IF IT COMES TO THAT, IT'LL TAKE A LOT OF TIME TO FIX...
MY PROMISE TO HOLO WAS TO BRING HER TO YOITSU...
...NOT ELIMINATE EVERYTHING THAT MIGHT POSSIBLY THREATEN HER HOMELAND.
EVEN HOLO WOULD THINK THAT'S UNREASONABLE.

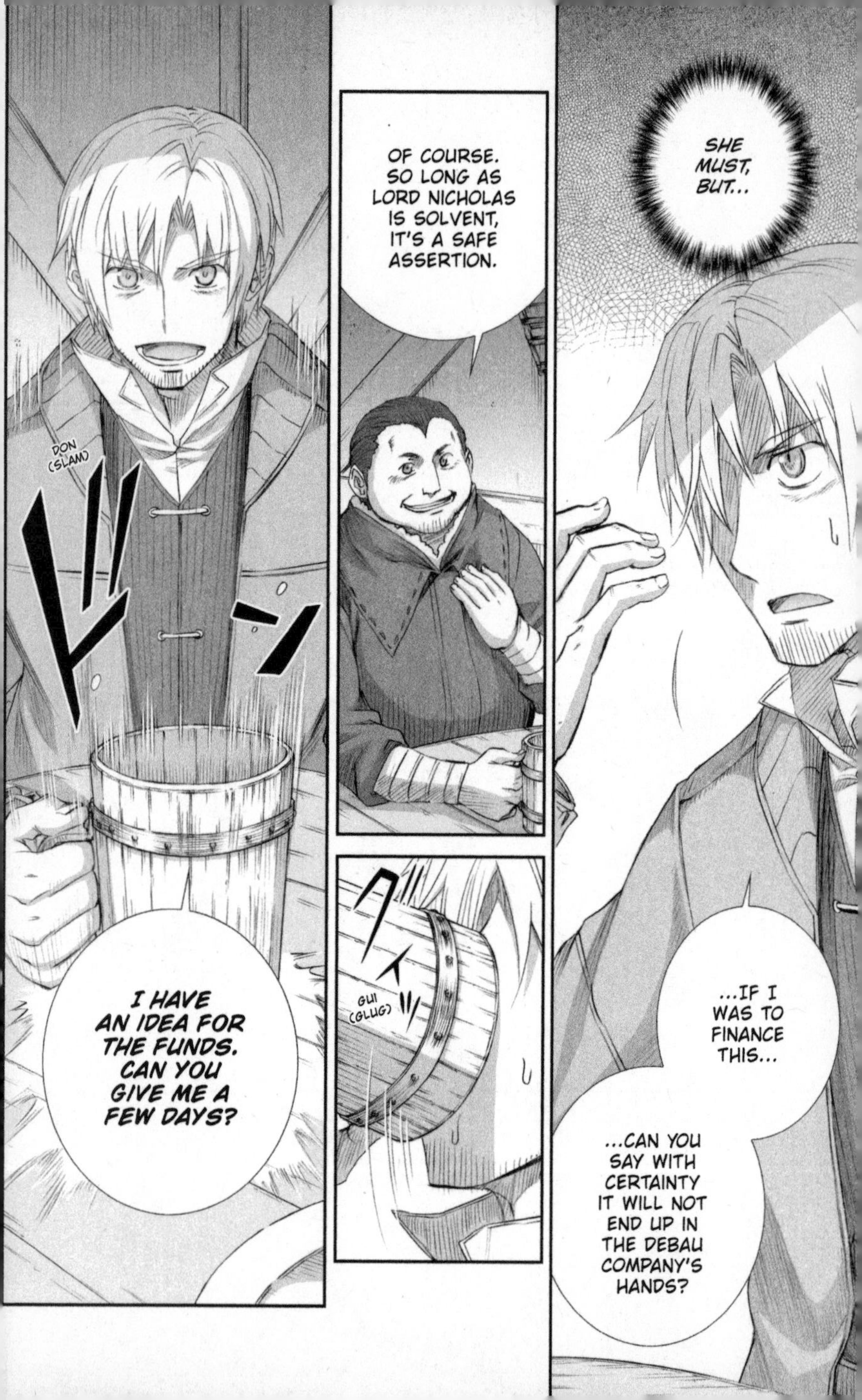
SHE MUST, BUT...
...IF I WAS TO FINANCE THIS...
...CAN YOU SAY WITH CERTAINTY IT WILL NOT END UP IN THE DEBAU COMPANY'S HANDS?
OF COURSE. SO LONG AS LORD NICHOLAS IS SOLVENT, IT'S A SAFE ASSERTION.
GUI (GLUG)
DON (SLAM)
I HAVE AN IDEA FOR THE FUNDS. CAN YOU GIVE ME A FEW DAYS?

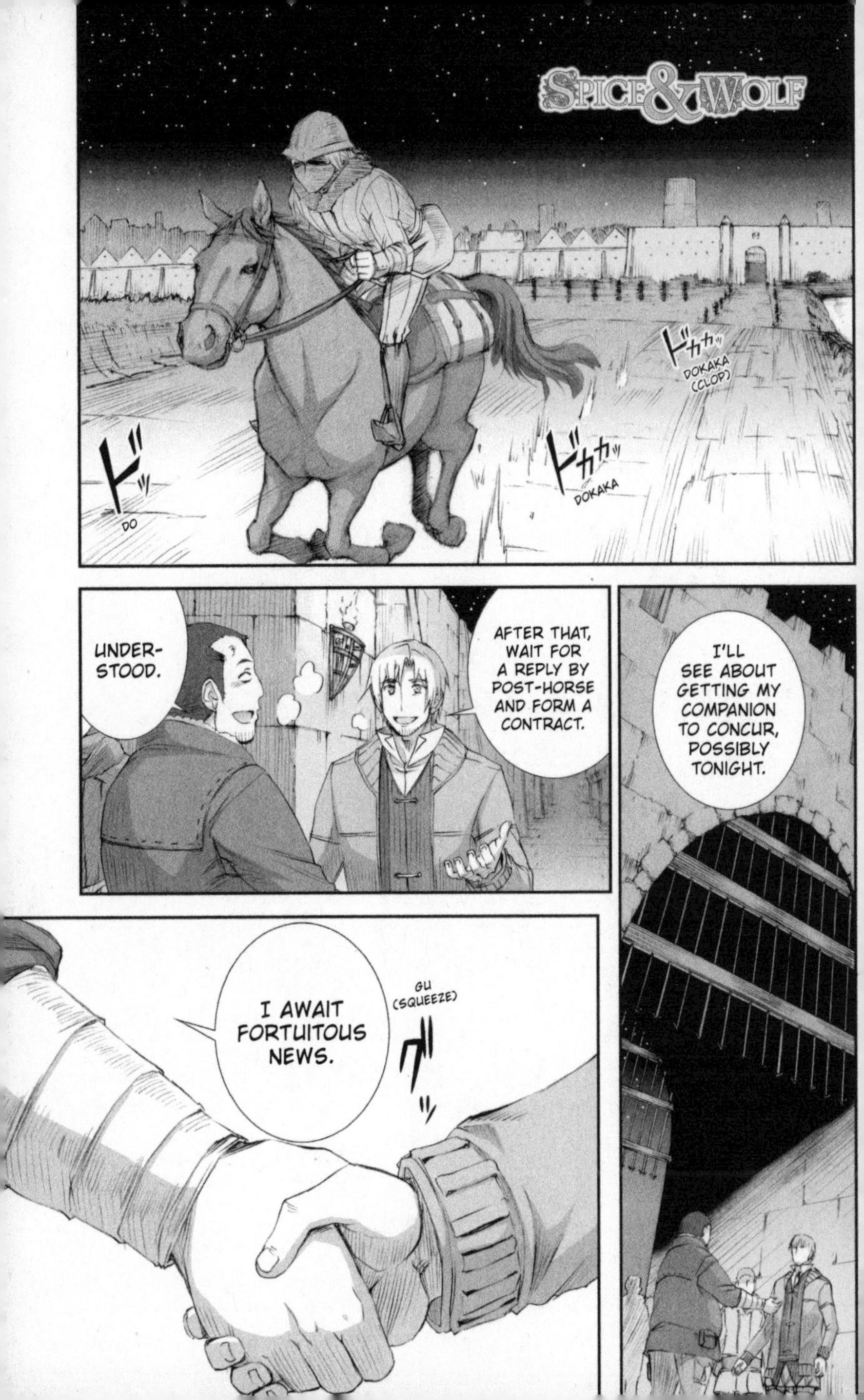
SPICE & WOLF
ドカカッ
DOKAKA (CLOP)
ドカカッ
DOKAKA
ドッ
DO
I'LL SEE ABOUT GETTING MY COMPANION TO CONCUR, POSSIBLY TONIGHT.
AFTER THAT, WAIT FOR A REPLY BY POST-HORSE AND FORM A CONTRACT.
UNDER-STOOD.
GU (SQUEEZE)
グッ
I AWAIT FORTUITOUS NEWS.

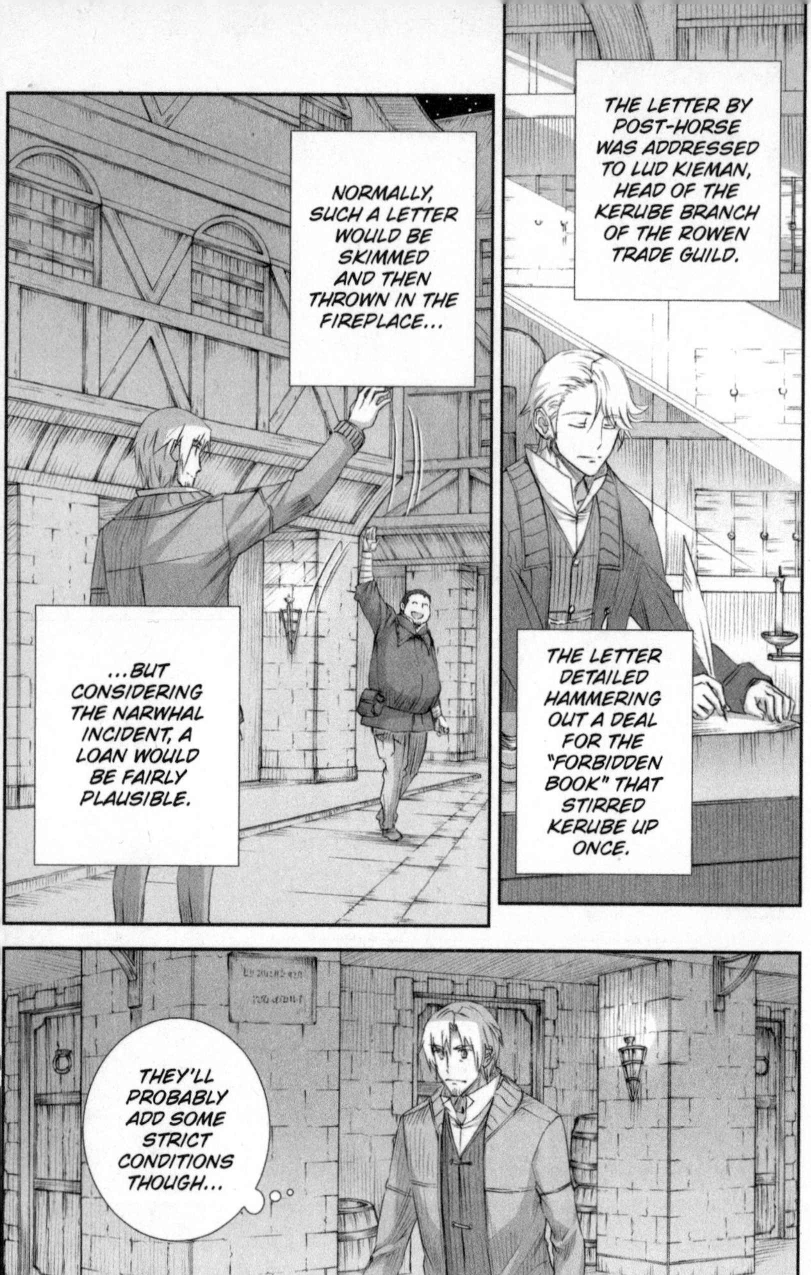
THE LETTER BY POST-HORSE WAS ADDRESSED TO LUD KIEMAN, HEAD OF THE KERUBE BRANCH OF THE ROWEN TRADE GUILD.
THE LETTER DETAILED HAMMERING OUT A DEAL FOR THE "FORBIDDEN BOOK" THAT STIRRED KERUBE UP ONCE.
NORMALLY, SUCH A LETTER WOULD BE SKIMMED AND THEN THROWN IN THE FIREPLACE...
...BUT CONSIDERING THE NARWHAL INCIDENT, A LOAN WOULD BE FAIRLY PLAUSIBLE.
THEY'LL PROBABLY ADD SOME STRICT CONDITIONS THOUGH...

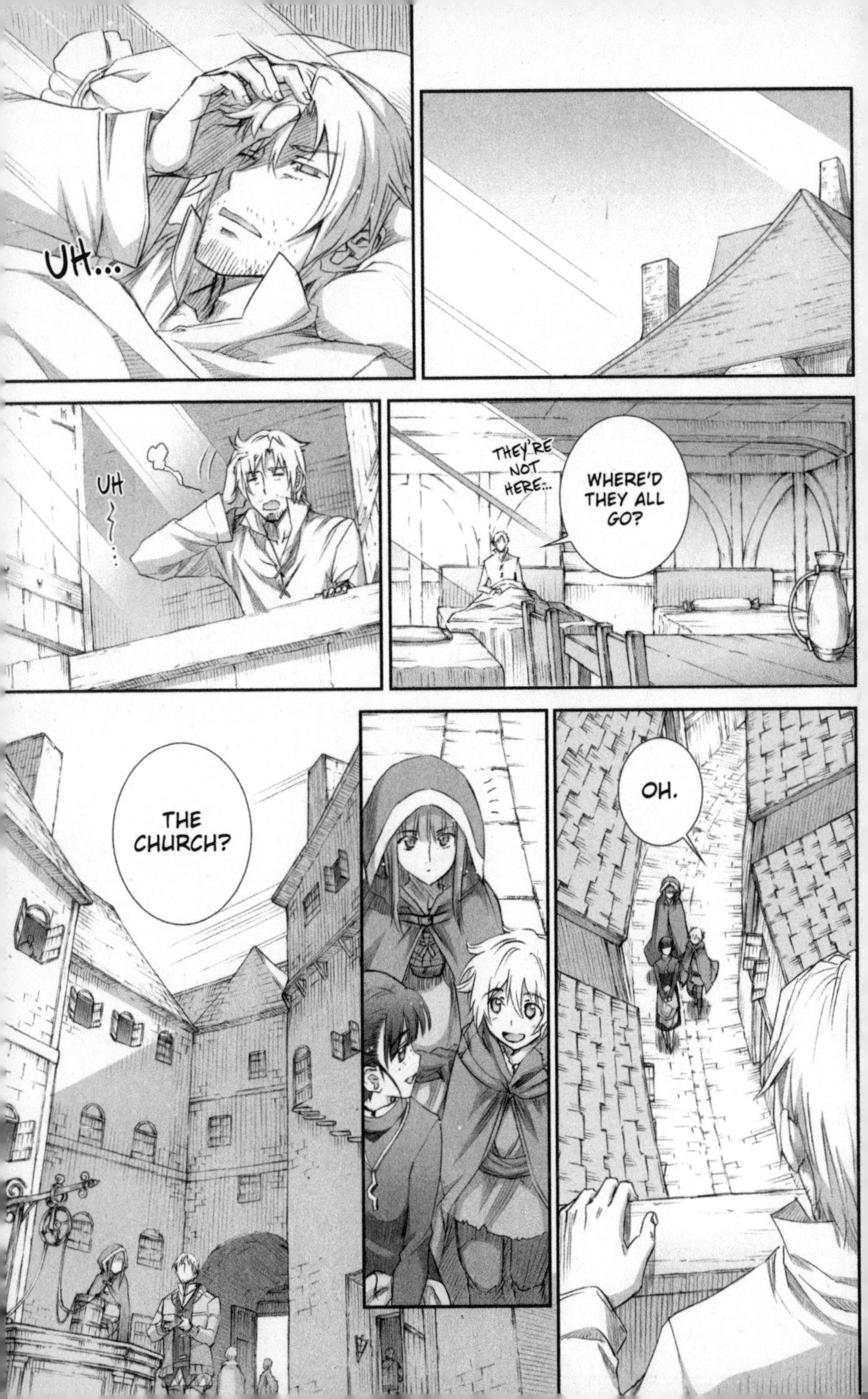
UH...
THEY'RE NOT HERE...
WHERE'D THEY ALL GO?
UH~...
OH.
THE CHURCH?

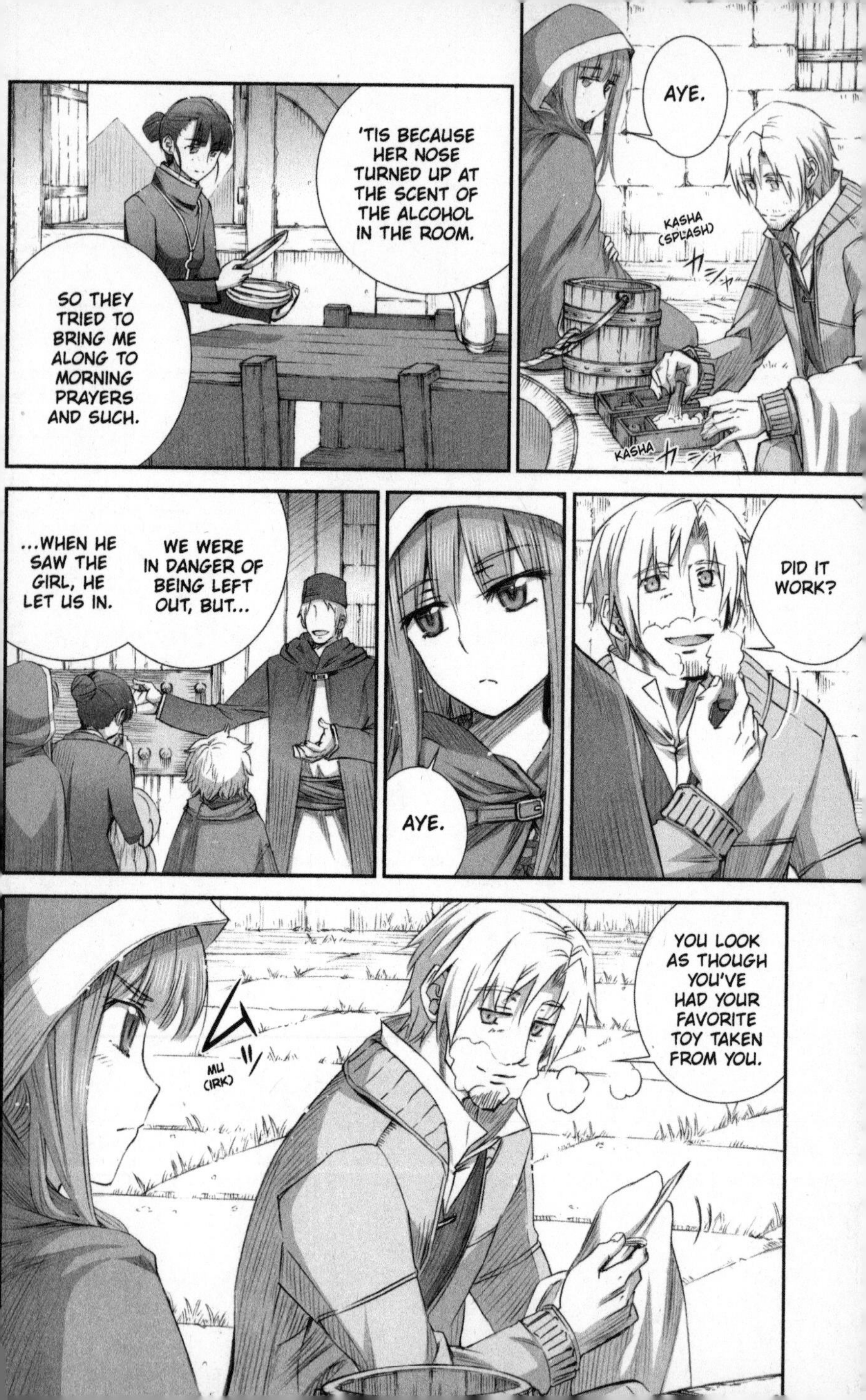
AYE.
KASHA (SPLASH)
KASHA
'TIS BECAUSE HER NOSE TURNED UP AT THE SCENT OF THE ALCOHOL IN THE ROOM.
SO THEY TRIED TO BRING ME ALONG TO MORNING PRAYERS AND SUCH.
DID IT WORK?
AYE.
WE WERE IN DANGER OF BEING LEFT OUT, BUT...
...WHEN HE SAW THE GIRL, HE LET US IN.
YOU LOOK AS THOUGH YOU'VE HAD YOUR FAVORITE TOY TAKEN FROM YOU.
MU (IRK)

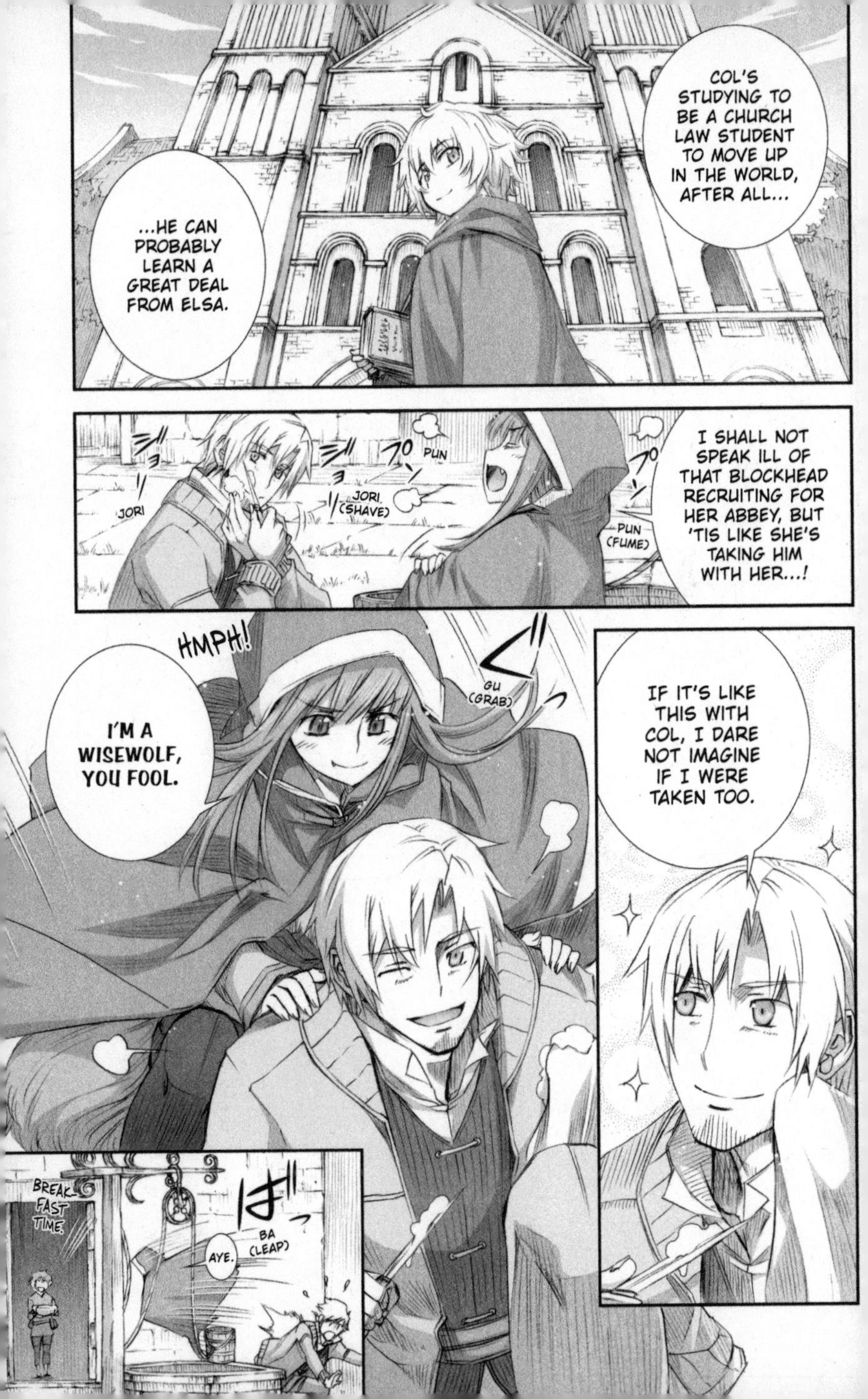
COL'S STUDYING TO BE A CHURCH LAW STUDENT TO MOVE UP IN THE WORLD, AFTER ALL...
...HE CAN PROBABLY LEARN A GREAT DEAL FROM ELSA.
I SHALL NOT SPEAK ILL OF THAT BLOCKHEAD RECRUITING FOR HER ABBEY, BUT 'TIS LIKE SHE'S TAKING HIM WITH HER...!
PUN (FUME)
PUN
JORI (SHAVE)
JORI
IF IT'S LIKE THIS WITH COL, I DARE NOT IMAGINE IF I WERE TAKEN TOO.
GU (GRAB)
HMPH!
I'M A WISEWOLF, YOU FOOL.
BA (LEAP)
AYE.
BREAK-FAST TIME.

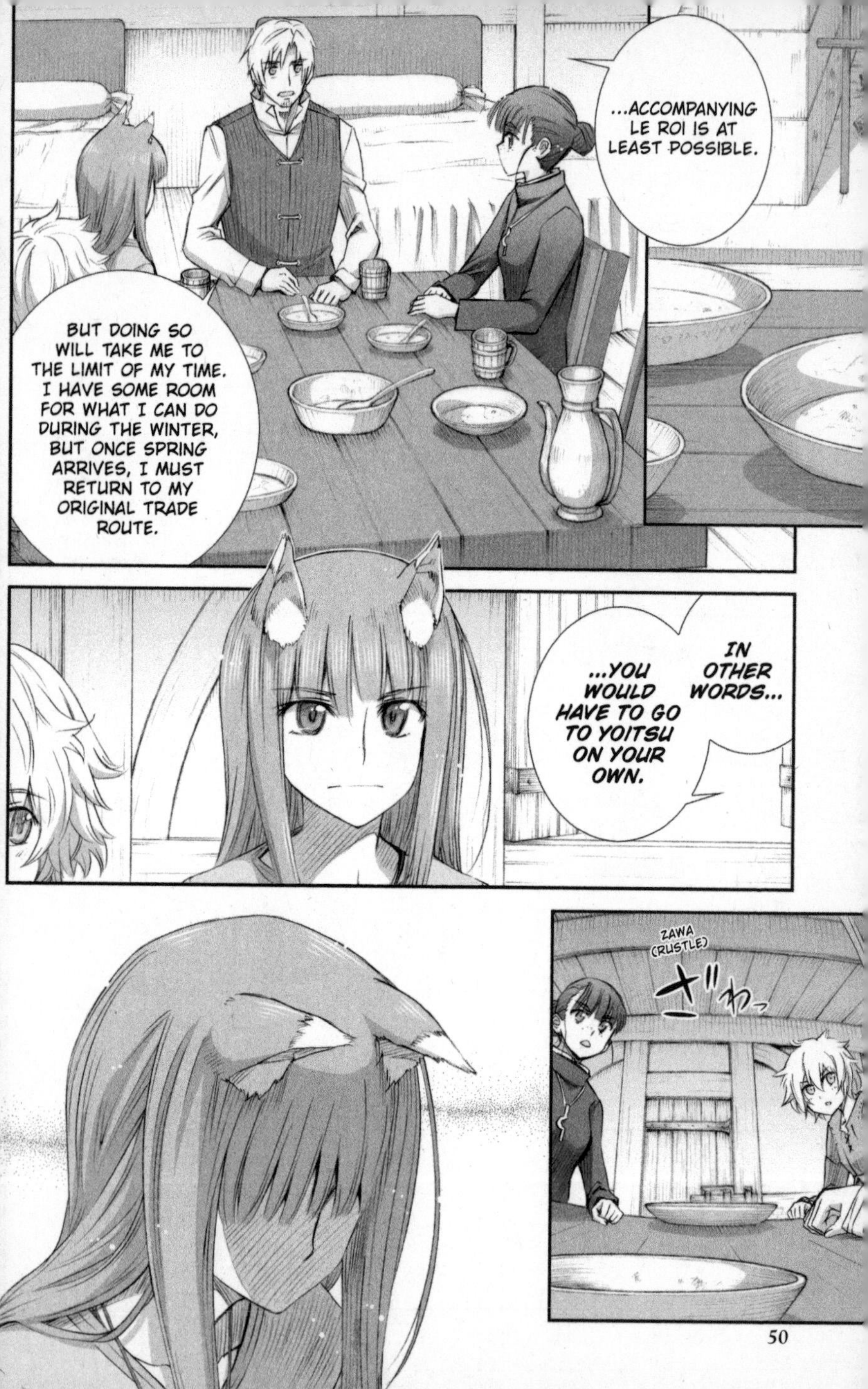
...ACCOMPANYING LE ROI IS AT LEAST POSSIBLE.
BUT DOING SO WILL TAKE ME TO THE LIMIT OF MY TIME. I HAVE SOME ROOM FOR WHAT I CAN DO DURING THE WINTER, BUT ONCE SPRING ARRIVES, I MUST RETURN TO MY ORIGINAL TRADE ROUTE.
IN OTHER WORDS...
...YOU WOULD HAVE TO GO TO YOITSU ON YOUR OWN.
ZAWA (RUSTLE)

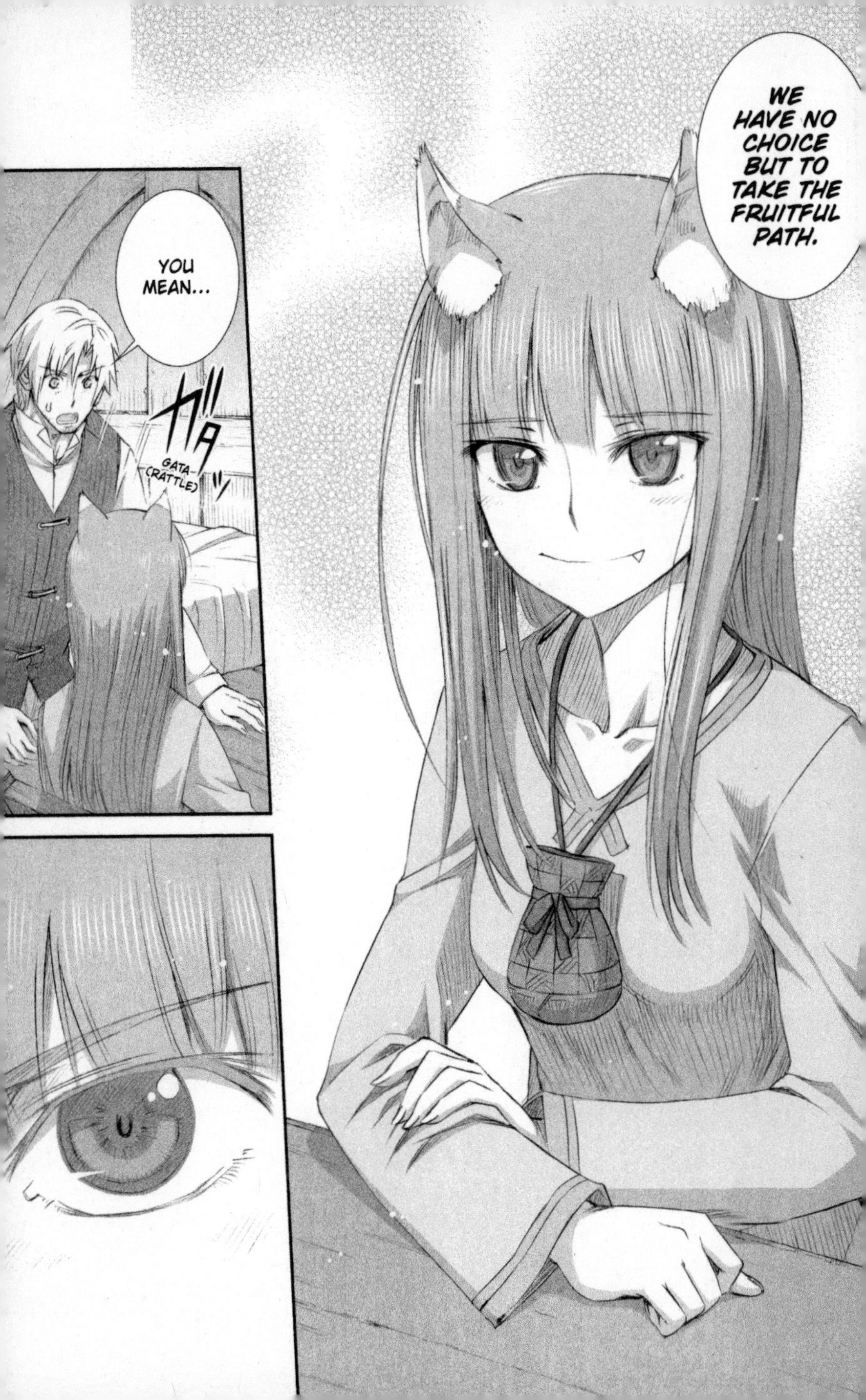
WE HAVE NO CHOICE BUT TO TAKE THE FRUITFUL PATH.
YOU MEAN...
ガタッ
GATA (RATTLE)

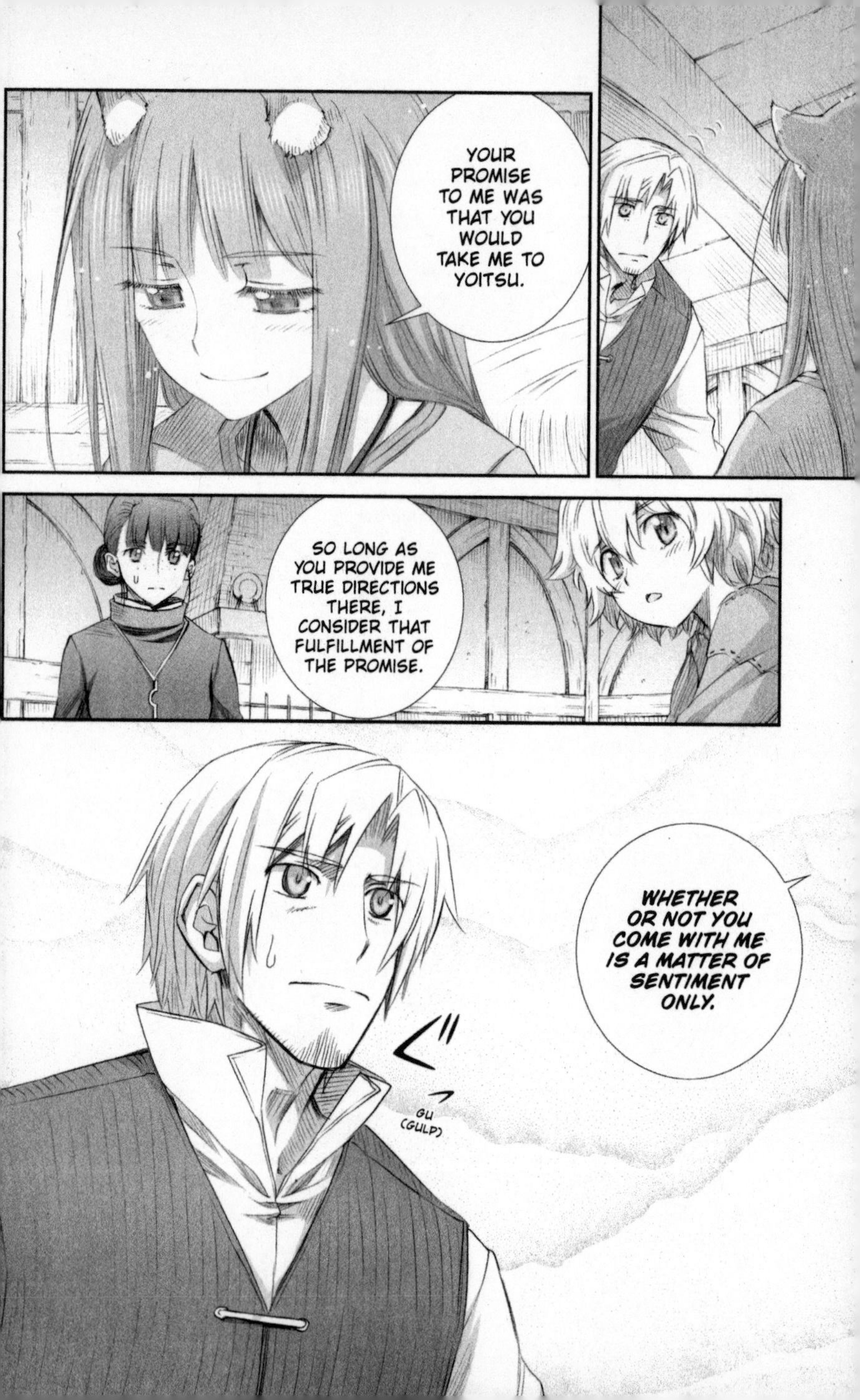
YOUR PROMISE TO ME WAS THAT YOU WOULD TAKE ME TO YOITSU.
SO LONG AS YOU PROVIDE ME TRUE DIRECTIONS THERE, I CONSIDER THAT FULFILLMENT OF THE PROMISE.
WHETHER OR NOT YOU COME WITH ME IS A MATTER OF SENTIMENT ONLY.
GU (GULP)

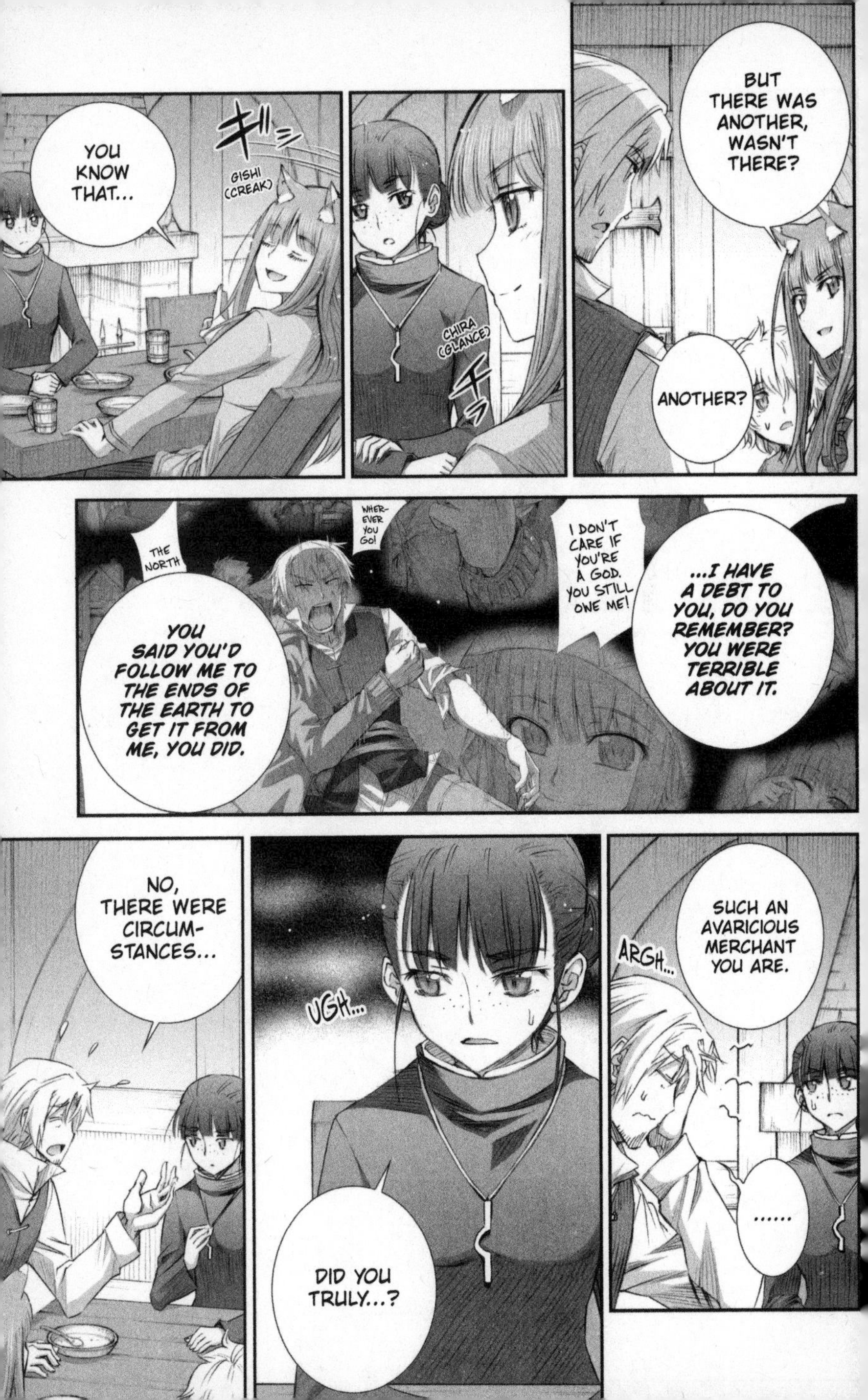
BUT THERE WAS ANOTHER, WASN'T THERE?
ANOTHER?
チラ
CHIRA (GLANCE)
ギシ
GISHI (CREAK)
YOU KNOW THAT...
...I HAVE A DEBT TO YOU, DO YOU REMEMBER? YOU WERE TERRIBLE ABOUT IT.
I DON'T CARE IF YOU'RE A GOD. YOU STILL OWE ME!
WHER-EVER YOU GO!
THE NORTH
YOU SAID YOU'D FOLLOW ME TO THE ENDS OF THE EARTH TO GET IT FROM ME, YOU DID.
SUCH AN AVARICIOUS MERCHANT YOU ARE.
ARGH...
......
UGH...
DID YOU TRULY...?
NO, THERE WERE CIRCUM-STANCES...

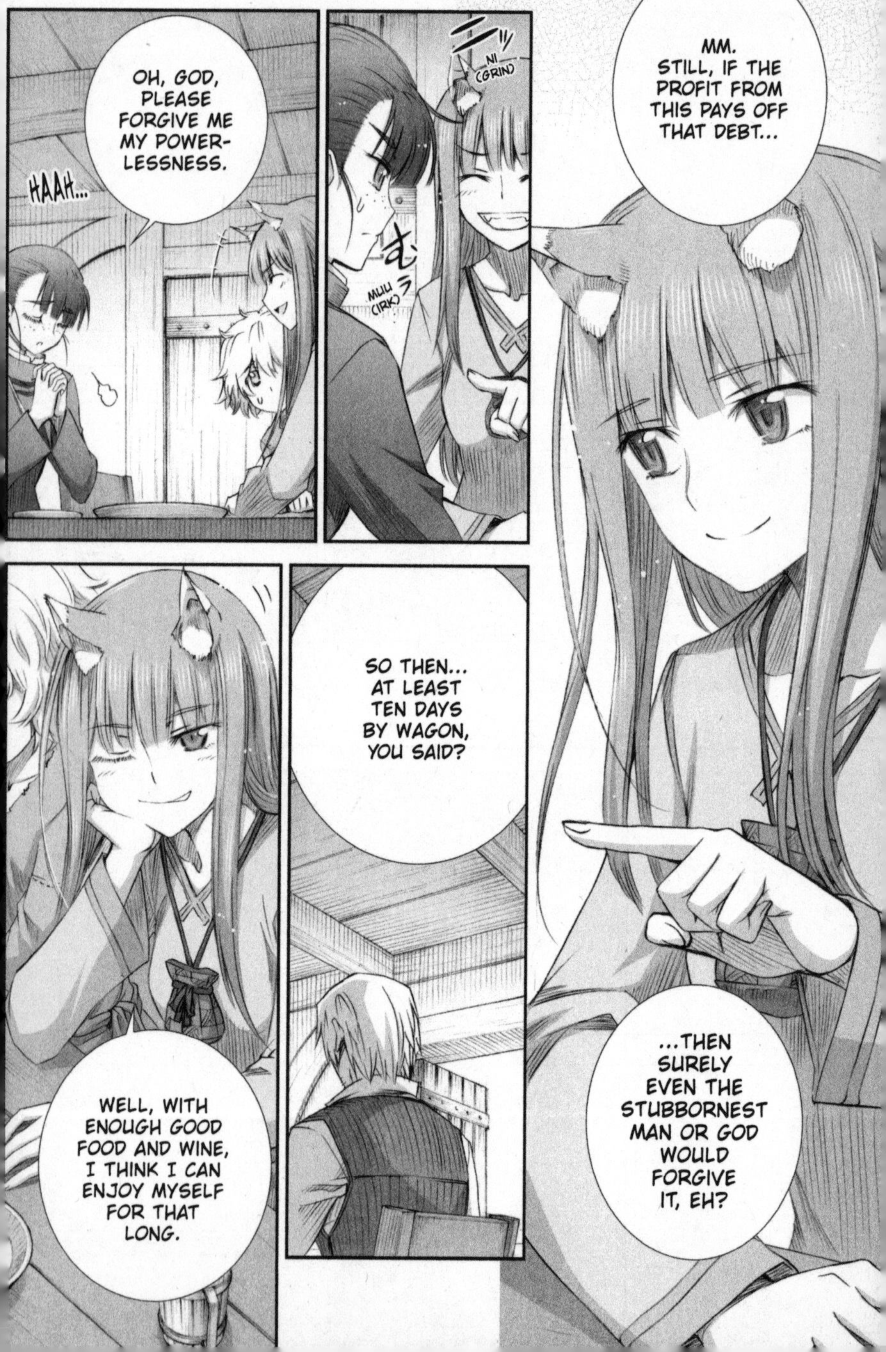
MM. STILL, IF THE PROFIT FROM THIS PAYS OFF THAT DEBT...
...THEN SURELY EVEN THE STUBBORNEST MAN OR GOD WOULD FORGIVE IT, EH?
OH, GOD, PLEASE FORGIVE ME MY POWER-LESSNESS.
HAAAH...
NI (GRIN)
MUU (IRK)
SO THEN... AT LEAST TEN DAYS BY WAGON, YOU SAID?
WELL, WITH ENOUGH GOOD FOOD AND WINE, I THINK I CAN ENJOY MYSELF FOR THAT LONG.

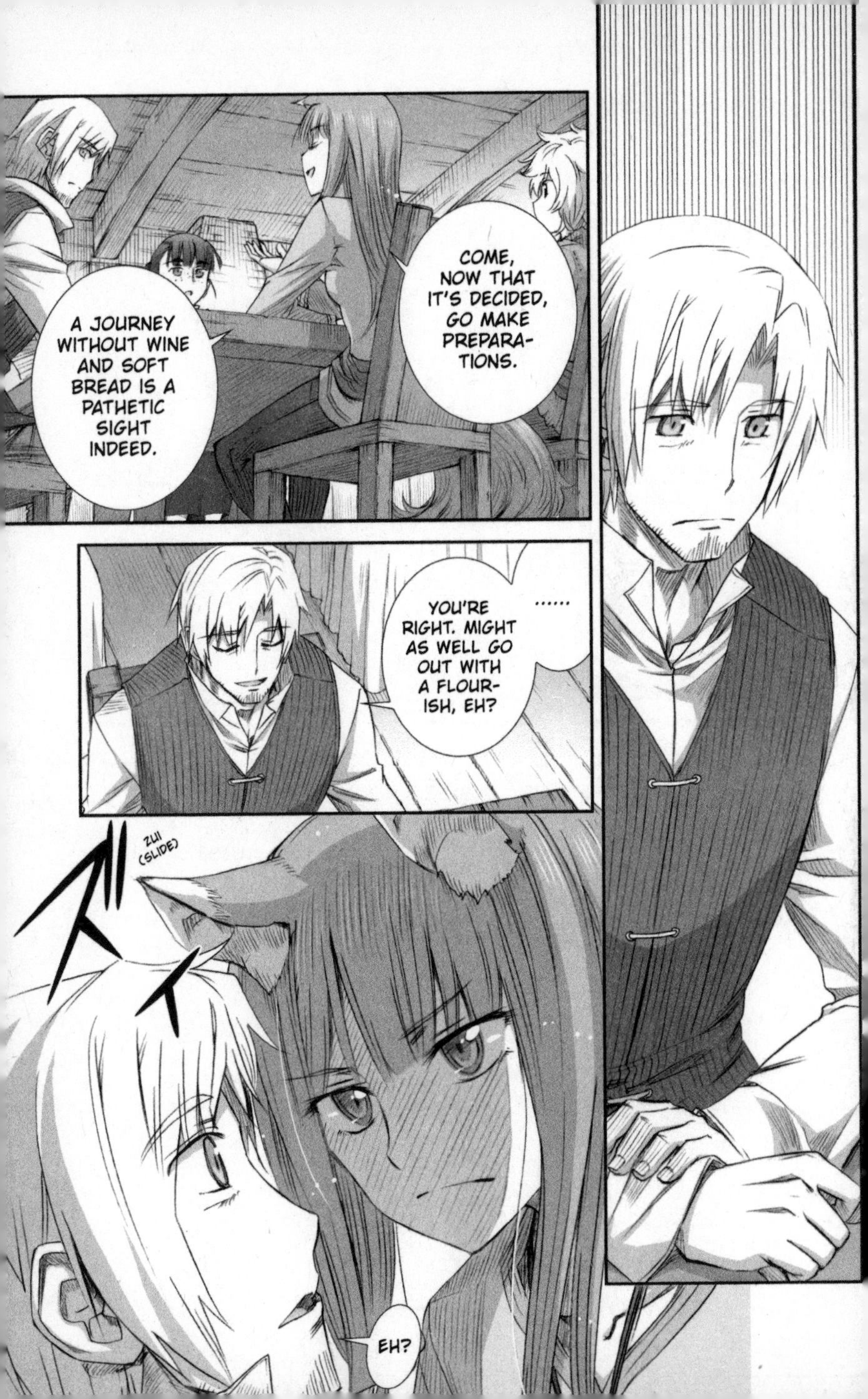
COME, NOW THAT IT'S DECIDED, GO MAKE PREPARATIONS.
A JOURNEY WITHOUT WINE AND SOFT BREAD IS A PATHETIC SIGHT INDEED.
......
YOU'RE RIGHT. MIGHT AS WELL GO OUT WITH A FLOURISH, EH?
ZUI (SLIDE)
EH?

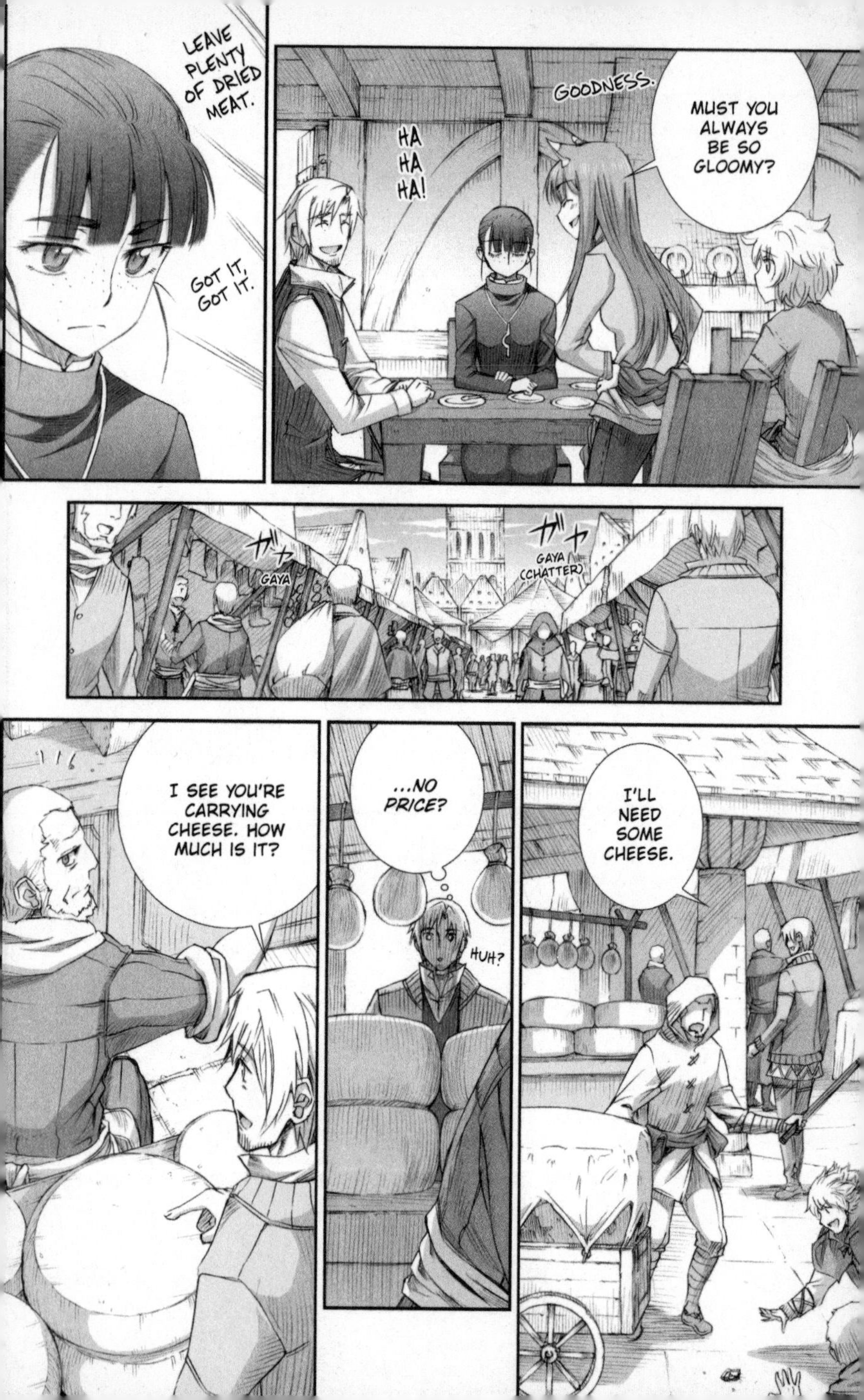
GOODNESS.
MUST YOU ALWAYS BE SO GLOOMY?
HA HA HA!
LEAVE PLENTY OF DRIED MEAT.
GOT IT, GOT IT.
ガヤ
GAYA (CHATTER)
ガヤ
GAYA
I'LL NEED SOME CHEESE.
HUH?
...NO PRICE?
I SEE YOU'RE CARRYING CHEESE. HOW MUCH IS IT?

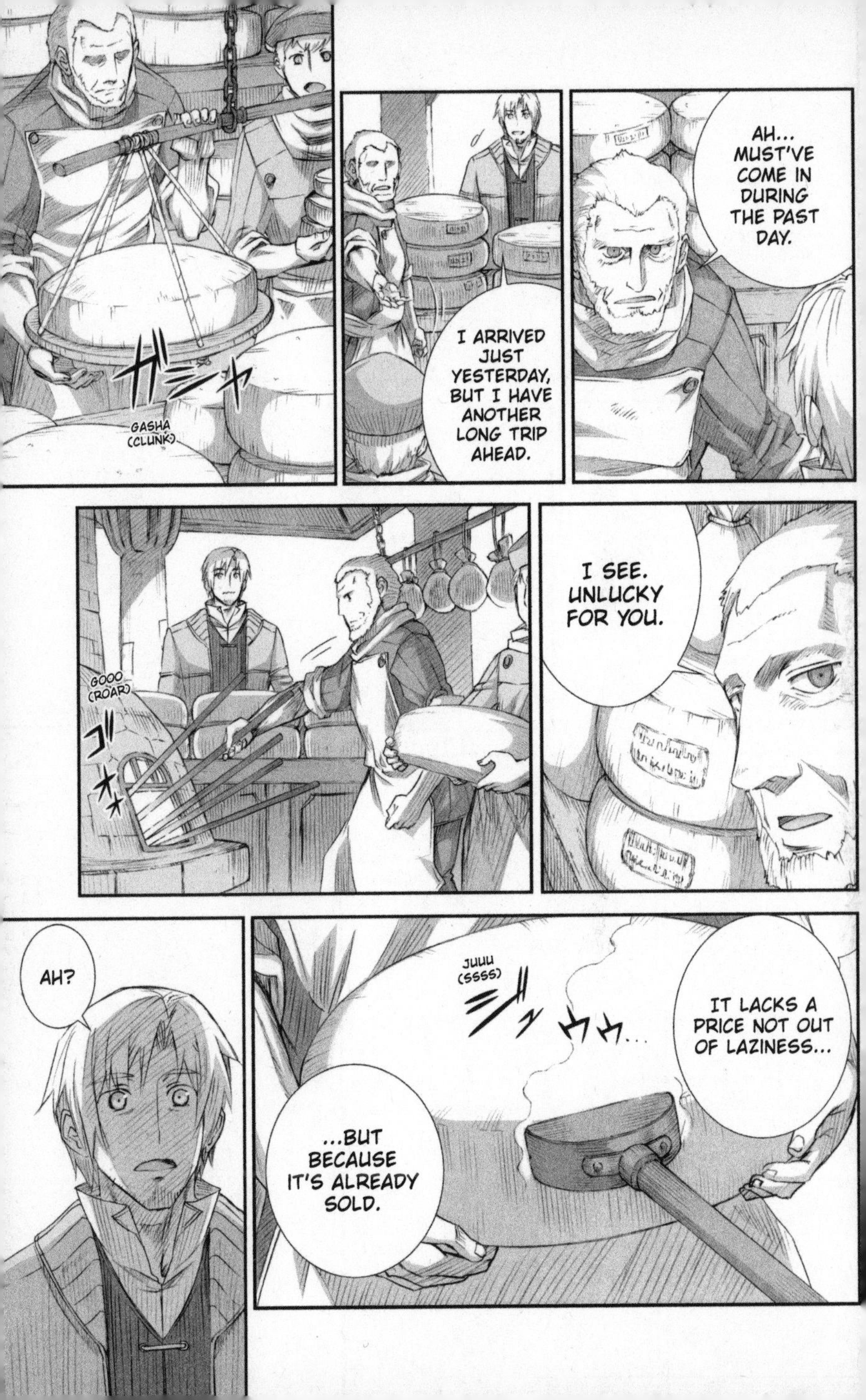
AH... MUST'VE COME IN DURING THE PAST DAY.
I ARRIVED JUST YESTERDAY, BUT I HAVE ANOTHER LONG TRIP AHEAD.
GASHA (CLUNK)
I SEE. UNLUCKY FOR YOU.
GOOO (ROAR)
JUUU (SSSS)
IT LACKS A PRICE NOT OUT OF LAZINESS...
...BUT BECAUSE IT'S ALREADY SOLD.
AH?

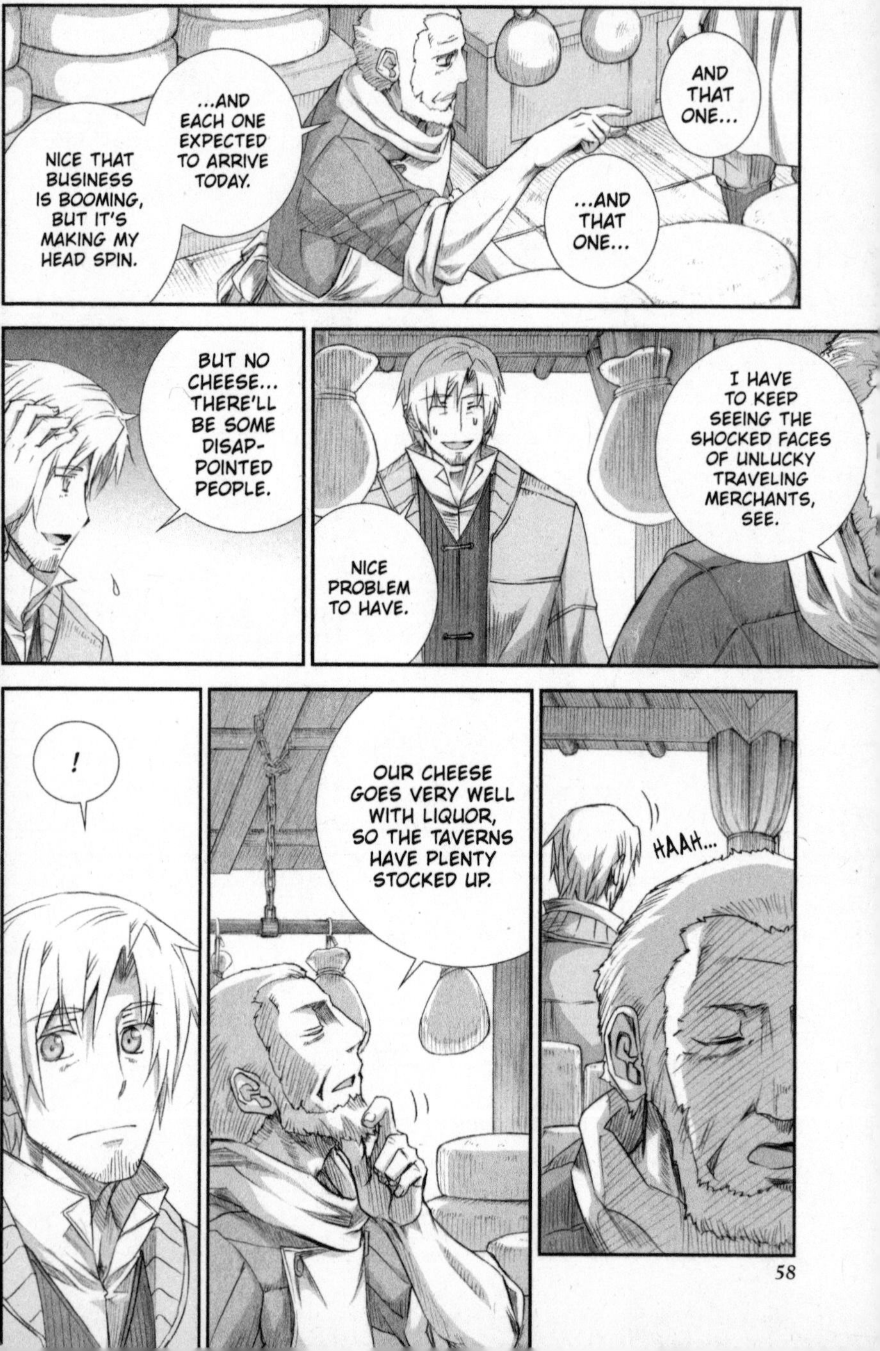
AND THAT ONE...
...AND THAT ONE...
...AND EACH ONE EXPECTED TO ARRIVE TODAY.
NICE THAT BUSINESS IS BOOMING, BUT IT'S MAKING MY HEAD SPIN.
I HAVE TO KEEP SEEING THE SHOCKED FACES OF UNLUCKY TRAVELING MERCHANTS, SEE.
NICE PROBLEM TO HAVE.
BUT NO CHEESE... THERE'LL BE SOME DISAP-POINTED PEOPLE.
HAAH...
OUR CHEESE GOES VERY WELL WITH LIQUOR, SO THE TAVERNS HAVE PLENTY STOCKED UP.
!

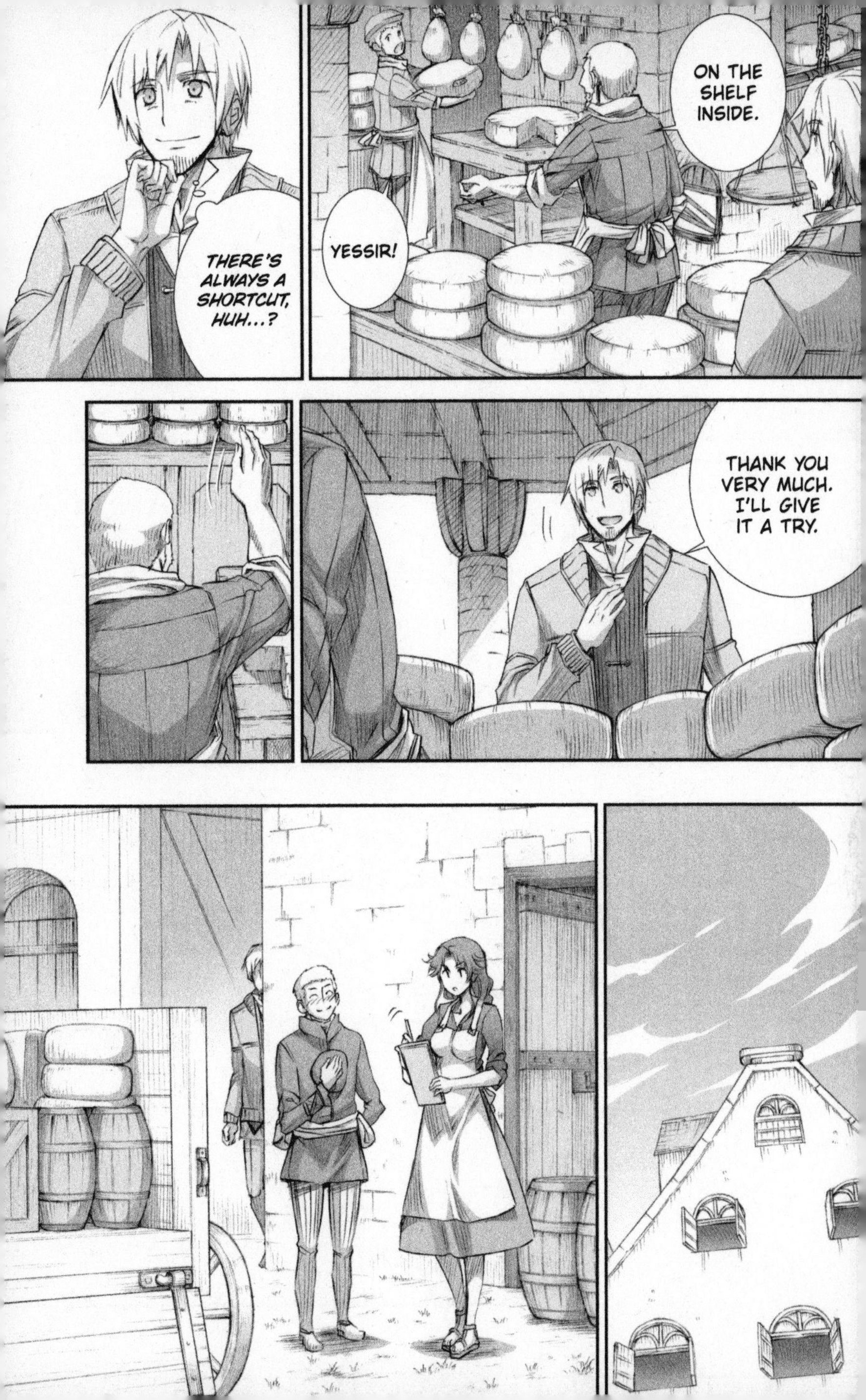
ON THE SHELF INSIDE.
YESSIR!
THERE'S ALWAYS A SHORTCUT, HUH...?
THANK YOU VERY MUCH. I'LL GIVE IT A TRY.

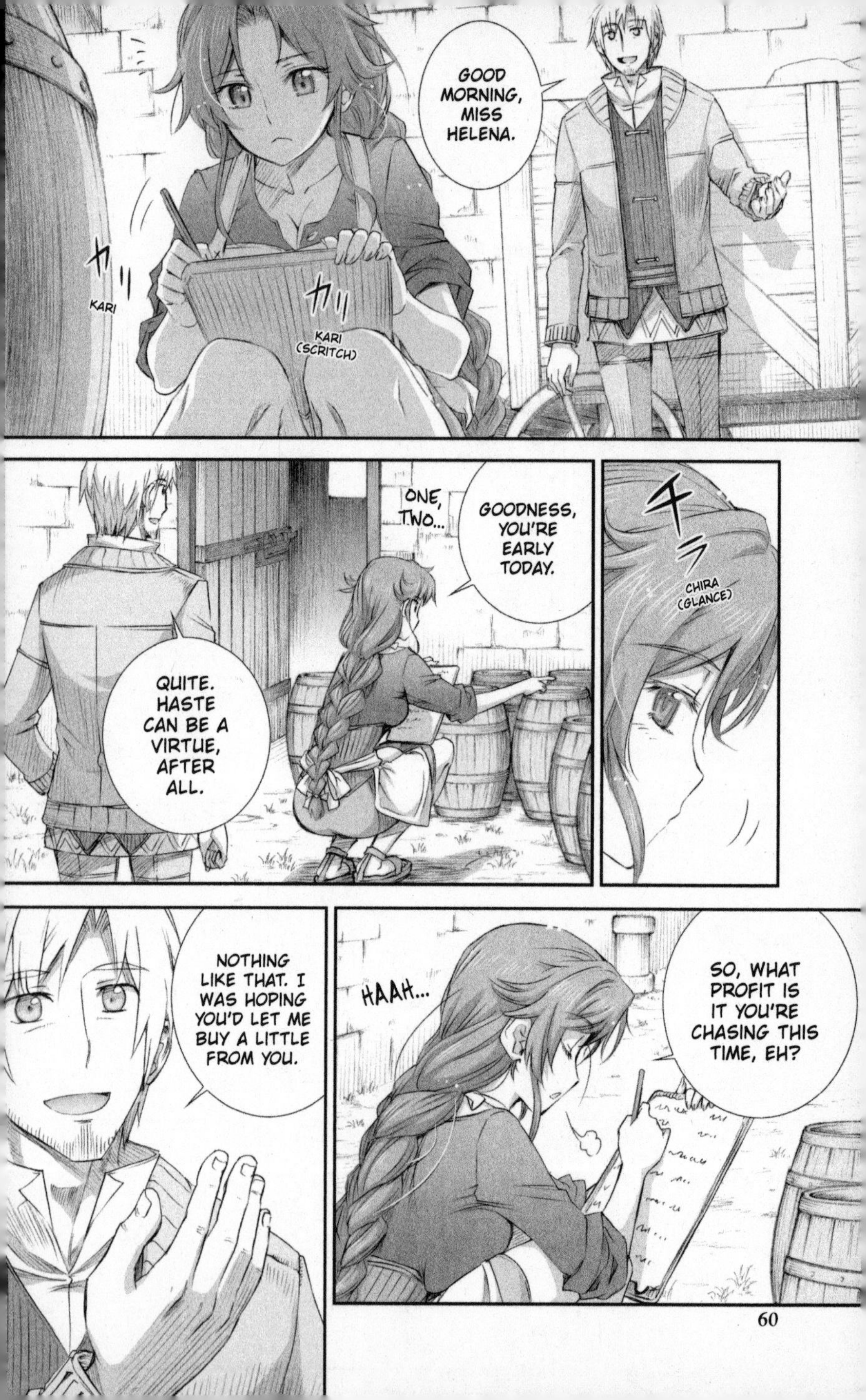
GOOD MORNING, MISS HELENA.
カリ
KARI (SCRITCH)
カリ
KARI
チラ
CHIRA (GLANCE)
GOODNESS, YOU'RE EARLY TODAY.
ONE, TWO...
QUITE. HASTE CAN BE A VIRTUE, AFTER ALL.
SO, WHAT PROFIT IS IT YOU'RE CHASING THIS TIME, EH?
HAAH...
NOTHING LIKE THAT. I WAS HOPING YOU'D LET ME BUY A LITTLE FROM YOU.

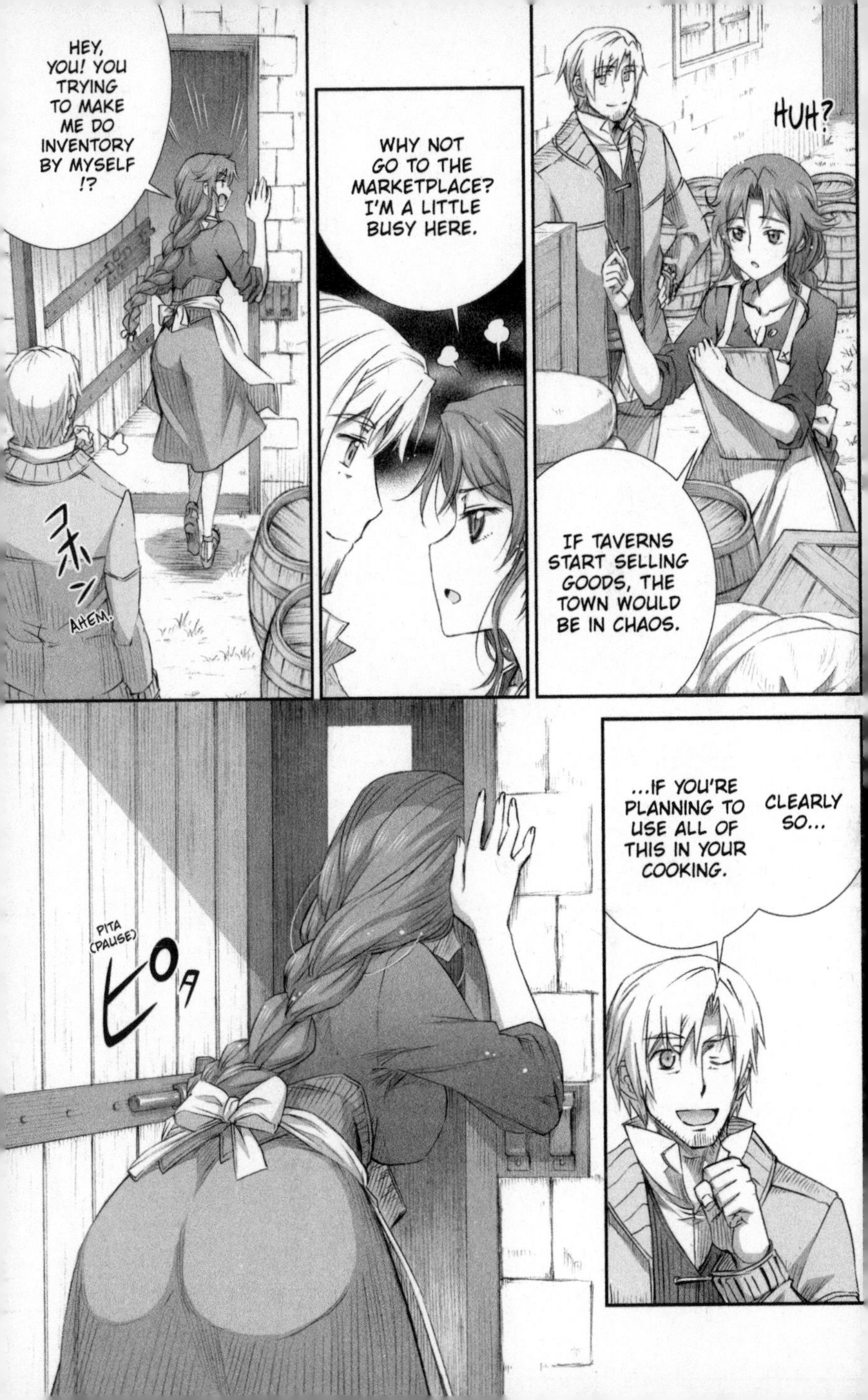
HUH?
IF TAVERNS START SELLING GOODS, THE TOWN WOULD BE IN CHAOS.
WHY NOT GO TO THE MARKETPLACE? I'M A LITTLE BUSY HERE.
HEY, YOU! YOU TRYING TO MAKE ME DO INVENTORY BY MYSELF !?
コホン
AHEM.
CLEARLY SO...
...IF YOU'RE PLANNING TO USE ALL OF THIS IN YOUR COOKING.
PITA (PAUSE)
ピタ

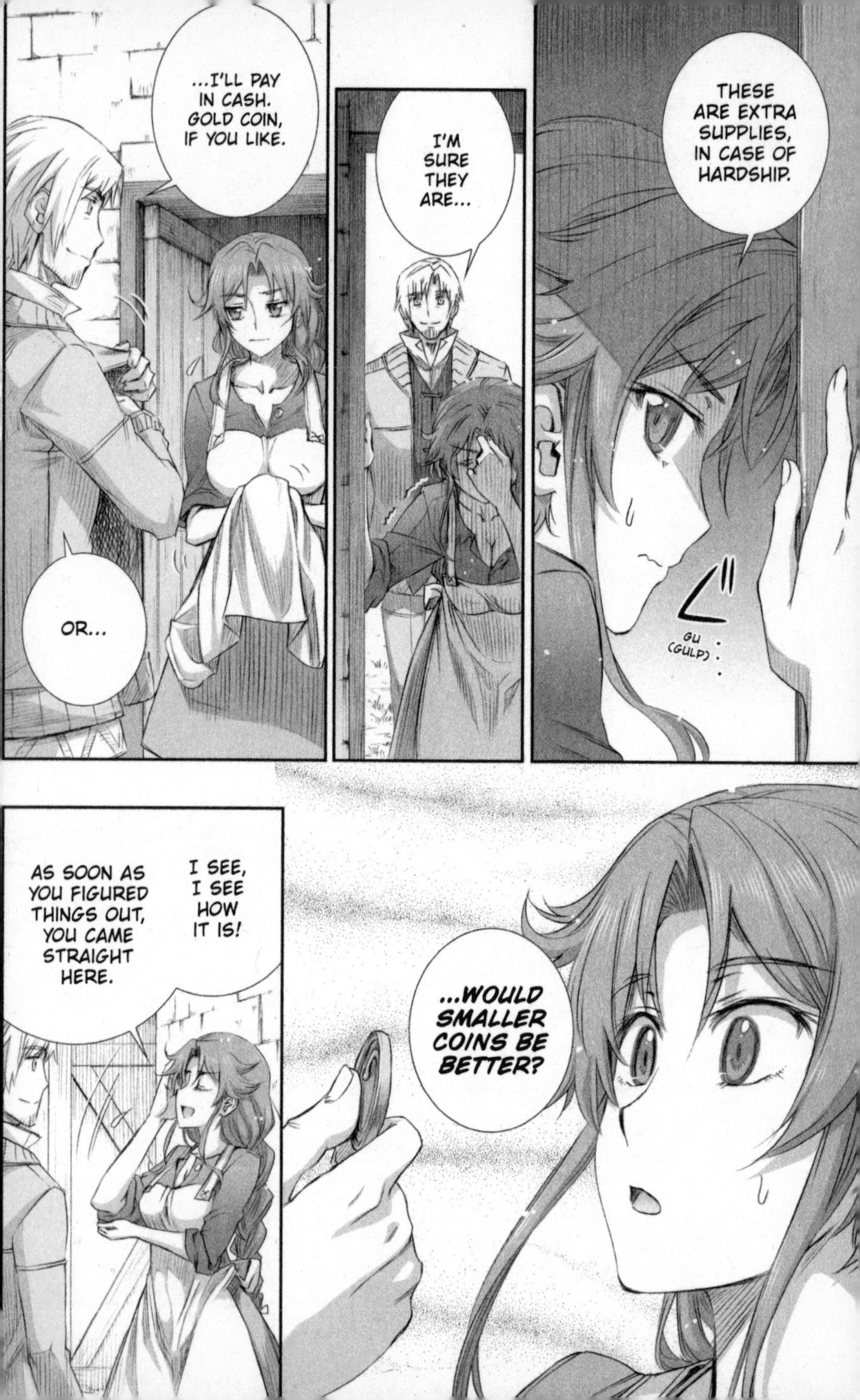
THESE ARE EXTRA SUPPLIES, IN CASE OF HARDSHIP.
ゴ
GU (GULP)...
I'M SURE THEY ARE...
...I'LL PAY IN CASH. GOLD COIN, IF YOU LIKE.
OR...
...WOULD SMALLER COINS BE BETTER?
I SEE, I SEE HOW IT IS!
AS SOON AS YOU FIGURED THINGS OUT, YOU CAME STRAIGHT HERE.

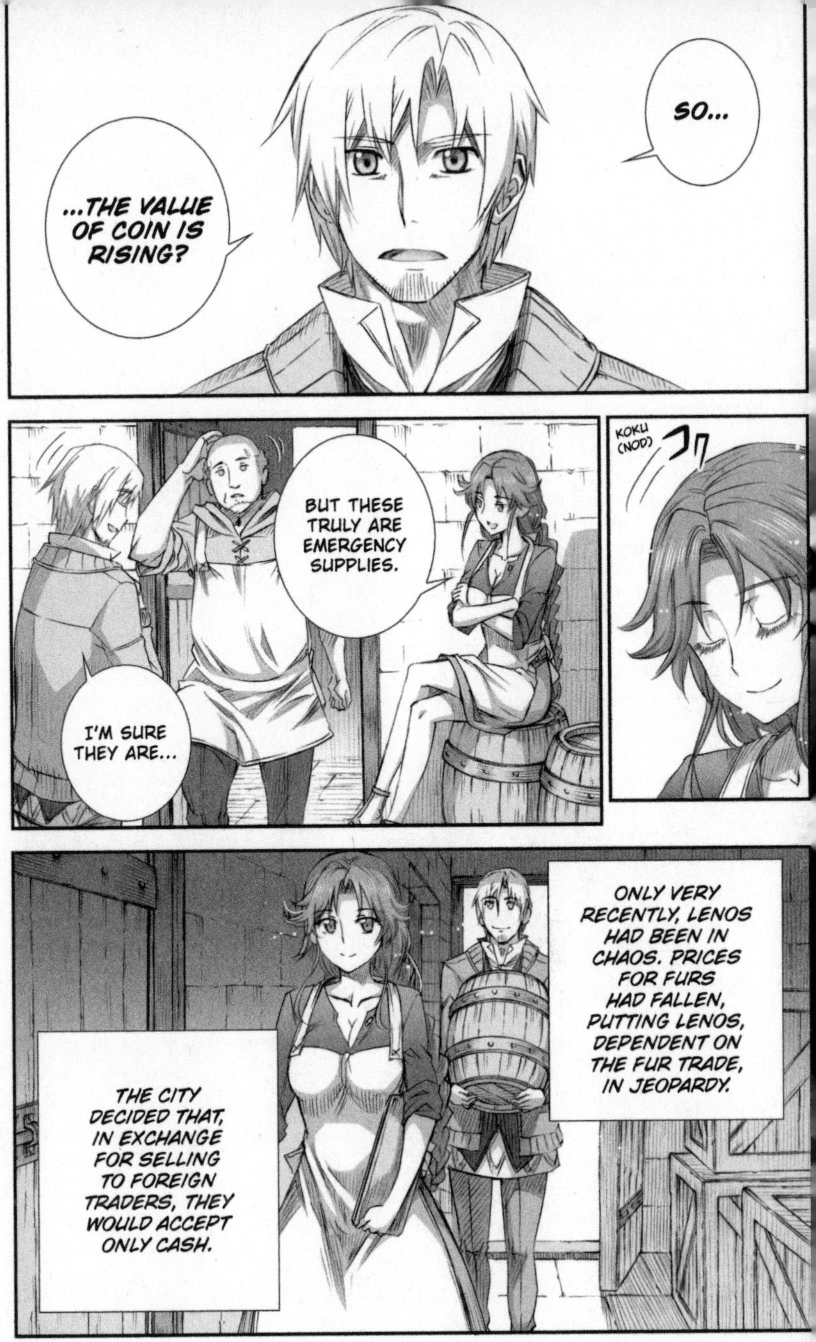
SO...
...THE VALUE OF COIN IS RISING?
KOKU (NOD)
BUT THESE TRULY ARE EMERGENCY SUPPLIES.
I'M SURE THEY ARE...
ONLY VERY RECENTLY, LENOS HAD BEEN IN CHAOS. PRICES FOR FURS HAD FALLEN, PUTTING LENOS, DEPENDENT ON THE FUR TRADE, IN JEOPARDY.
THE CITY DECIDED THAT, IN EXCHANGE FOR SELLING TO FOREIGN TRADERS, THEY WOULD ACCEPT ONLY CASH.

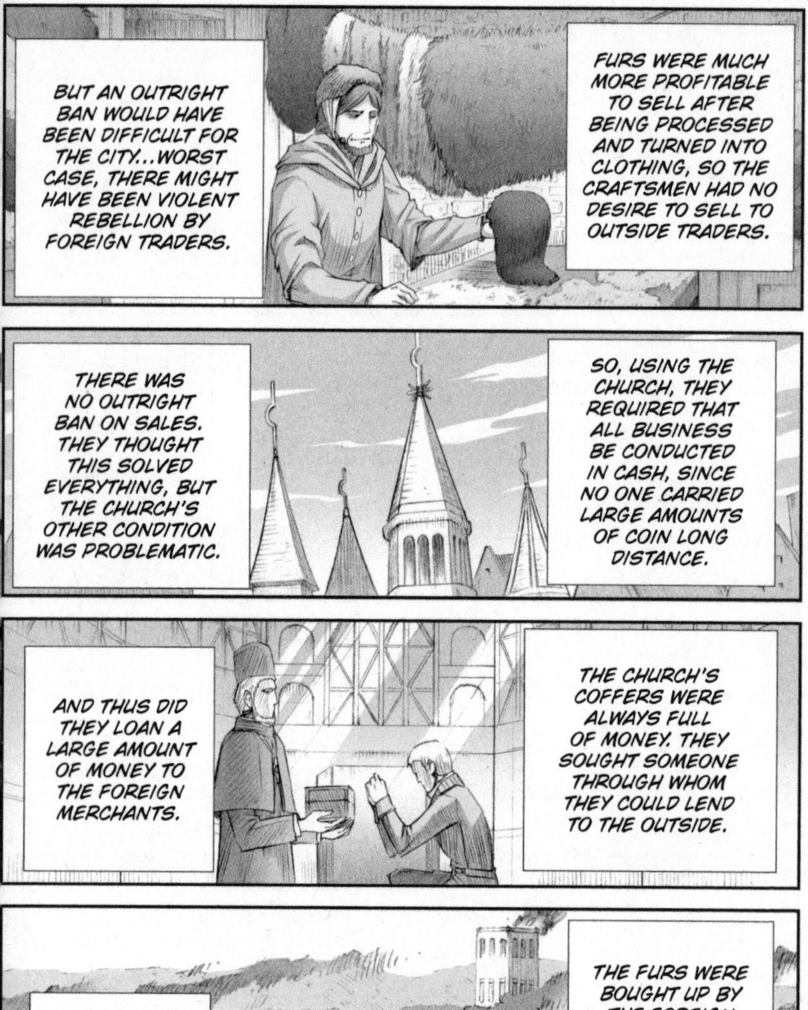
FURS WERE MUCH MORE PROFITABLE TO SELL AFTER BEING PROCESSED AND TURNED INTO CLOTHING, SO THE CRAFTSMEN HAD NO DESIRE TO SELL TO OUTSIDE TRADERS.
BUT AN OUTRIGHT BAN WOULD HAVE BEEN DIFFICULT FOR THE CITY...WORST CASE, THERE MIGHT HAVE BEEN VIOLENT REBELLION BY FOREIGN TRADERS.
SO, USING THE CHURCH, THEY REQUIRED THAT ALL BUSINESS BE CONDUCTED IN CASH, SINCE NO ONE CARRIED LARGE AMOUNTS OF COIN LONG DISTANCE.
THERE WAS NO OUTRIGHT BAN ON SALES. THEY THOUGHT THIS SOLVED EVERYTHING, BUT THE CHURCH'S OTHER CONDITION WAS PROBLEMATIC.
THE CHURCH'S COFFERS WERE ALWAYS FULL OF MONEY. THEY SOUGHT SOMEONE THROUGH WHOM THEY COULD LEND TO THE OUTSIDE.
AND THUS DID THEY LOAN A LARGE AMOUNT OF MONEY TO THE FOREIGN MERCHANTS.
THE FURS WERE BOUGHT UP BY THE FOREIGN MERCHANTS, AND THE ENRAGED CRAFTSMEN RIOTED.
AND SUCH DISUTES ALWAYS LEAVE THEIR CLAW MARKS BEHIND.

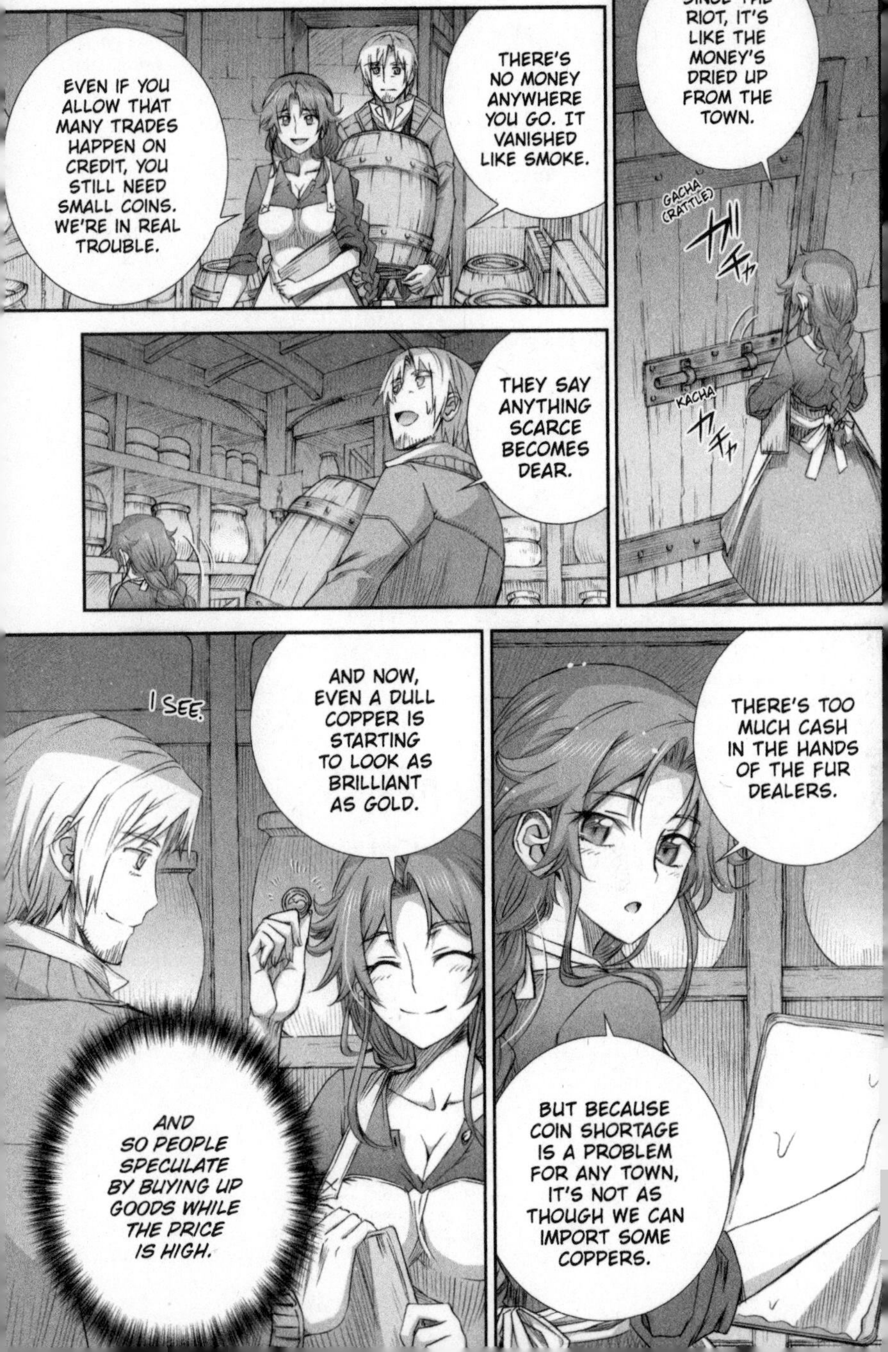
SINCE THE RIOT, IT'S LIKE THE MONEY'S DRIED UP FROM THE TOWN.
GACHA (RATTLE)
KACHA
THERE'S NO MONEY ANYWHERE YOU GO. IT VANISHED LIKE SMOKE.
EVEN IF YOU ALLOW THAT MANY TRADES HAPPEN ON CREDIT, YOU STILL NEED SMALL COINS. WE'RE IN REAL TROUBLE.
THEY SAY ANYTHING SCARCE BECOMES DEAR.
THERE'S TOO MUCH CASH IN THE HANDS OF THE FUR DEALERS.
BUT BECAUSE COIN SHORTAGE IS A PROBLEM FOR ANY TOWN, IT'S NOT AS THOUGH WE CAN IMPORT SOME COPPERS.
AND NOW, EVEN A DULL COPPER IS STARTING TO LOOK AS BRILLIANT AS GOLD.
I SEE.
AND SO PEOPLE SPECULATE BY BUYING UP GOODS WHILE THE PRICE IS HIGH.

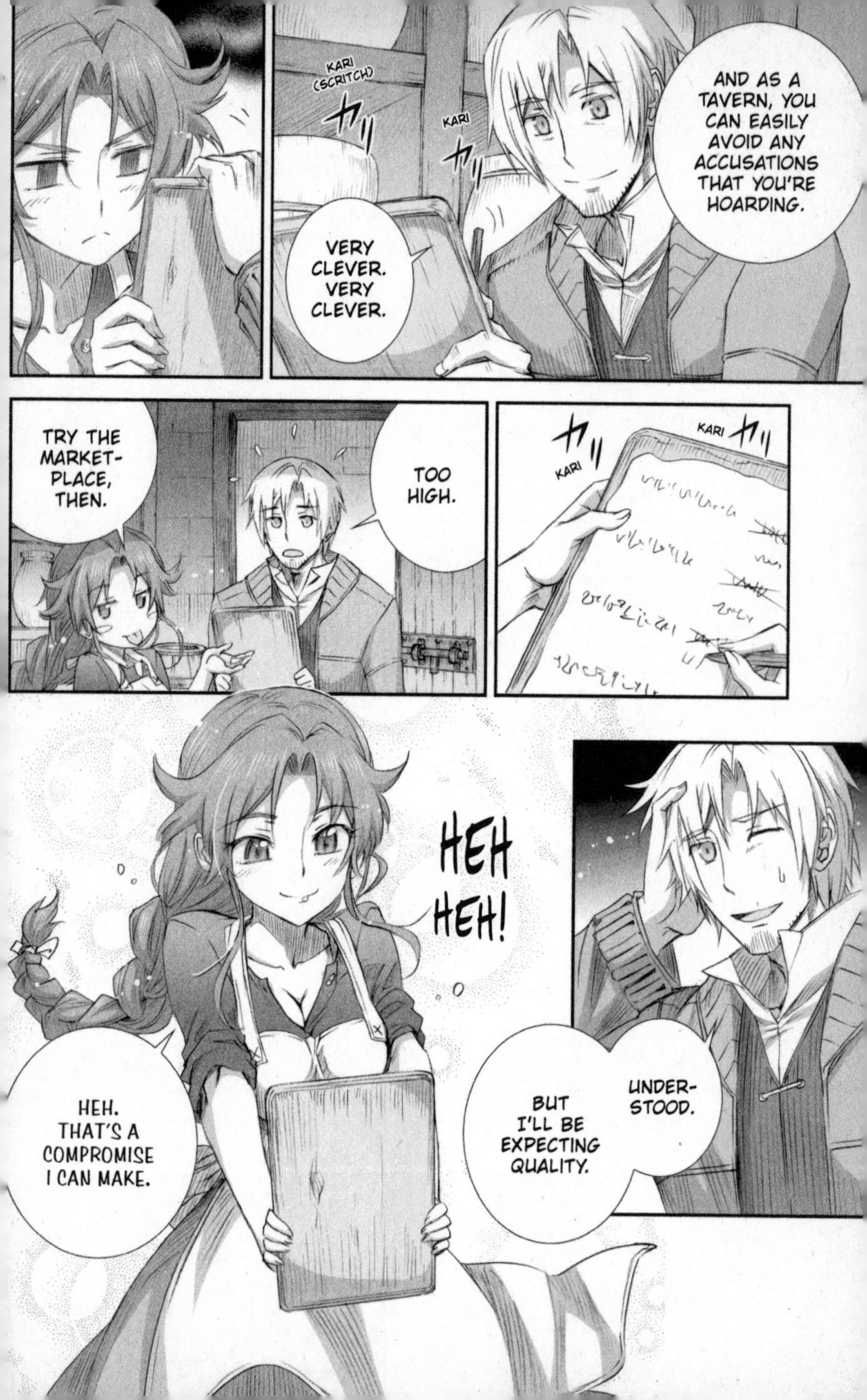
AND AS A TAVERN, YOU CAN EASILY AVOID ANY ACCUSATIONS THAT YOU'RE HOARDING.
KARI
カリ
KARI (SCRITCH)
カリ
VERY CLEVER. VERY CLEVER.
KARI
カリ
KARI
カリ
TOO HIGH.
TRY THE MARKET-PLACE, THEN.
UNDER-STOOD.
BUT I'LL BE EXPECTING QUALITY.
HEH HEH!
HEH. THAT'S A COMPROMISE I CAN MAKE.

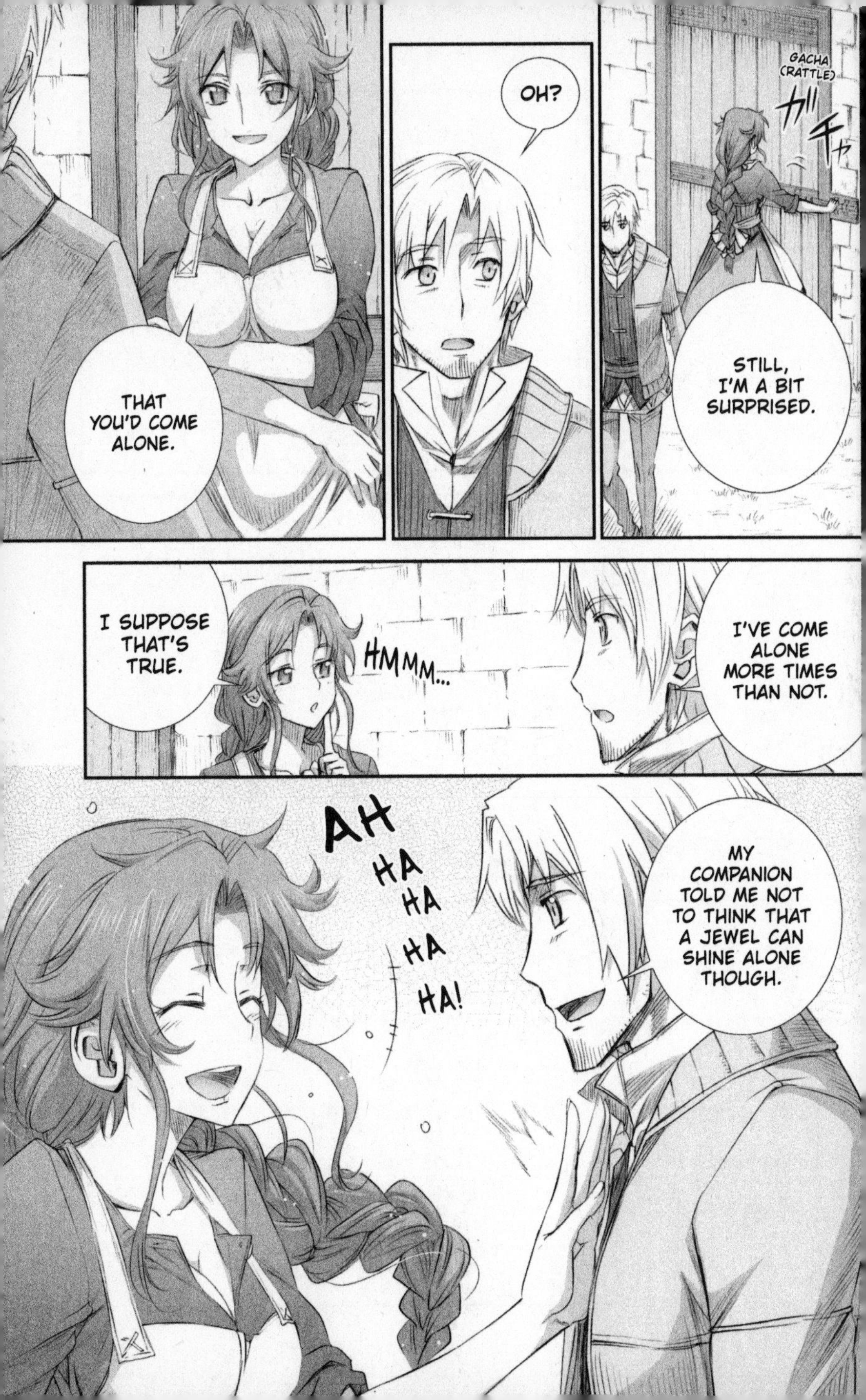
GACHA (RATTLE)
ガチャ
STILL, I'M A BIT SURPRISED.
OH?
THAT YOU'D COME ALONE.
I'VE COME ALONE MORE TIMES THAN NOT.
HMMM...
I SUPPOSE THAT'S TRUE.
MY COMPANION TOLD ME NOT TO THINK THAT A JEWEL CAN SHINE ALONE THOUGH.
AH HA HA HA HA!

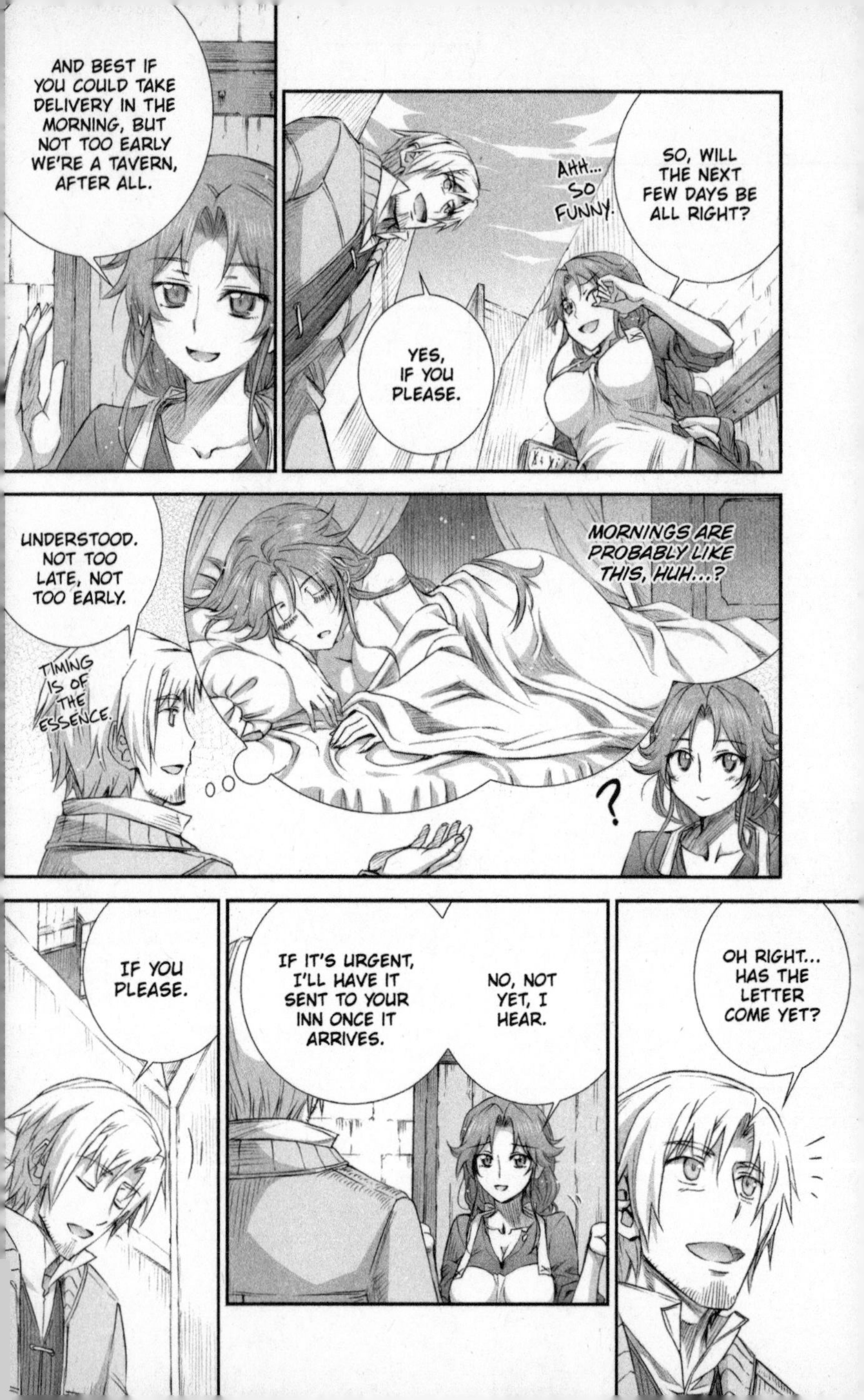
SO, WILL THE NEXT FEW DAYS BE ALL RIGHT?
AHH... SO FUNNY.
YES, IF YOU PLEASE.
AND BEST IF YOU COULD TAKE DELIVERY IN THE MORNING, BUT NOT TOO EARLY WE'RE A TAVERN, AFTER ALL.
MORNINGS ARE PROBABLY LIKE THIS, HUH...?
UNDERSTOOD. NOT TOO LATE, NOT TOO EARLY.
TIMING IS OF THE ESSENCE.
?
OH RIGHT... HAS THE LETTER COME YET?
NO, NOT YET, I HEAR.
IF IT'S URGENT, I'LL HAVE IT SENT TO YOUR INN ONCE IT ARRIVES.
IF YOU PLEASE.

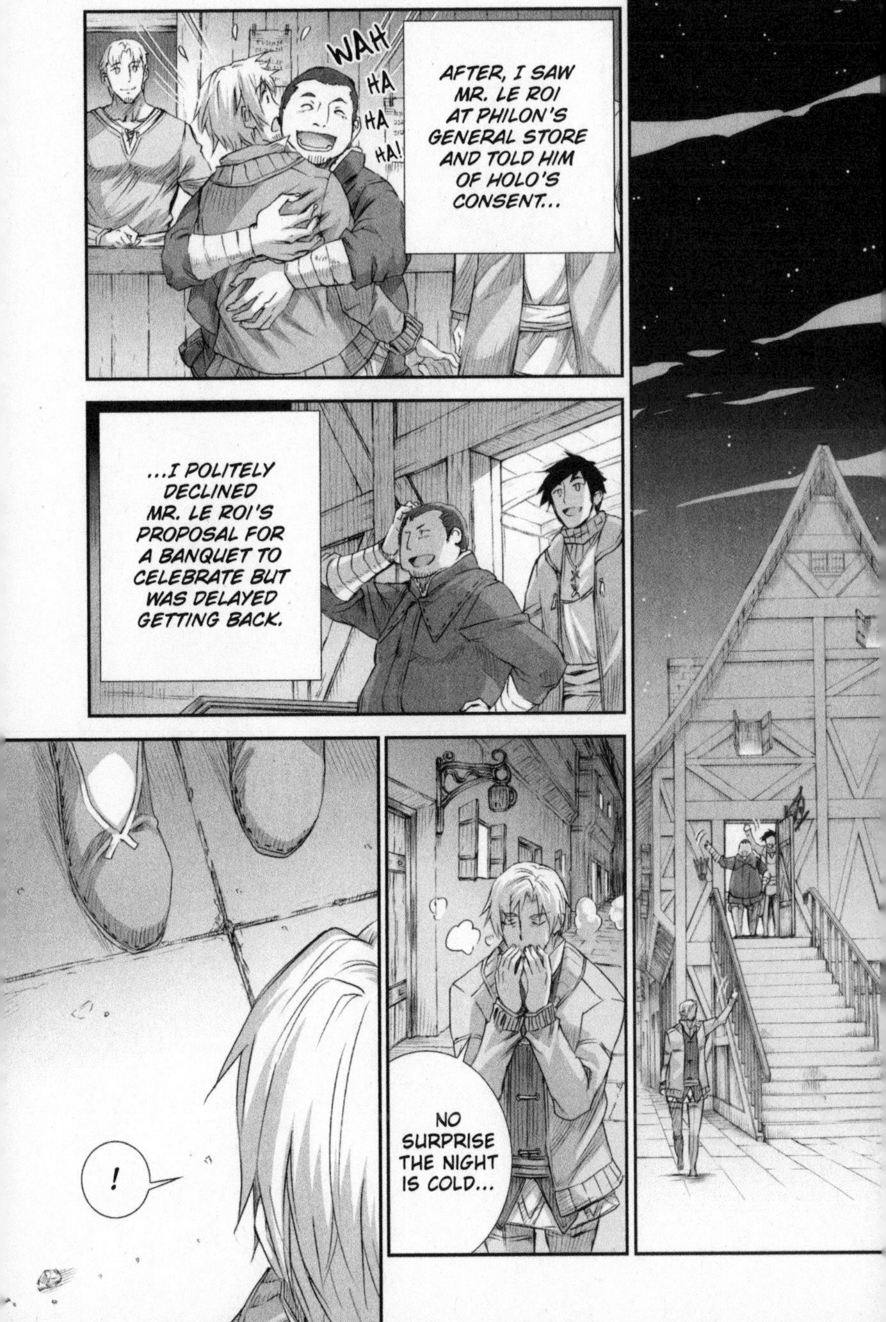
AFTER, I SAW MR. LE ROI AT PHILON'S GENERAL STORE AND TOLD HIM OF HOLO'S CONSENT...
WAH HA HA HA!
...I POLITELY DECLINED MR. LE ROI'S PROPOSAL FOR A BANQUET TO CELEBRATE BUT WAS DELAYED GETTING BACK.
NO SURPRISE THE NIGHT IS COLD...
!

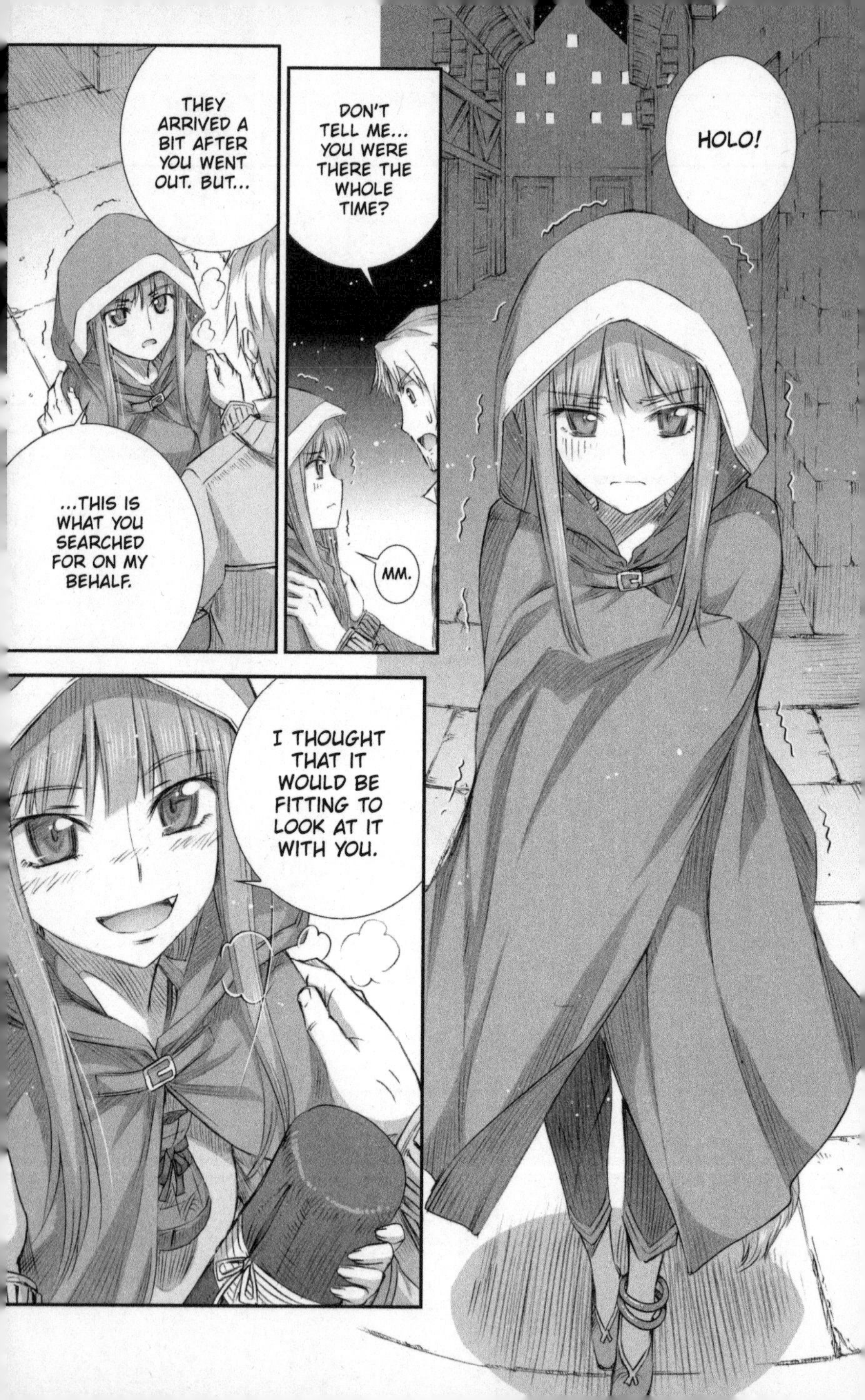
HOLO!
DON'T TELL ME... YOU WERE THERE THE WHOLE TIME?
MM.
THEY ARRIVED A BIT AFTER YOU WENT OUT. BUT...
...THIS IS WHAT YOU SEARCHED FOR ON MY BEHALF.
I THOUGHT THAT IT WOULD BE FITTING TO LOOK AT IT WITH YOU.

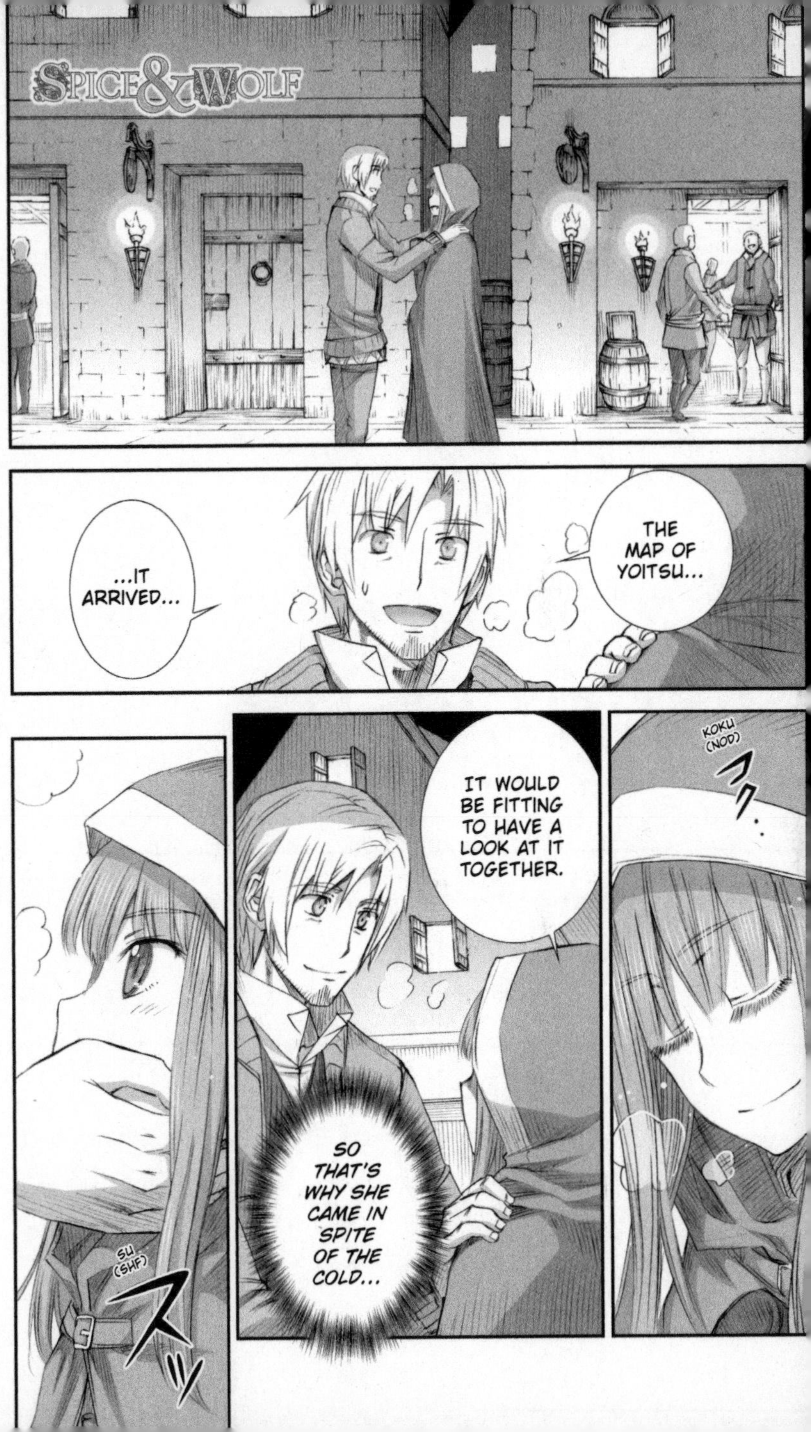
SPICE & WOLF
THE MAP OF YOITSU...
...IT ARRIVED...
KOKU (NOD)
IT WOULD BE FITTING TO HAVE A LOOK AT IT TOGETHER.
SO THAT'S WHY SHE CAME IN SPITE OF THE COLD...
SU (SHF)

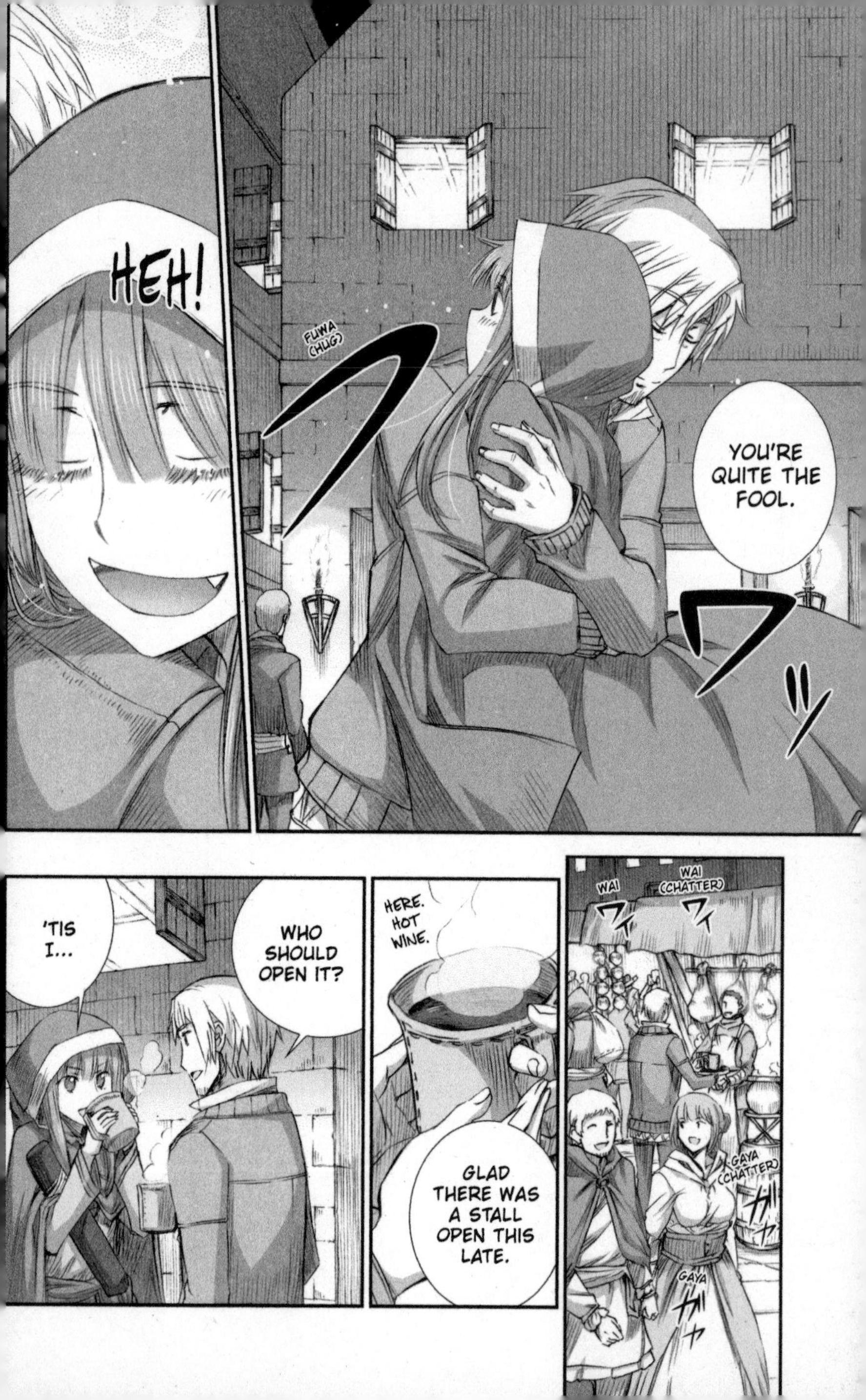
FUWA (HUG)
YOU'RE QUITE THE FOOL.
HEH!
WAI (CHATTER)
WAI
GAYA (CHATTER)
GAYA
HERE. HOT WINE.
GLAD THERE WAS A STALL OPEN THIS LATE.
WHO SHOULD OPEN IT?
'TIS I...

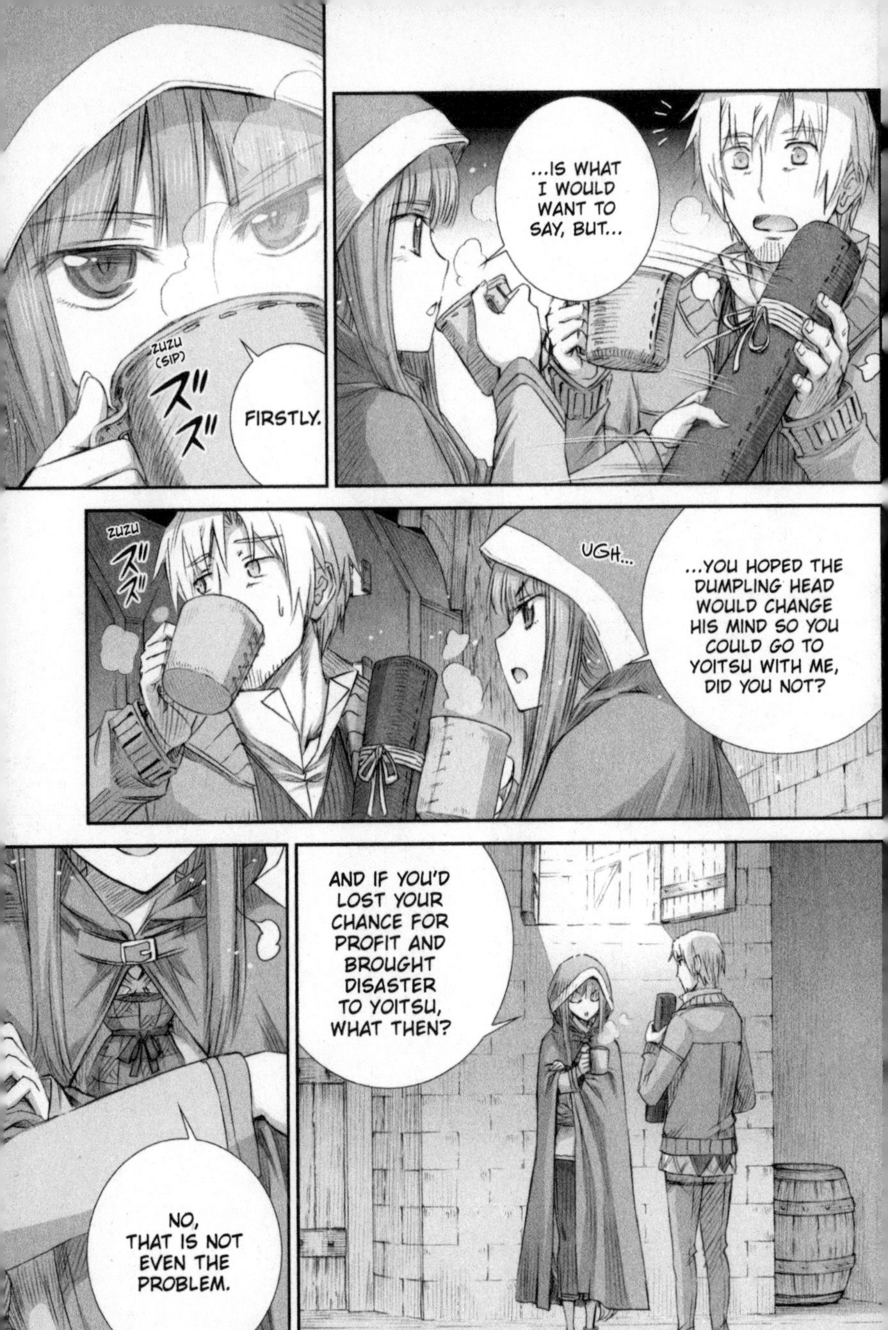
...IS WHAT I WOULD WANT TO SAY, BUT...
ZUZU (SIP)
ズズ
FIRSTLY.
...YOU HOPED THE DUMPLING HEAD WOULD CHANGE HIS MIND SO YOU COULD GO TO YOITSU WITH ME, DID YOU NOT?
UGH...
ZUZU
ズズ
AND IF YOU'D LOST YOUR CHANCE FOR PROFIT AND BROUGHT DISASTER TO YOITSU, WHAT THEN?
NO, THAT IS NOT EVEN THE PROBLEM.

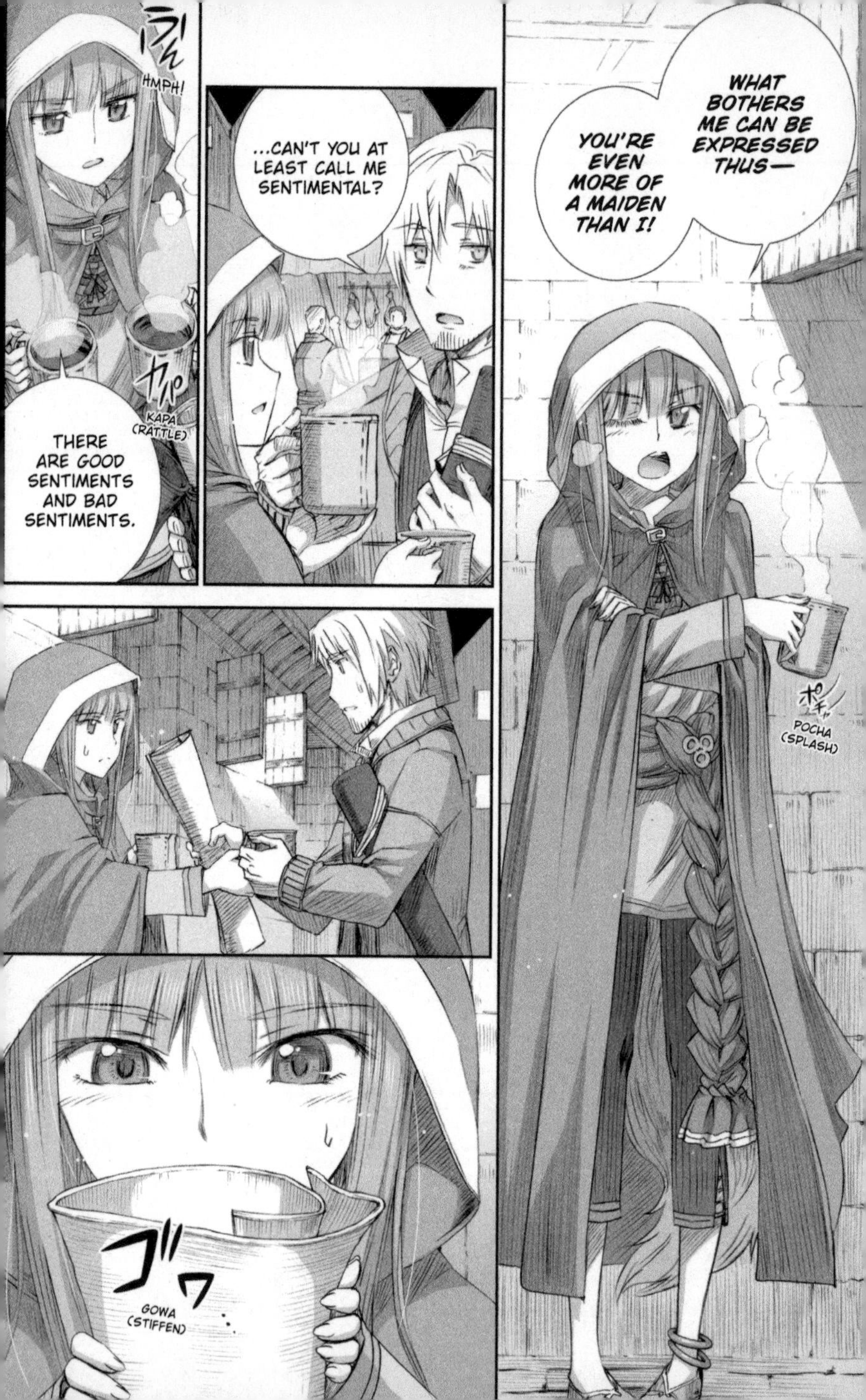
WHAT BOTHERS ME CAN BE EXPRESSED THUS—
YOU'RE EVEN MORE OF A MAIDEN THAN I!
POCHA (SPLASH)
...CAN'T YOU AT LEAST CALL ME SENTIMENTAL?
HMPH!
KAPA (RATTLE)
THERE ARE GOOD SENTIMENTS AND BAD SENTIMENTS.
GOWA (STIFFEN)

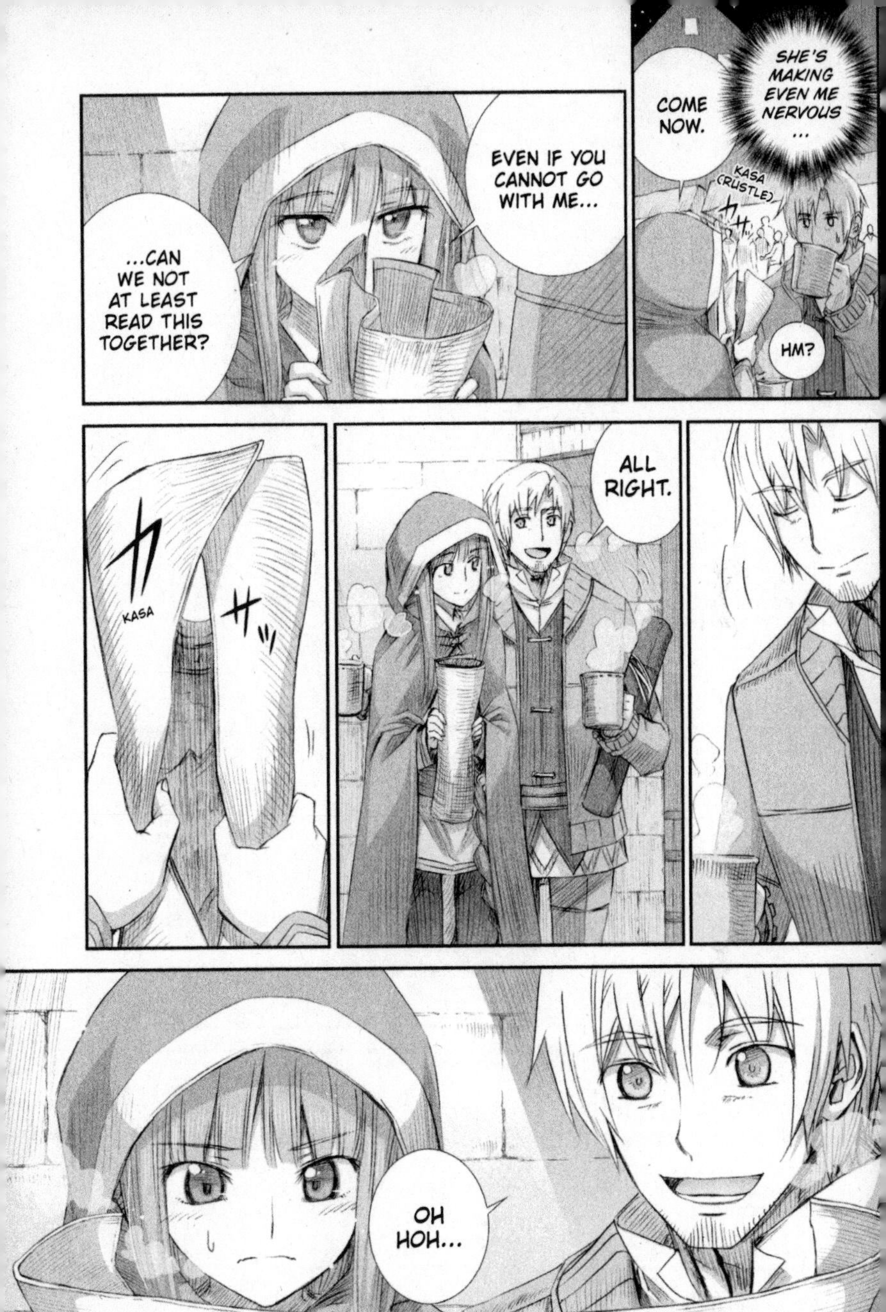
SHE'S MAKING EVEN ME NERVOUS...
COME NOW.
KASA (RUSTLE)
HM?
EVEN IF YOU CANNOT GO WITH ME...
...CAN WE NOT AT LEAST READ THIS TOGETHER?
ALL RIGHT.
KASA
OH HOH...

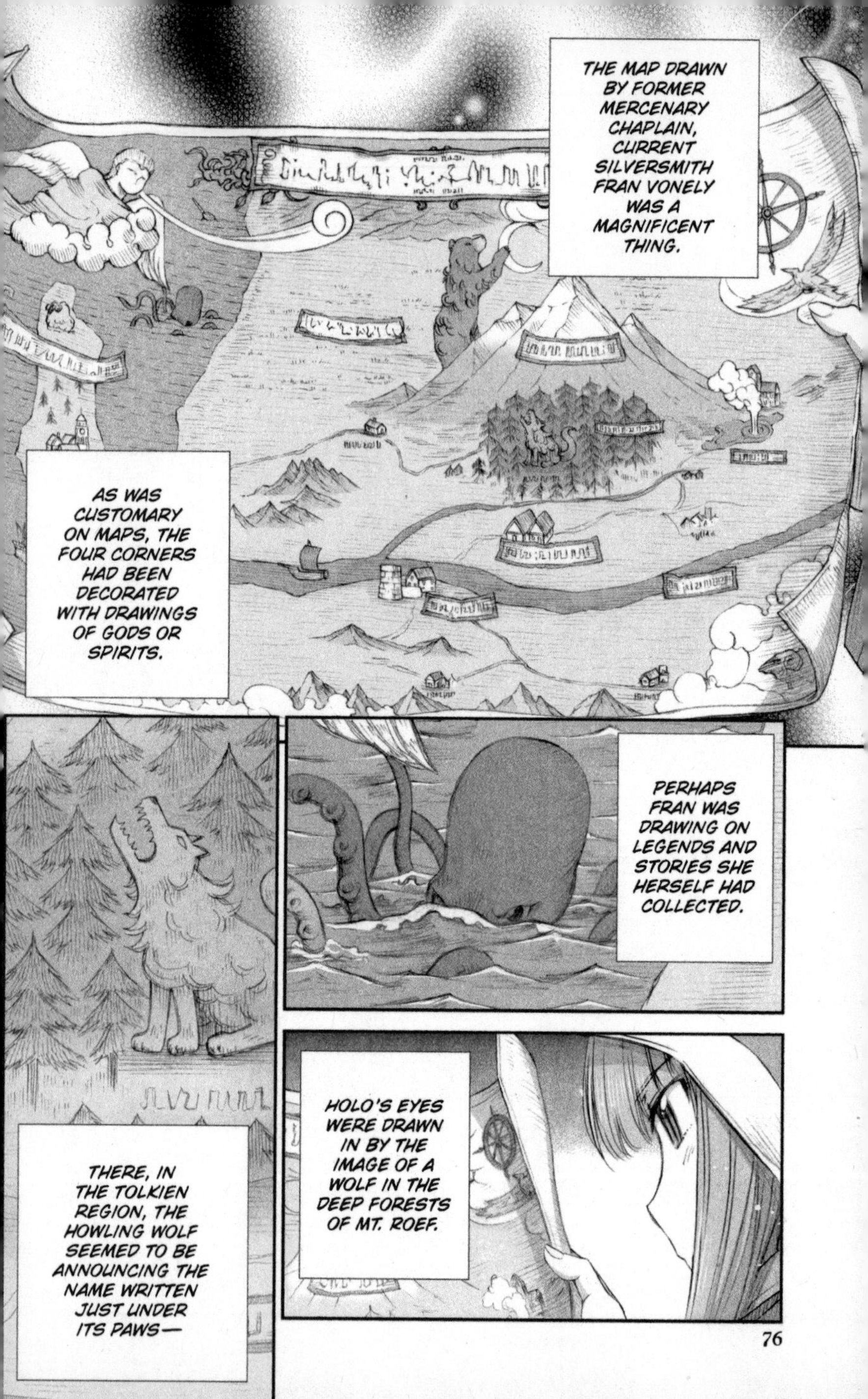
THE MAP DRAWN BY FORMER MERCENARY CHAPLAIN, CURRENT SILVERSMITH FRAN VONELY WAS A MAGNIFICENT THING.
AS WAS CUSTOMARY ON MAPS, THE FOUR CORNERS HAD BEEN DECORATED WITH DRAWINGS OF GODS OR SPIRITS.
PERHAPS FRAN WAS DRAWING ON LEGENDS AND STORIES SHE HERSELF HAD COLLECTED.
HOLO'S EYES WERE DRAWN IN BY THE IMAGE OF A WOLF IN THE DEEP FORESTS OF MT. ROEF.
THERE, IN THE TOLKIEN REGION, THE HOWLING WOLF SEEMED TO BE ANNOUNCING THE NAME WRITTEN JUST UNDER ITS PAWS—

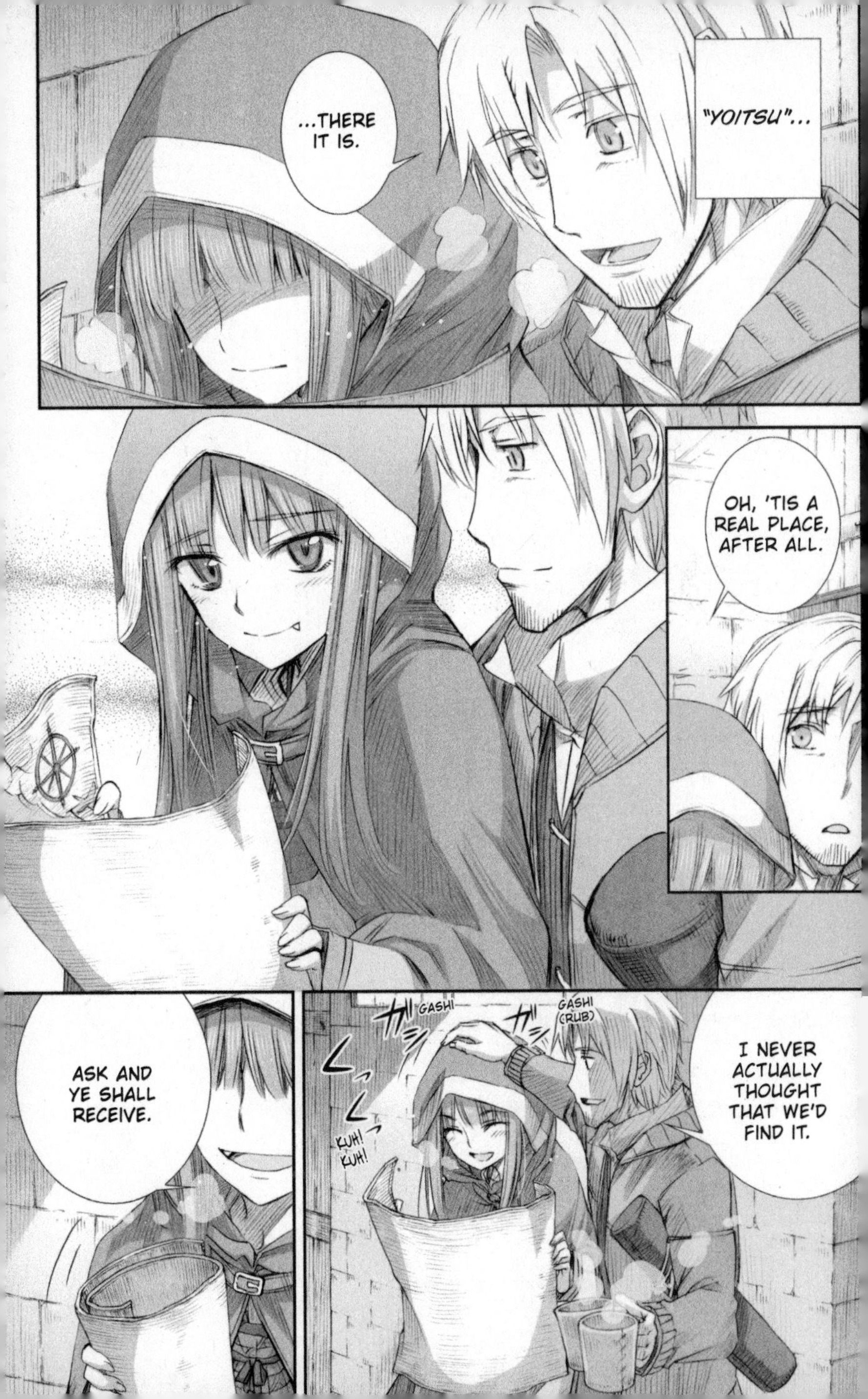
"YOITSU"...
...THERE IT IS.
OH, 'TIS A REAL PLACE, AFTER ALL.
I NEVER ACTUALLY THOUGHT THAT WE'D FIND IT.
GASHI (RUB)
GASHI
KUH! KUH!
ASK AND YE SHALL RECEIVE.

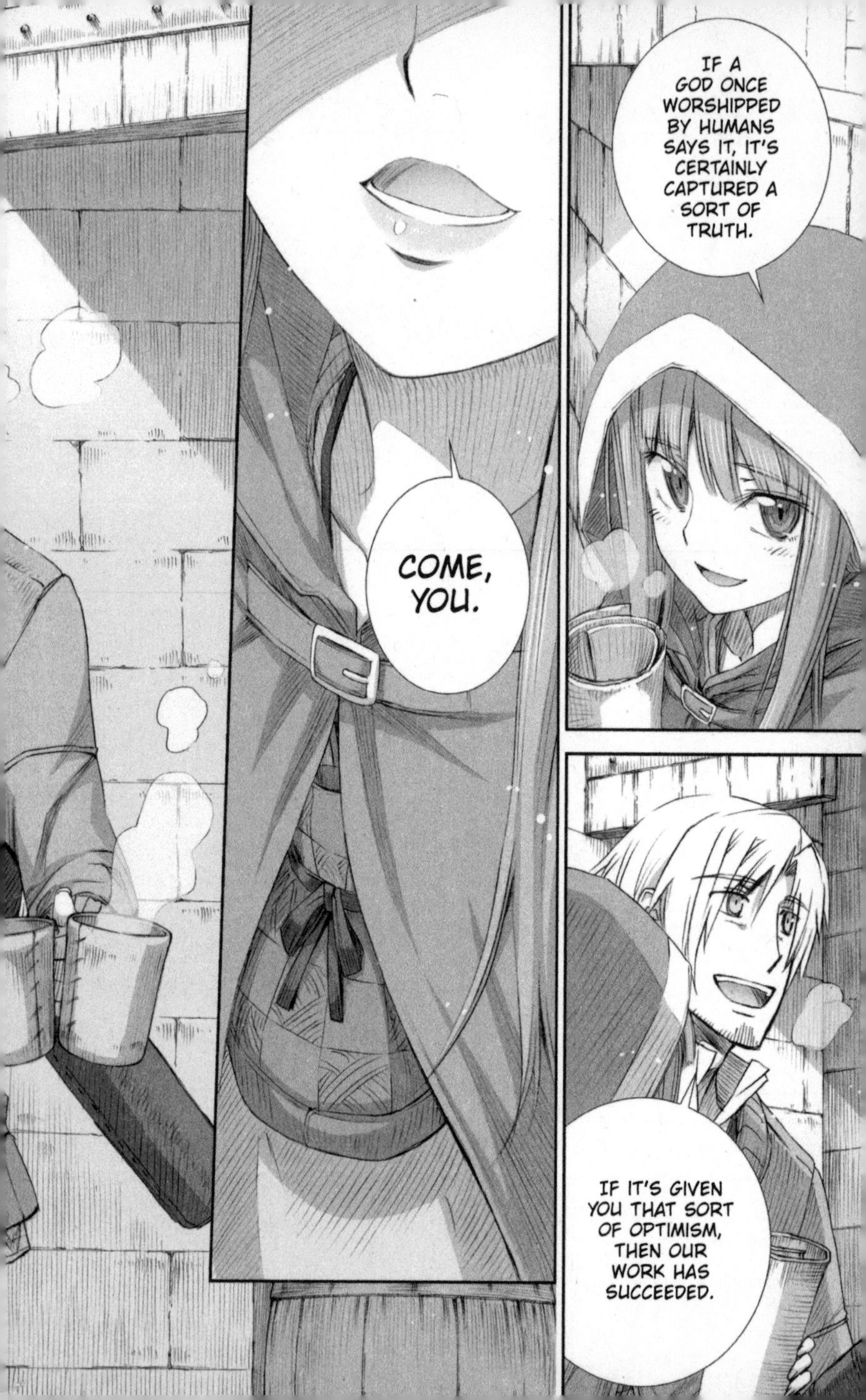
IF A GOD ONCE WORSHIPPED BY HUMANS SAYS IT, IT'S CERTAINLY CAPTURED A SORT OF TRUTH.
IF IT'S GIVEN YOU THAT SORT OF OPTIMISM, THEN OUR WORK HAS SUCCEEDED.
COME, YOU.

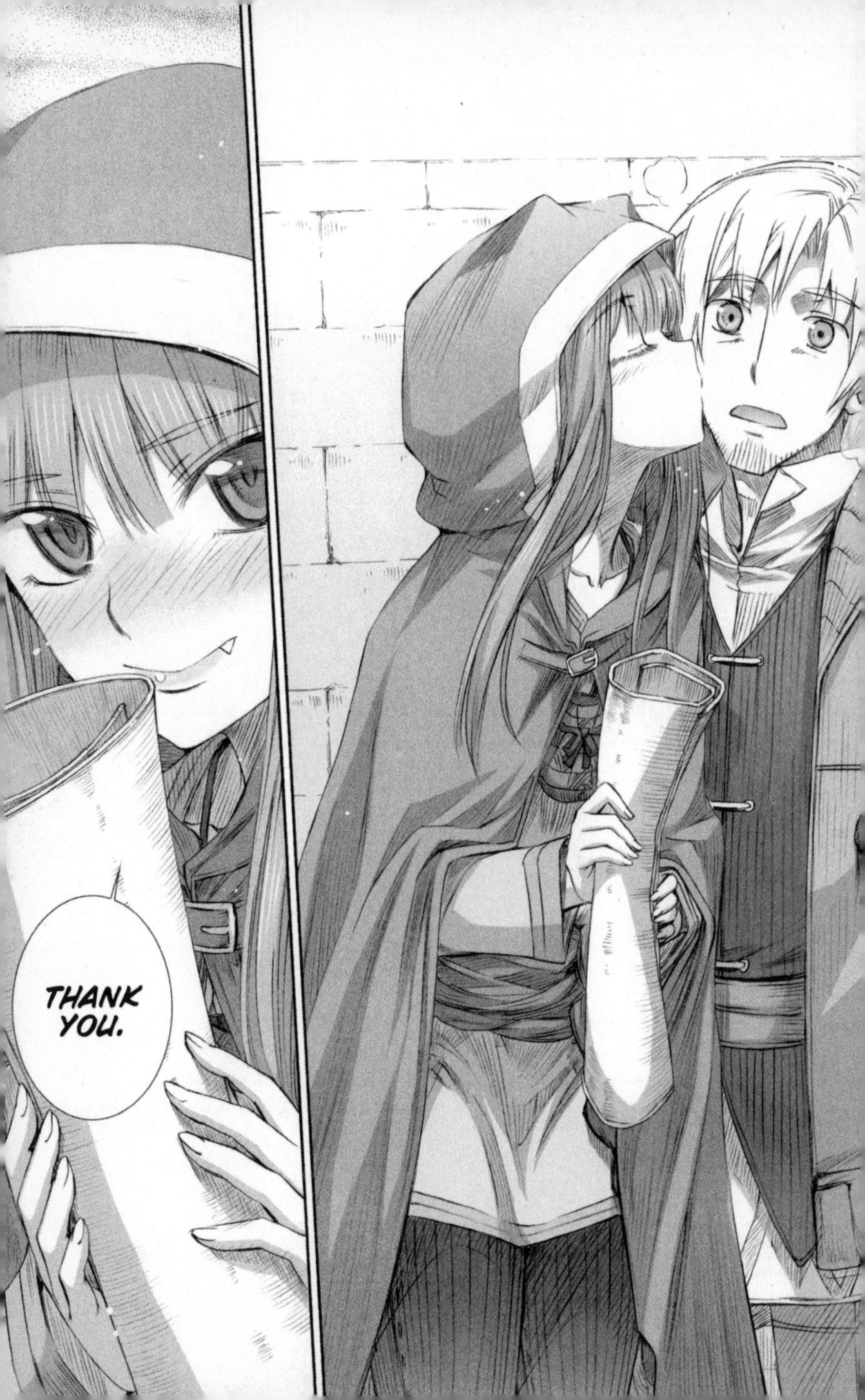
THANK YOU.

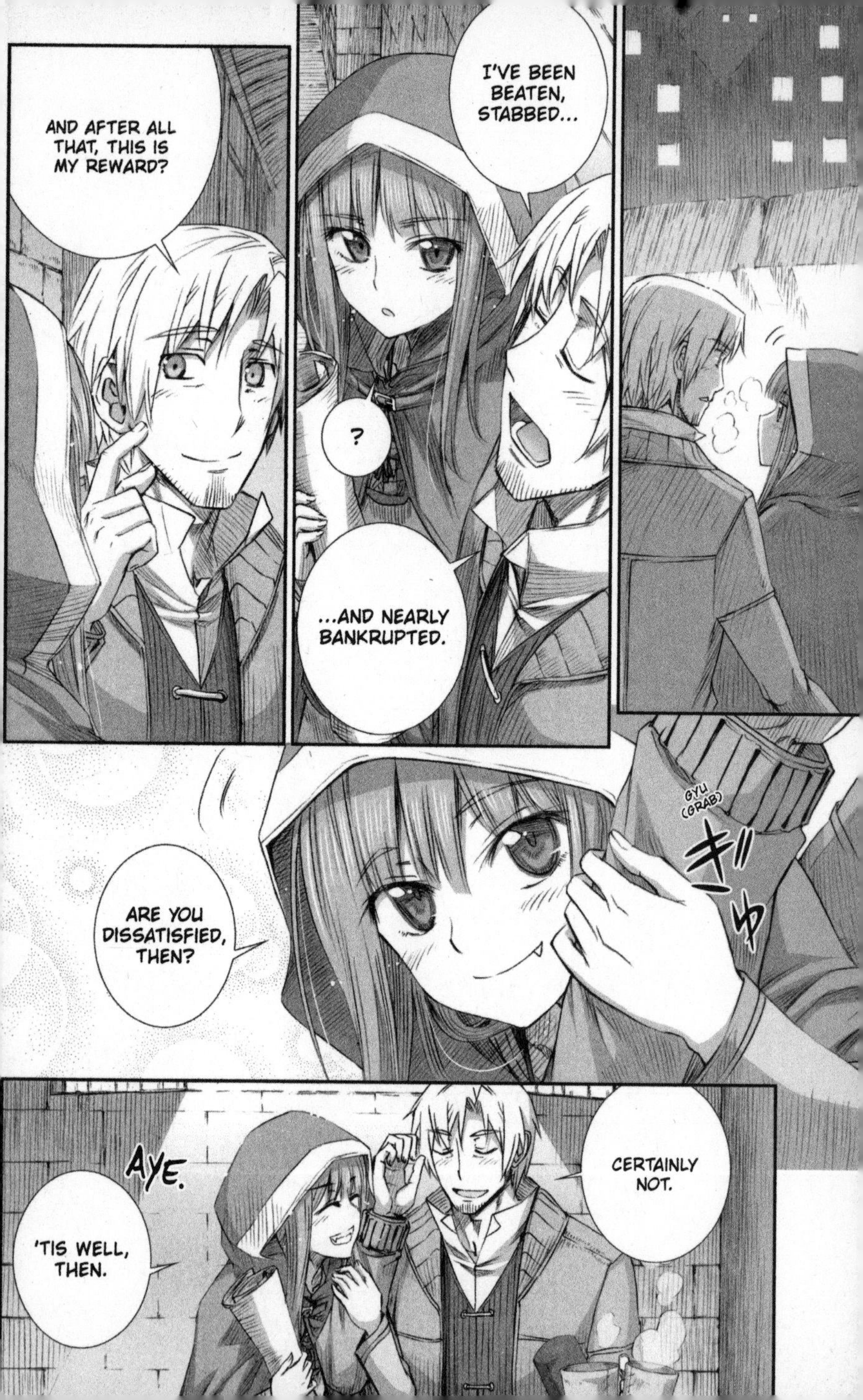
I'VE BEEN BEATEN, STABBED...
?
...AND NEARLY BANKRUPTED.
AND AFTER ALL THAT, THIS IS MY REWARD?
GYU (GRAB)
ぎゅ
ARE YOU DISSATISFIED, THEN?
CERTAINLY NOT.
AYE.
'TIS WELL, THEN.

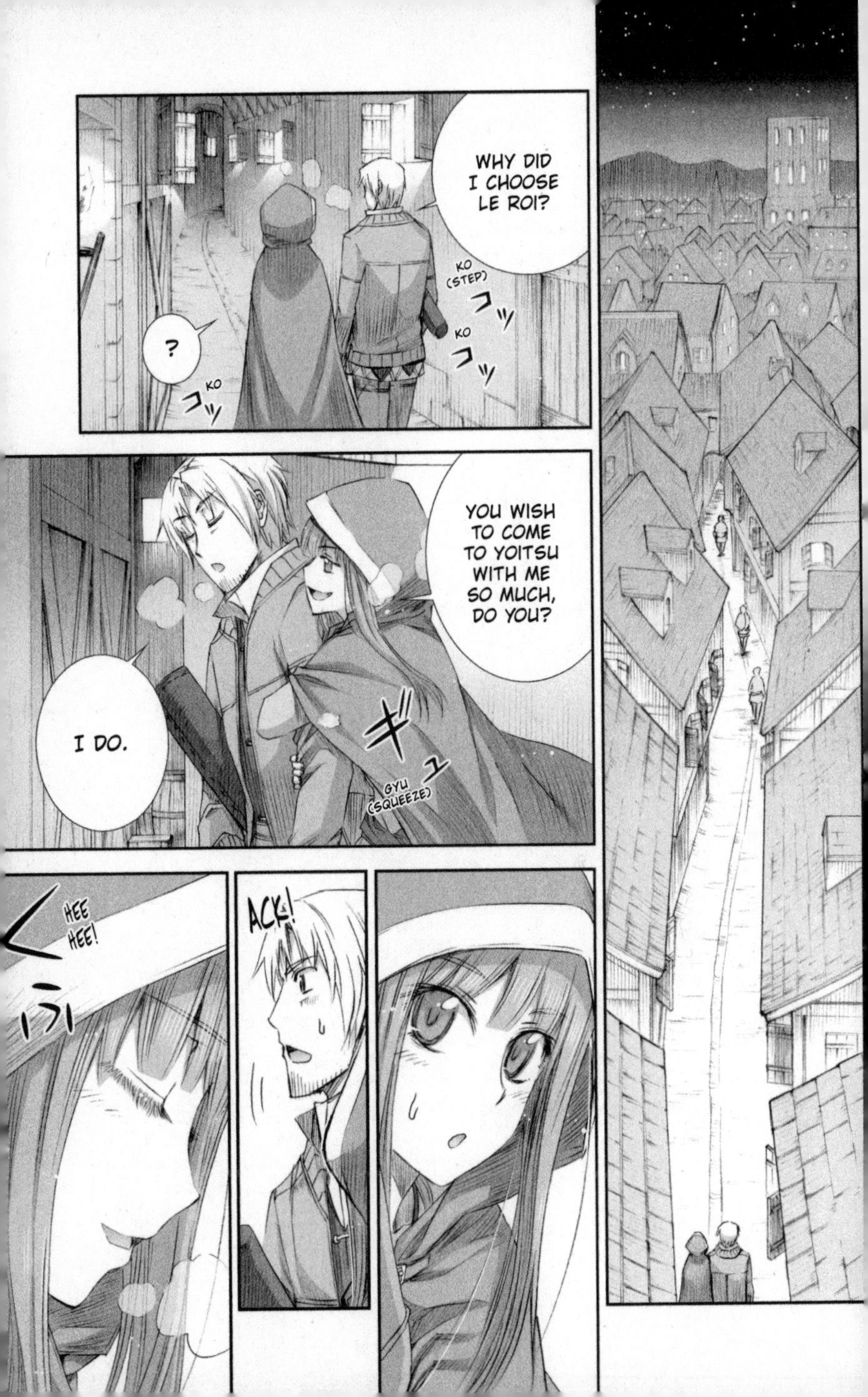
WHY DID I CHOOSE LE ROI?
KO (STEP)
コッ
KO
コッ
?
KO
コッ
YOU WISH TO COME TO YOITSU WITH ME SO MUCH, DO YOU?
ギュ
GYU (SQUEEZE)
I DO.
ACK!
HEE HEE!

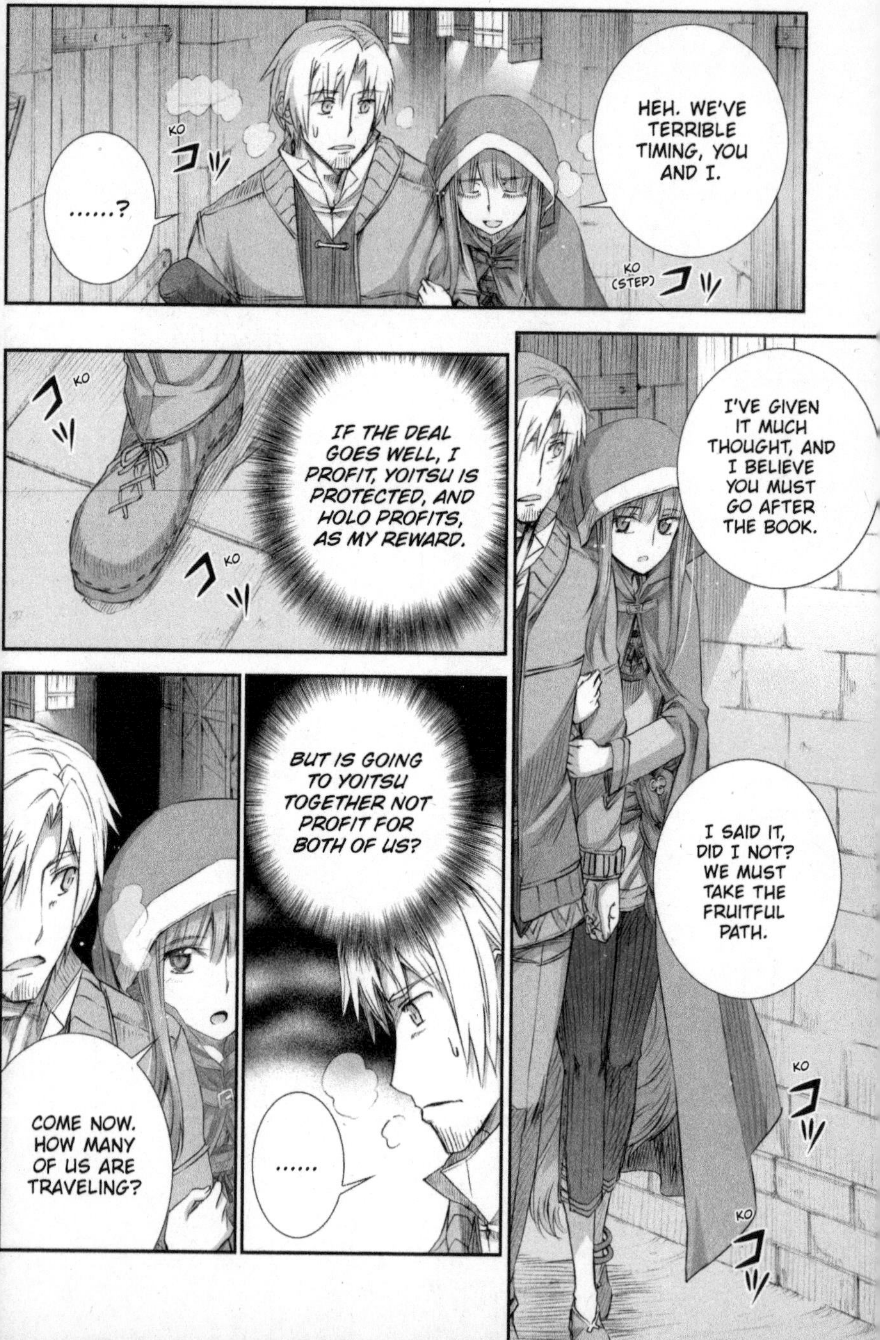
HEH. WE'VE TERRIBLE TIMING, YOU AND I.
KO (STEP)
KO
......?
I'VE GIVEN IT MUCH THOUGHT, AND I BELIEVE YOU MUST GO AFTER THE BOOK.
I SAID IT, DID I NOT? WE MUST TAKE THE FRUITFUL PATH.
KO
KO
KO
IF THE DEAL GOES WELL, I PROFIT, YOITSU IS PROTECTED, AND HOLO PROFITS, AS MY REWARD.
KO
BUT IS GOING TO YOITSU TOGETHER NOT PROFIT FOR BOTH OF US?
......
COME NOW. HOW MANY OF US ARE TRAVELING?

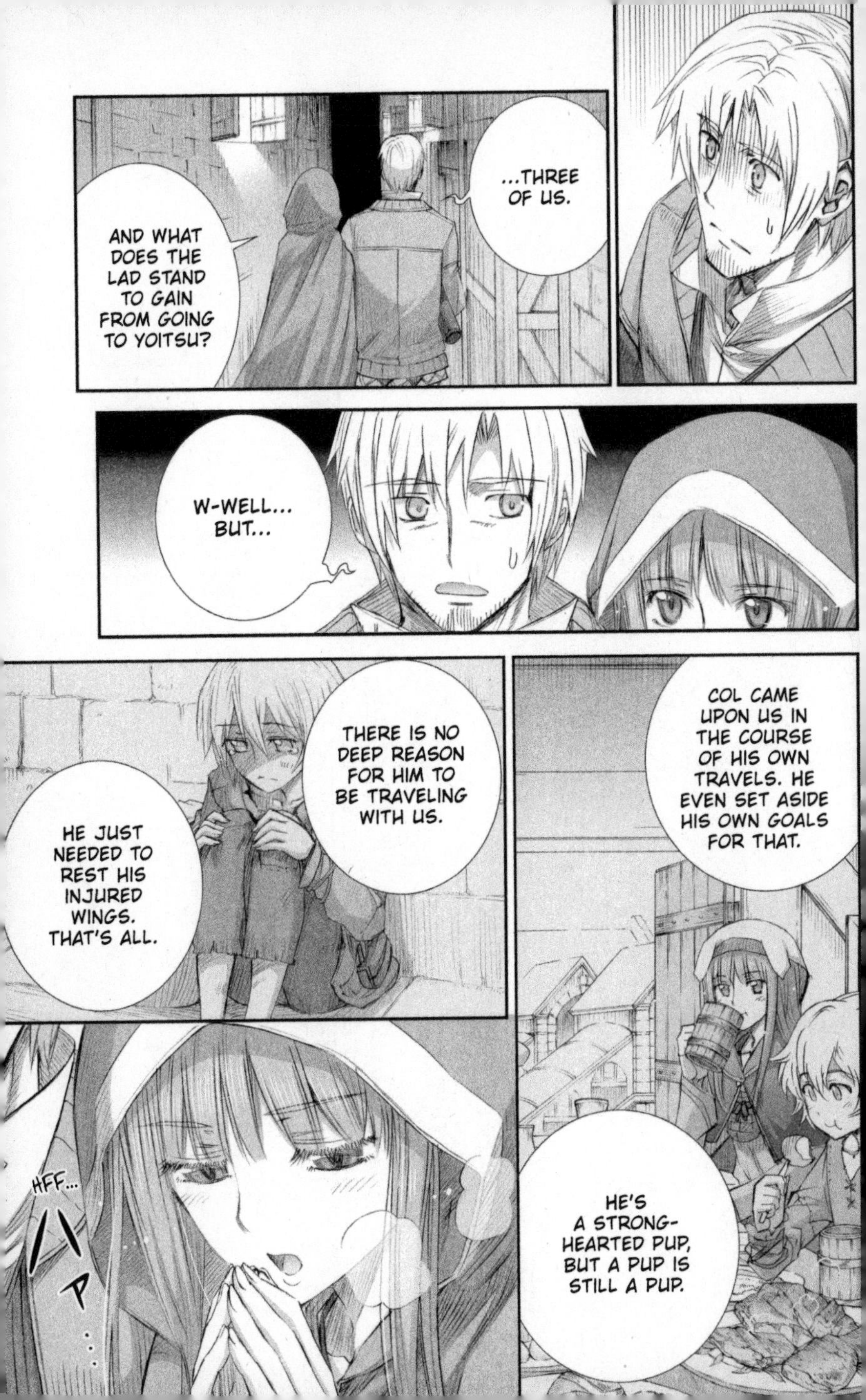
...THREE OF US.
AND WHAT DOES THE LAD STAND TO GAIN FROM GOING TO YOITSU?
W-WELL... BUT...
COL CAME UPON US IN THE COURSE OF HIS OWN TRAVELS. HE EVEN SET ASIDE HIS OWN GOALS FOR THAT.
HE'S A STRONG-HEARTED PUP, BUT A PUP IS STILL A PUP.
THERE IS NO DEEP REASON FOR HIM TO BE TRAVELING WITH US.
HE JUST NEEDED TO REST HIS INJURED WINGS. THAT'S ALL.
HFF...
ハァ...

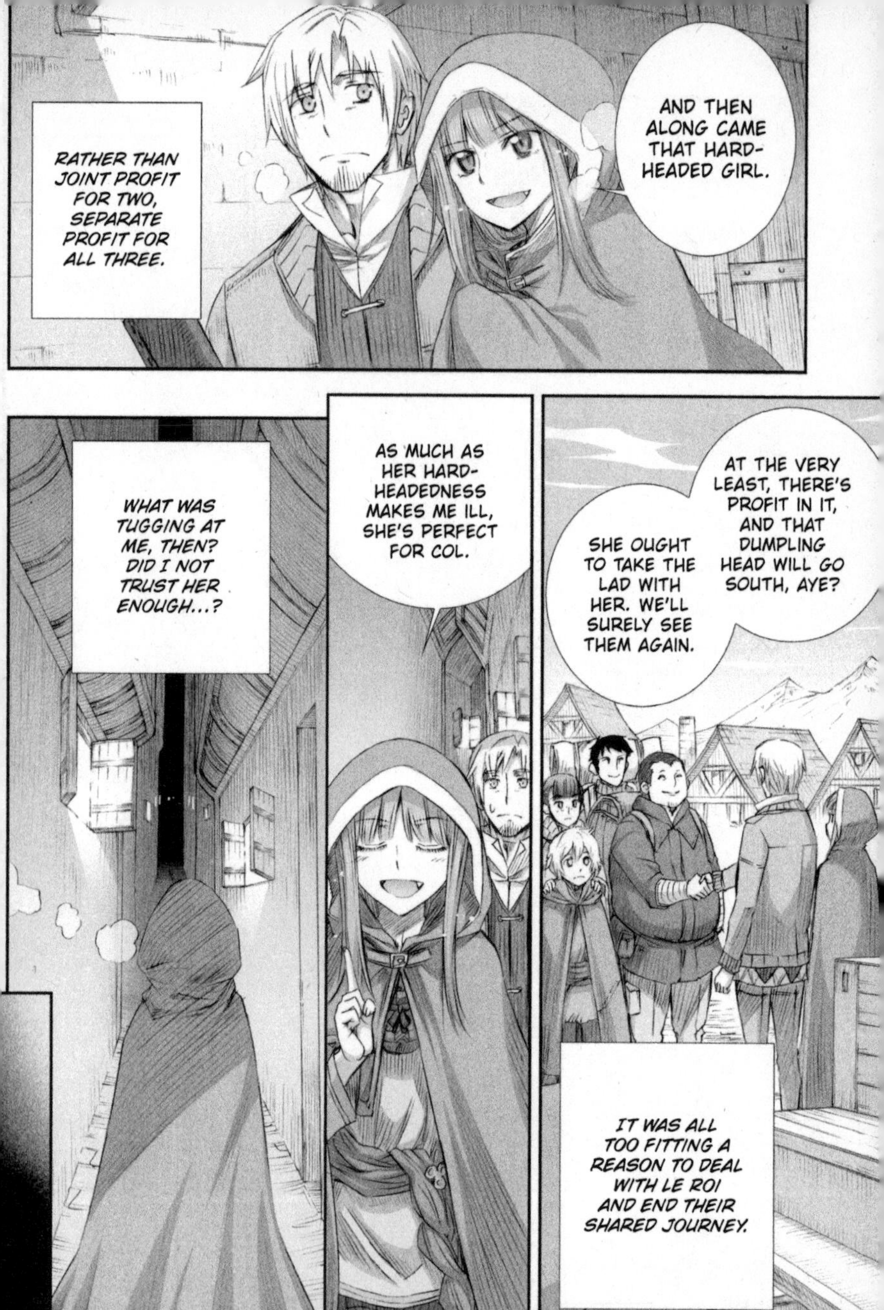
AND THEN ALONG CAME THAT HARD-HEADED GIRL.
RATHER THAN JOINT PROFIT FOR TWO, SEPARATE PROFIT FOR ALL THREE.
AT THE VERY LEAST, THERE'S PROFIT IN IT, AND THAT DUMPLING HEAD WILL GO SOUTH, AYE?
SHE OUGHT TO TAKE THE LAD WITH HER. WE'LL SURELY SEE THEM AGAIN.
IT WAS ALL TOO FITTING A REASON TO DEAL WITH LE ROI AND END THEIR SHARED JOURNEY.
AS MUCH AS HER HARD-HEADEDNESS MAKES ME ILL, SHE'S PERFECT FOR COL.
WHAT WAS TUGGING AT ME, THEN? DID I NOT TRUST HER ENOUGH...?

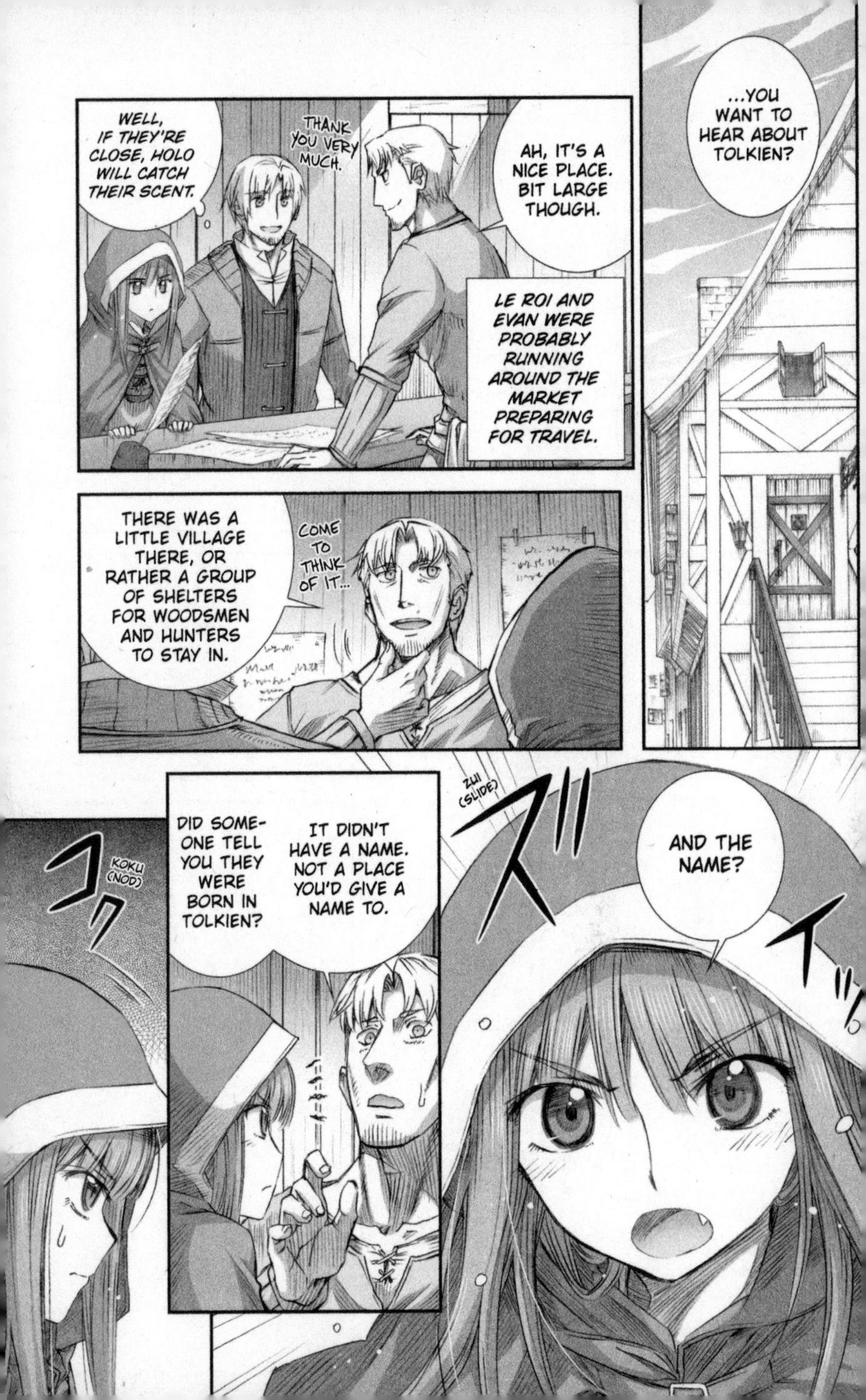
...YOU WANT TO HEAR ABOUT TOLKIEN?
AH, IT'S A NICE PLACE. BIT LARGE THOUGH.
THANK YOU VERY MUCH.
WELL, IF THEY'RE CLOSE, HOLO WILL CATCH THEIR SCENT.
LE ROI AND EVAN WERE PROBABLY RUNNING AROUND THE MARKET PREPARING FOR TRAVEL.
COME TO THINK OF IT...
THERE WAS A LITTLE VILLAGE THERE, OR RATHER A GROUP OF SHELTERS FOR WOODSMEN AND HUNTERS TO STAY IN.
ZUI (SLIDE)
AND THE NAME?
IT DIDN'T HAVE A NAME. NOT A PLACE YOU'D GIVE A NAME TO.
DID SOME-ONE TELL YOU THEY WERE BORN IN TOLKIEN?
KOKU (NOD)

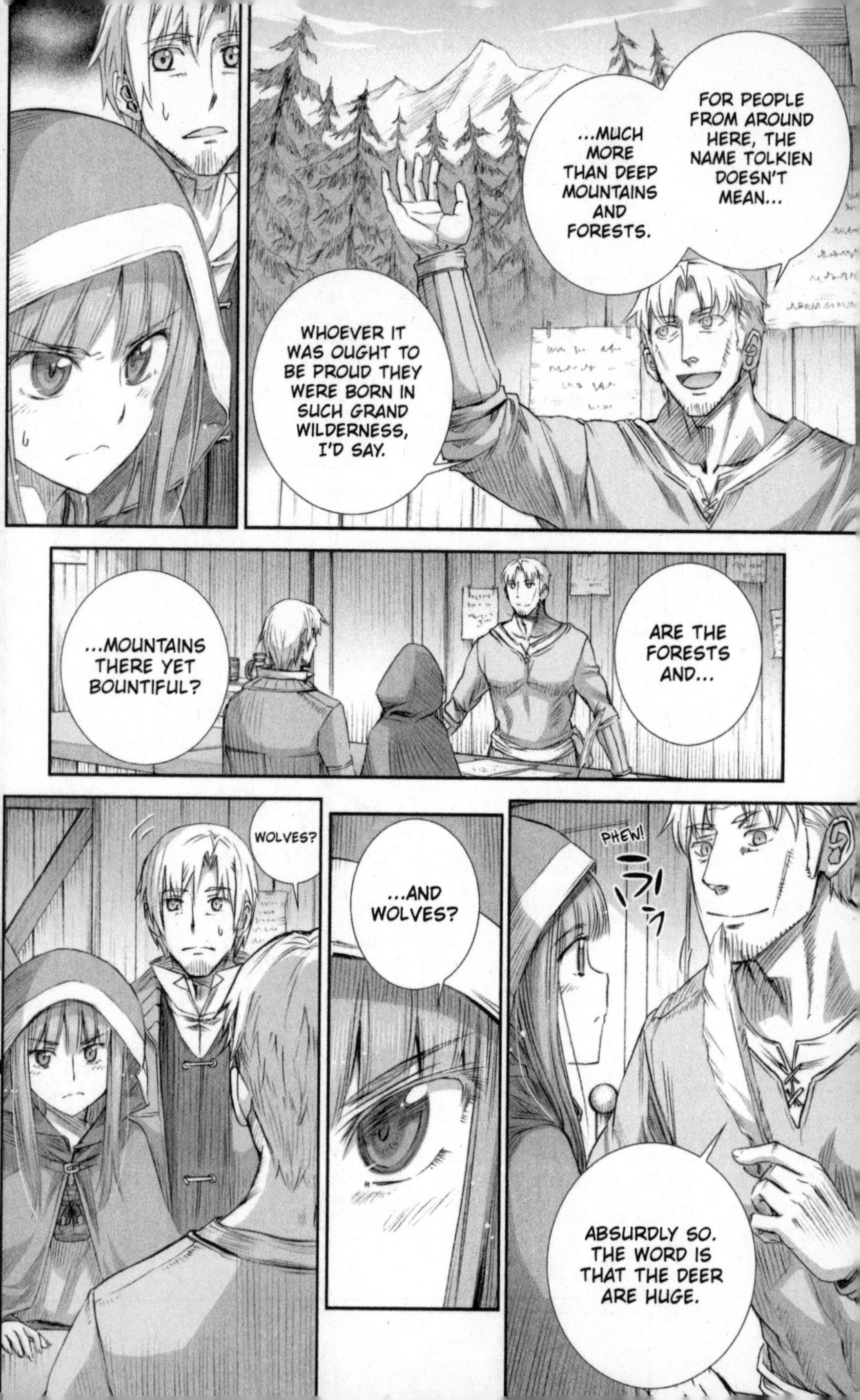
FOR PEOPLE FROM AROUND HERE, THE NAME TOLKIEN DOESN'T MEAN...
...MUCH MORE THAN DEEP MOUNTAINS AND FORESTS.
WHOEVER IT WAS OUGHT TO BE PROUD THEY WERE BORN IN SUCH GRAND WILDERNESS, I'D SAY.
ARE THE FORESTS AND...
...MOUNTAINS THERE YET BOUNTIFUL?
PHEW!
ABSURDLY SO. THE WORD IS THAT THE DEER ARE HUGE.
...AND WOLVES?
WOLVES?

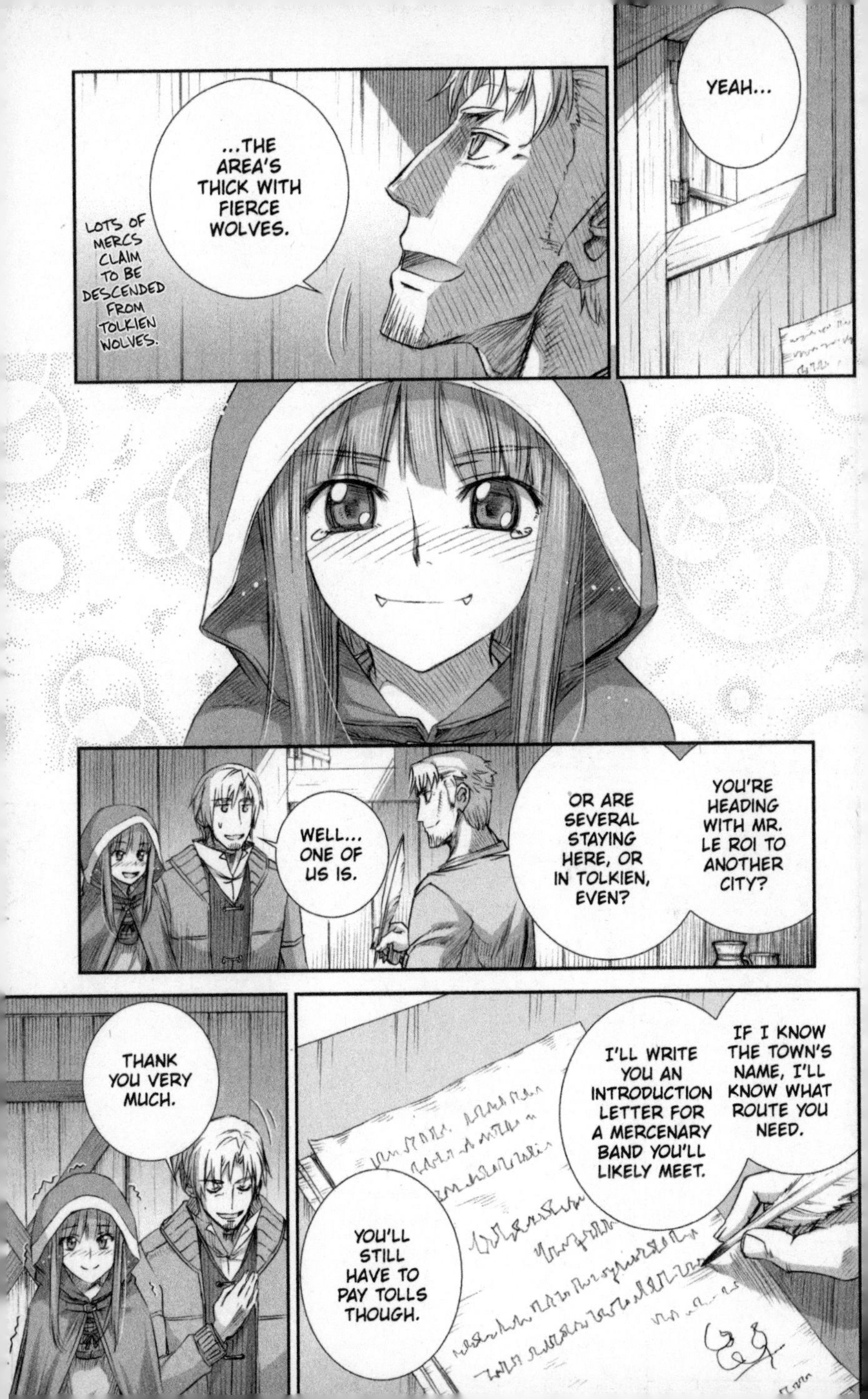
YEAH...
...THE AREA'S THICK WITH FIERCE WOLVES.
LOTS OF MERCS CLAIM TO BE DESCENDED FROM TOLKIEN WOLVES.
YOU'RE HEADING WITH MR. LE ROI TO ANOTHER CITY?
OR ARE SEVERAL STAYING HERE, OR IN TOLKIEN, EVEN?
WELL... ONE OF US IS.
IF I KNOW THE TOWN'S NAME, I'LL KNOW WHAT ROUTE YOU NEED.
I'LL WRITE YOU AN INTRODUCTION LETTER FOR A MERCENARY BAND YOU'LL LIKELY MEET.
YOU'LL STILL HAVE TO PAY TOLLS THOUGH.
THANK YOU VERY MUCH.

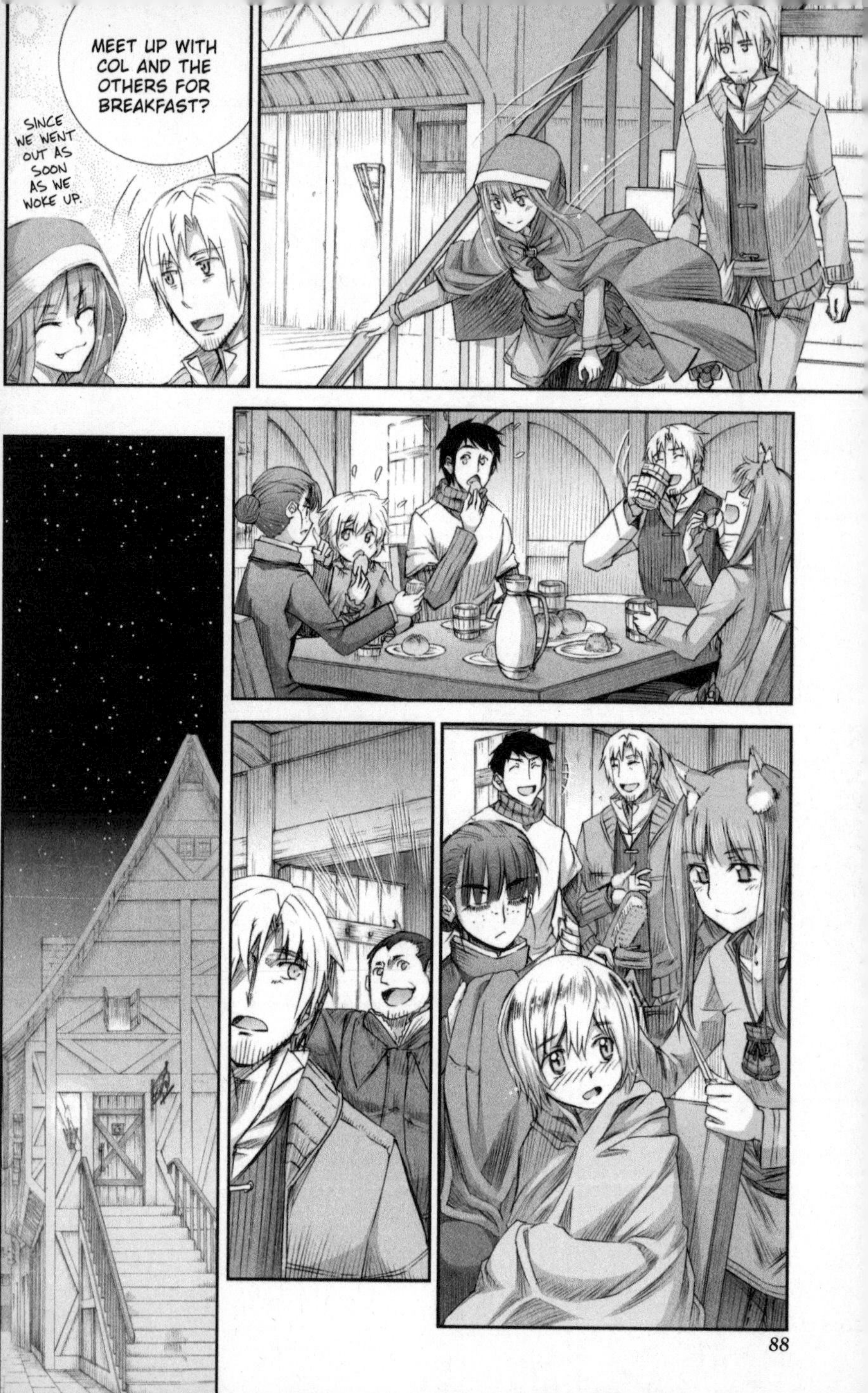
MEET UP WITH COL AND THE OTHERS FOR BREAKFAST?
SINCE WE WENT OUT AS SOON AS WE WOKE UP.

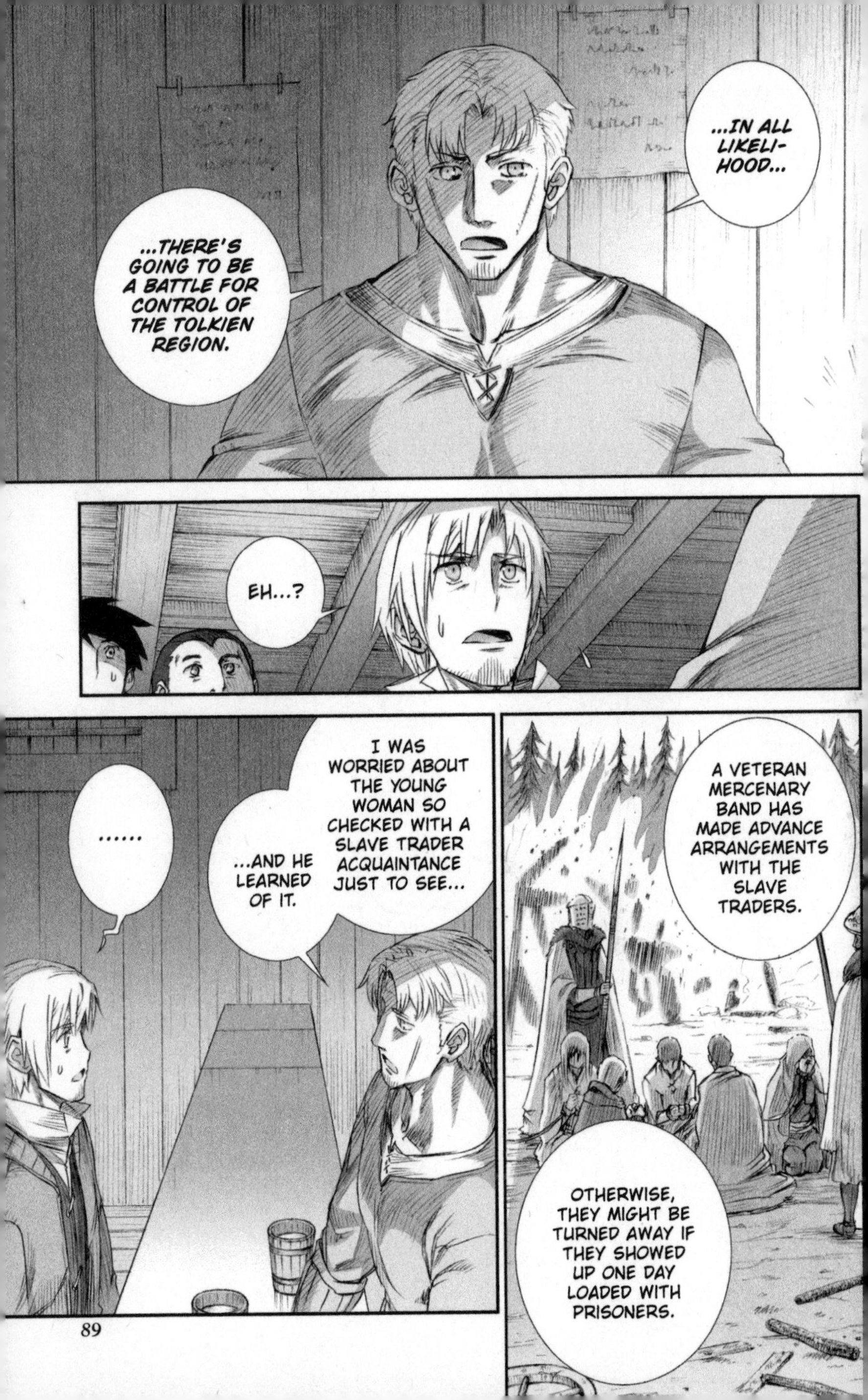
...IN ALL LIKELIHOOD...
...THERE'S GOING TO BE A BATTLE FOR CONTROL OF THE TOLKIEN REGION.
EH...?
A VETERAN MERCENARY BAND HAS MADE ADVANCE ARRANGEMENTS WITH THE SLAVE TRADERS.
OTHERWISE, THEY MIGHT BE TURNED AWAY IF THEY SHOWED UP ONE DAY LOADED WITH PRISONERS.
I WAS WORRIED ABOUT THE YOUNG WOMAN SO CHECKED WITH A SLAVE TRADER ACQUAINTANCE JUST TO SEE...
...AND HE LEARNED OF IT.
......

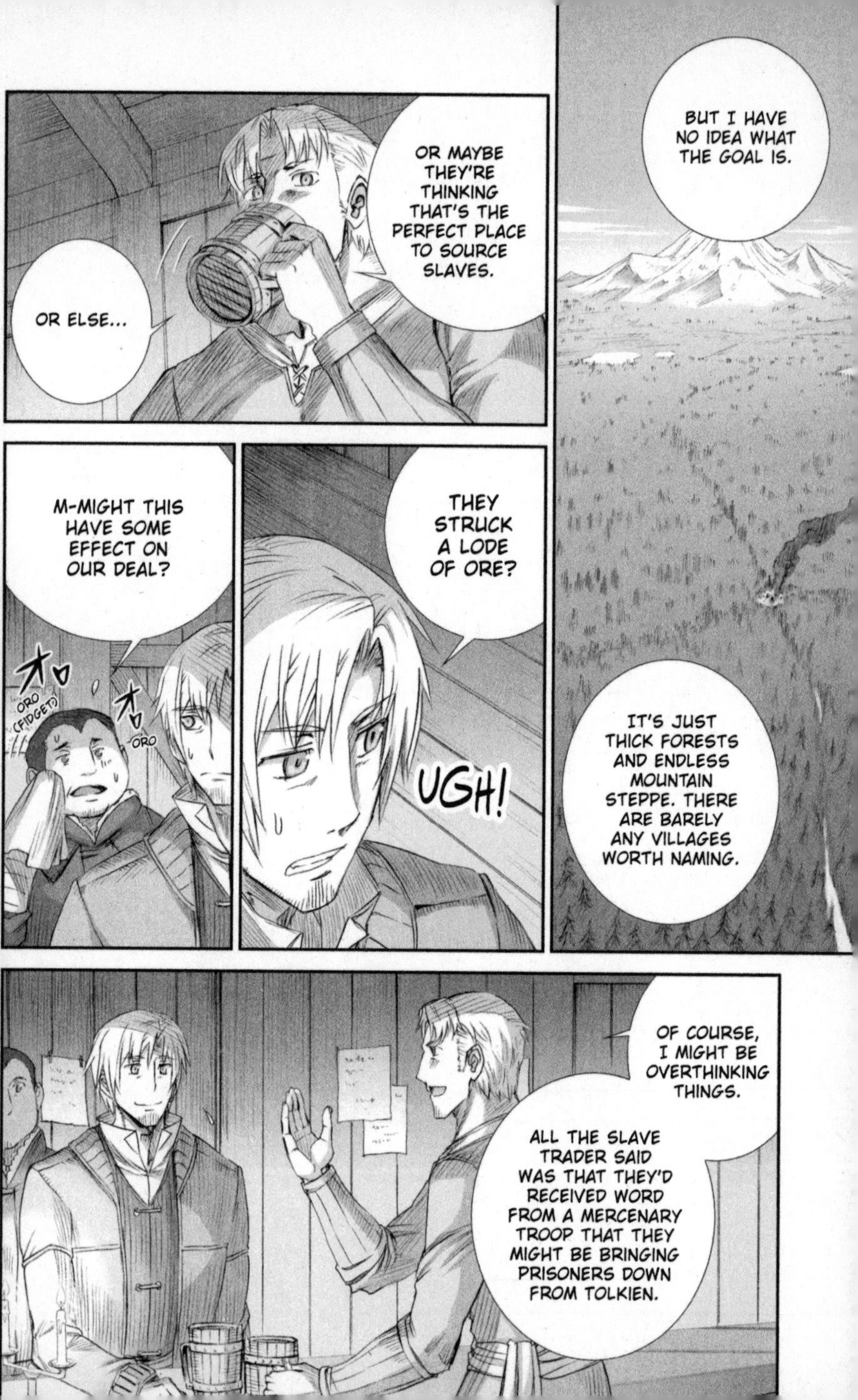

BUT I HAVE NO IDEA WHAT THE GOAL IS.
IT'S JUST THICK FORESTS AND ENDLESS MOUNTAIN STEPPE. THERE ARE BARELY ANY VILLAGES WORTH NAMING.
OR MAYBE THEY'RE THINKING THAT'S THE PERFECT PLACE TO SOURCE SLAVES.
OR ELSE...
THEY STRUCK A LODE OF ORE?
UGH!
M-MIGHT THIS HAVE SOME EFFECT ON OUR DEAL?
ORO
ORO (FIDGET)
OF COURSE, I MIGHT BE OVERTHINKING THINGS.
ALL THE SLAVE TRADER SAID WAS THAT THEY'D RECEIVED WORD FROM A MERCENARY TROOP THAT THEY MIGHT BE BRINGING PRISONERS DOWN FROM TOLKIEN.

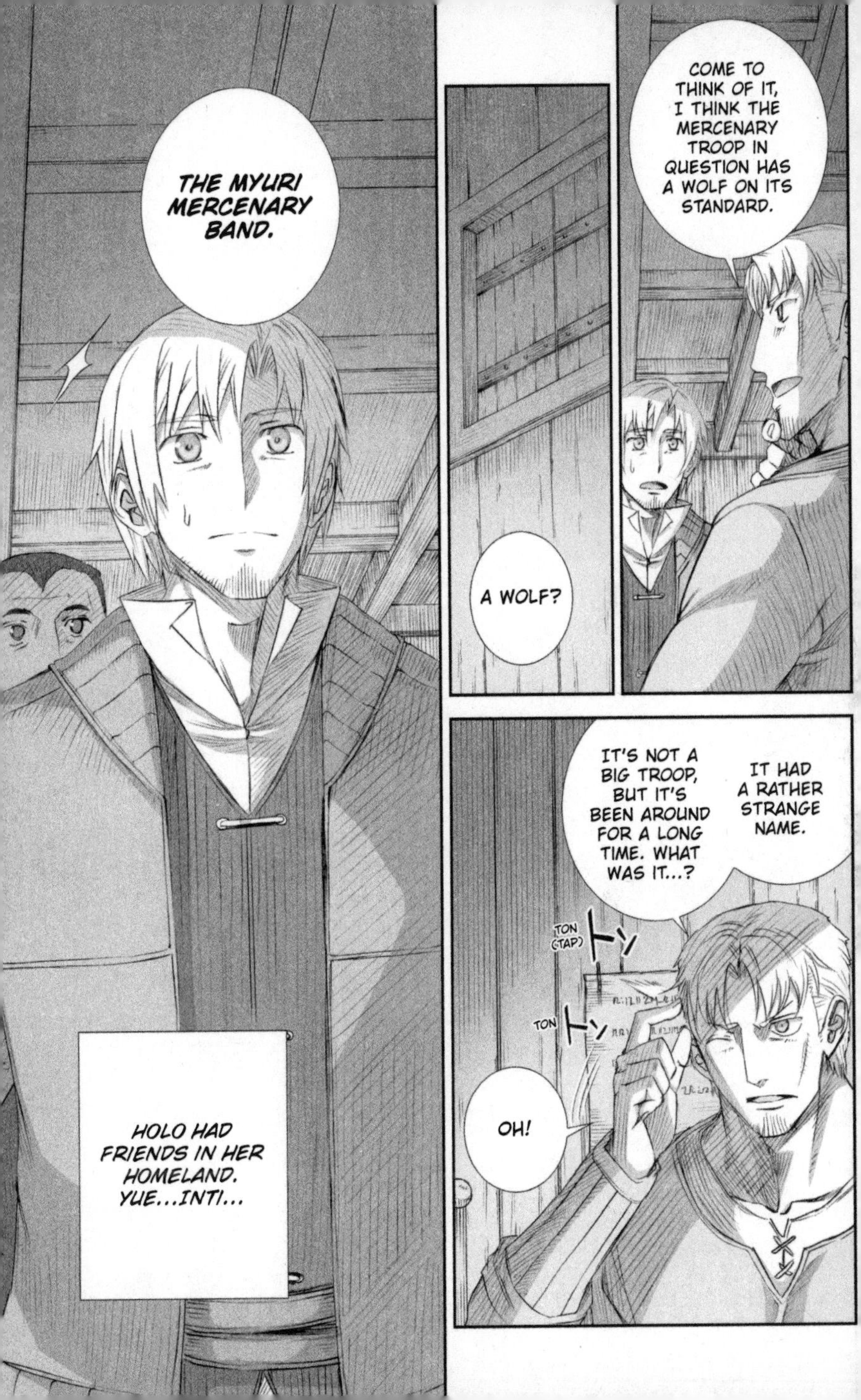
COME TO THINK OF IT, I THINK THE MERCENARY TROOP IN QUESTION HAS A WOLF ON ITS STANDARD.
A WOLF?
IT HAD A RATHER STRANGE NAME.
IT'S NOT A BIG TROOP, BUT IT'S BEEN AROUND FOR A LONG TIME. WHAT WAS IT...?
TON (TAP)
TON
OH!
THE MYURI MERCENARY BAND.
HOLO HAD FRIENDS IN HER HOMELAND. YUE...INTI...

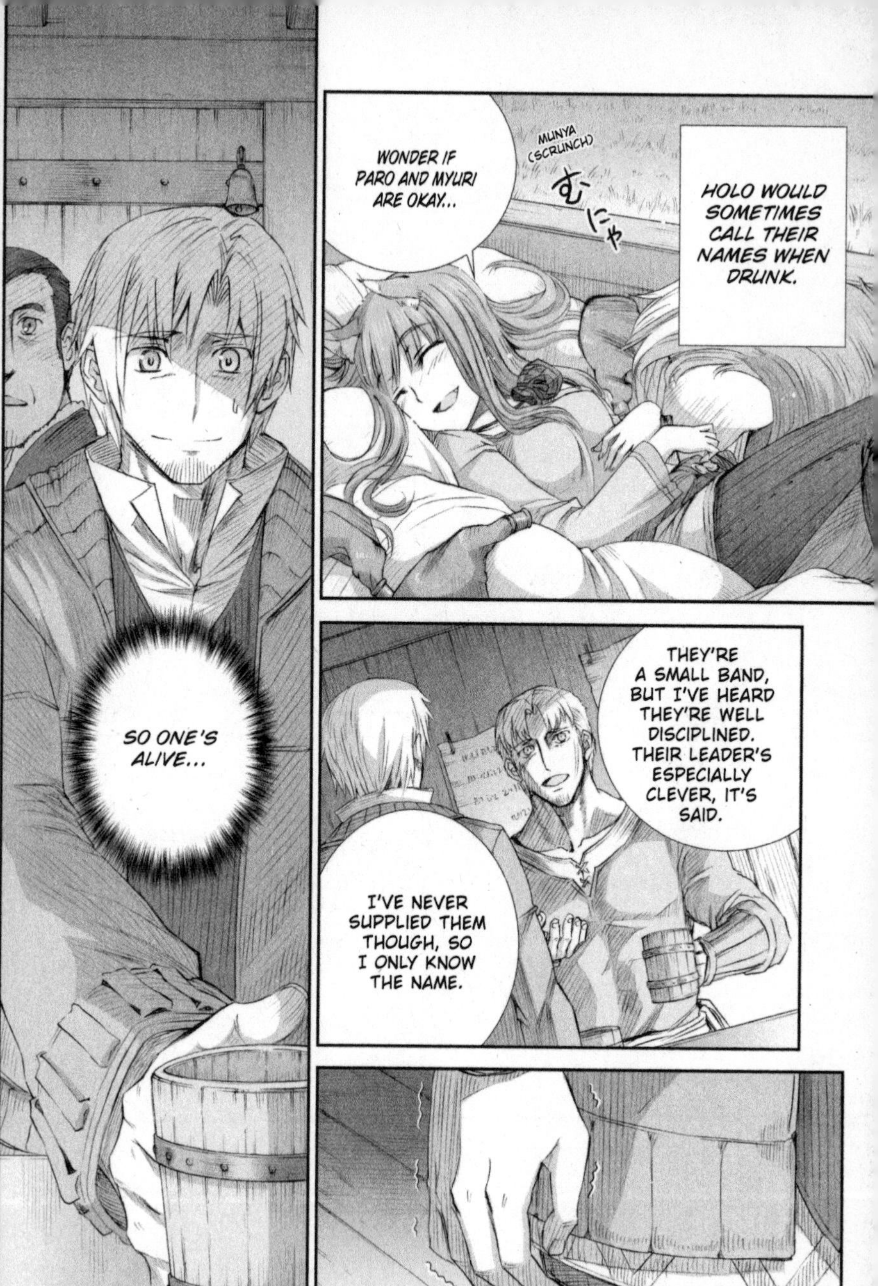
HOLO WOULD SOMETIMES CALL THEIR NAMES WHEN DRUNK.
MUNYA (SCRUNCH)
むにゃ
WONDER IF PARO AND MYURI ARE OKAY...
THEY'RE A SMALL BAND, BUT I'VE HEARD THEY'RE WELL DISCIPLINED. THEIR LEADER'S ESPECIALLY CLEVER, IT'S SAID.
I'VE NEVER SUPPLIED THEM THOUGH, SO I ONLY KNOW THE NAME.
SO ONE'S ALIVE...

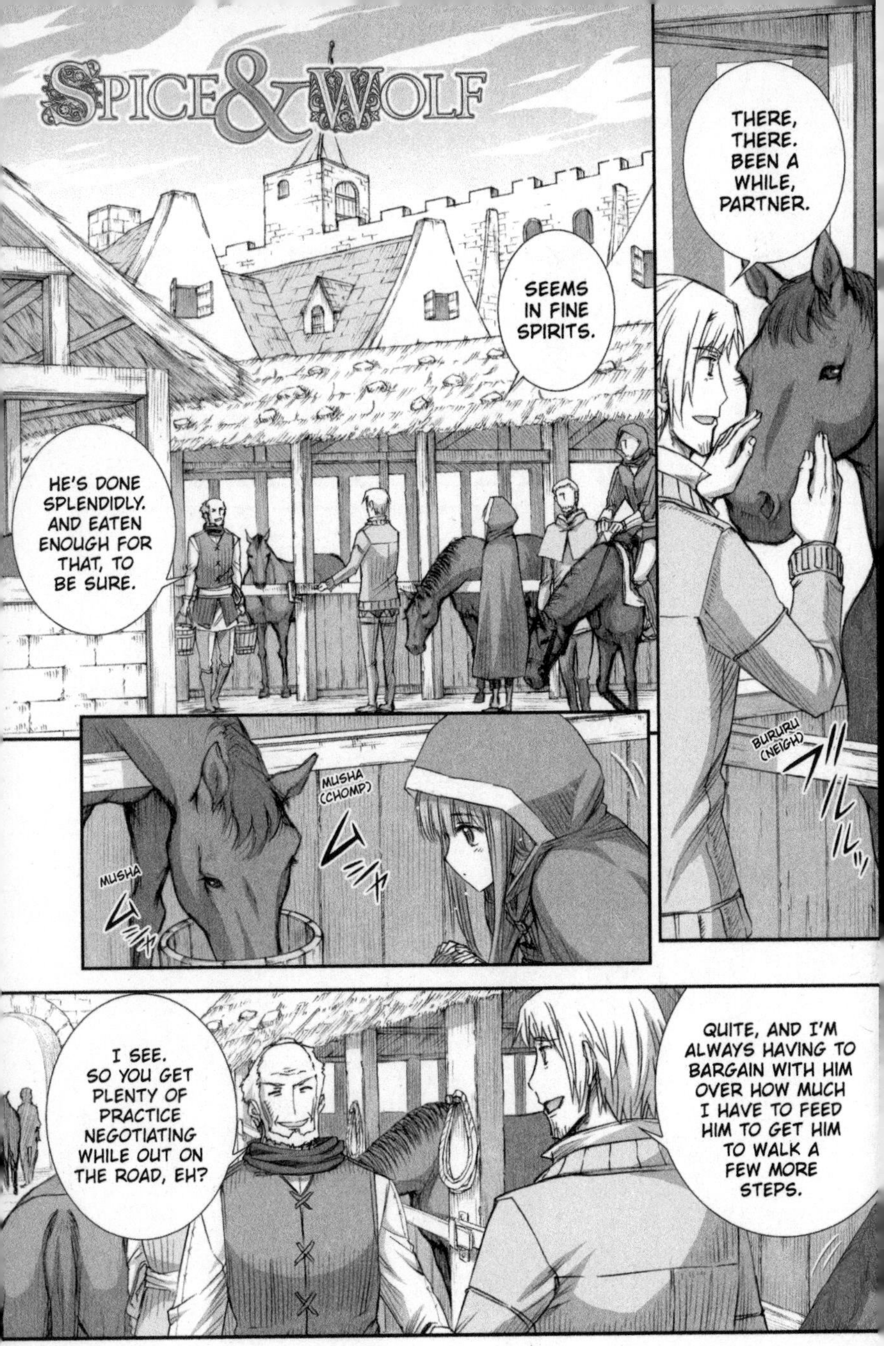
THERE, THERE. BEEN A WHILE, PARTNER.
BURURU (NEIGH)
SPICE & WOLF
SEEMS IN FINE SPIRITS.
HE'S DONE SPLENDIDLY. AND EATEN ENOUGH FOR THAT, TO BE SURE.
MUSHA (CHOMP)
MUSHA
QUITE, AND I'M ALWAYS HAVING TO BARGAIN WITH HIM OVER HOW MUCH I HAVE TO FEED HIM TO GET HIM TO WALK A FEW MORE STEPS.
I SEE. SO YOU GET PLENTY OF PRACTICE NEGOTIATING WHILE OUT ON THE ROAD, EH?

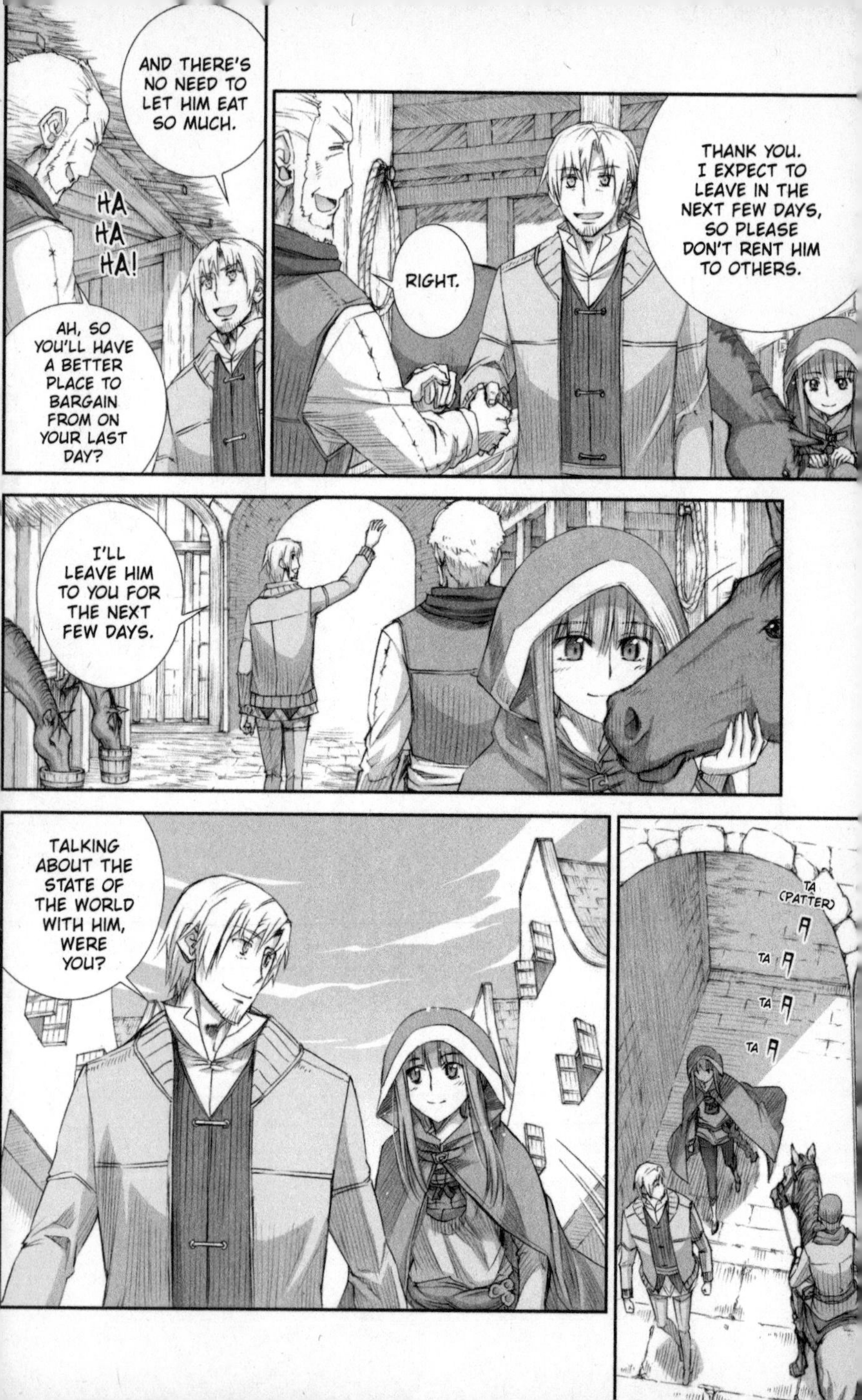
THANK YOU. I EXPECT TO LEAVE IN THE NEXT FEW DAYS, SO PLEASE DON'T RENT HIM TO OTHERS.
RIGHT.
AND THERE'S NO NEED TO LET HIM EAT SO MUCH.
HA HA HA!
AH, SO YOU'LL HAVE A BETTER PLACE TO BARGAIN FROM ON YOUR LAST DAY?
I'LL LEAVE HIM TO YOU FOR THE NEXT FEW DAYS.
TA (PATTER)
TA
TA
TA
TALKING ABOUT THE STATE OF THE WORLD WITH HIM, WERE YOU?

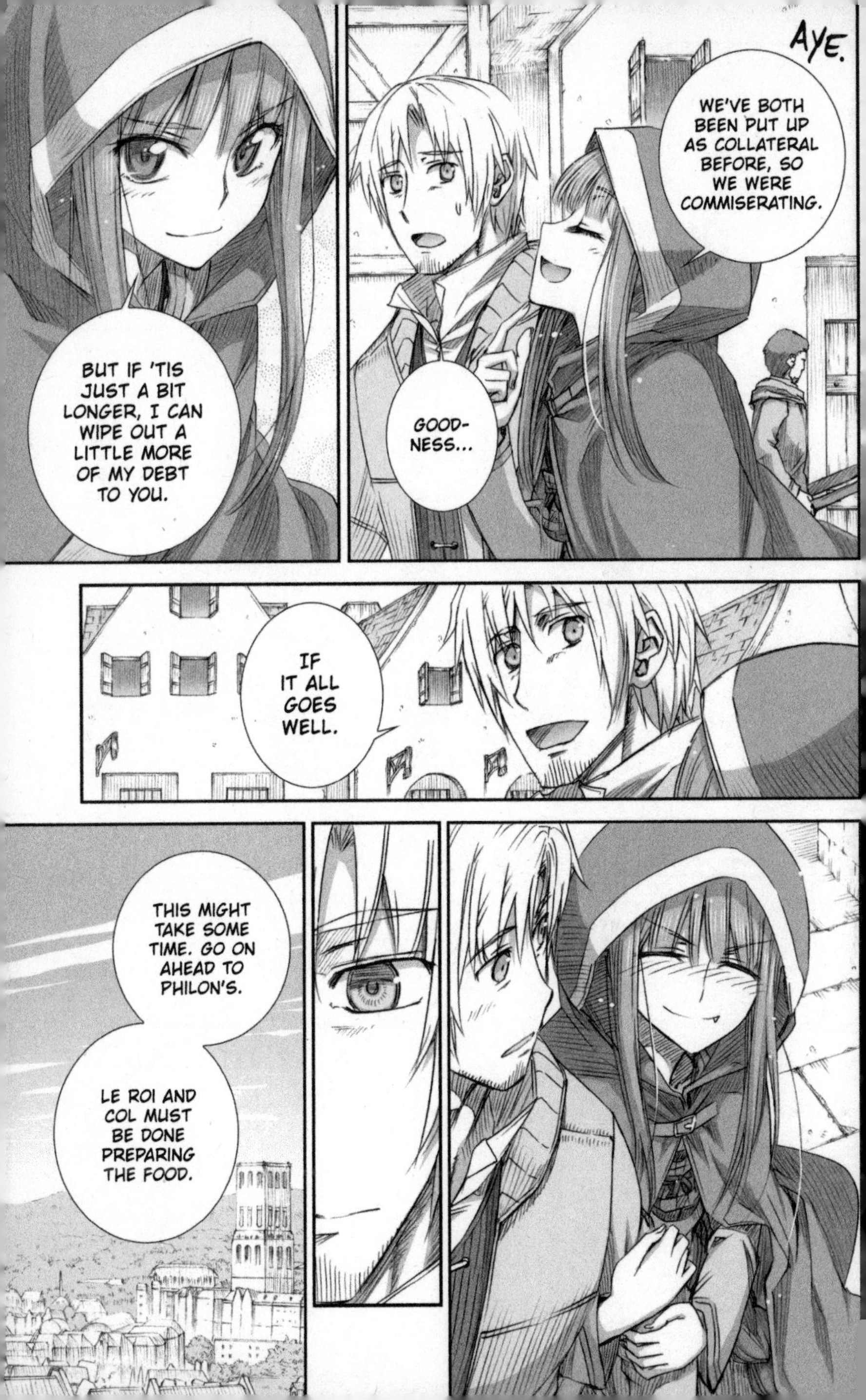
AYE.
WE'VE BOTH BEEN PUT UP AS COLLATERAL BEFORE, SO WE WERE COMMISERATING.
GOOD-NESS...
BUT IF 'TIS JUST A BIT LONGER, I CAN WIPE OUT A LITTLE MORE OF MY DEBT TO YOU.
IF IT ALL GOES WELL.
THIS MIGHT TAKE SOME TIME. GO ON AHEAD TO PHILON'S.
LE ROI AND COL MUST BE DONE PREPARING THE FOOD.

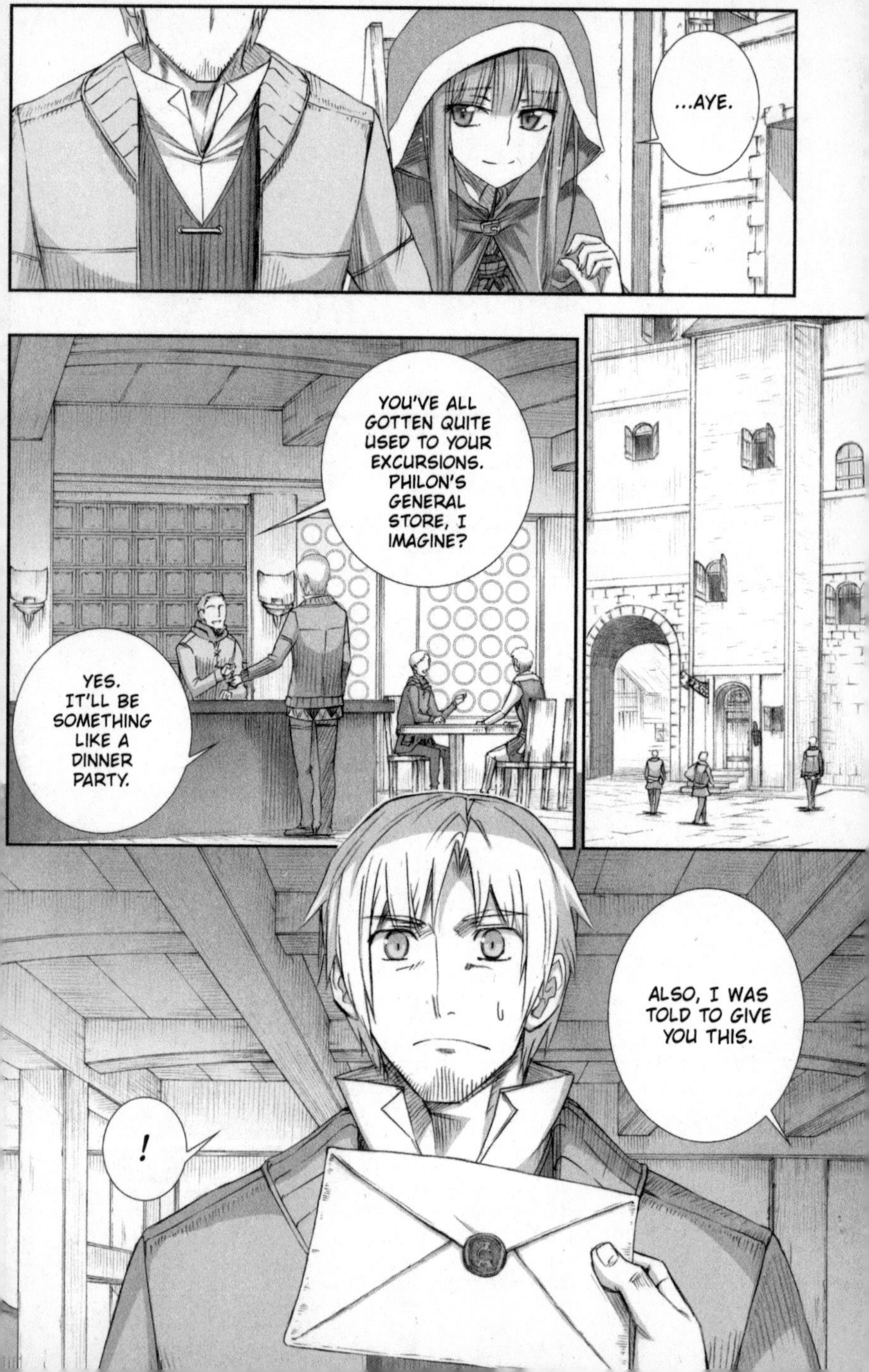
...AYE.
YOU'VE ALL GOTTEN QUITE USED TO YOUR EXCURSIONS. PHILON'S GENERAL STORE, I IMAGINE?
YES. IT'LL BE SOMETHING LIKE A DINNER PARTY.
ALSO, I WAS TOLD TO GIVE YOU THIS.
!

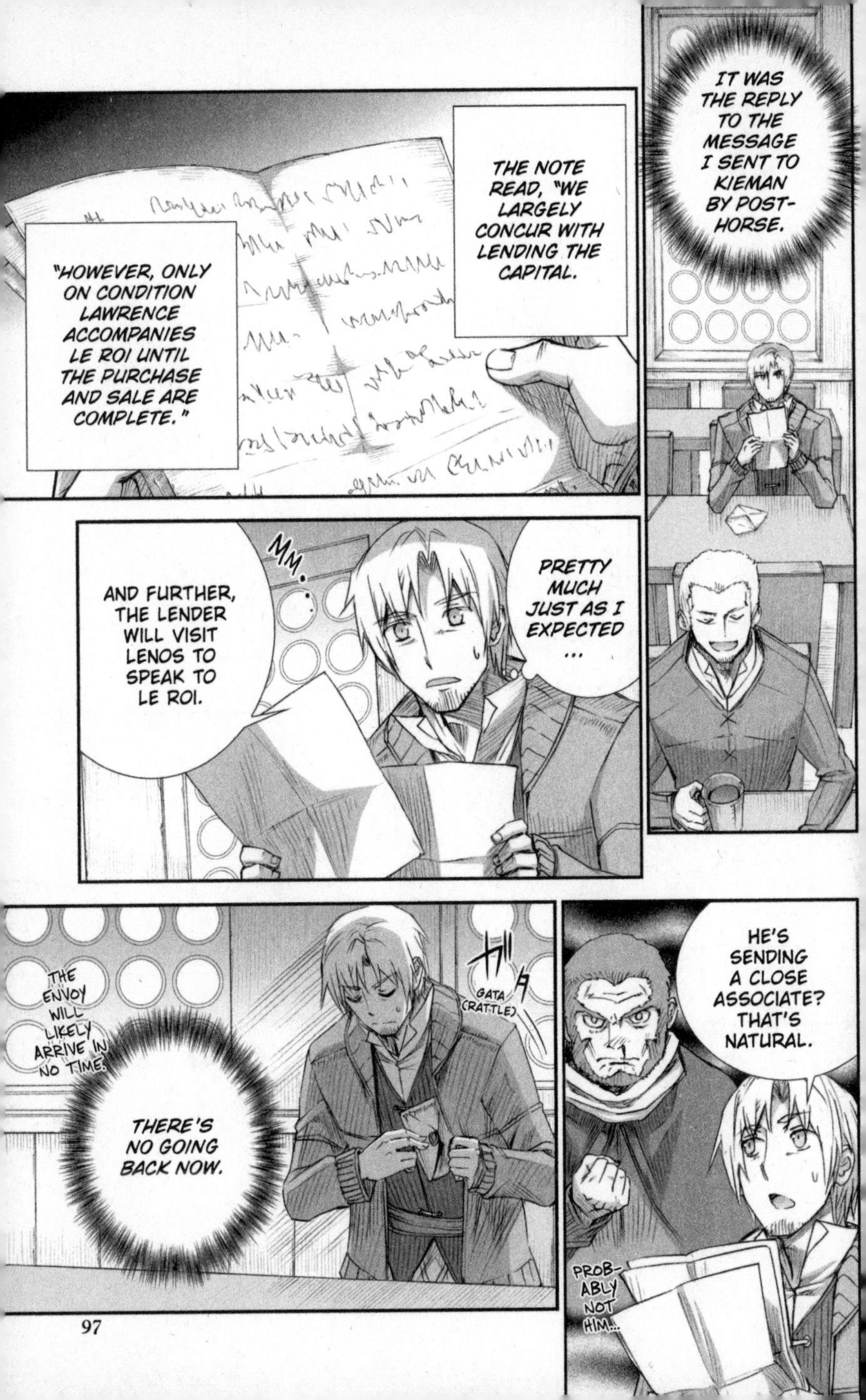
IT WAS THE REPLY TO THE MESSAGE I SENT TO KIEMAN BY POST-HORSE.
THE NOTE READ, "WE LARGELY CONCUR WITH LENDING THE CAPITAL.
"HOWEVER, ONLY ON CONDITION LAWRENCE ACCOMPANIES LE ROI UNTIL THE PURCHASE AND SALE ARE COMPLETE."
PRETTY MUCH JUST AS I EXPECTED...
MM.
AND FURTHER, THE LENDER WILL VISIT LENOS TO SPEAK TO LE ROI.
HE'S SENDING A CLOSE ASSOCIATE? THAT'S NATURAL.
PROB-ABLY NOT HIM...
GATA (RATTLE)
THE ENVOY WILL LIKELY ARRIVE IN NO TIME.
THERE'S NO GOING BACK NOW.

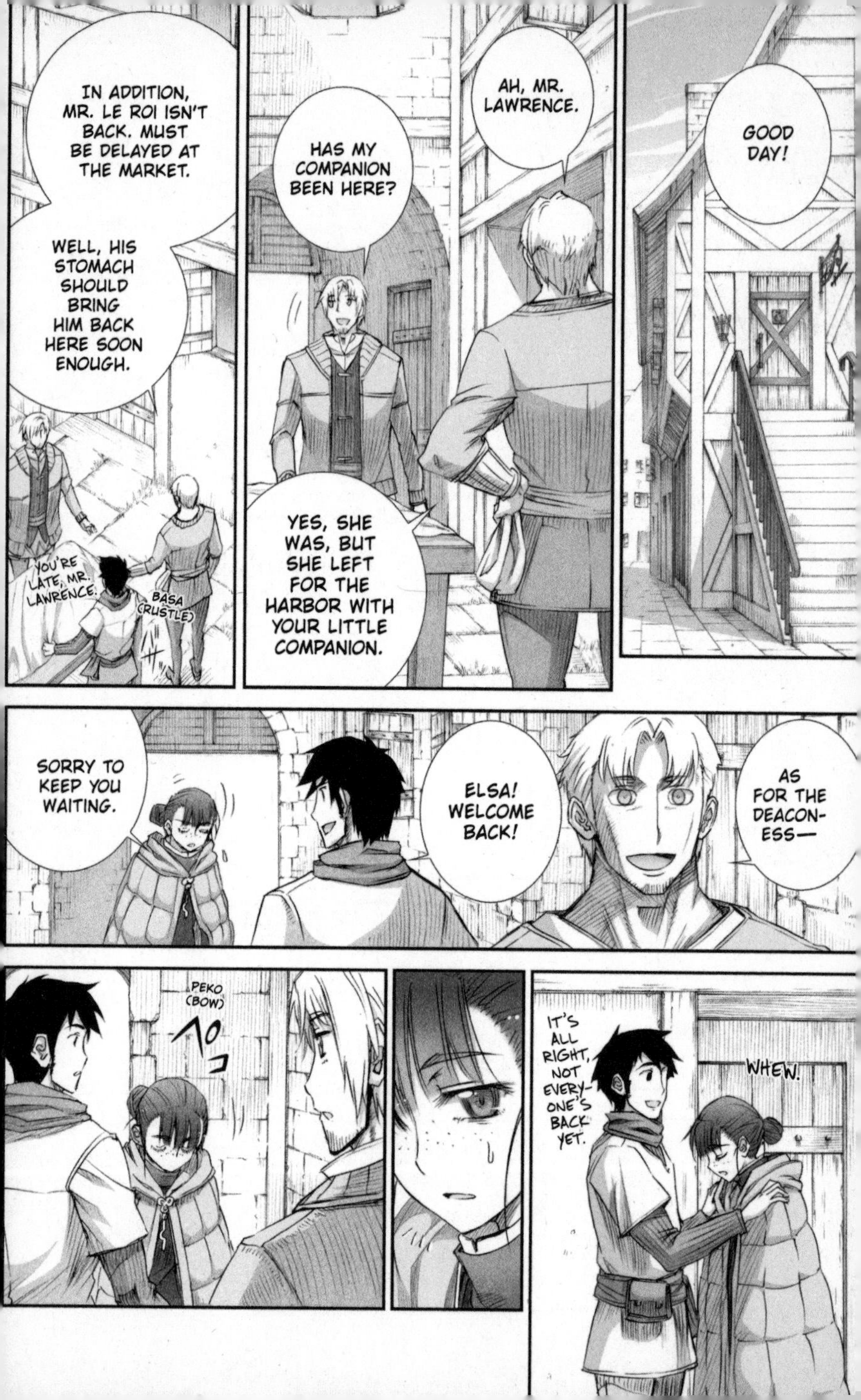
GOOD DAY!
AH, MR. LAWRENCE.
HAS MY COMPANION BEEN HERE?
YES, SHE WAS, BUT SHE LEFT FOR THE HARBOR WITH YOUR LITTLE COMPANION.
IN ADDITION, MR. LE ROI ISN'T BACK. MUST BE DELAYED AT THE MARKET.
WELL, HIS STOMACH SHOULD BRING HIM BACK HERE SOON ENOUGH.
YOU'RE LATE, MR. LAWRENCE.
BASA (RUSTLE)
AS FOR THE DEACONESS—
ELSA! WELCOME BACK!
SORRY TO KEEP YOU WAITING.
IT'S ALL RIGHT, NOT EVERYONE'S BACK YET.
WHEW.
PEKO (BOW)

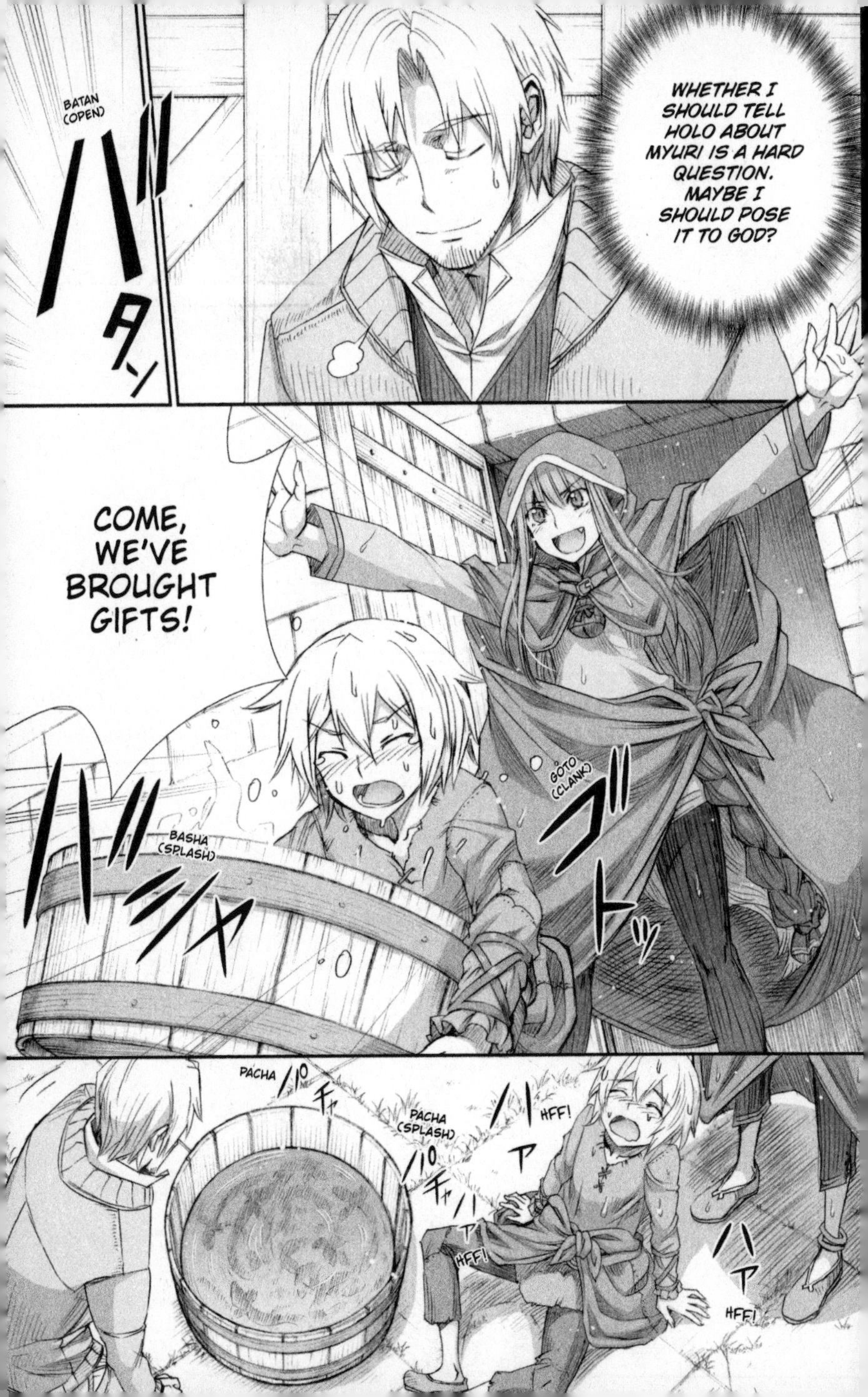
WHETHER I SHOULD TELL HOLO ABOUT MYURI IS A HARD QUESTION. MAYBE I SHOULD POSE IT TO GOD?
BATAN (OPEN)
COME, WE'VE BROUGHT GIFTS!
GOTO (CLANK)
BASHA (SPLASH)
HFF!
HFF!
PACHA (SPLASH)
PACHA
HFF!

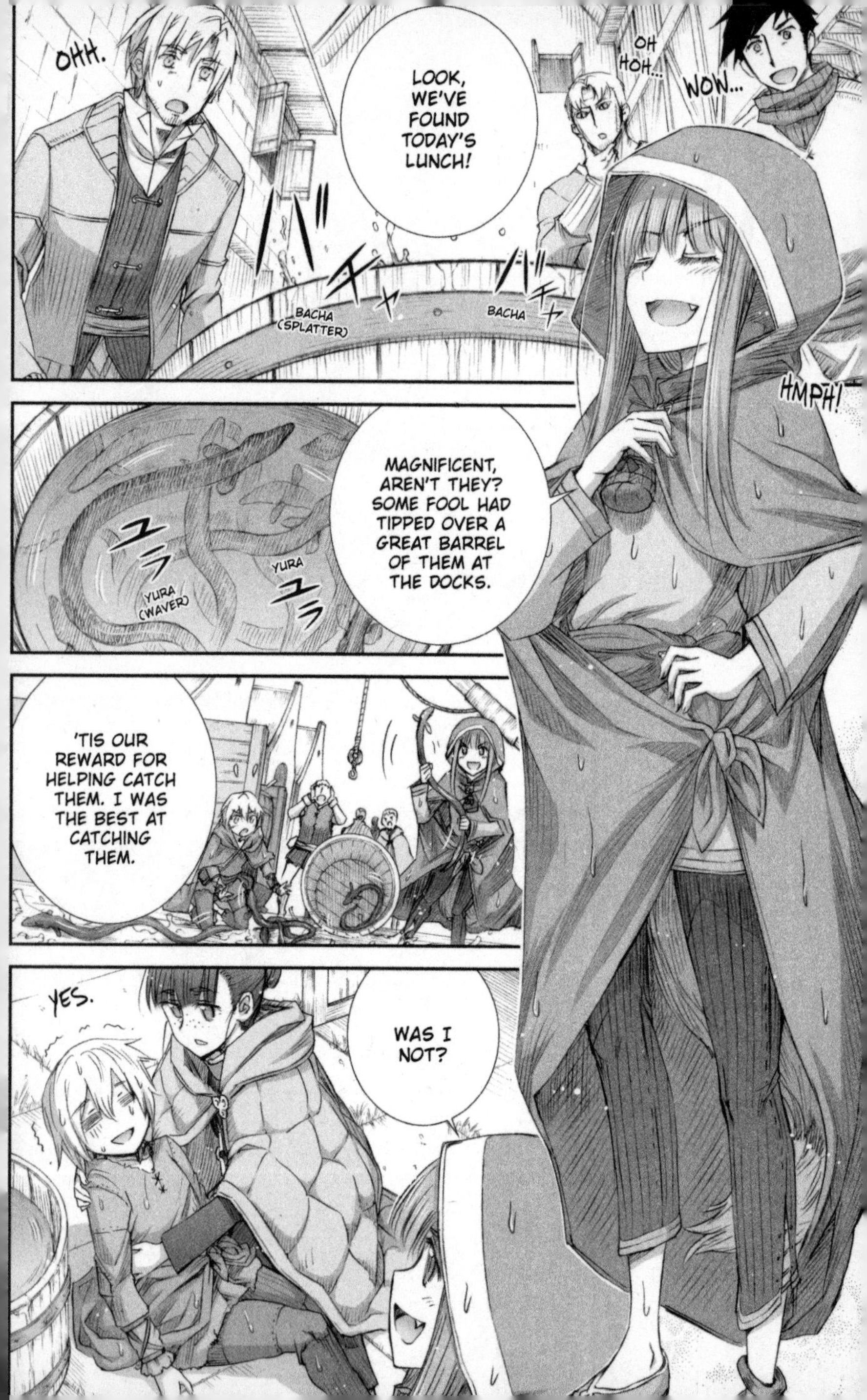
OH HOH...
WOW...
LOOK, WE'VE FOUND TODAY'S LUNCH!
BACHA
BACHA (SPLATTER)
OHH.
HMPH!
MAGNIFICENT, AREN'T THEY? SOME FOOL HAD TIPPED OVER A GREAT BARREL OF THEM AT THE DOCKS.
YURA
YURA (WAVER)
'TIS OUR REWARD FOR HELPING CATCH THEM. I WAS THE BEST AT CATCHING THEM.
WAS I NOT?
YES.

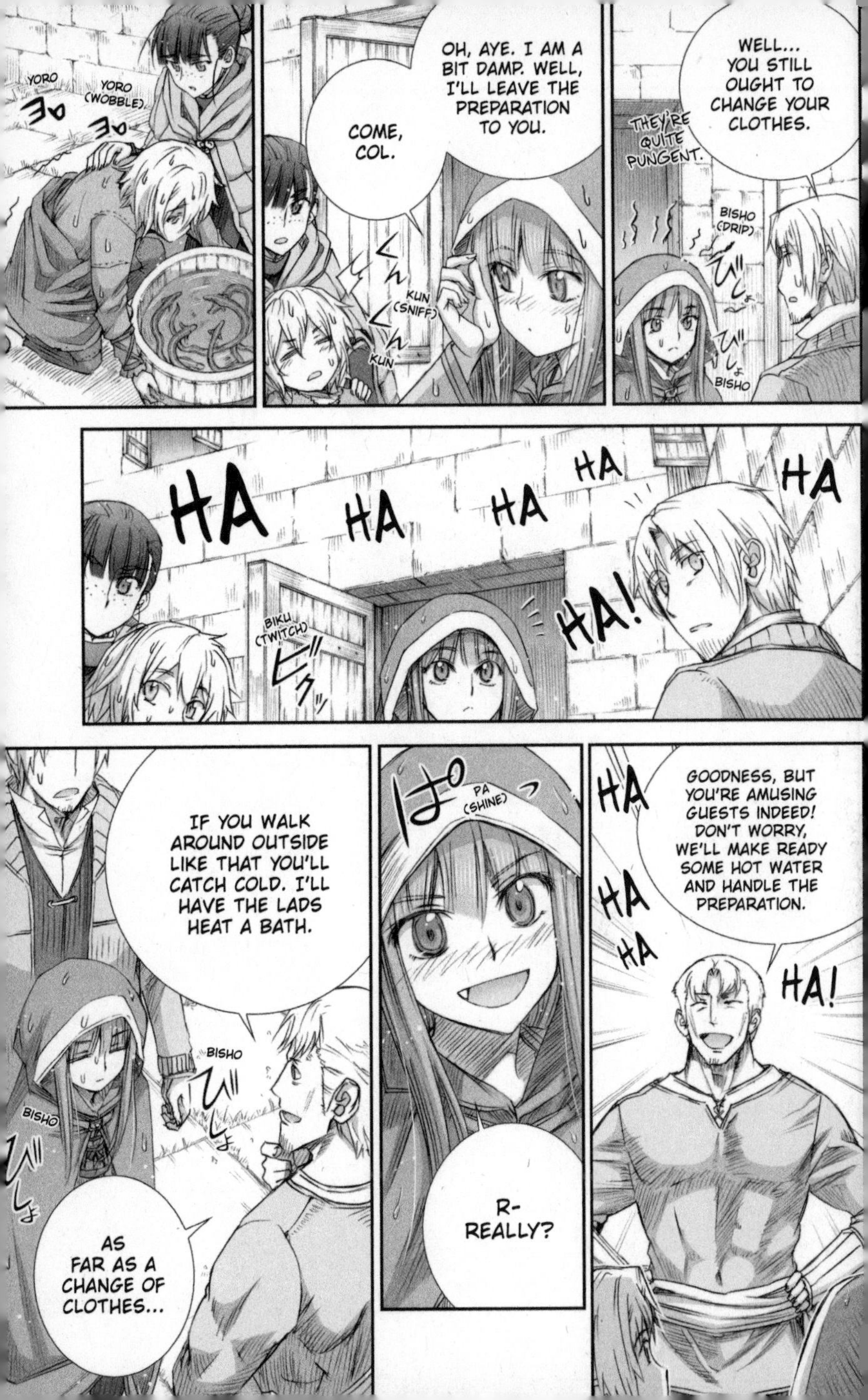
WELL... YOU STILL OUGHT TO CHANGE YOUR CLOTHES.
THEY'RE QUITE PUNGENT.
BISHO (DRIP)
BISHO
OH, AYE. I AM A BIT DAMP. WELL, I'LL LEAVE THE PREPARATION TO YOU.
COME, COL.
KUN (SNIFF)
KUN
YORO (WOBBLE)
YORO
HA
HA!
HA
HA
HA
HA
BIKU (TWITCH)
GOODNESS, BUT YOU'RE AMUSING GUESTS INDEED! DON'T WORRY, WE'LL MAKE READY SOME HOT WATER AND HANDLE THE PREPARATION.
HA
HA
HA
HA!
PA (SHINE)
R- REALLY?
IF YOU WALK AROUND OUTSIDE LIKE THAT YOU'LL CATCH COLD. I'LL HAVE THE LADS HEAT A BATH.
BISHO
BISHO
AS FAR AS A CHANGE OF CLOTHES...

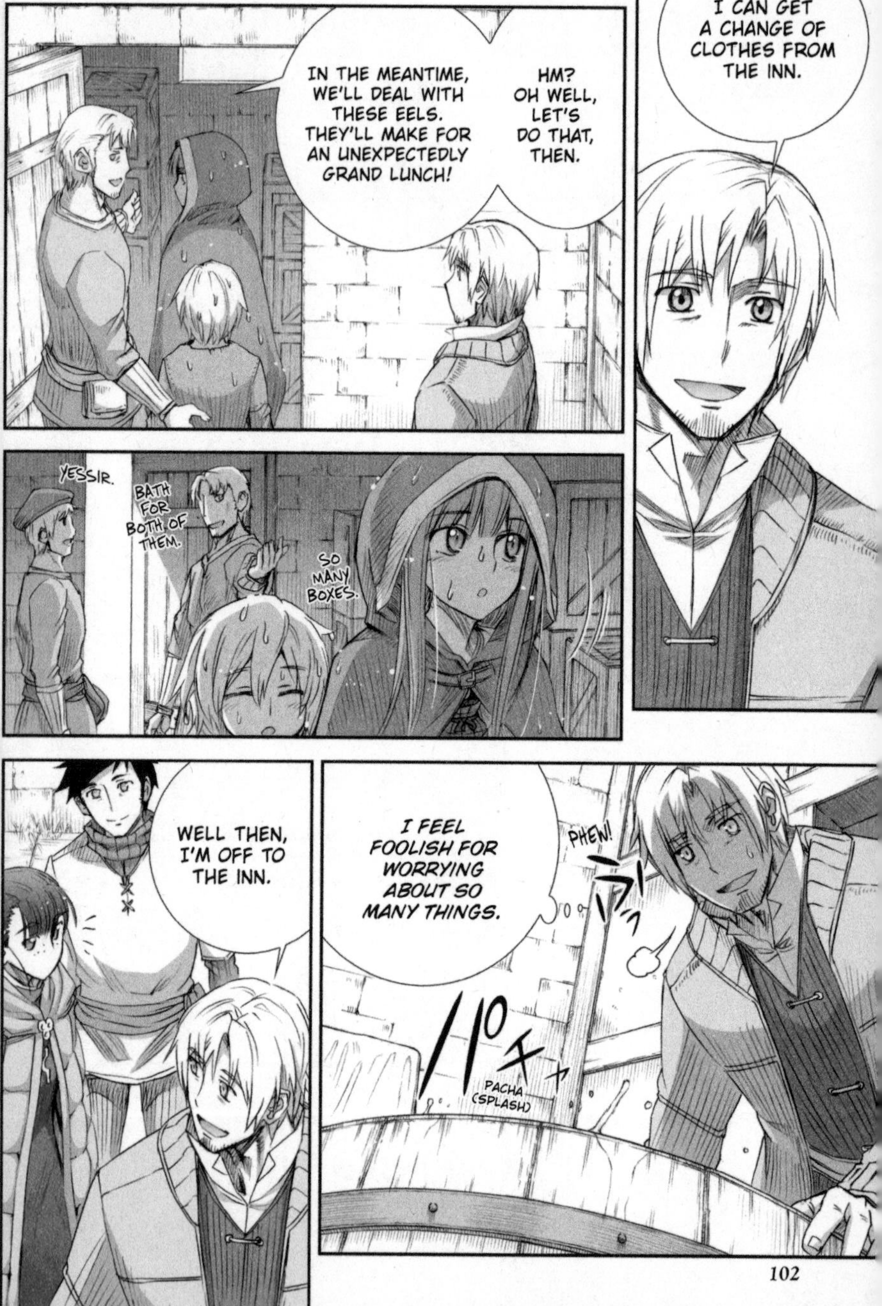
I CAN GET A CHANGE OF CLOTHES FROM THE INN.
HM? OH WELL, LET'S DO THAT, THEN.
IN THE MEANTIME, WE'LL DEAL WITH THESE EELS. THEY'LL MAKE FOR AN UNEXPECTEDLY GRAND LUNCH!
SO MANY BOXES.
BATH FOR BOTH OF THEM.
YESSIR.
PHEW!
I FEEL FOOLISH FOR WORRYING ABOUT SO MANY THINGS.
PACHA (SPLASH)
WELL THEN, I'M OFF TO THE INN.

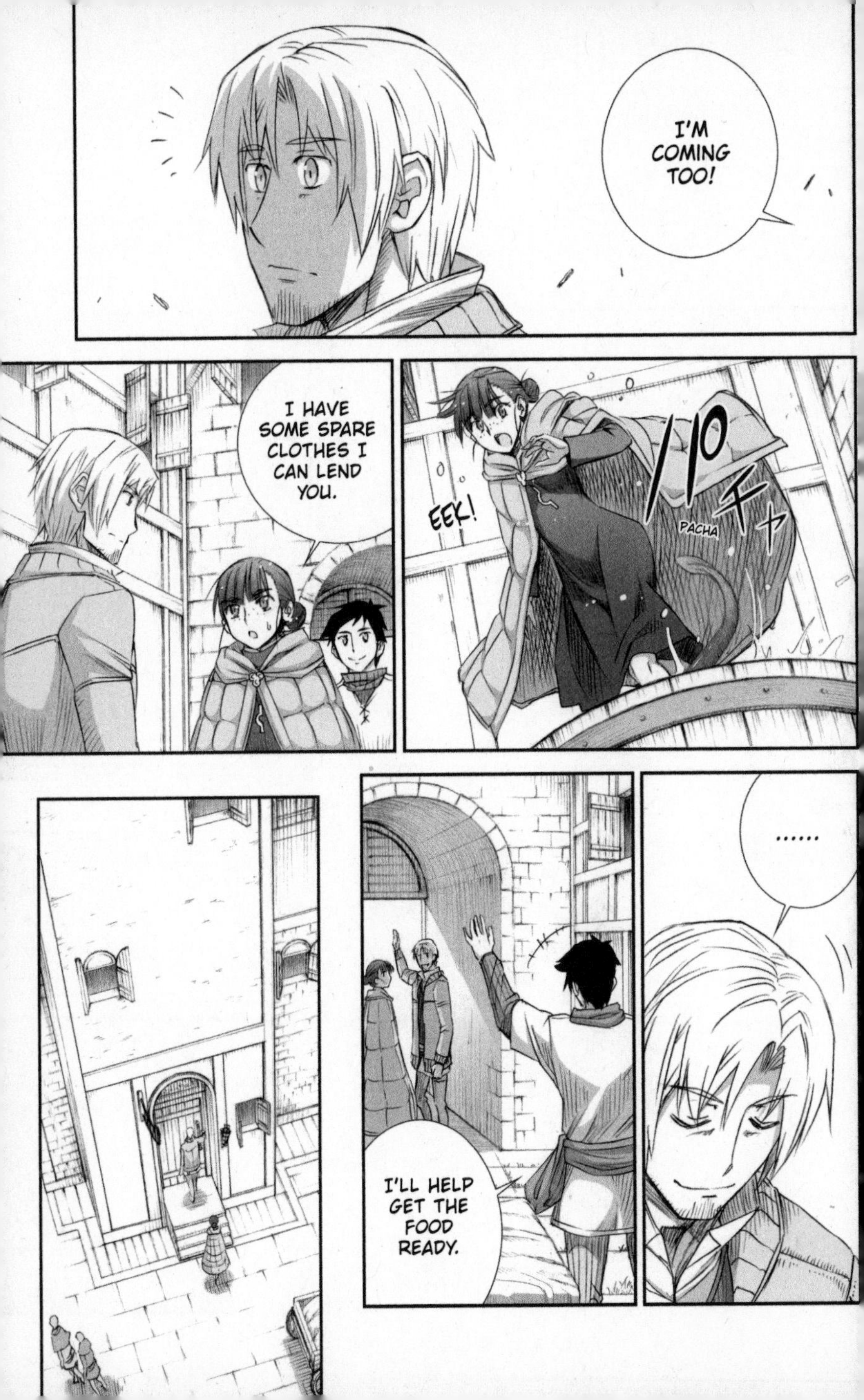
I'M COMING TOO!
EEK!
PACHA
I HAVE SOME SPARE CLOTHES I CAN LEND YOU.
......
I'LL HELP GET THE FOOD READY.

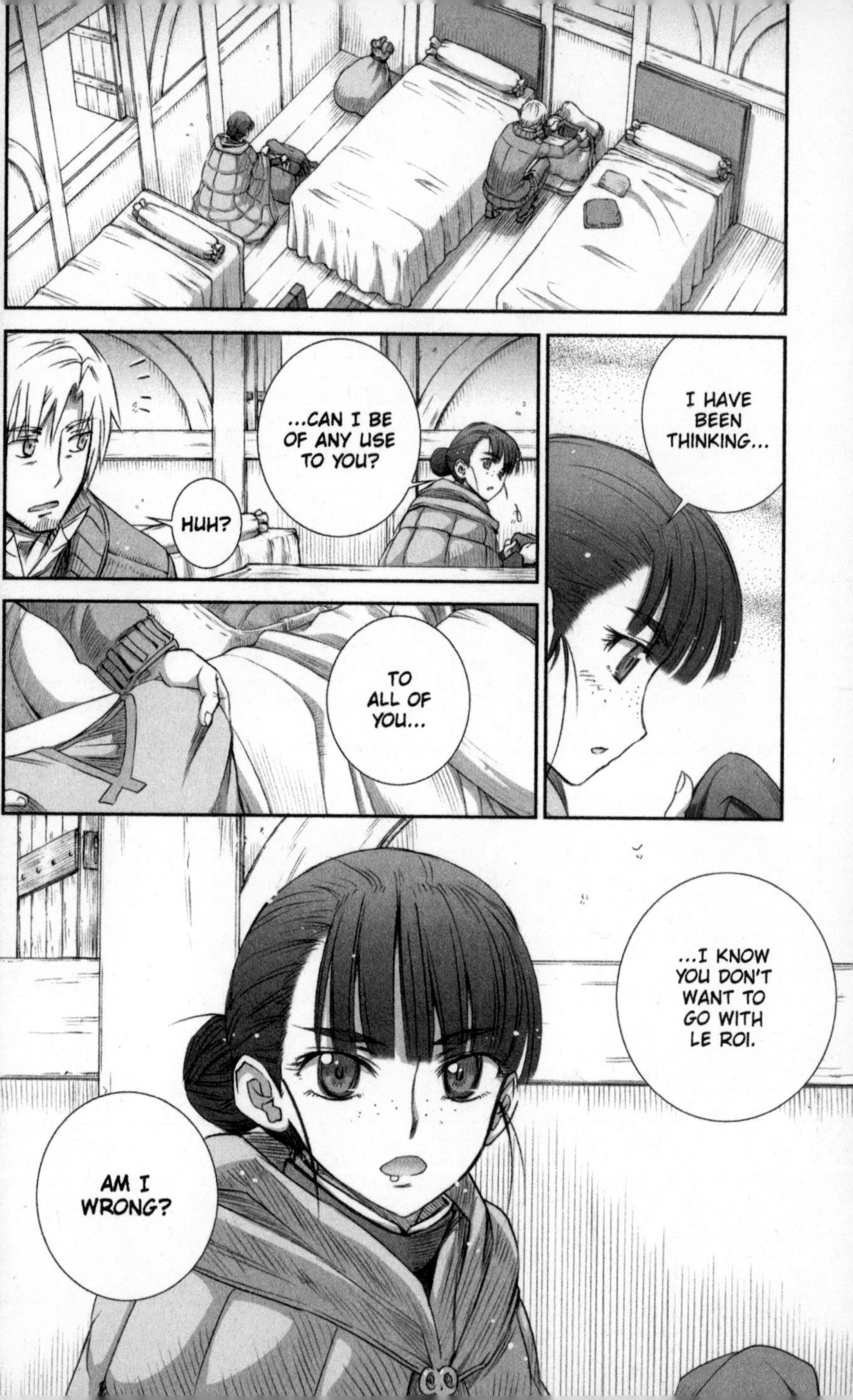
I HAVE BEEN THINKING...
...CAN I BE OF ANY USE TO YOU?
HUH?
TO ALL OF YOU...
...I KNOW YOU DON'T WANT TO GO WITH LE ROI.
AM I WRONG?

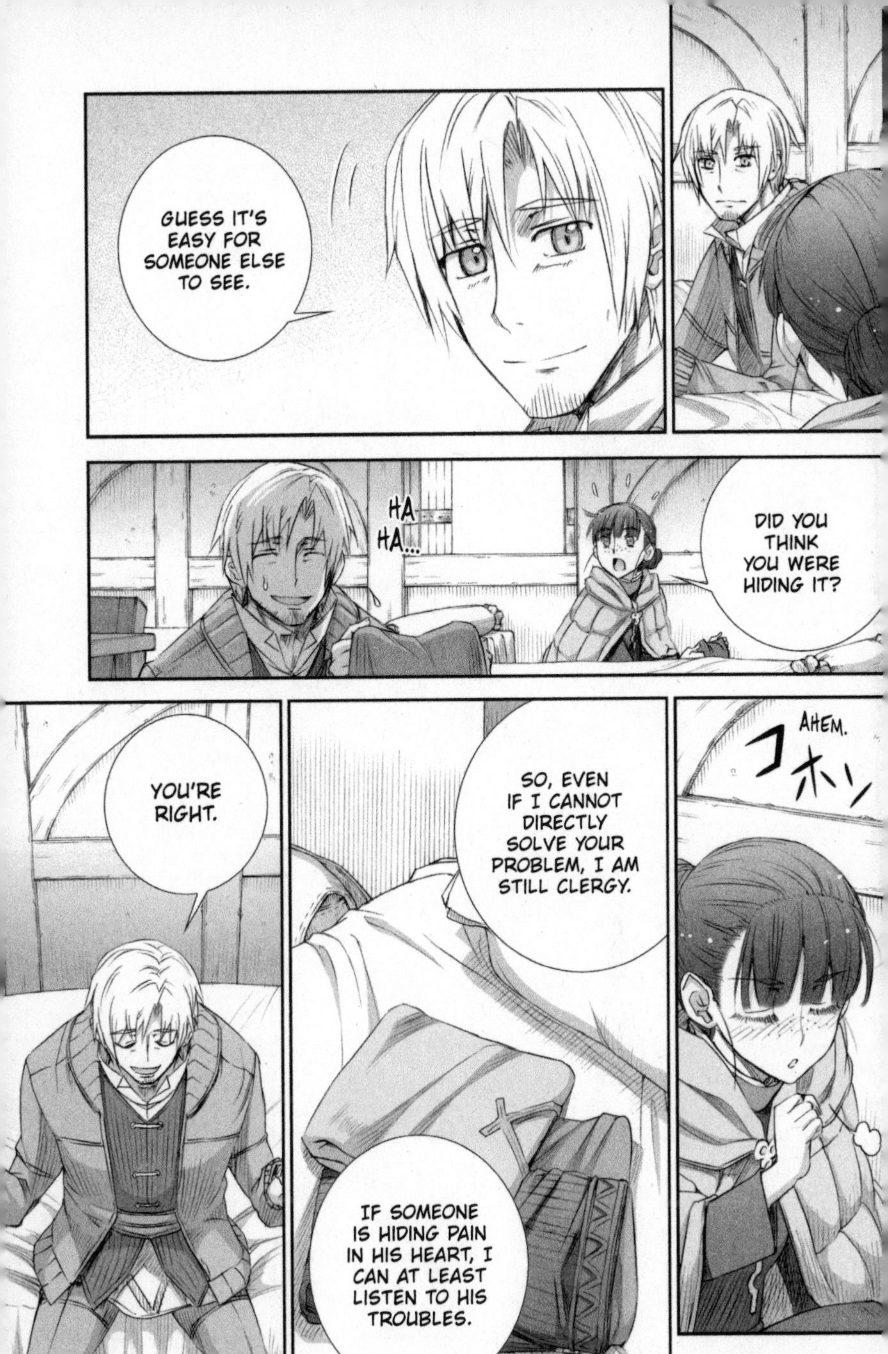
GUESS IT'S EASY FOR SOMEONE ELSE TO SEE.
DID YOU THINK YOU WERE HIDING IT?
HA HA...
AHEM.
コホン
SO, EVEN IF I CANNOT DIRECTLY SOLVE YOUR PROBLEM, I AM STILL CLERGY.
IF SOMEONE IS HIDING PAIN IN HIS HEART, I CAN AT LEAST LISTEN TO HIS TROUBLES.
YOU'RE RIGHT.

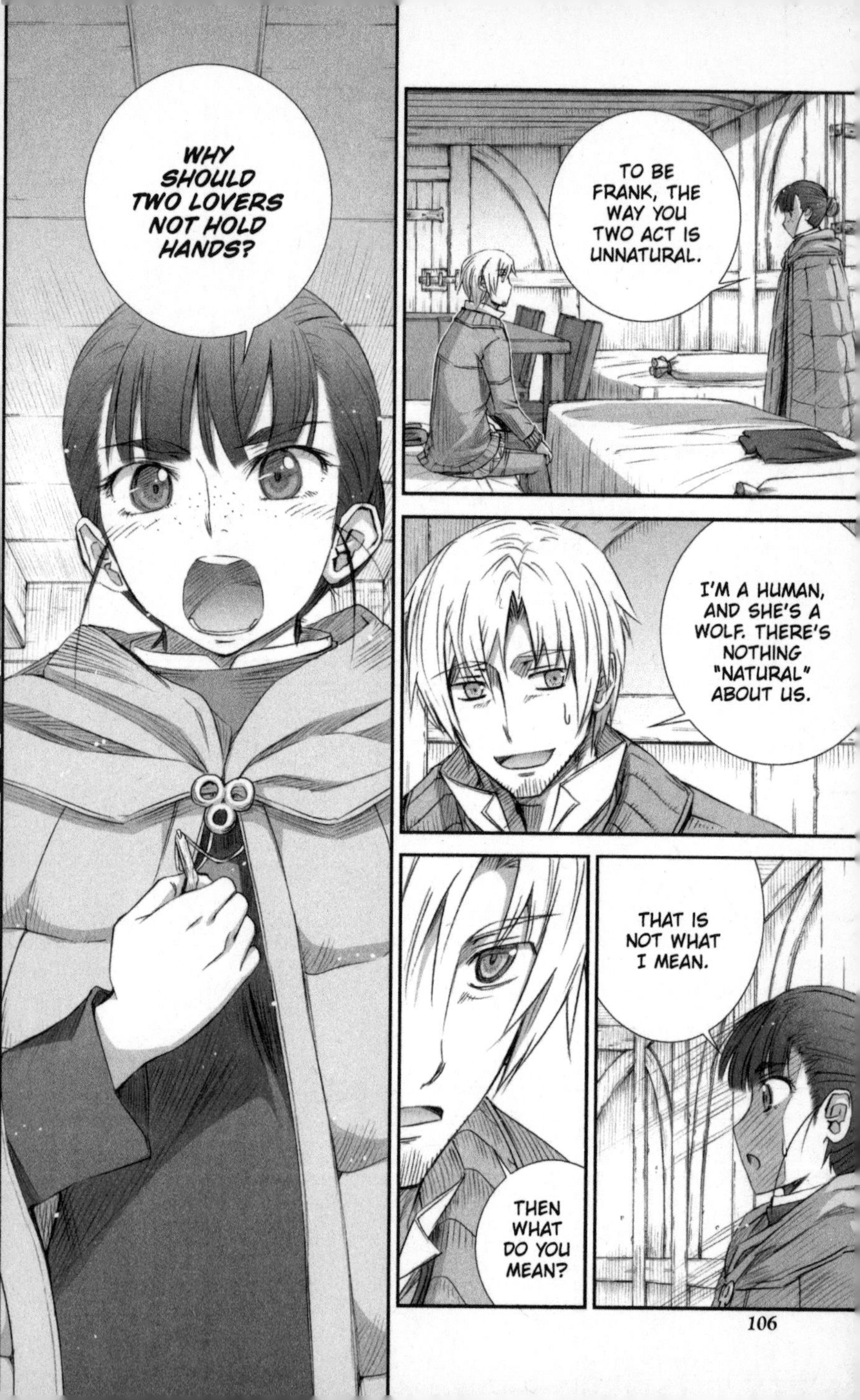
TO BE FRANK, THE WAY YOU TWO ACT IS UNNATURAL.
I'M A HUMAN, AND SHE'S A WOLF. THERE'S NOTHING "NATURAL" ABOUT US.
THAT IS NOT WHAT I MEAN.
THEN WHAT DO YOU MEAN?
WHY SHOULD TWO LOVERS NOT HOLD HANDS?

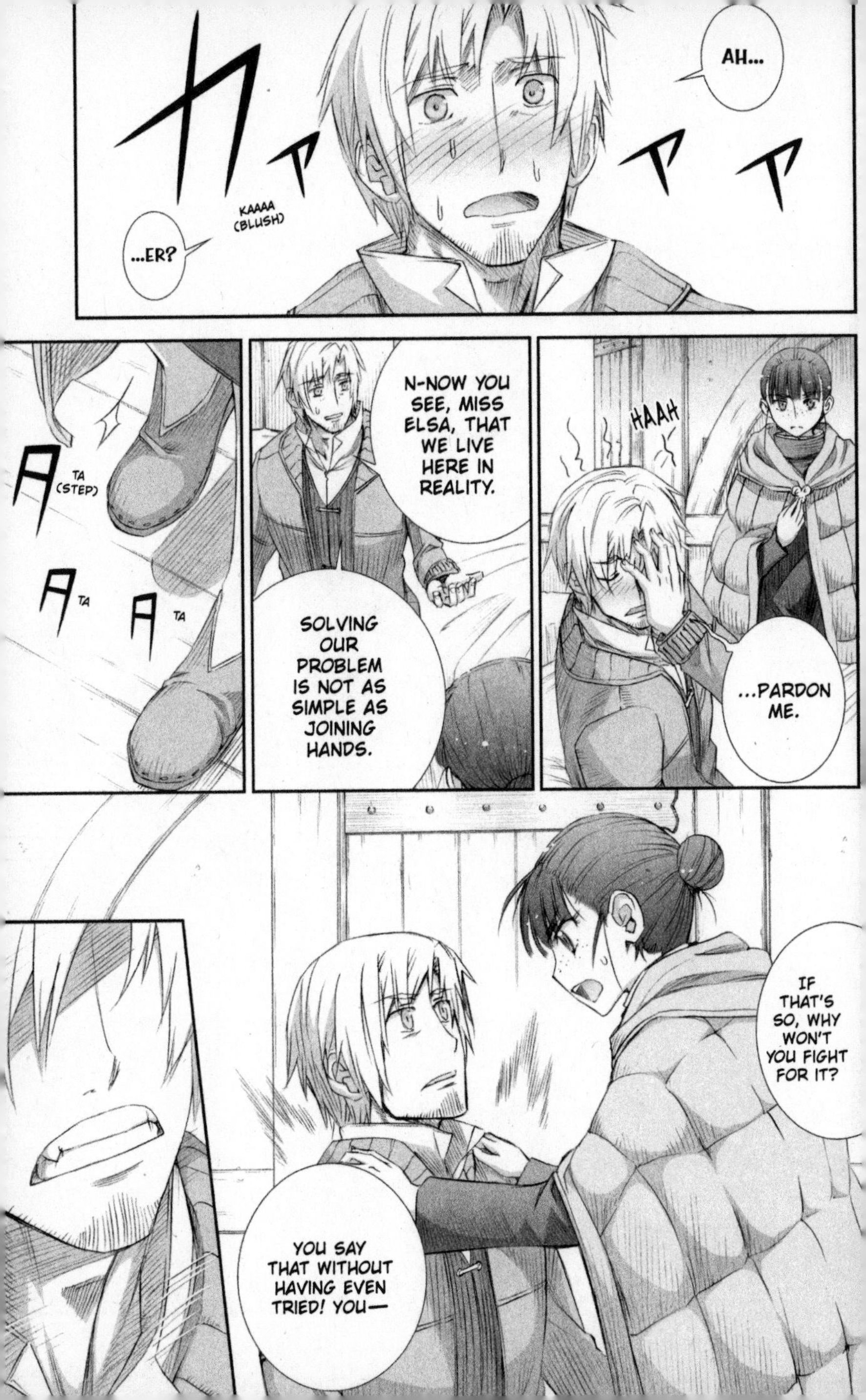
AH...
KAAAA (BLUSH)
...ER?
HAAH
...PARDON ME.
N-NOW YOU SEE, MISS ELSA, THAT WE LIVE HERE IN REALITY.
SOLVING OUR PROBLEM IS NOT AS SIMPLE AS JOINING HANDS.
TA (STEP)
TA
TA
IF THAT'S SO, WHY WON'T YOU FIGHT FOR IT?
YOU SAY THAT WITHOUT HAVING EVEN TRIED! YOU—

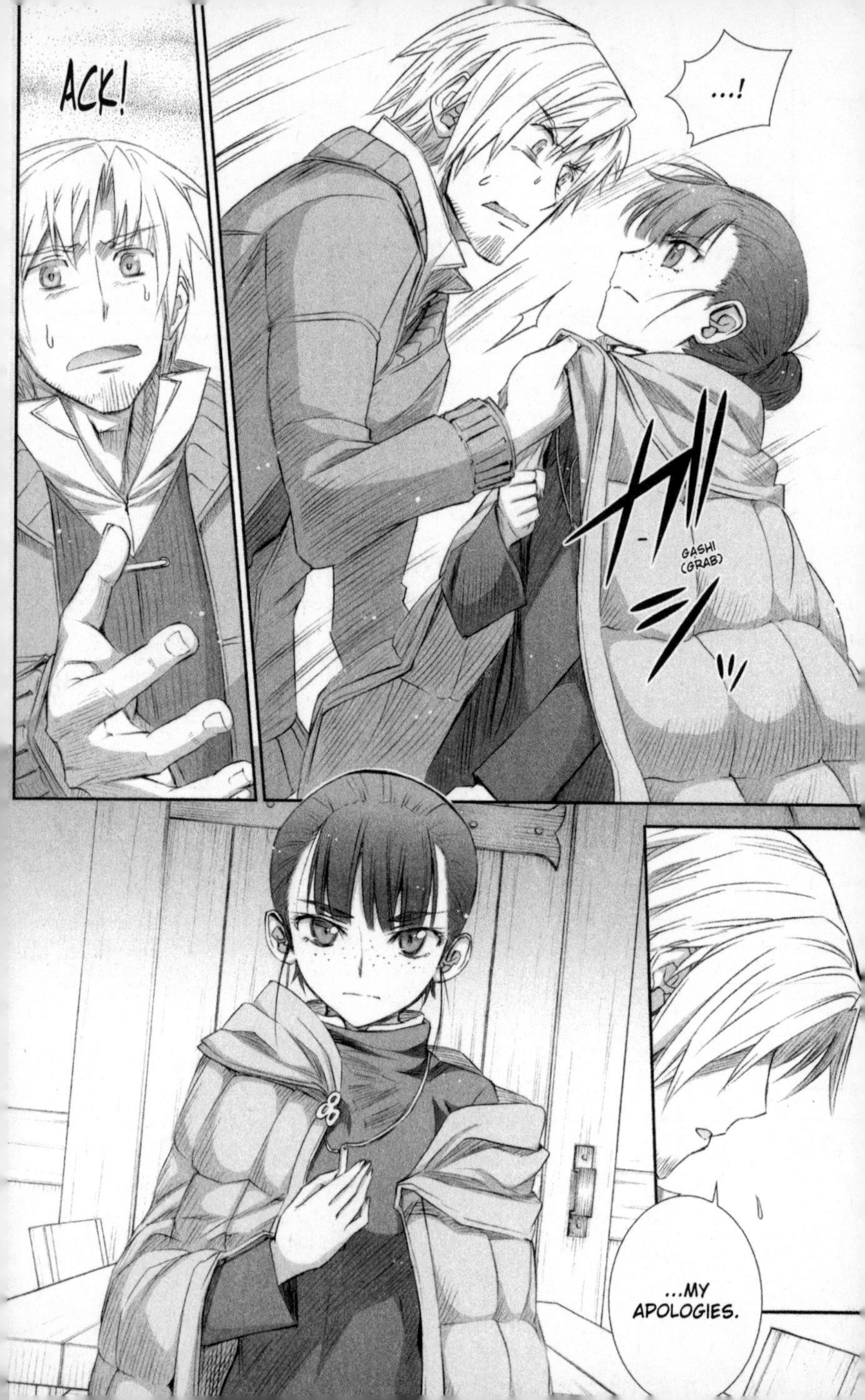
...!
GASHI (GRAB)
ACK!
...MY APOLOGIES.

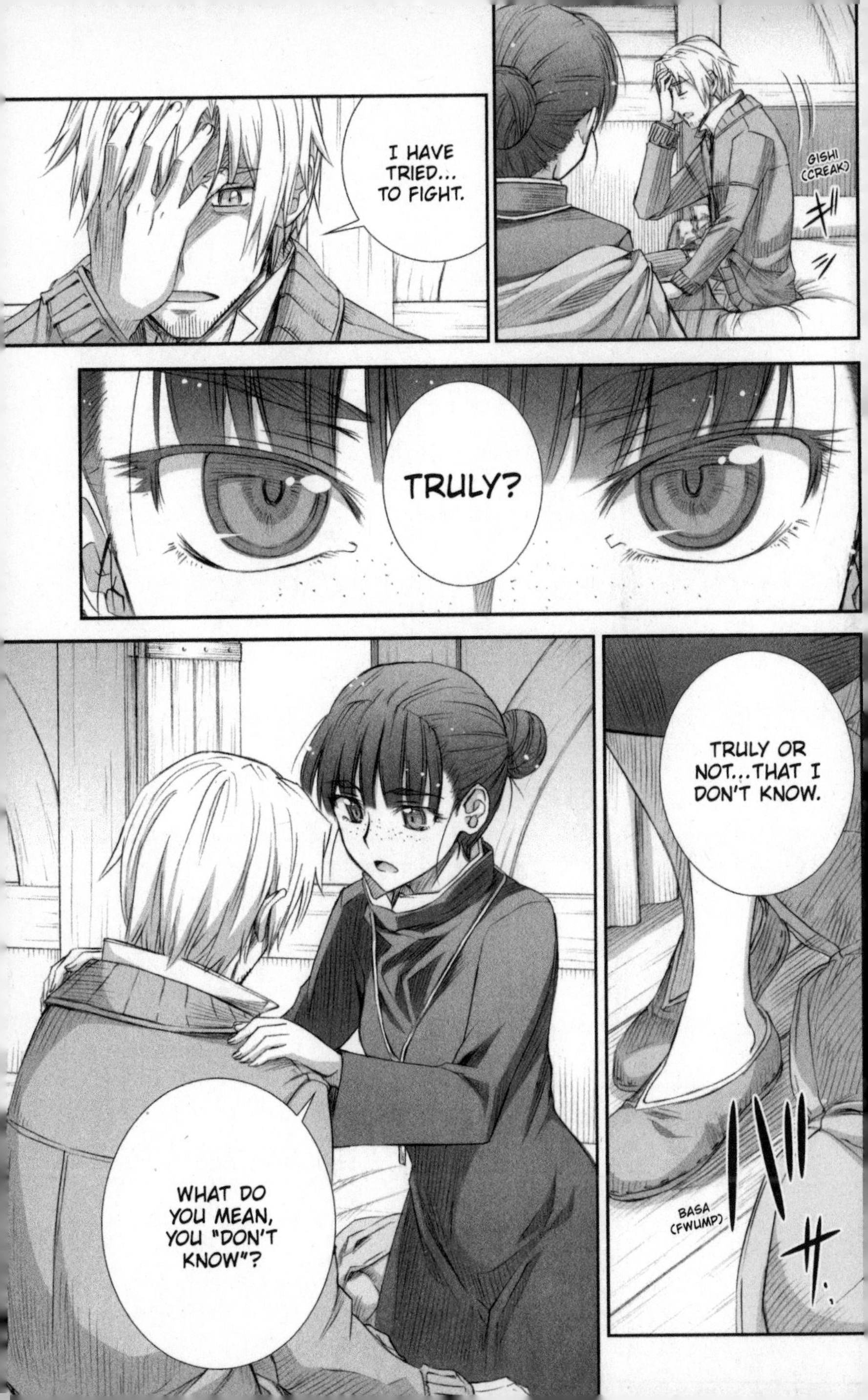
GISHI (CREAK)
I HAVE TRIED... TO FIGHT.
TRULY?
TRULY OR NOT...THAT I DON'T KNOW.
BASA (FWUMP)
WHAT DO YOU MEAN, YOU "DON'T KNOW"?

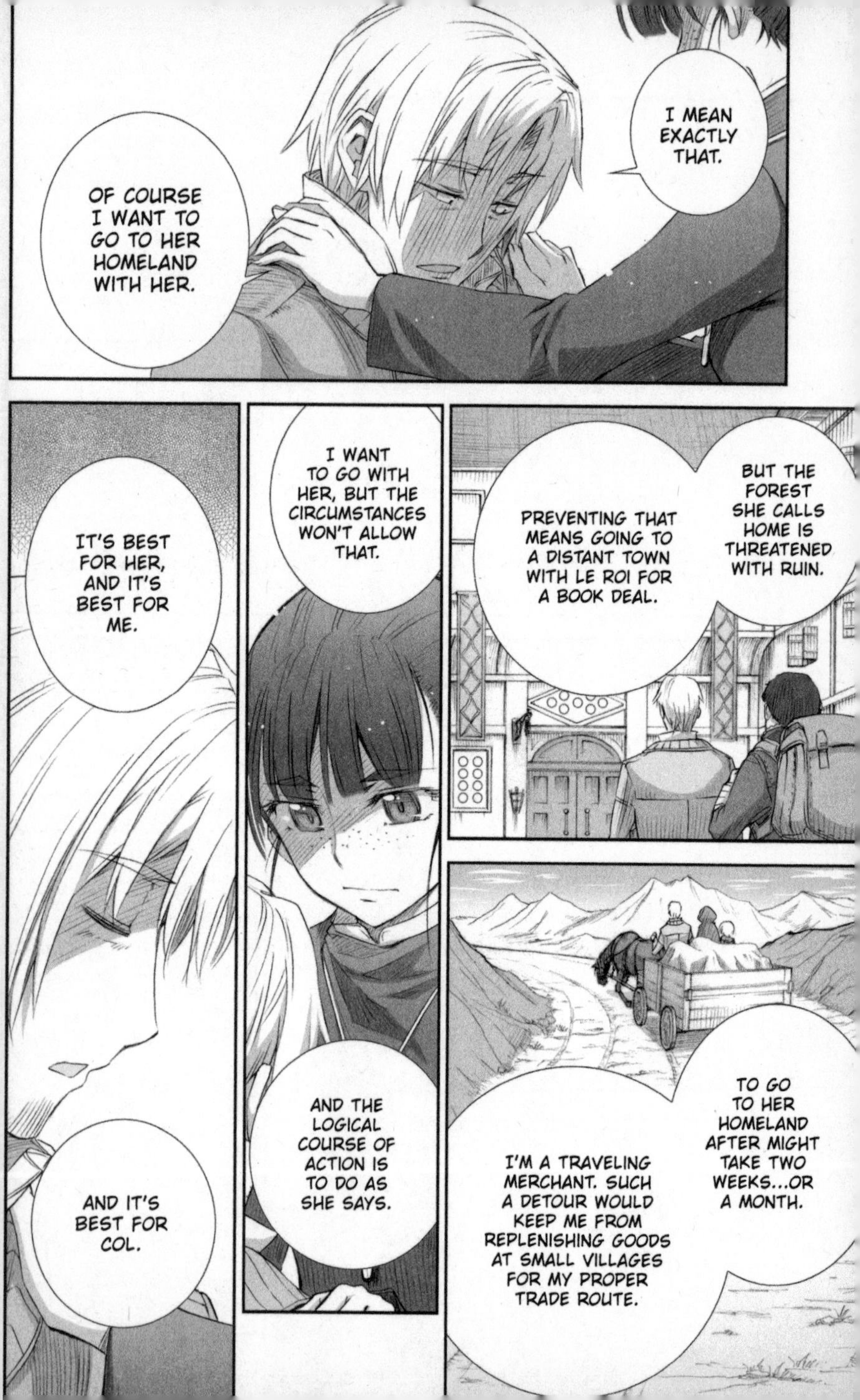
I MEAN EXACTLY THAT.
OF COURSE I WANT TO GO TO HER HOMELAND WITH HER.
BUT THE FOREST SHE CALLS HOME IS THREATENED WITH RUIN.
PREVENTING THAT MEANS GOING TO A DISTANT TOWN WITH LE ROI FOR A BOOK DEAL.
TO GO TO HER HOMELAND AFTER MIGHT TAKE TWO WEEKS...OR A MONTH.
I'M A TRAVELING MERCHANT. SUCH A DETOUR WOULD KEEP ME FROM REPLENISHING GOODS AT SMALL VILLAGES FOR MY PROPER TRADE ROUTE.
I WANT TO GO WITH HER, BUT THE CIRCUMSTANCES WON'T ALLOW THAT.
AND THE LOGICAL COURSE OF ACTION IS TO DO AS SHE SAYS.
IT'S BEST FOR HER, AND IT'S BEST FOR ME.
AND IT'S BEST FOR COL.

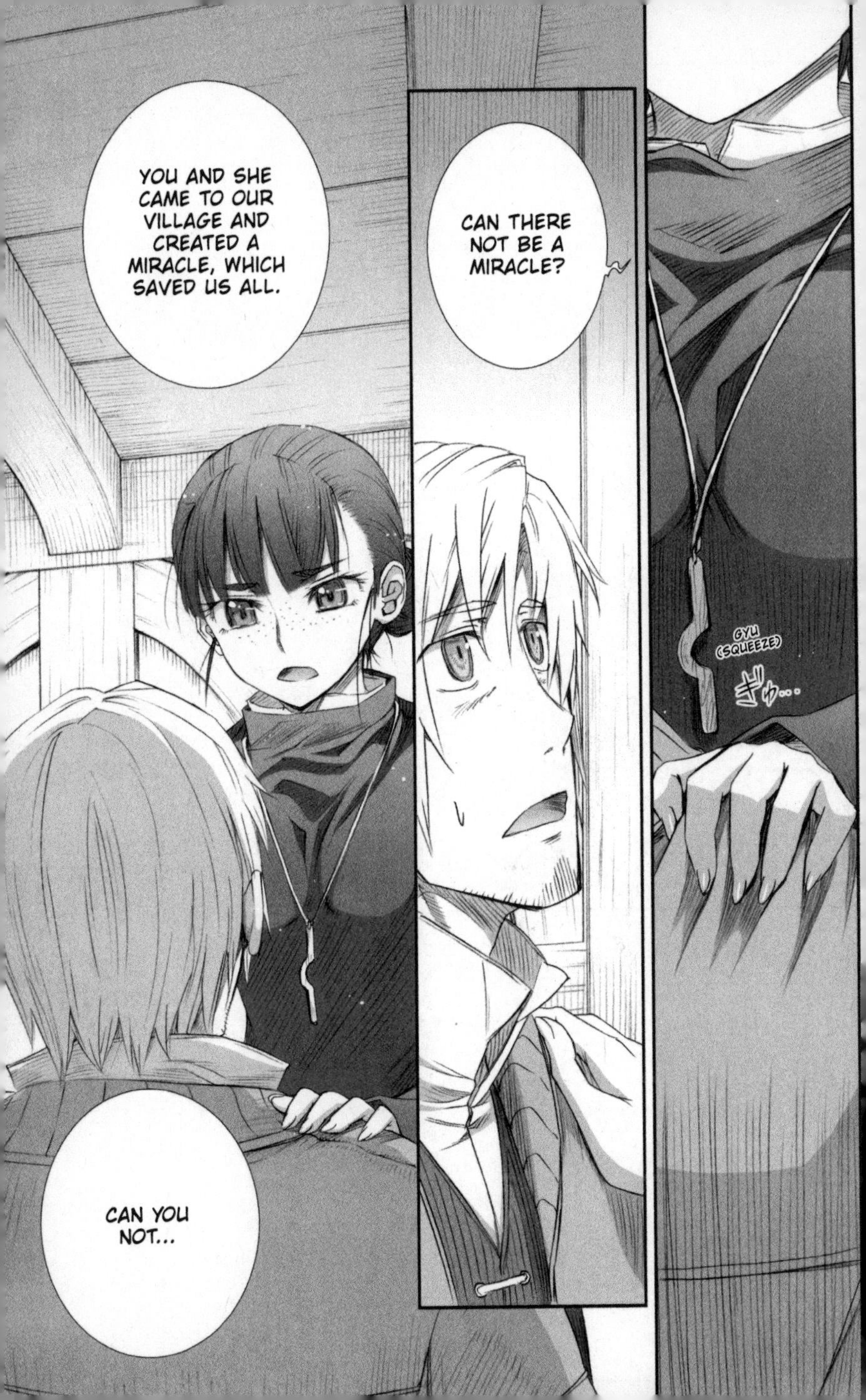
GYU (SQUEEZE)
ぎゅ…
CAN THERE NOT BE A MIRACLE?
YOU AND SHE CAME TO OUR VILLAGE AND CREATED A MIRACLE, WHICH SAVED US ALL.
CAN YOU NOT...

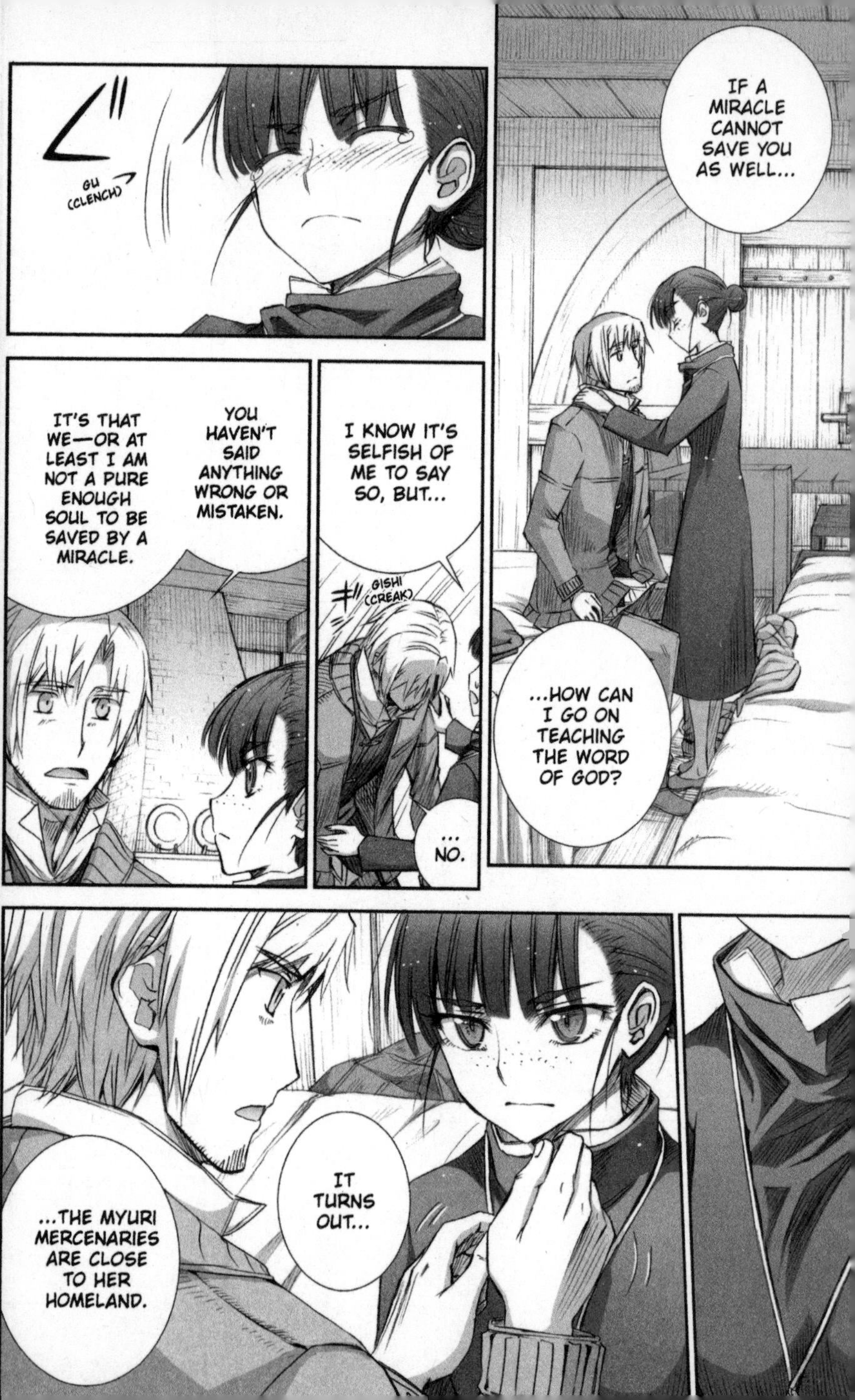
IF A MIRACLE CANNOT SAVE YOU AS WELL...
...HOW CAN I GO ON TEACHING THE WORD OF GOD?
GU (CLENCH)
I KNOW IT'S SELFISH OF ME TO SAY SO, BUT...
GISHI (CREAK)
... NO.
YOU HAVEN'T SAID ANYTHING WRONG OR MISTAKEN.
IT'S THAT WE—OR AT LEAST I AM NOT A PURE ENOUGH SOUL TO BE SAVED BY A MIRACLE.
IT TURNS OUT...
...THE MYURI MERCENARIES ARE CLOSE TO HER HOMELAND.

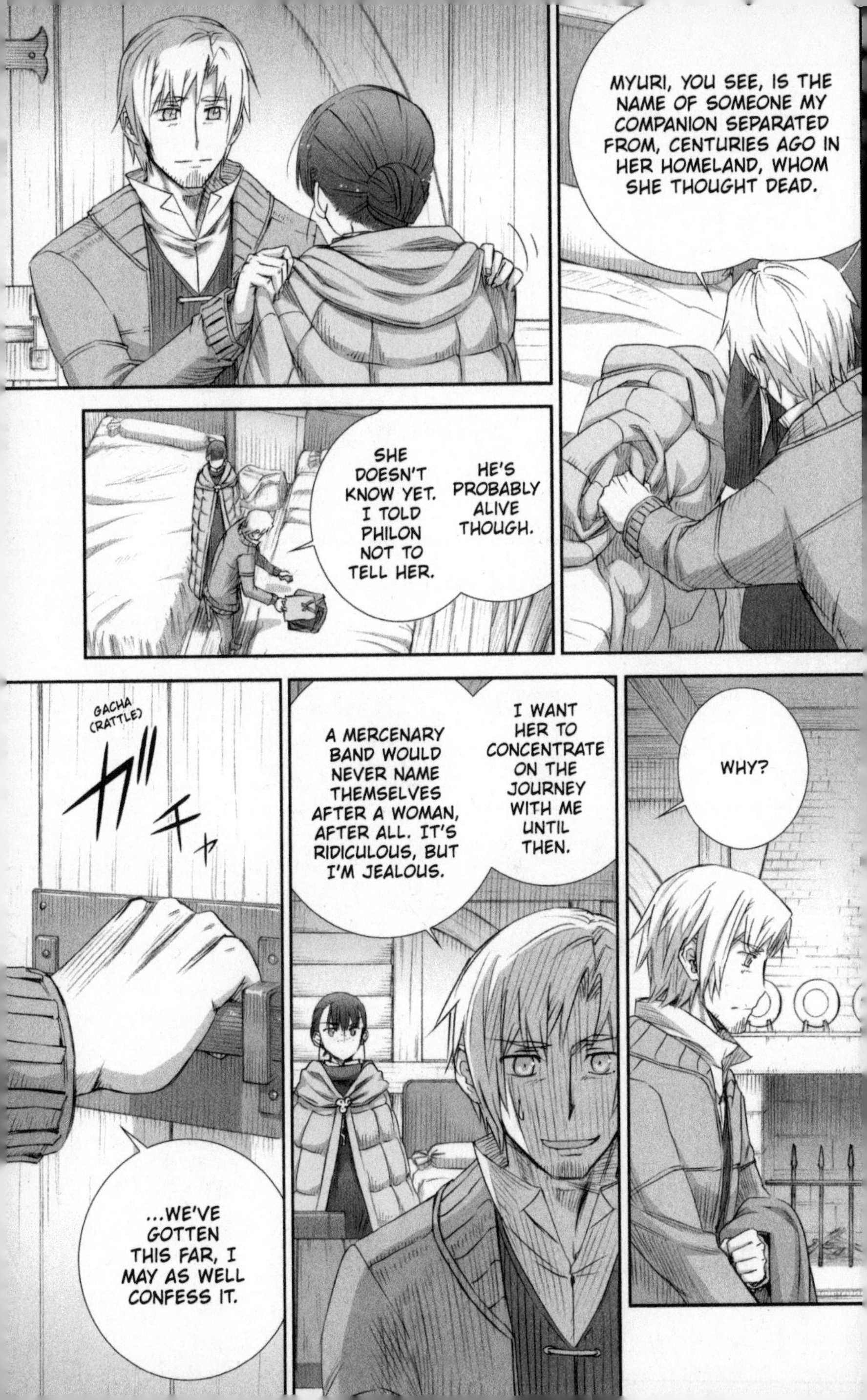

MYURI, YOU SEE, IS THE NAME OF SOMEONE MY COMPANION SEPARATED FROM, CENTURIES AGO IN HER HOMELAND, WHOM SHE THOUGHT DEAD.
HE'S PROBABLY ALIVE THOUGH.
SHE DOESN'T KNOW YET. I TOLD PHILON NOT TO TELL HER.
WHY?
I WANT HER TO CONCENTRATE ON THE JOURNEY WITH ME UNTIL THEN.
A MERCENARY BAND WOULD NEVER NAME THEMSELVES AFTER A WOMAN, AFTER ALL. IT'S RIDICULOUS, BUT I'M JEALOUS.
GACHA (RATTLE)
ガチャ
...WE'VE GOTTEN THIS FAR, I MAY AS WELL CONFESS IT.

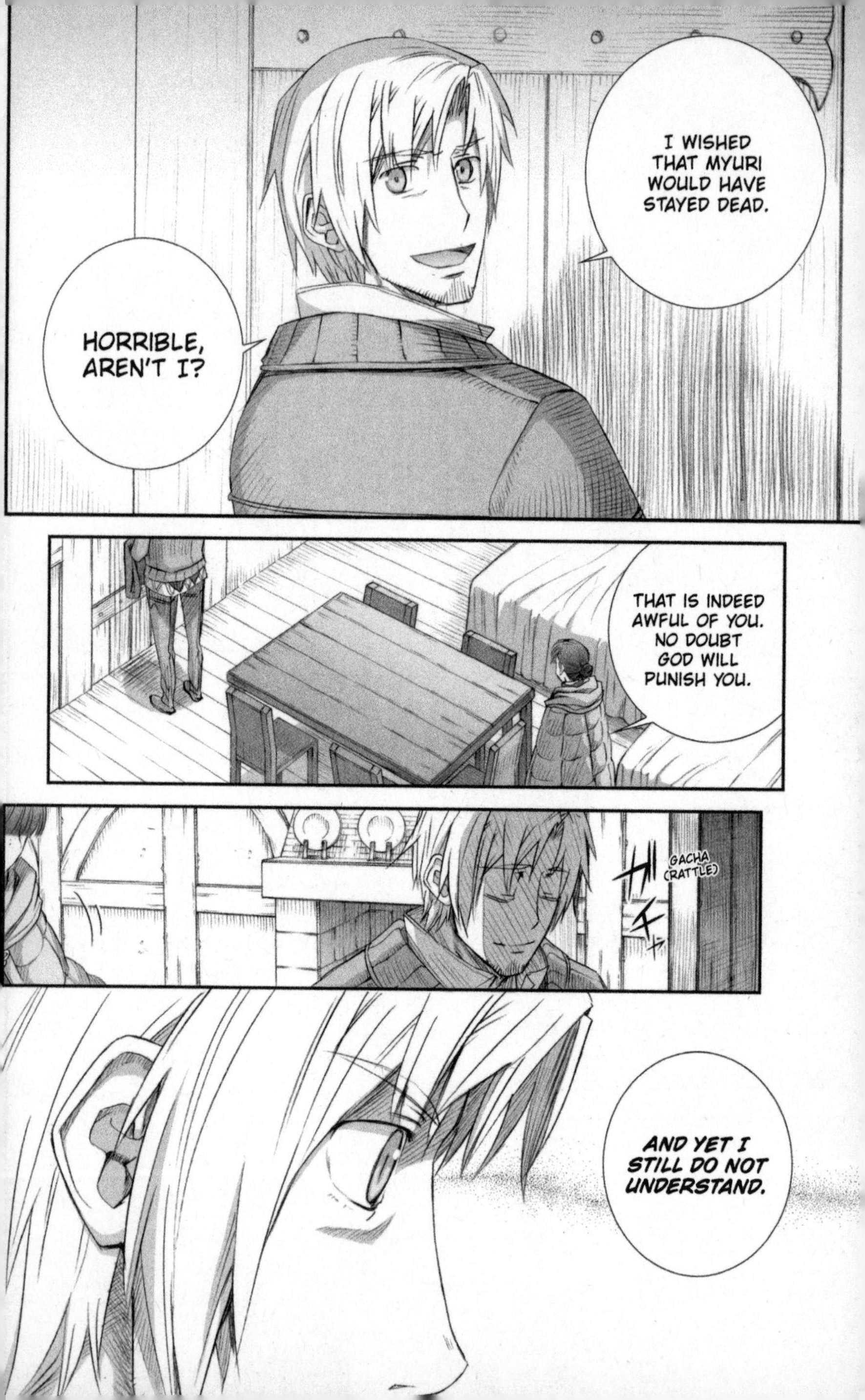
I WISHED THAT MYURI WOULD HAVE STAYED DEAD.
HORRIBLE, AREN'T I?
THAT IS INDEED AWFUL OF YOU. NO DOUBT GOD WILL PUNISH YOU.
GACHA (RATTLE)
AND YET I STILL DO NOT UNDERSTAND.

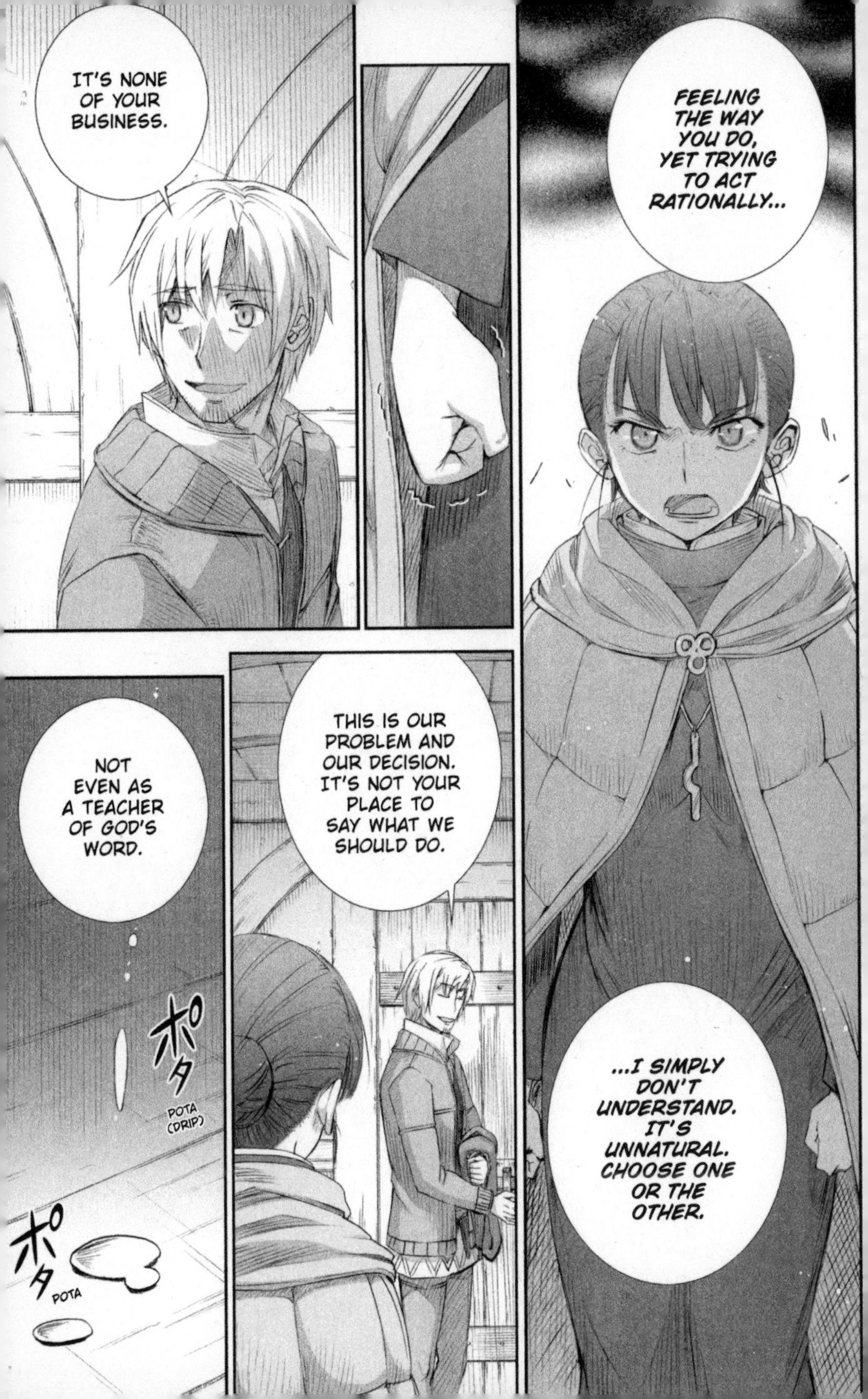
FEELING THE WAY YOU DO, YET TRYING TO ACT RATIONALLY...
...I SIMPLY DON'T UNDERSTAND. IT'S UNNATURAL. CHOOSE ONE OR THE OTHER.
IT'S NONE OF YOUR BUSINESS.
THIS IS OUR PROBLEM AND OUR DECISION. IT'S NOT YOUR PLACE TO SAY WHAT WE SHOULD DO.
NOT EVEN AS A TEACHER OF GOD'S WORD.
ポタ
POTA (DRIP)
ポタ
POTA

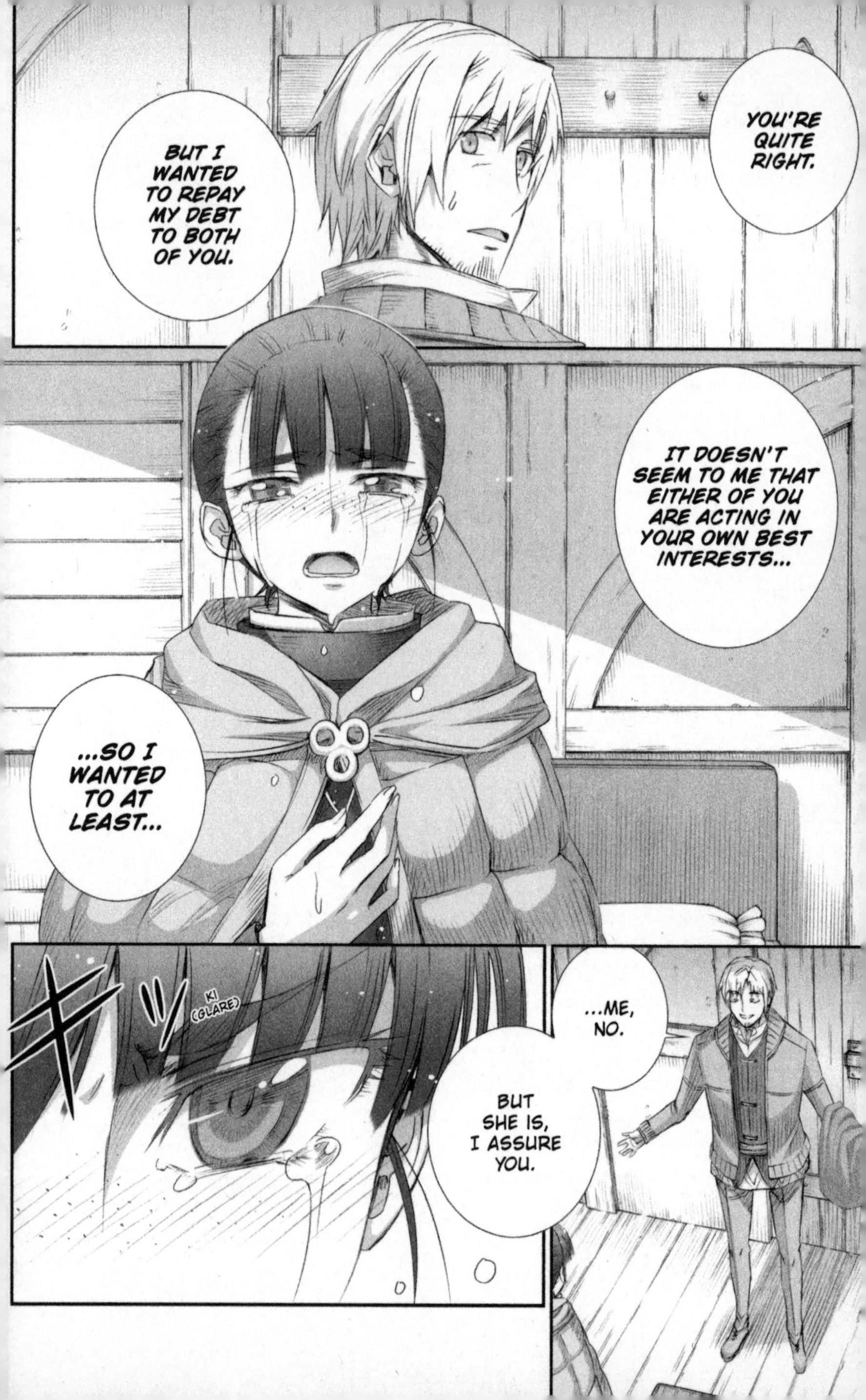
YOU'RE QUITE RIGHT.
BUT I WANTED TO REPAY MY DEBT TO BOTH OF YOU.
IT DOESN'T SEEM TO ME THAT EITHER OF YOU ARE ACTING IN YOUR OWN BEST INTERESTS...
...SO I WANTED TO AT LEAST...
...ME, NO.
BUT SHE IS, I ASSURE YOU.
KI (GLARE)

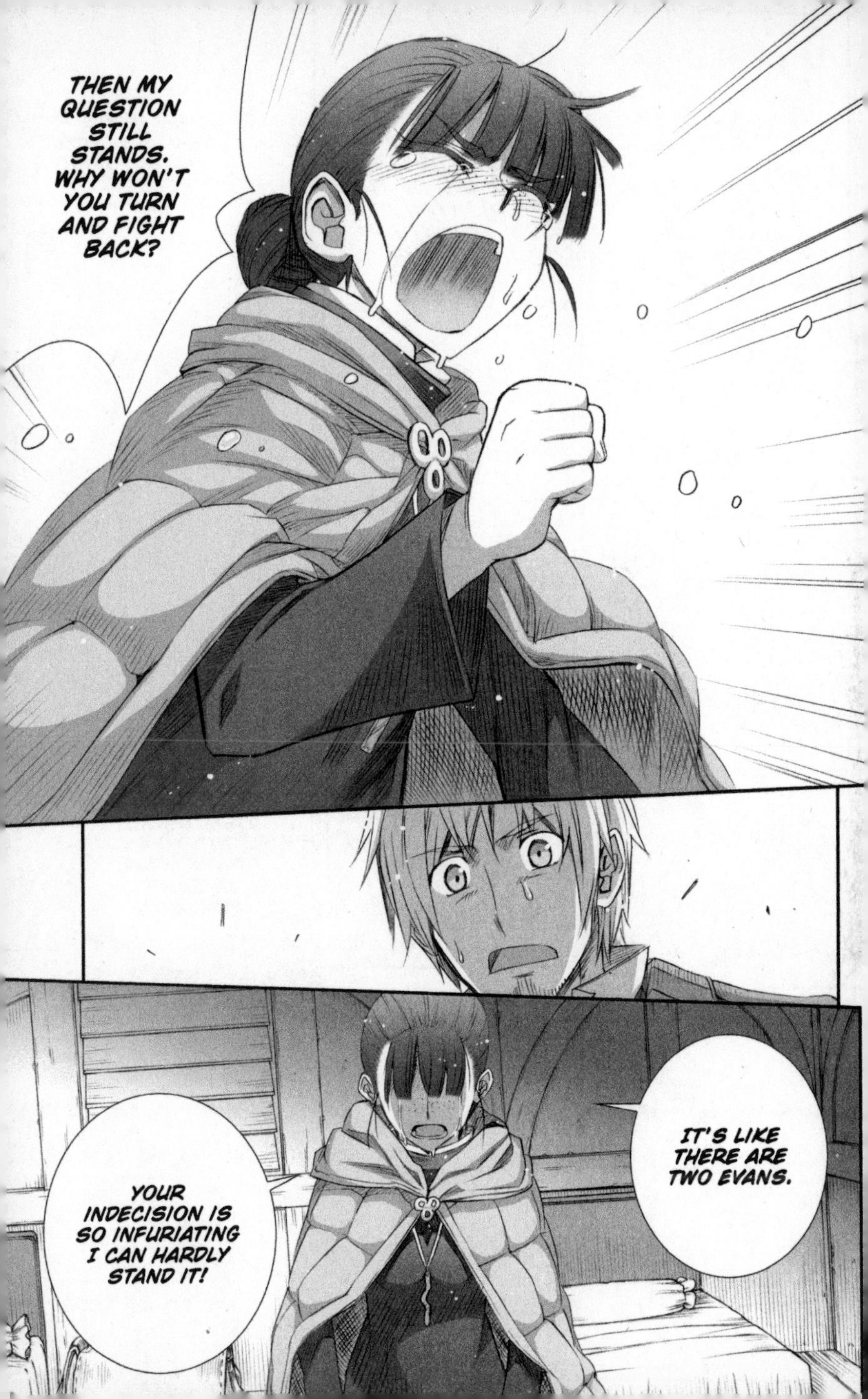
THEN MY QUESTION STILL STANDS. WHY WON'T YOU TURN AND FIGHT BACK?
IT'S LIKE THERE ARE TWO EVANS.
YOUR INDECISION IS SO INFURIATING I CAN HARDLY STAND IT!

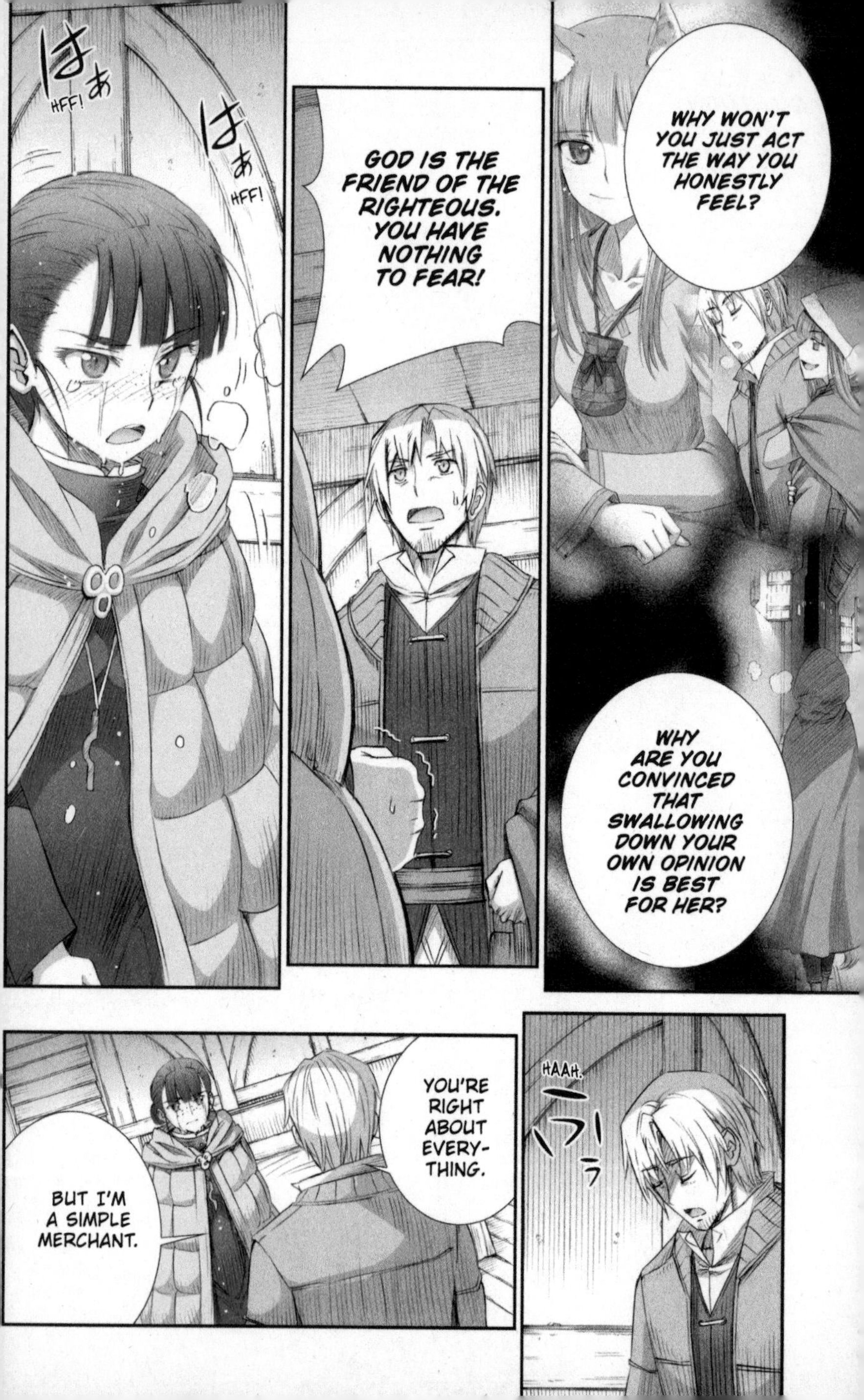
WHY WON'T YOU JUST ACT THE WAY YOU HONESTLY FEEL?
WHY ARE YOU CONVINCED THAT SWALLOWING DOWN YOUR OWN OPINION IS BEST FOR HER?
GOD IS THE FRIEND OF THE RIGHTEOUS. YOU HAVE NOTHING TO FEAR!
はぁ
HFF!
はぁ
HFF!
HAAH.
YOU'RE RIGHT ABOUT EVERY-THING.
BUT I'M A SIMPLE MERCHANT.

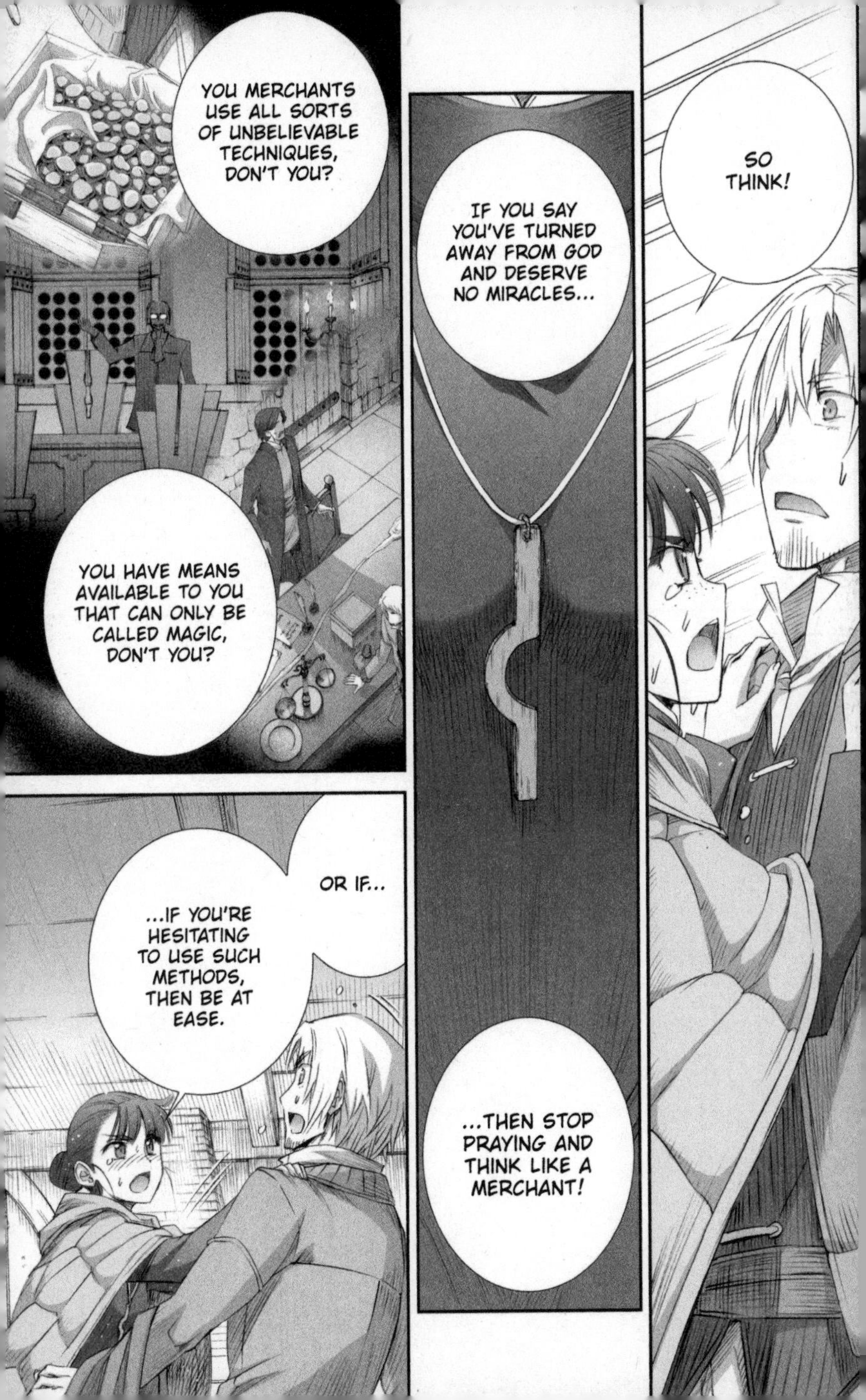
SO THINK!
IF YOU SAY YOU'VE TURNED AWAY FROM GOD AND DESERVE NO MIRACLES...
...THEN STOP PRAYING AND THINK LIKE A MERCHANT!
YOU MERCHANTS USE ALL SORTS OF UNBELIEVABLE TECHNIQUES, DON'T YOU?
YOU HAVE MEANS AVAILABLE TO YOU THAT CAN ONLY BE CALLED MAGIC, DON'T YOU?
OR IF...
...IF YOU'RE HESITATING TO USE SUCH METHODS, THEN BE AT EASE.

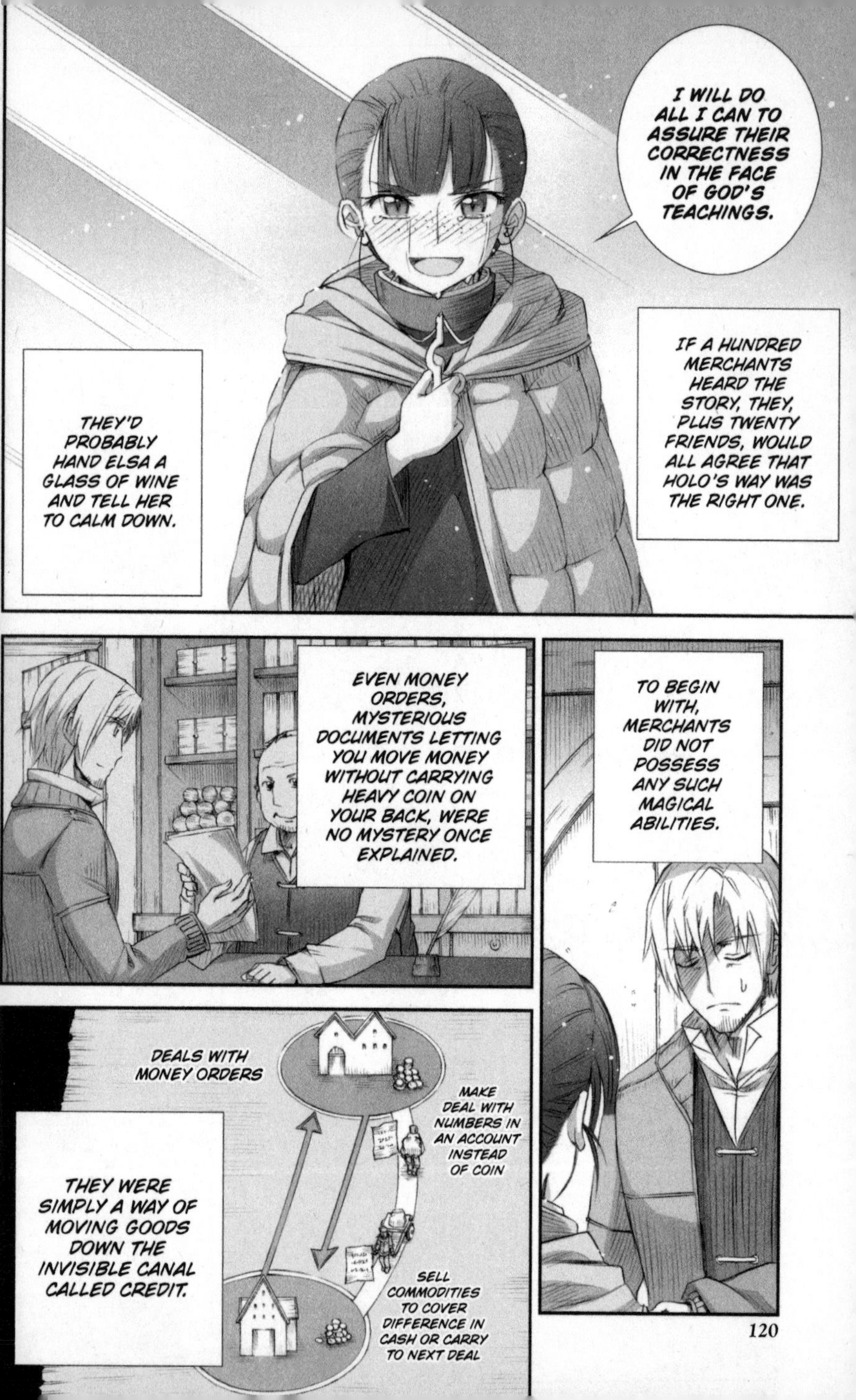
I WILL DO ALL I CAN TO ASSURE THEIR CORRECTNESS IN THE FACE OF GOD'S TEACHINGS.
IF A HUNDRED MERCHANTS HEARD THE STORY, THEY, PLUS TWENTY FRIENDS, WOULD ALL AGREE THAT HOLO'S WAY WAS THE RIGHT ONE.
THEY'D PROBABLY HAND ELSA A GLASS OF WINE AND TELL HER TO CALM DOWN.
TO BEGIN WITH, MERCHANTS DID NOT POSSESS ANY SUCH MAGICAL ABILITIES.
EVEN MONEY ORDERS, MYSTERIOUS DOCUMENTS LETTING YOU MOVE MONEY WITHOUT CARRYING HEAVY COIN ON YOUR BACK, WERE NO MYSTERY ONCE EXPLAINED.
DEALS WITH MONEY ORDERS
MAKE DEAL WITH NUMBERS IN AN ACCOUNT INSTEAD OF COIN
THEY WERE SIMPLY A WAY OF MOVING GOODS DOWN THE INVISIBLE CANAL CALLED CREDIT.
SELL COMMODITIES TO COVER DIFFERENCE IN CASH OR CARRY TO NEXT DEAL

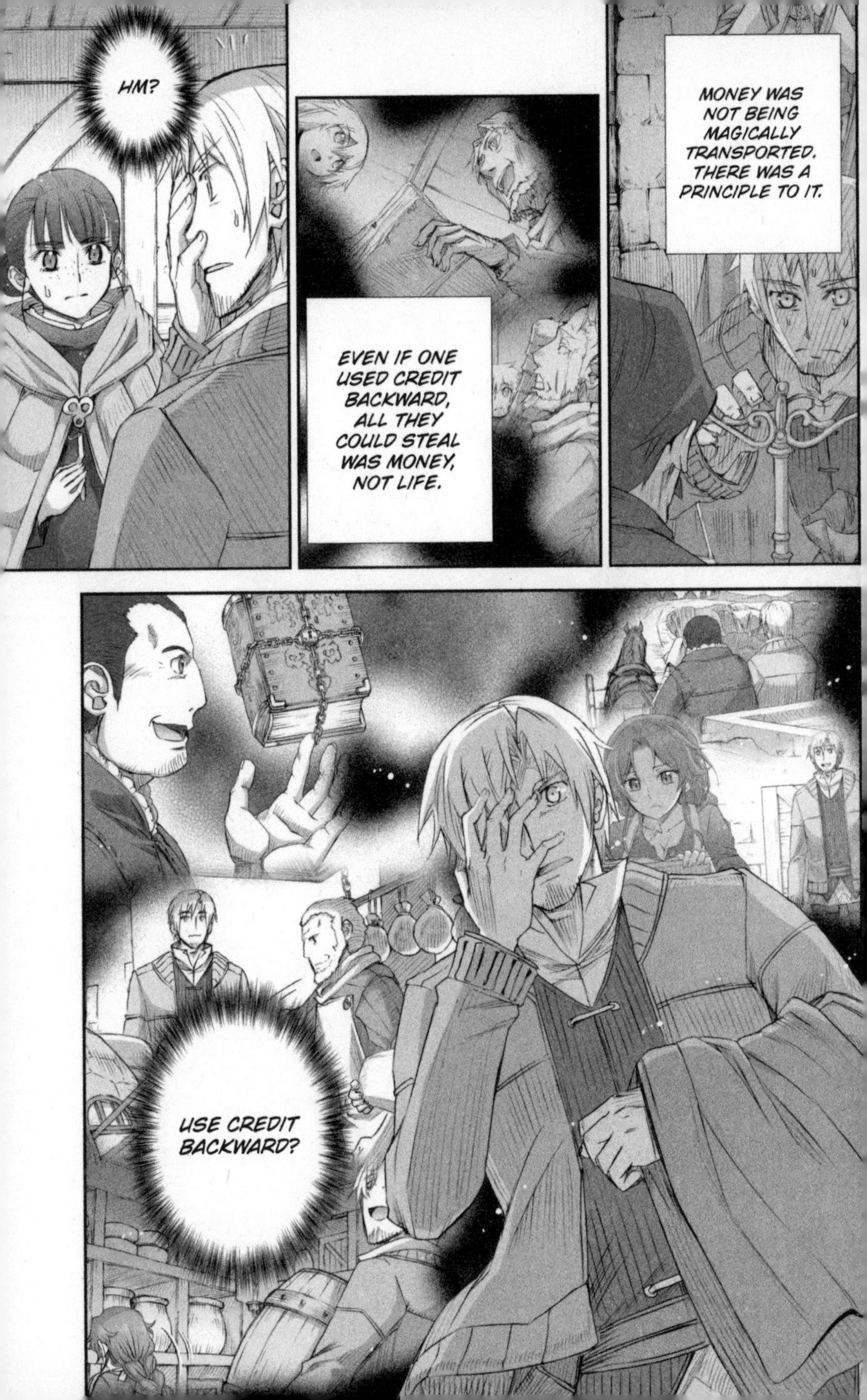
MONEY WAS NOT BEING MAGICALLY TRANSPORTED. THERE WAS A PRINCIPLE TO IT.
EVEN IF ONE USED CREDIT BACKWARD, ALL THEY COULD STEAL WAS MONEY, NOT LIFE.
HM?
USE CREDIT BACKWARD?

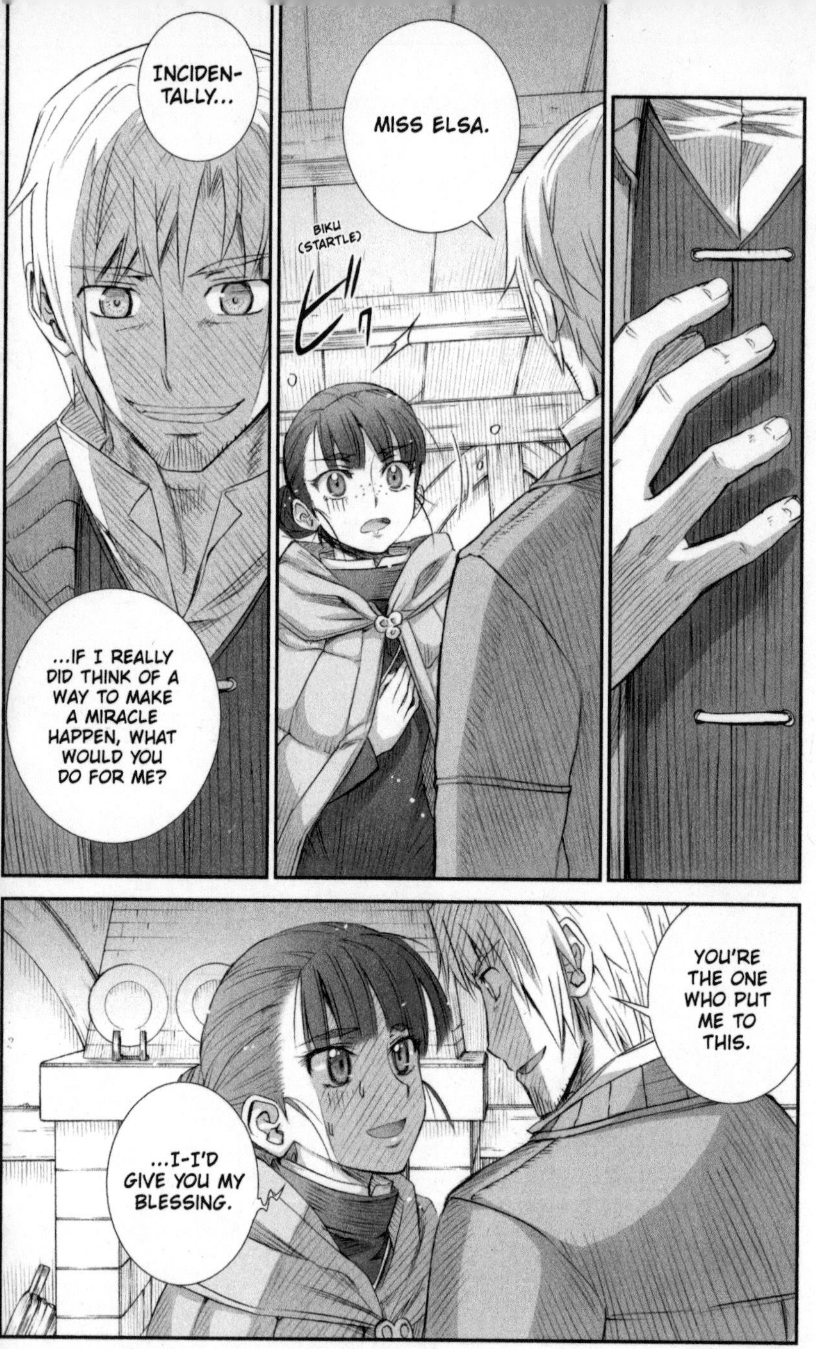
MISS ELSA.
BIKU (STARTLE)
INCIDEN-TALLY...
...IF I REALLY DID THINK OF A WAY TO MAKE A MIRACLE HAPPEN, WHAT WOULD YOU DO FOR ME?
YOU'RE THE ONE WHO PUT ME TO THIS.
...I-I'D GIVE YOU MY BLESSING.

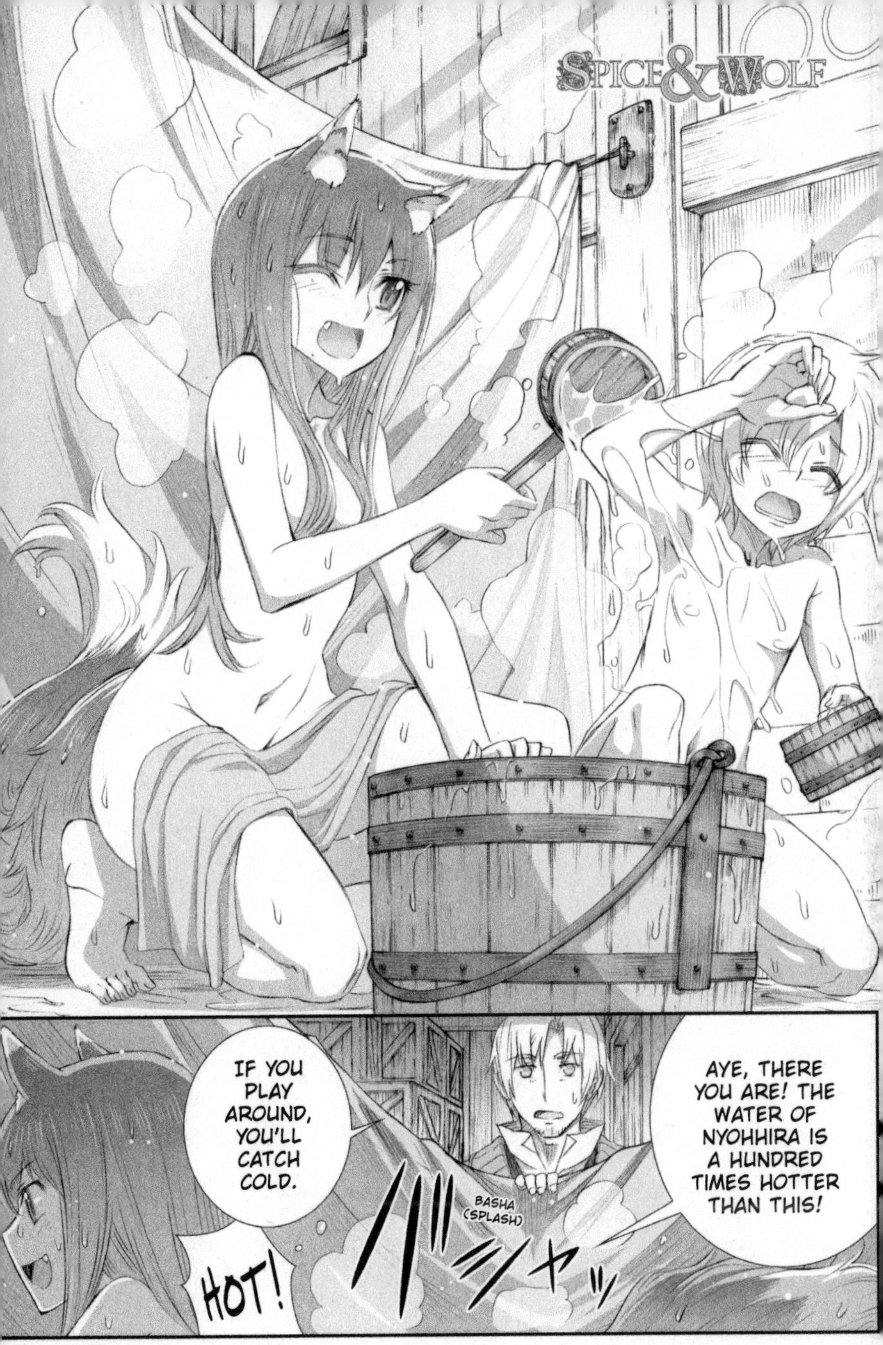
SPICE & WOLF
AYE, THERE YOU ARE! THE WATER OF NYOHHIRA IS A HUNDRED TIMES HOTTER THAN THIS!
BASHA (SPLASH)
IF YOU PLAY AROUND, YOU'LL CATCH COLD.
HOT!

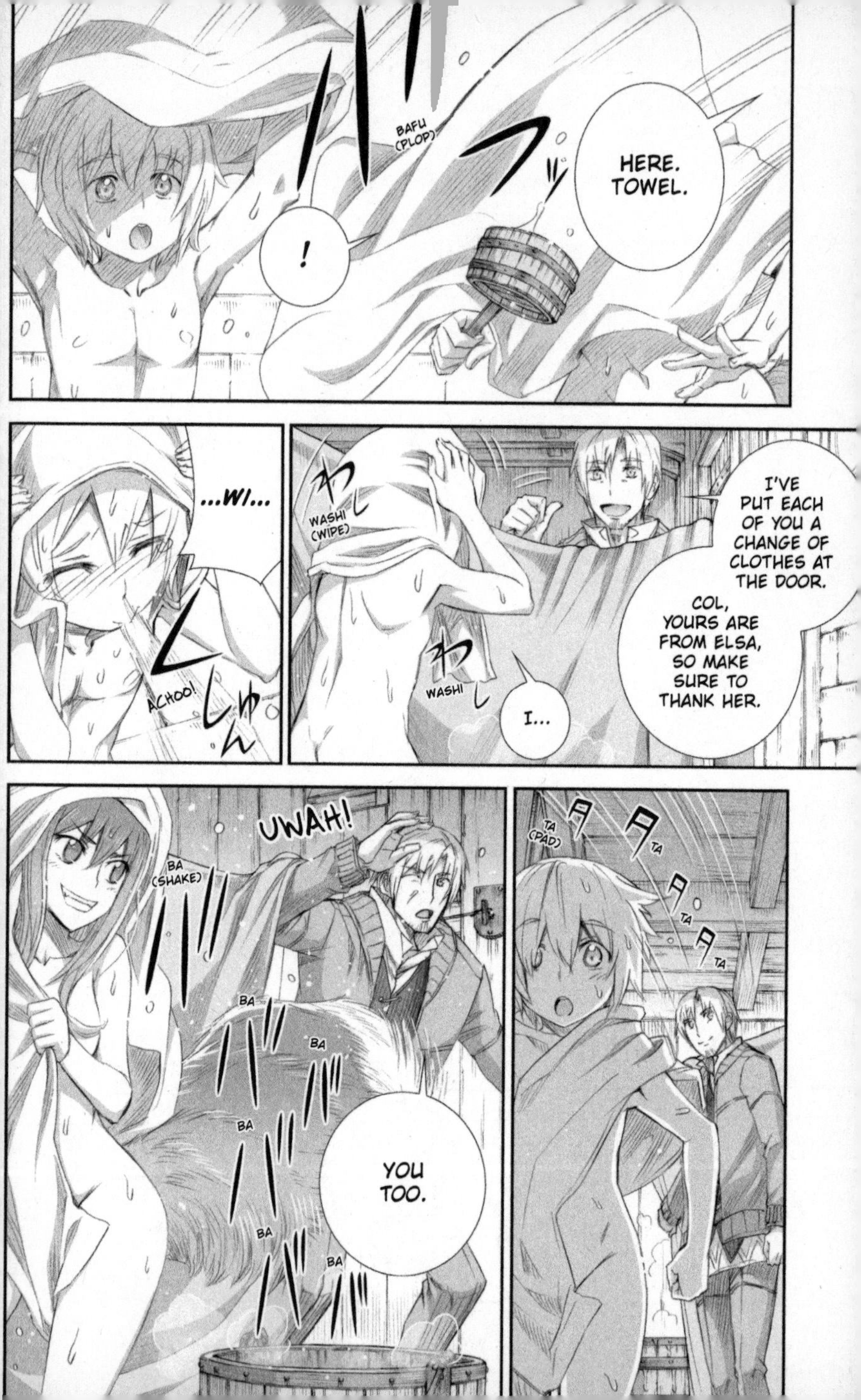
HERE. TOWEL.
BAFU (PLOP)
!
I'VE PUT EACH OF YOU A CHANGE OF CLOTHES AT THE DOOR.
COL, YOURS ARE FROM ELSA, SO MAKE SURE TO THANK HER.
WASHI (WIPE)
WASHI
I...
...WI...
ACHOO!
TA (PAD)
TA
TA
TA
TA
UWAH!
BA (SHAKE)
BA
BA
BA
BA
BA
YOU TOO.

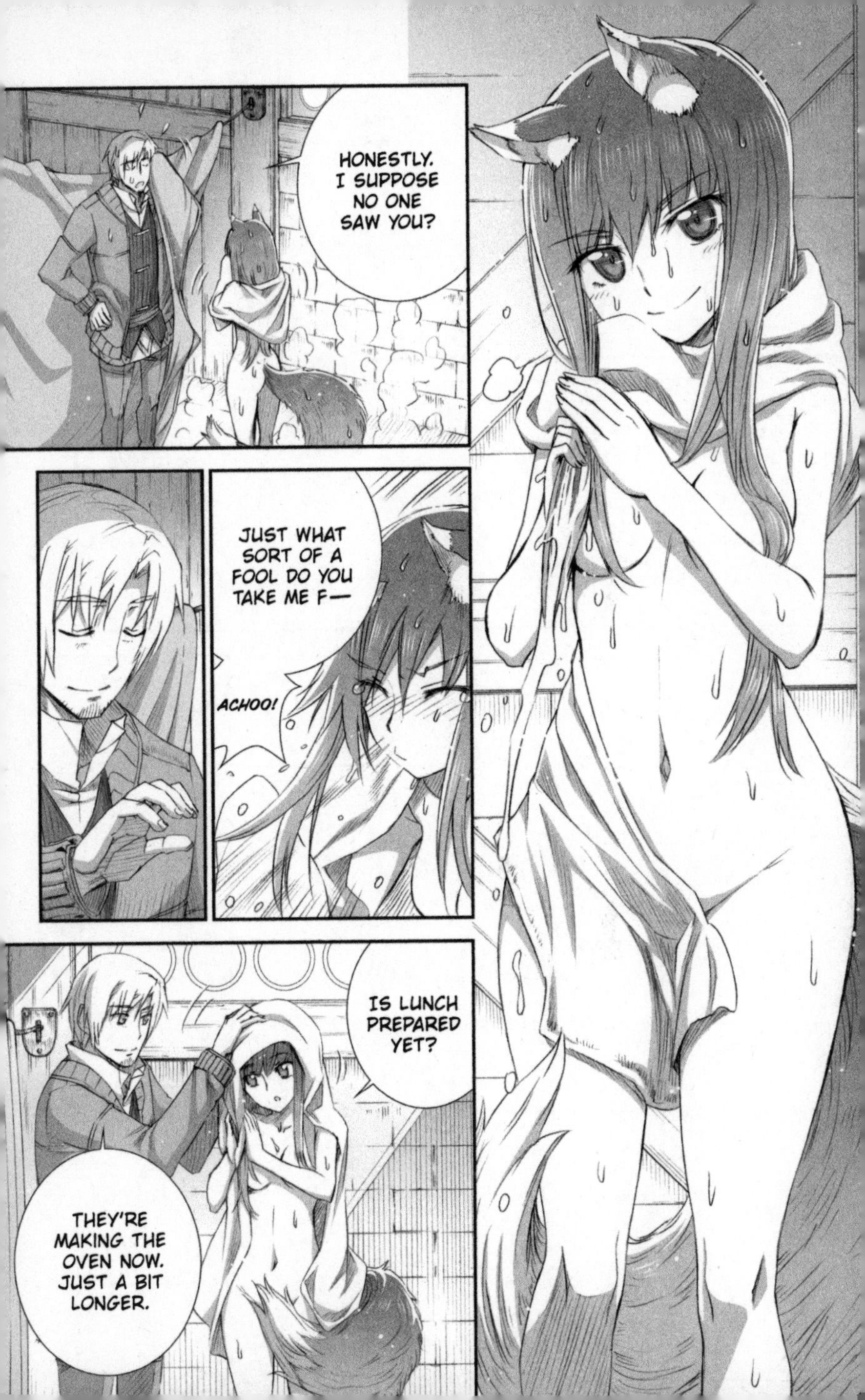
HONESTLY. I SUPPOSE NO ONE SAW YOU?
JUST WHAT SORT OF A FOOL DO YOU TAKE ME F—
ACHOO!
IS LUNCH PREPARED YET?
THEY'RE MAKING THE OVEN NOW. JUST A BIT LONGER.

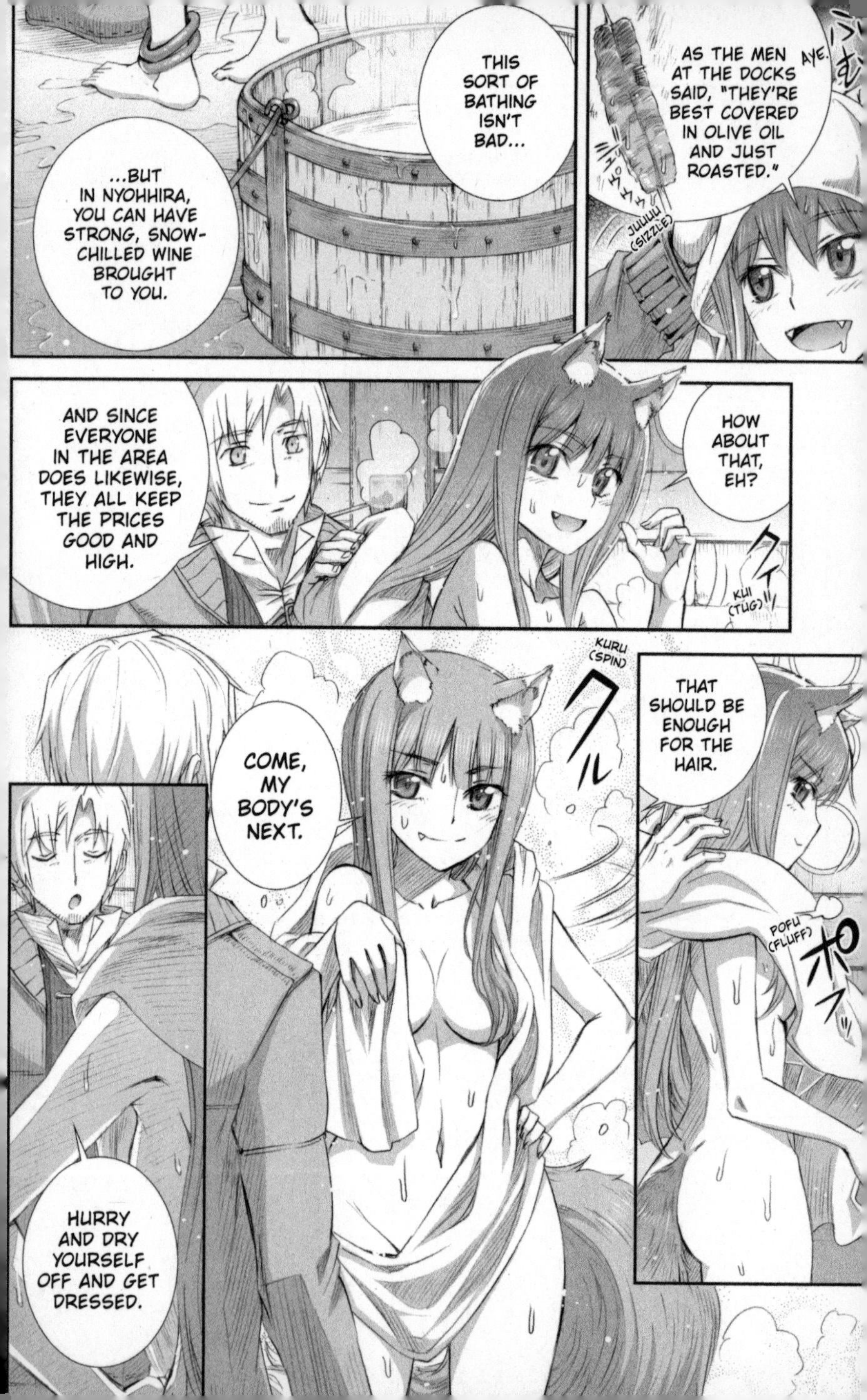
AYE.
AS THE MEN AT THE DOCKS SAID, "THEY'RE BEST COVERED IN OLIVE OIL AND JUST ROASTED."
JUUUU (SIZZLE)
THIS SORT OF BATHING ISN'T BAD...
...BUT IN NYOHHIRA, YOU CAN HAVE STRONG, SNOW-CHILLED WINE BROUGHT TO YOU.
AND SINCE EVERYONE IN THE AREA DOES LIKEWISE, THEY ALL KEEP THE PRICES GOOD AND HIGH.
HOW ABOUT THAT, EH?
KUI (TUG)
THAT SHOULD BE ENOUGH FOR THE HAIR.
POFU (FLUFF)
KURU (SPIN)
COME, MY BODY'S NEXT.
HURRY AND DRY YOURSELF OFF AND GET DRESSED.

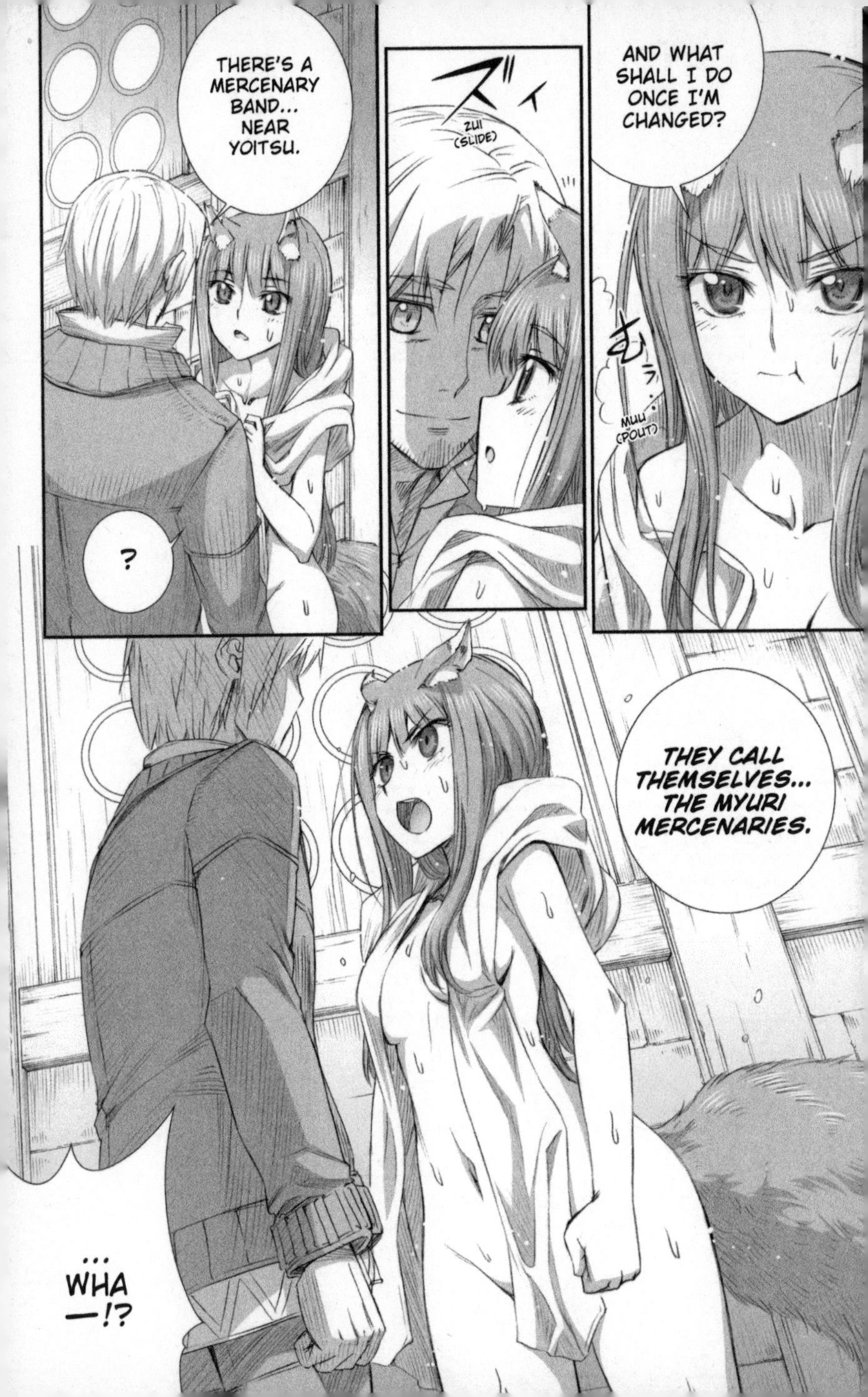
AND WHAT SHALL I DO ONCE I'M CHANGED?
MUU (POUT)
ZUI (SLIDE)
THERE'S A MERCENARY BAND... NEAR YOITSU.
?
THEY CALL THEMSELVES... THE MYURI MERCENARIES.
...WHA—!?

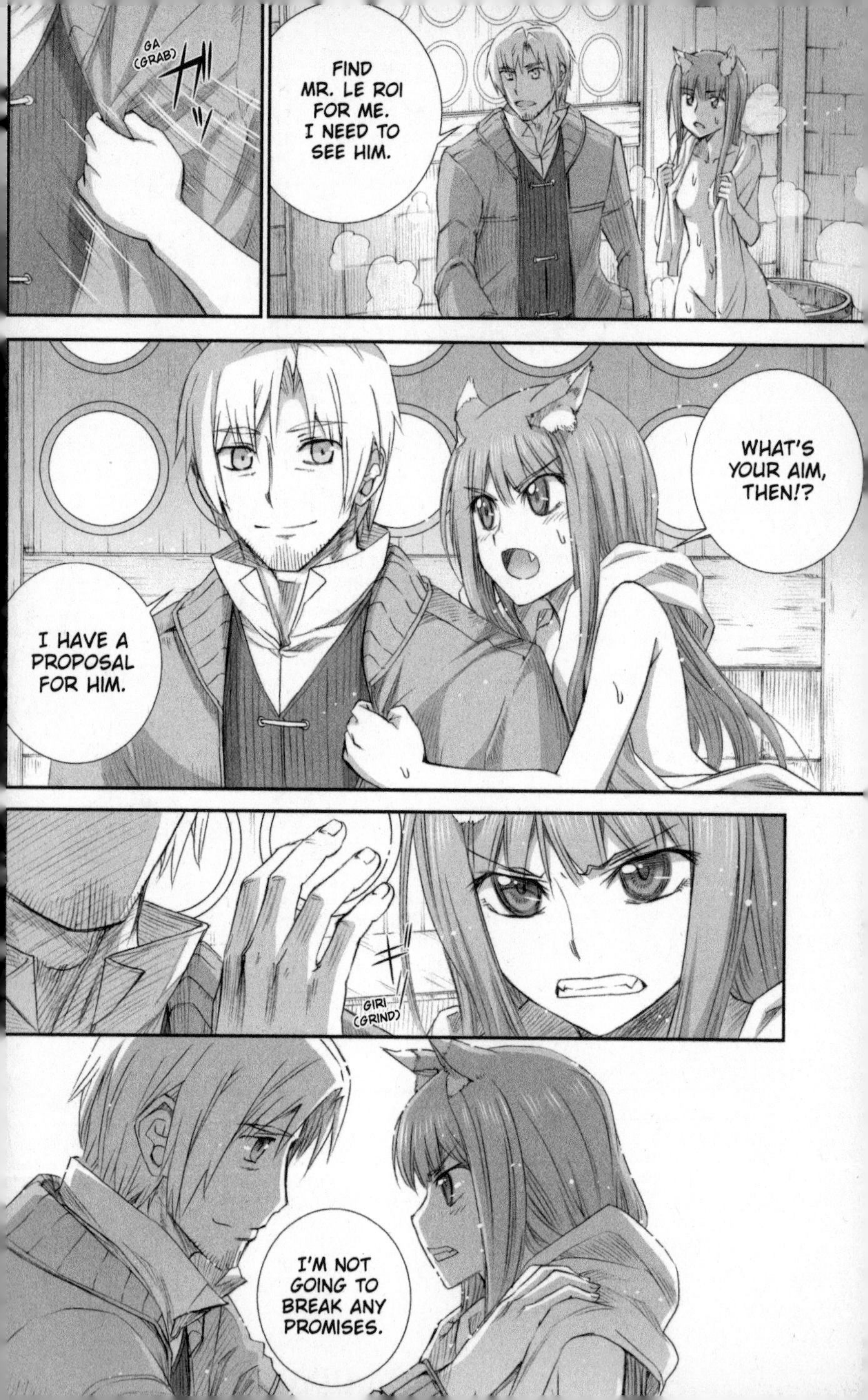
FIND MR. LE ROI FOR ME. I NEED TO SEE HIM.
GA (GRAB)
WHAT'S YOUR AIM, THEN!?
I HAVE A PROPOSAL FOR HIM.
GIRI (GRIND)
I'M NOT GOING TO BREAK ANY PROMISES.

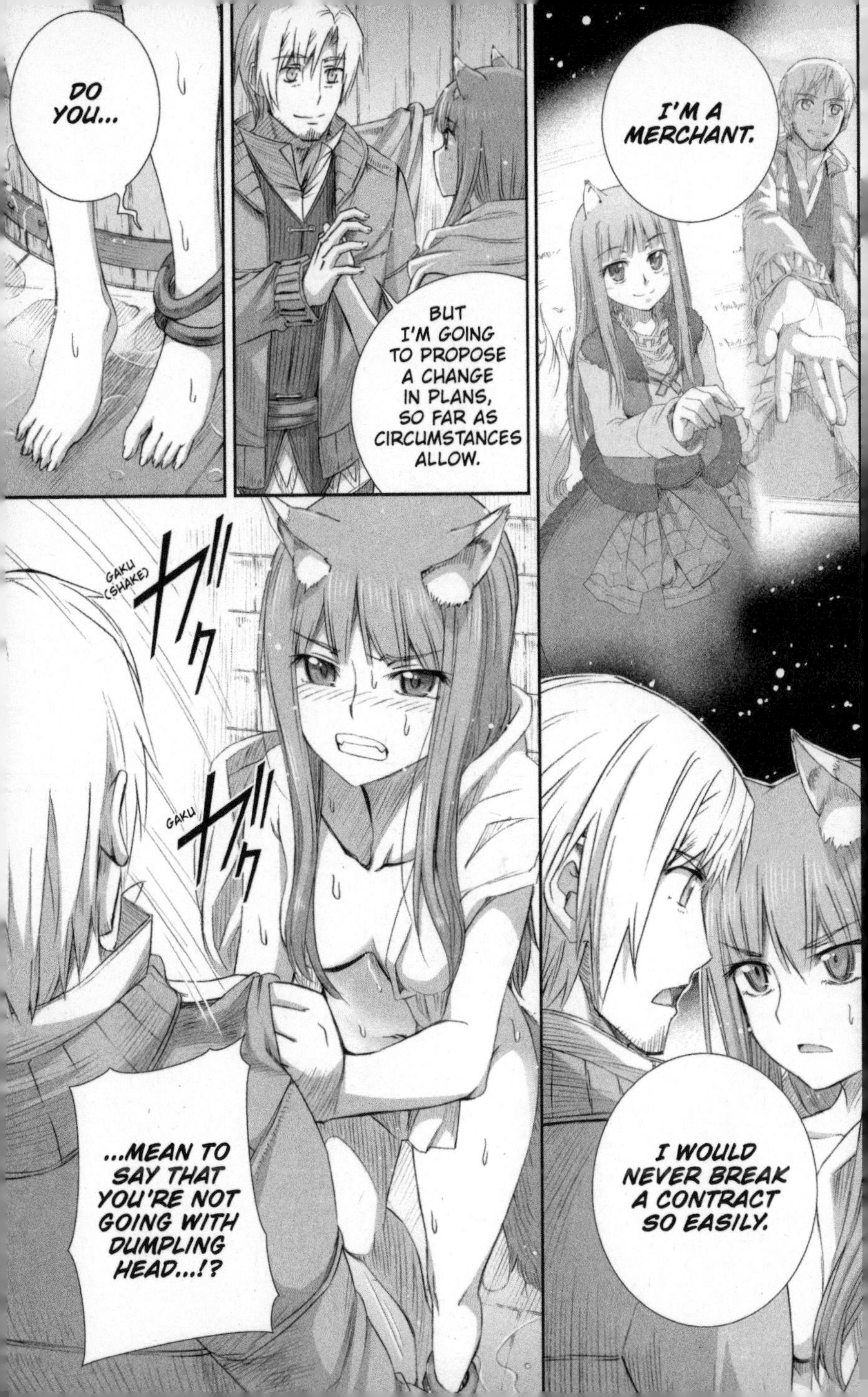
DO YOU...
GAKU (SHAKE)
GAKU
...MEAN TO SAY THAT YOU'RE NOT GOING WITH DUMPLING HEAD...!?
I'M A MERCHANT.
I WOULD NEVER BREAK A CONTRACT SO EASILY.
BUT I'M GOING TO PROPOSE A CHANGE IN PLANS, SO FAR AS CIRCUMSTANCES ALLOW.

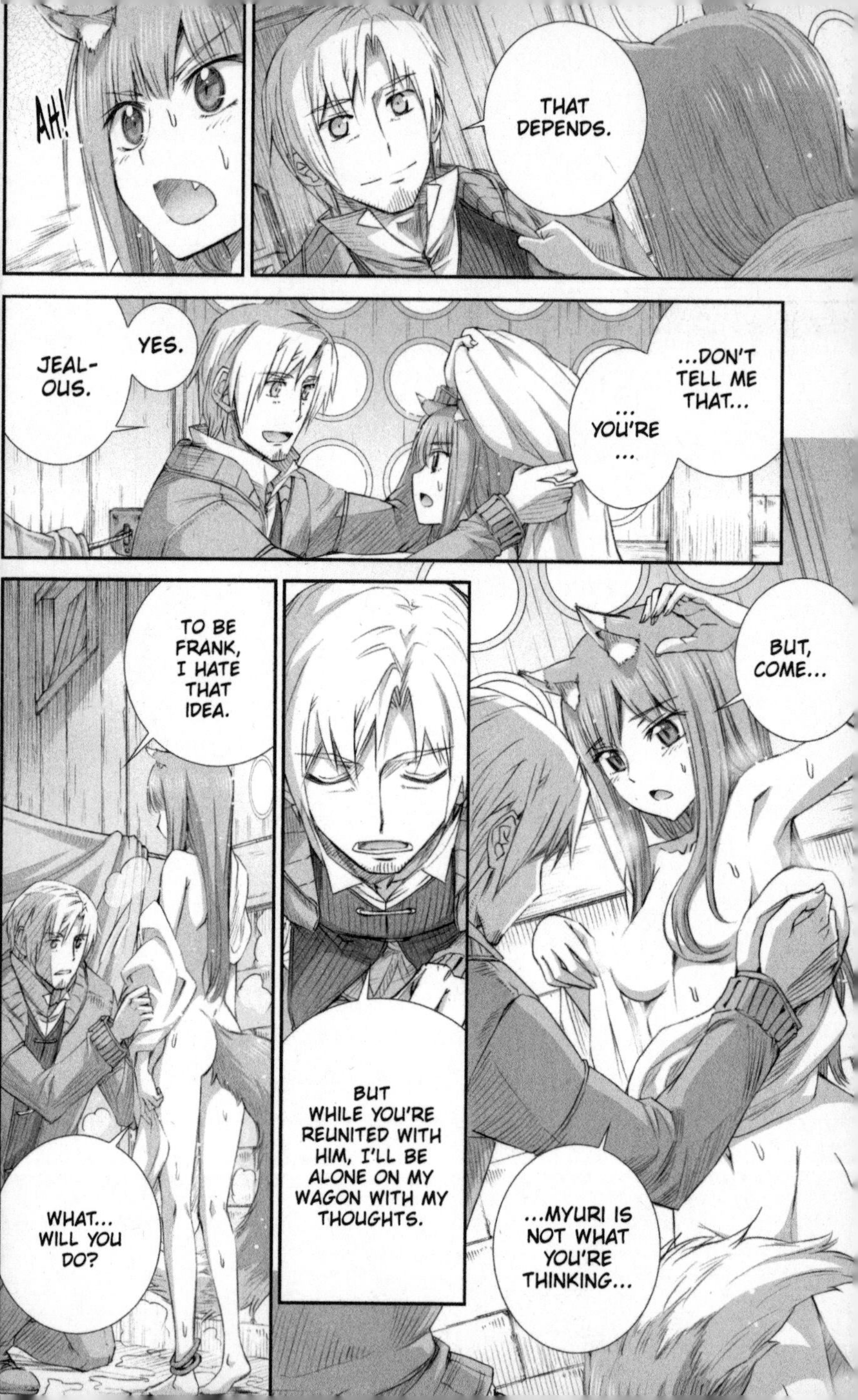
THAT DEPENDS.
AH!
...DON'T TELL ME THAT...
... YOU'RE ...
YES.
JEAL-OUS.
BUT, COME...
...MYURI IS NOT WHAT YOU'RE THINKING...
BUT WHILE YOU'RE REUNITED WITH HIM, I'LL BE ALONE ON MY WAGON WITH MY THOUGHTS.
TO BE FRANK, I HATE THAT IDEA.
WHAT... WILL YOU DO?

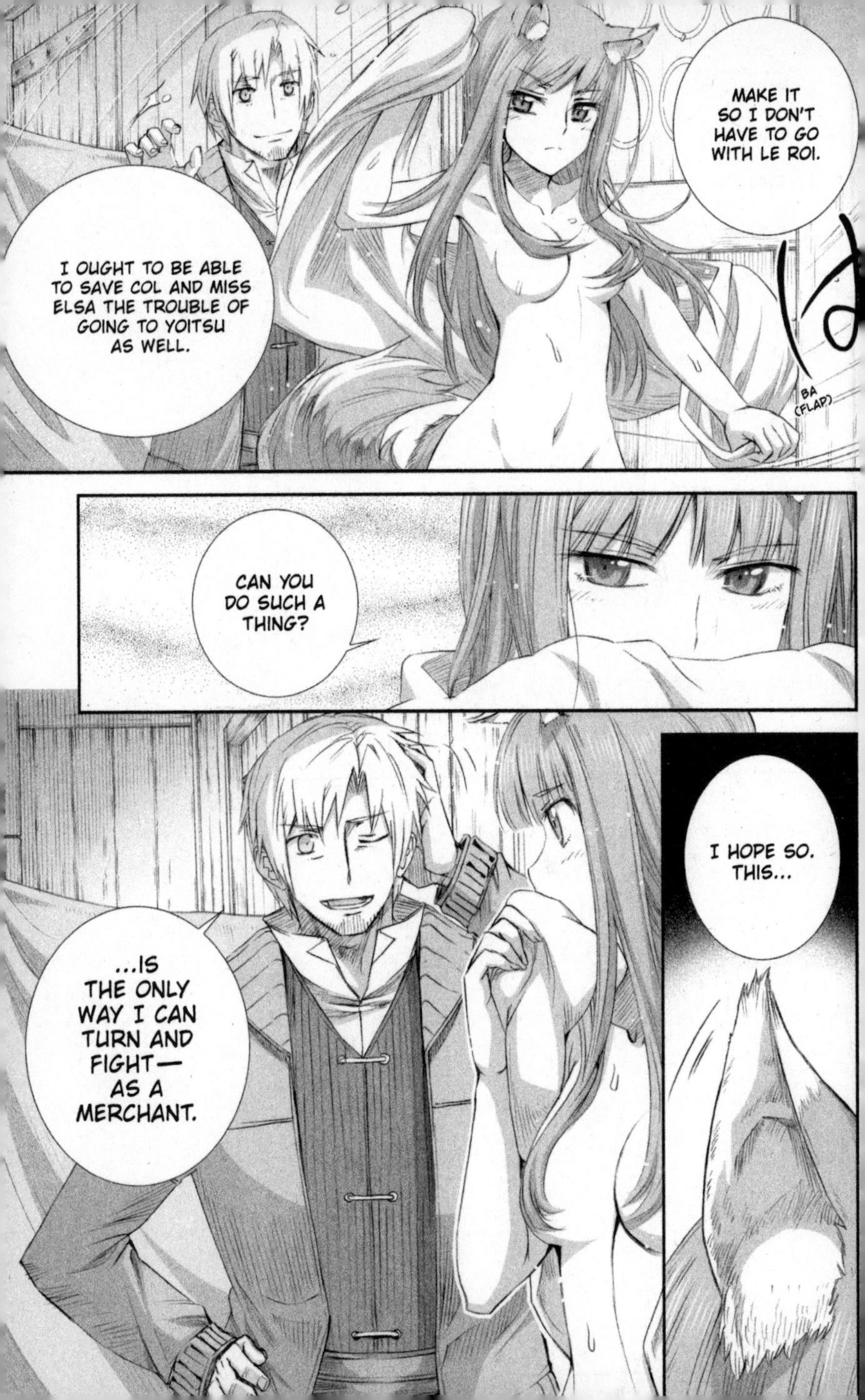
MAKE IT SO I DON'T HAVE TO GO WITH LE ROI.
BA (FLAP)
I OUGHT TO BE ABLE TO SAVE COL AND MISS ELSA THE TROUBLE OF GOING TO YOITSU AS WELL.
CAN YOU DO SUCH A THING?
I HOPE SO. THIS...
...IS THE ONLY WAY I CAN TURN AND FIGHT—AS A MERCHANT.

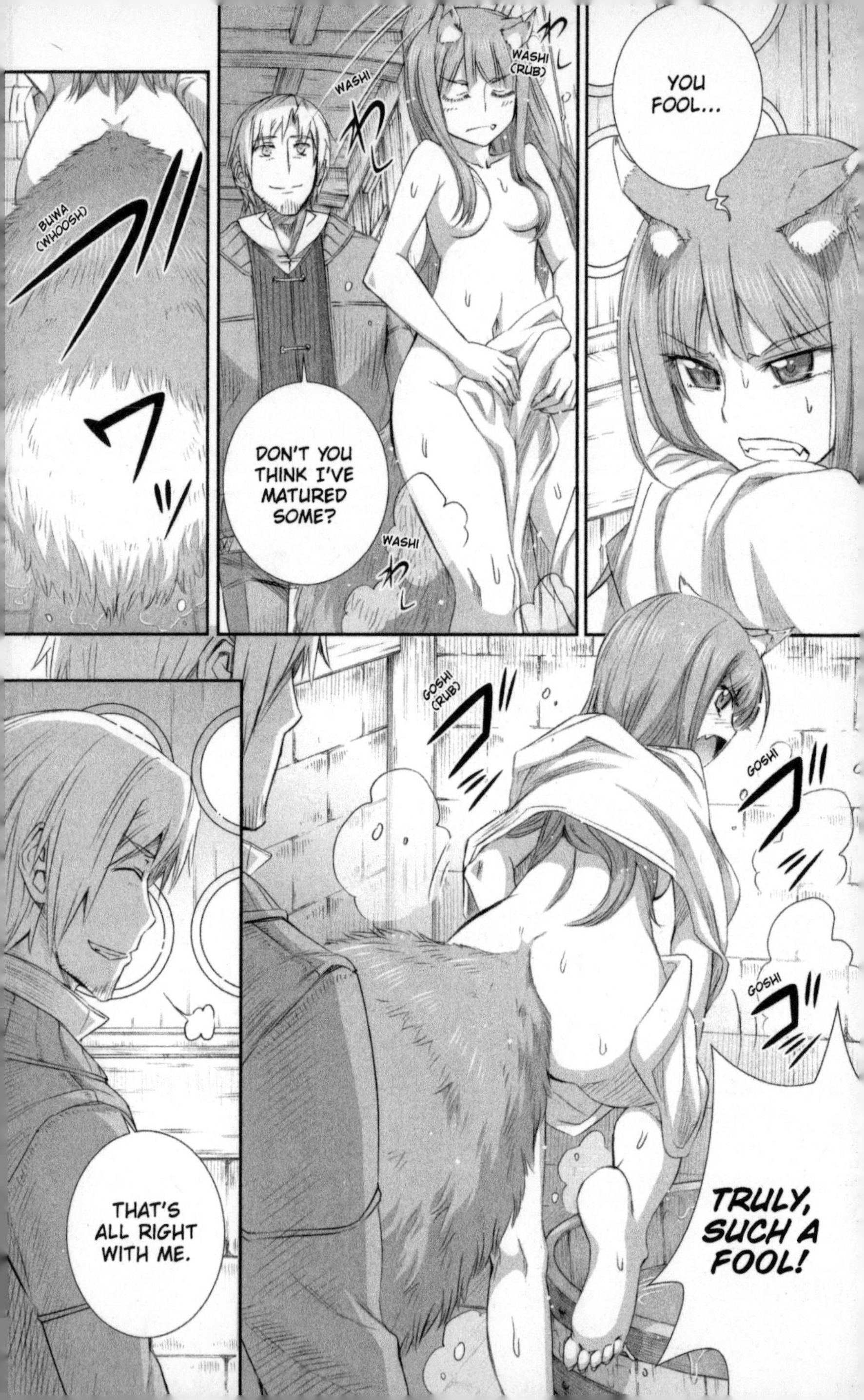
YOU FOOL...
WASHI (RUB)
WASHI
DON'T YOU THINK I'VE MATURED SOME?
WASHI
BUWA (WHOOSH)
GOSHI (RUB)
GOSHI
GOSHI
TRULY, SUCH A FOOL!
THAT'S ALL RIGHT WITH ME.

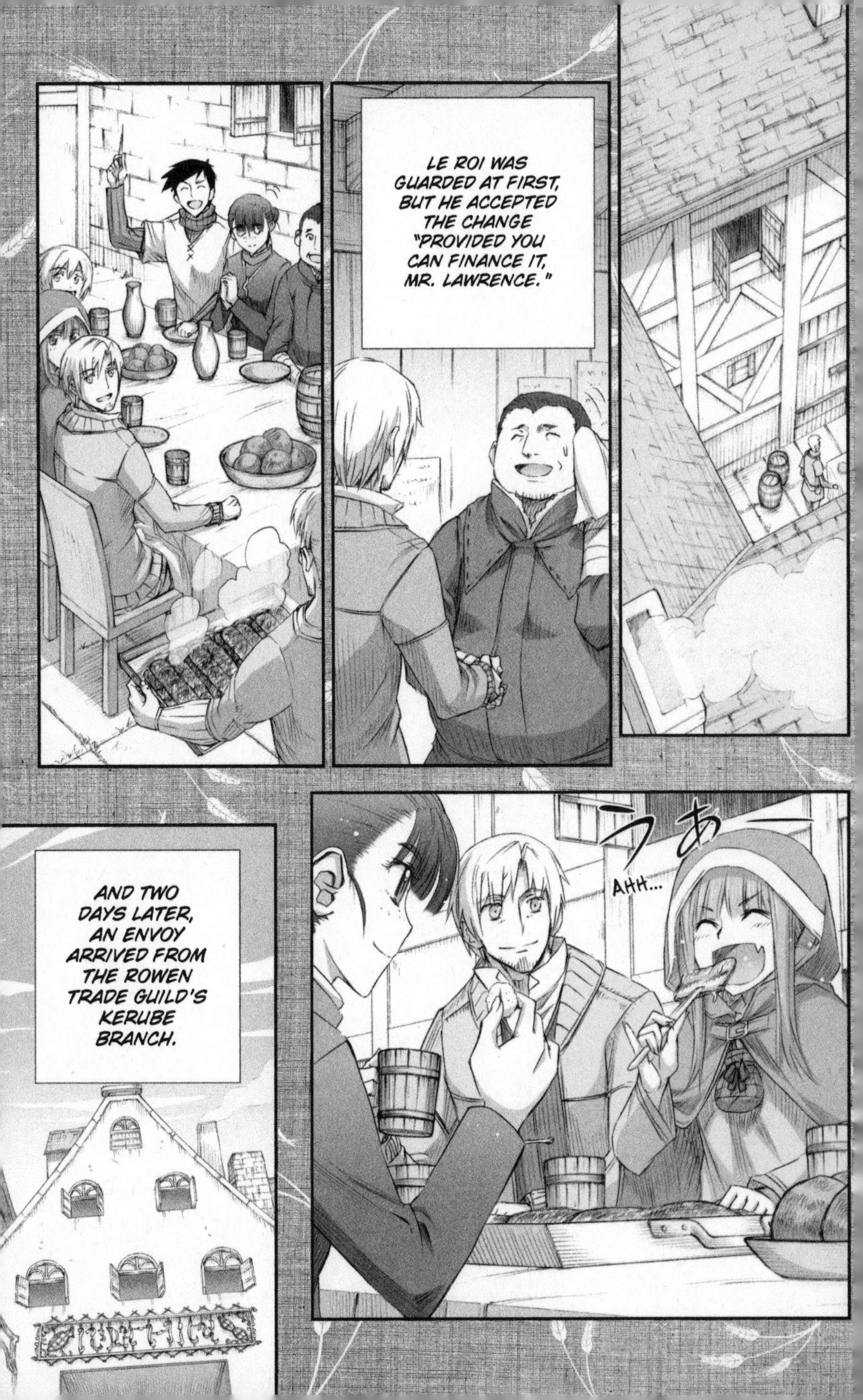
LE ROI WAS GUARDED AT FIRST, BUT HE ACCEPTED THE CHANGE "PROVIDED YOU CAN FINANCE IT, MR. LAWRENCE."
うあー
AHH...
AND TWO DAYS LATER, AN ENVOY ARRIVED FROM THE ROWEN TRADE GUILD'S KERUBE BRANCH.

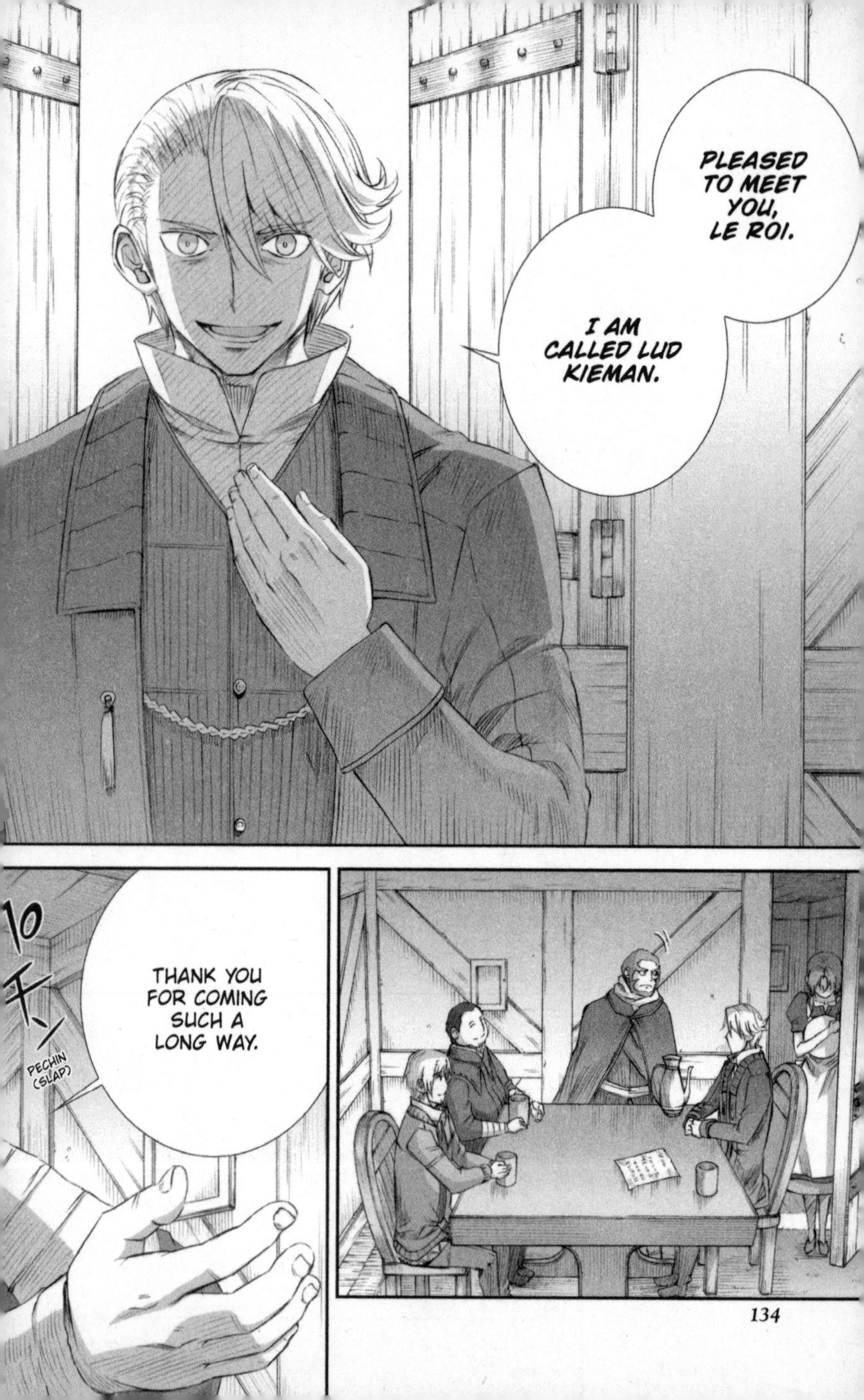
PLEASED TO MEET YOU, LE ROI.
I AM CALLED LUD KIEMAN.
THANK YOU FOR COMING SUCH A LONG WAY.
PECHIN (SLAP)

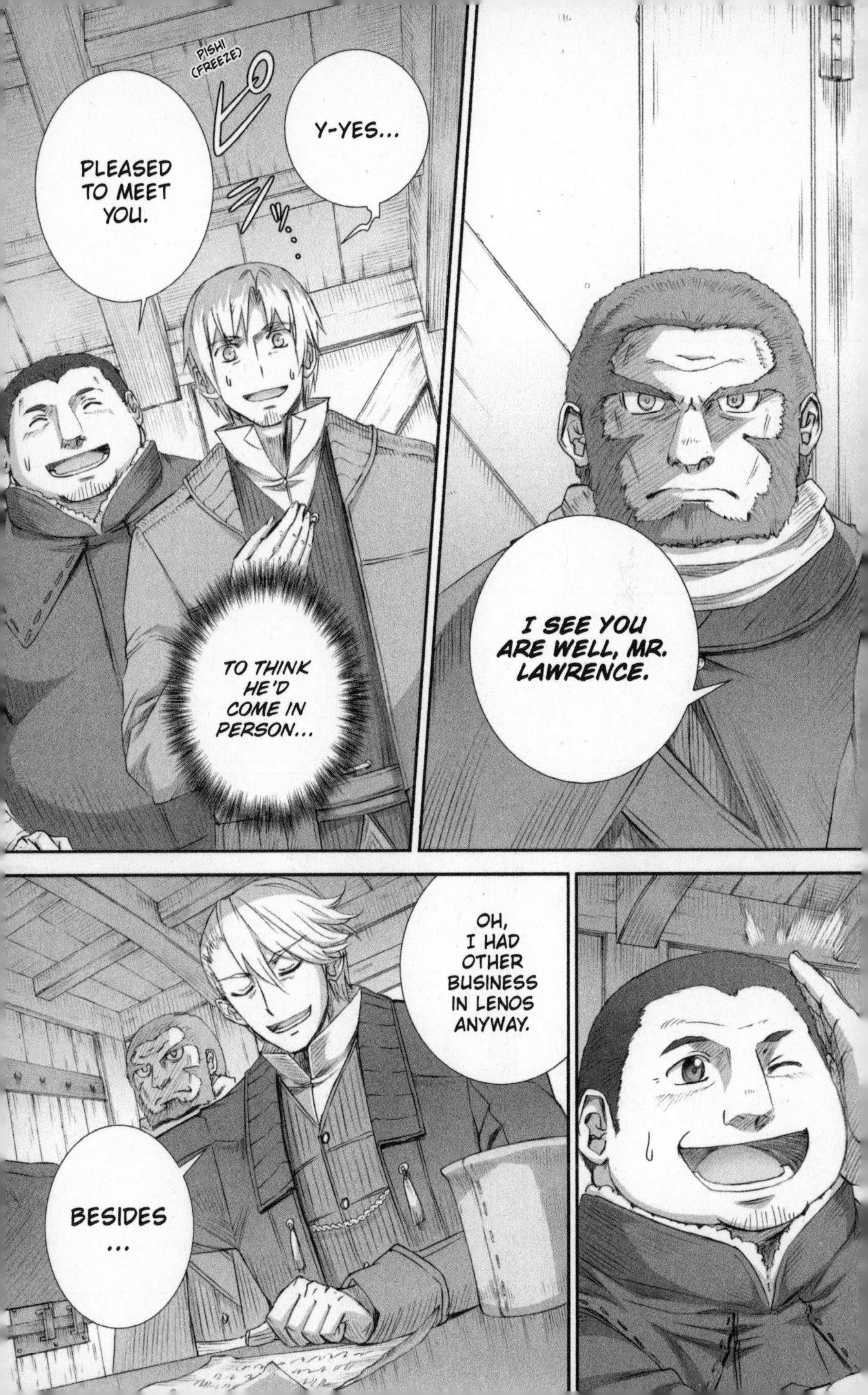
I SEE YOU ARE WELL, MR. LAWRENCE.
Y-YES...
PISHI (FREEZE)
PLEASED TO MEET YOU.
TO THINK HE'D COME IN PERSON...
OH, I HAD OTHER BUSINESS IN LENOS ANYWAY.
BESIDES...

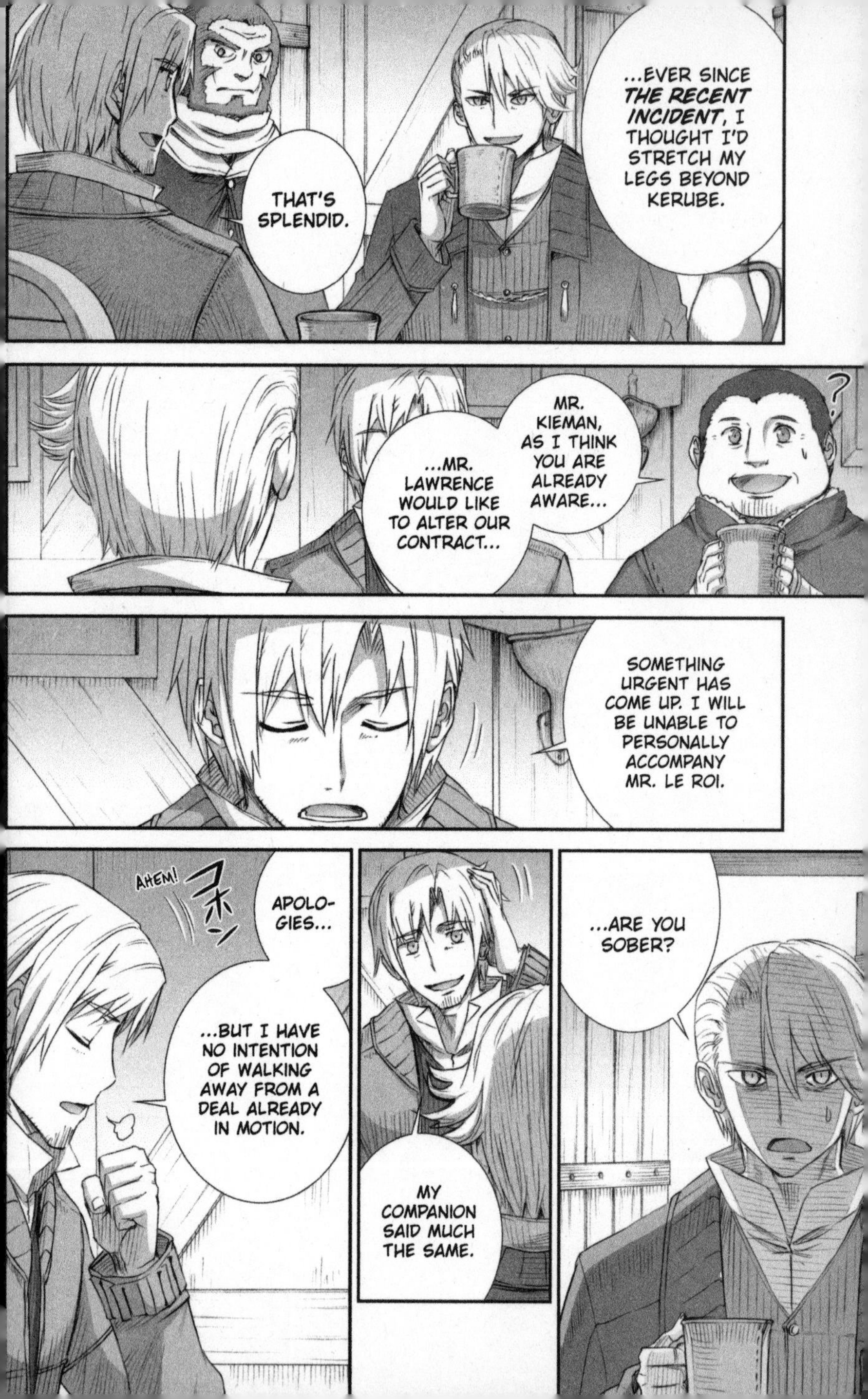
...EVER SINCE *THE RECENT INCIDENT*, I THOUGHT I'D STRETCH MY LEGS BEYOND KERUBE.
THAT'S SPLENDID.
MR. KIEMAN, AS I THINK YOU ARE ALREADY AWARE...
...MR. LAWRENCE WOULD LIKE TO ALTER OUR CONTRACT...
SOMETHING URGENT HAS COME UP. I WILL BE UNABLE TO PERSONALLY ACCOMPANY MR. LE ROI.
...ARE YOU SOBER?
MY COMPANION SAID MUCH THE SAME.
コホン
AHEM!
APOLOGIES...
...BUT I HAVE NO INTENTION OF WALKING AWAY FROM A DEAL ALREADY IN MOTION.

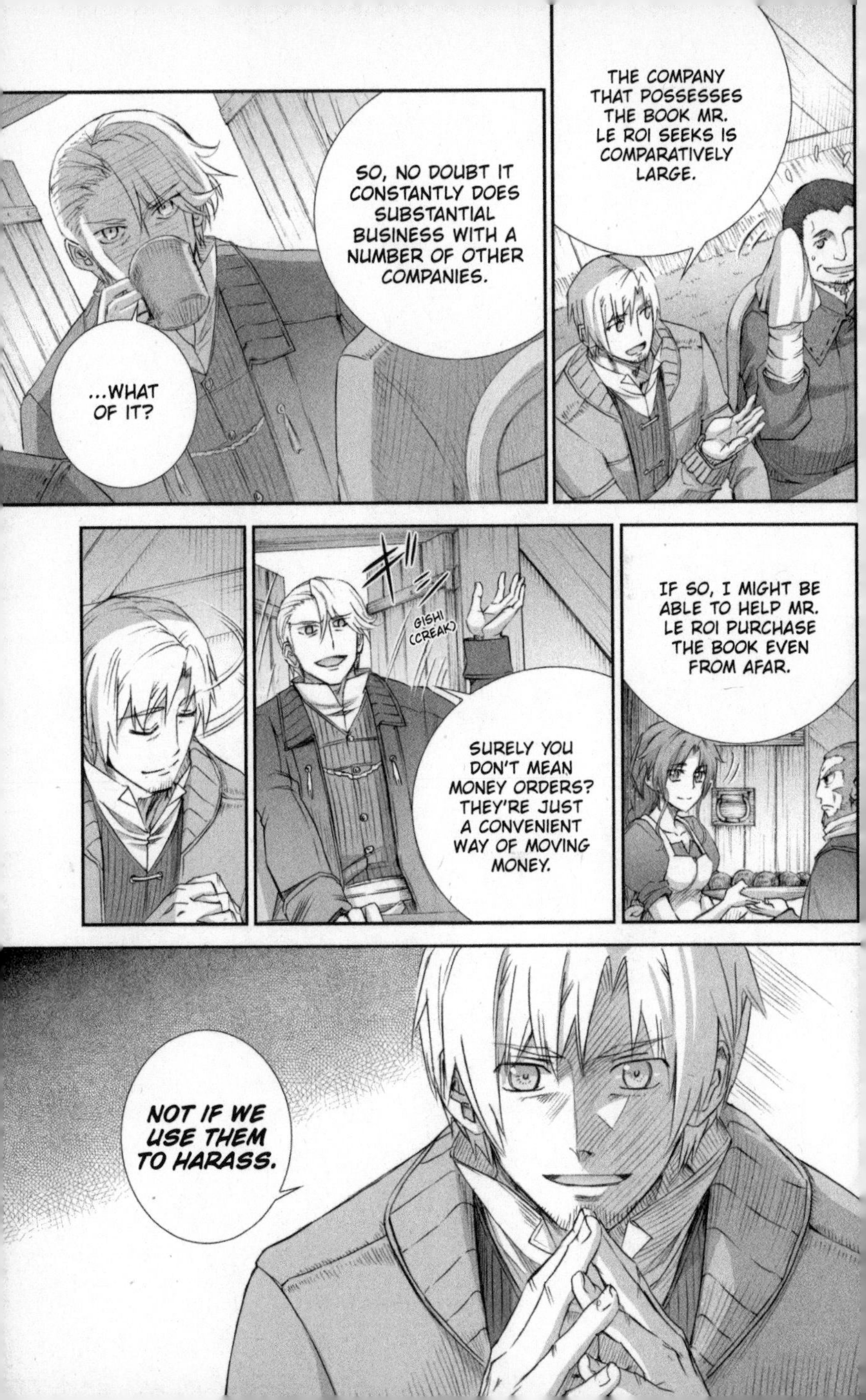
THE COMPANY THAT POSSESSES THE BOOK MR. LE ROI SEEKS IS COMPARATIVELY LARGE.
SO, NO DOUBT IT CONSTANTLY DOES SUBSTANTIAL BUSINESS WITH A NUMBER OF OTHER COMPANIES.
...WHAT OF IT?
IF SO, I MIGHT BE ABLE TO HELP MR. LE ROI PURCHASE THE BOOK EVEN FROM AFAR.
GISHI (CREAK)
SURELY YOU DON'T MEAN MONEY ORDERS? THEY'RE JUST A CONVENIENT WAY OF MOVING MONEY.
NOT IF WE USE THEM TO HARASS.

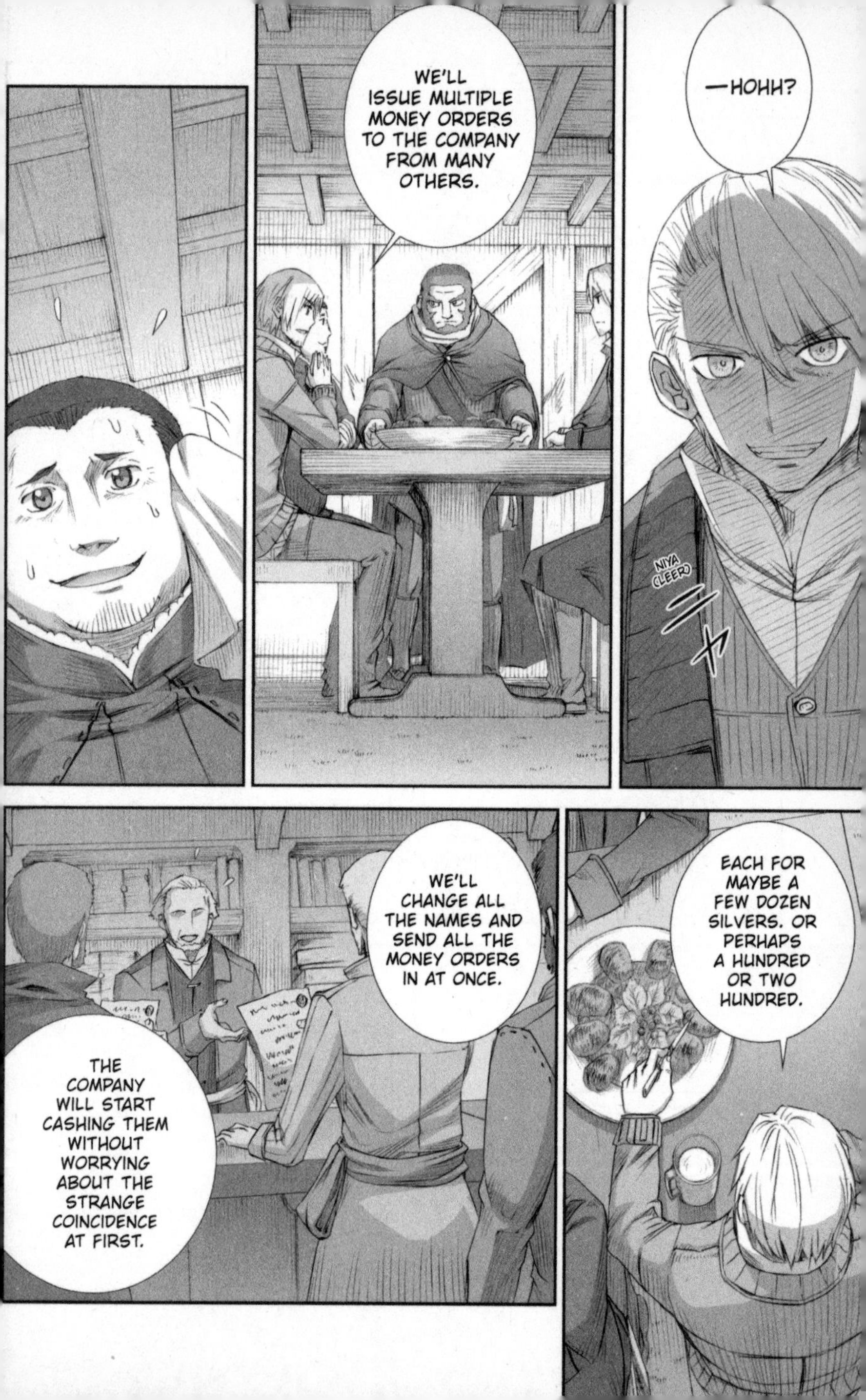
—HOHH?
NIYA (LEER)
WE'LL ISSUE MULTIPLE MONEY ORDERS TO THE COMPANY FROM MANY OTHERS.
EACH FOR MAYBE A FEW DOZEN SILVERS. OR PERHAPS A HUNDRED OR TWO HUNDRED.
WE'LL CHANGE ALL THE NAMES AND SEND ALL THE MONEY ORDERS IN AT ONCE.
THE COMPANY WILL START CASHING THEM WITHOUT WORRYING ABOUT THE STRANGE COINCIDENCE AT FIRST.

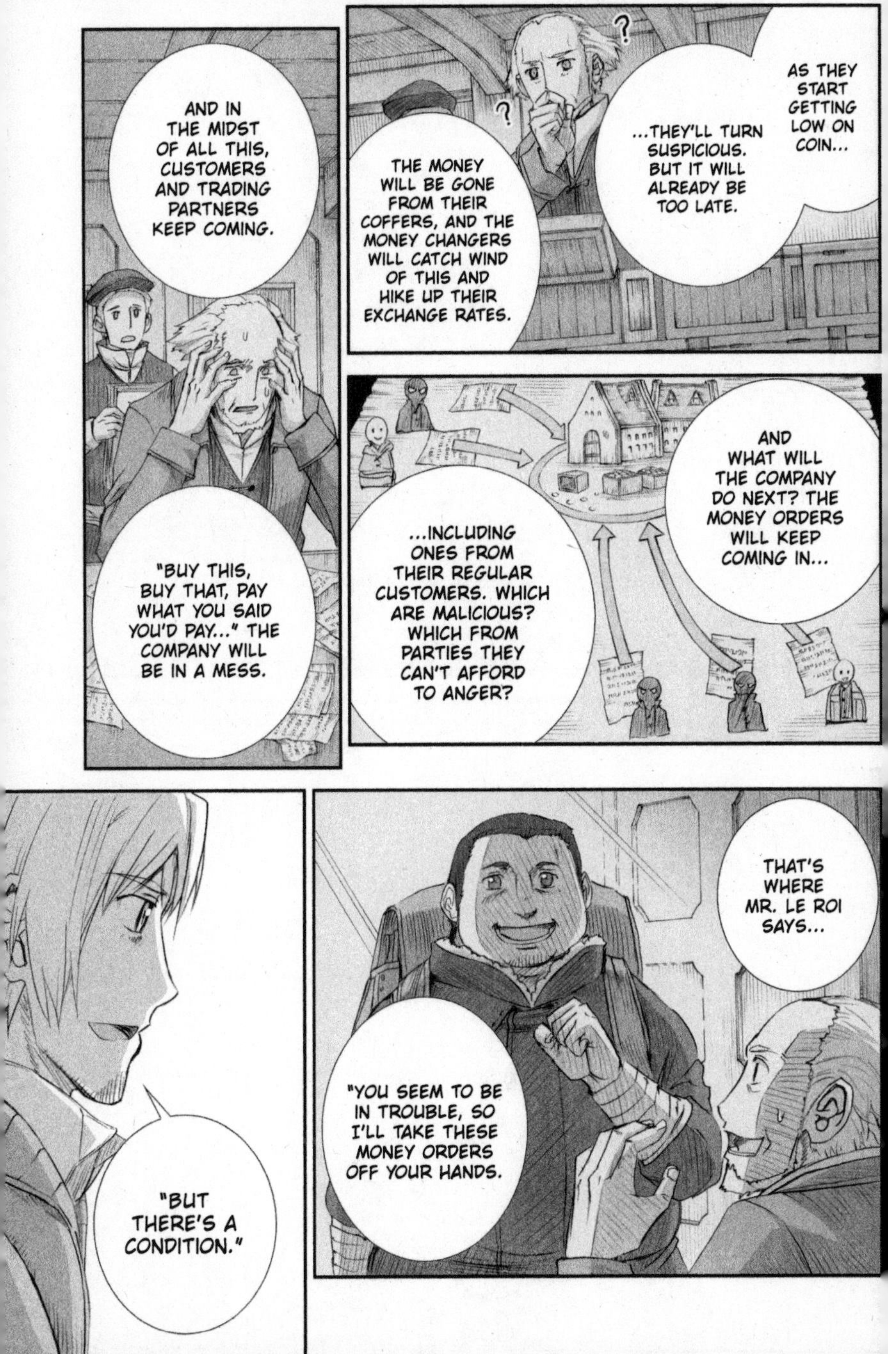
AS THEY START GETTING LOW ON COIN...
...THEY'LL TURN SUSPICIOUS. BUT IT WILL ALREADY BE TOO LATE.
THE MONEY WILL BE GONE FROM THEIR COFFERS, AND THE MONEY CHANGERS WILL CATCH WIND OF THIS AND HIKE UP THEIR EXCHANGE RATES.
AND WHAT WILL THE COMPANY DO NEXT? THE MONEY ORDERS WILL KEEP COMING IN...
...INCLUDING ONES FROM THEIR REGULAR CUSTOMERS. WHICH ARE MALICIOUS? WHICH FROM PARTIES THEY CAN'T AFFORD TO ANGER?
AND IN THE MIDST OF ALL THIS, CUSTOMERS AND TRADING PARTNERS KEEP COMING.
"BUY THIS, BUY THAT, PAY WHAT YOU SAID YOU'D PAY..." THE COMPANY WILL BE IN A MESS.
THAT'S WHERE MR. LE ROI SAYS...
"YOU SEEM TO BE IN TROUBLE, SO I'LL TAKE THESE MONEY ORDERS OFF YOUR HANDS.
"BUT THERE'S A CONDITION."

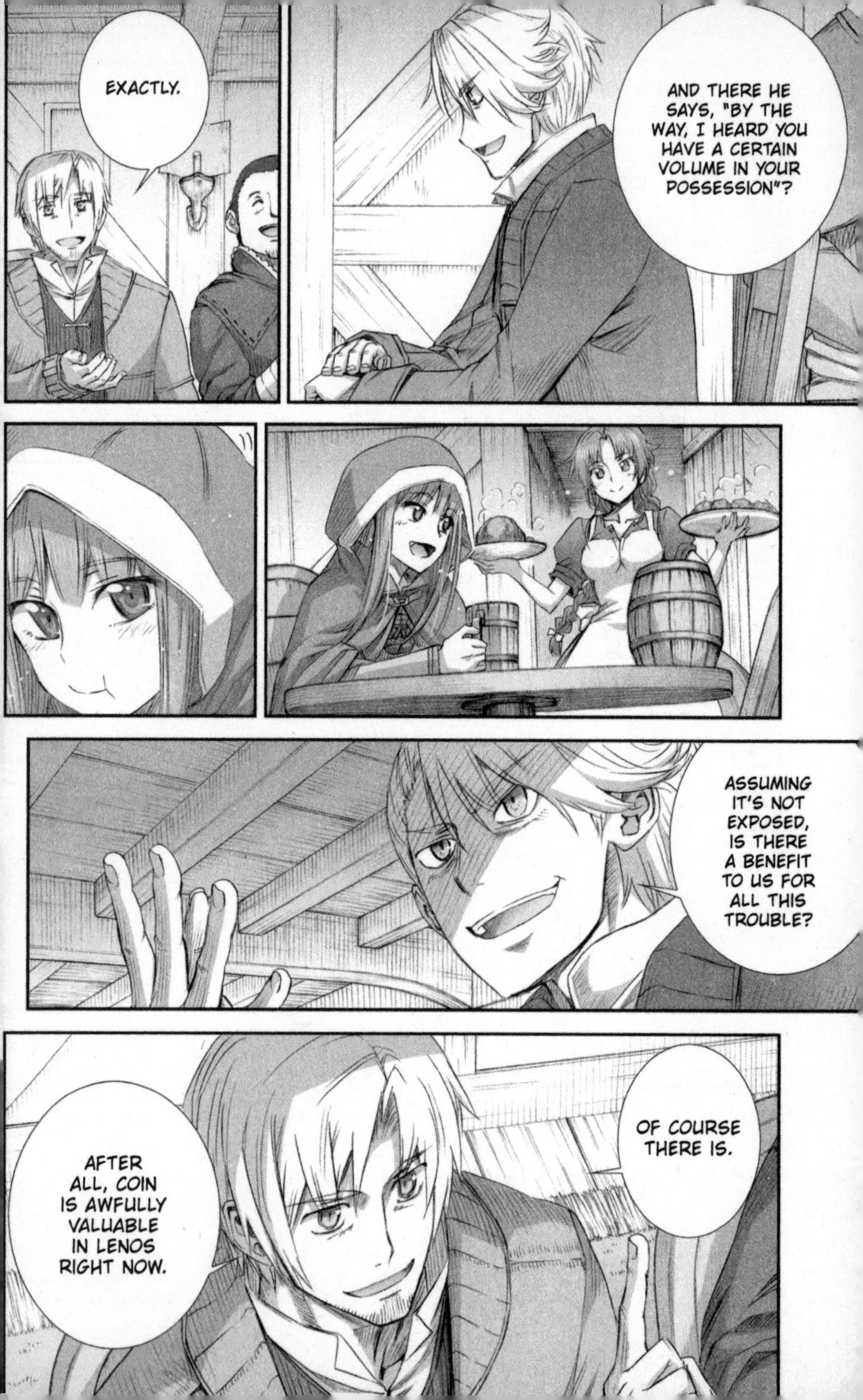
AND THERE HE SAYS, "BY THE WAY, I HEARD YOU HAVE A CERTAIN VOLUME IN YOUR POSSESSION"?
EXACTLY.
ASSUMING IT'S NOT EXPOSED, IS THERE A BENEFIT TO US FOR ALL THIS TROUBLE?
OF COURSE THERE IS.
AFTER ALL, COIN IS AWFULLY VALUABLE IN LENOS RIGHT NOW.

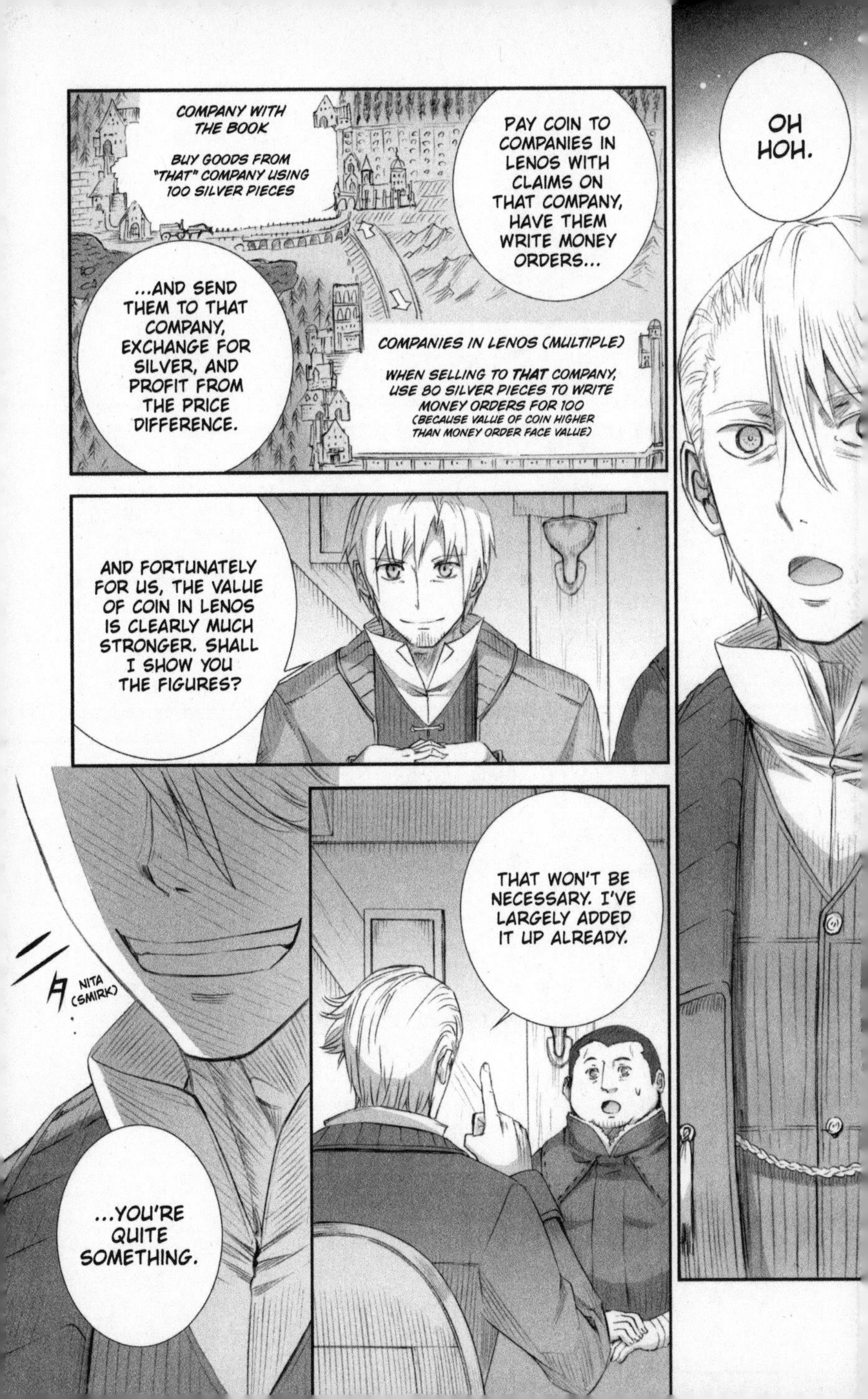
OH HOH.
PAY COIN TO COMPANIES IN LENOS WITH CLAIMS ON THAT COMPANY, HAVE THEM WRITE MONEY ORDERS...
COMPANY WITH THE BOOK
BUY GOODS FROM "THAT" COMPANY USING 100 SILVER PIECES
...AND SEND THEM TO THAT COMPANY, EXCHANGE FOR SILVER, AND PROFIT FROM THE PRICE DIFFERENCE.
COMPANIES IN LENOS (MULTIPLE)
WHEN SELLING TO THAT COMPANY, USE 80 SILVER PIECES TO WRITE MONEY ORDERS FOR 100 (BECAUSE VALUE OF COIN HIGHER THAN MONEY ORDER FACE VALUE)
AND FORTUNATELY FOR US, THE VALUE OF COIN IN LENOS IS CLEARLY MUCH STRONGER. SHALL I SHOW YOU THE FIGURES?
THAT WON'T BE NECESSARY. I'VE LARGELY ADDED IT UP ALREADY.
NITA (SMIRK)
...YOU'RE QUITE SOMETHING.

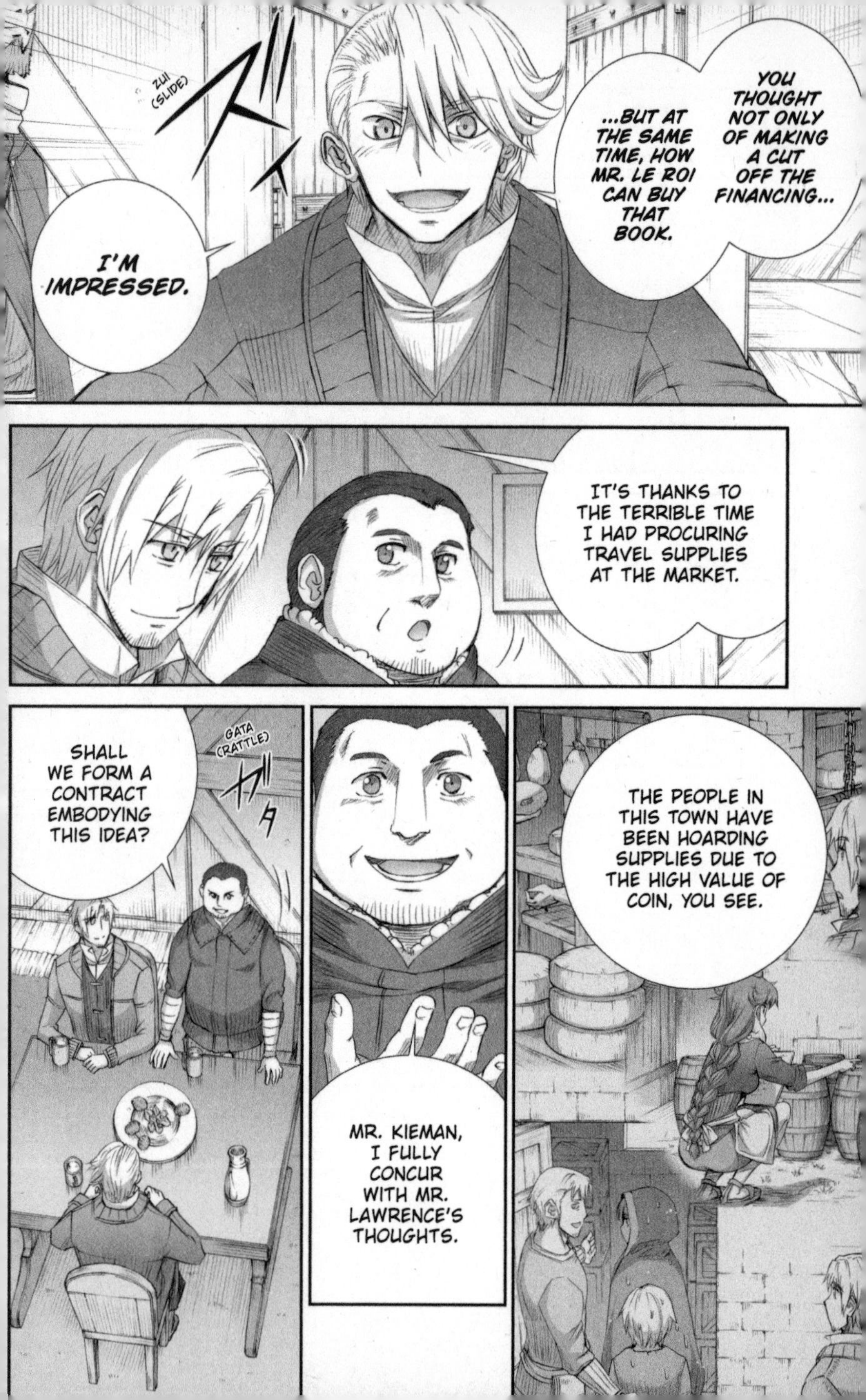
YOU THOUGHT NOT ONLY OF MAKING A CUT OFF THE FINANCING...
...BUT AT THE SAME TIME, HOW MR. LE ROI CAN BUY THAT BOOK.
ZUI (SLIDE)
I'M IMPRESSED.
IT'S THANKS TO THE TERRIBLE TIME I HAD PROCURING TRAVEL SUPPLIES AT THE MARKET.
THE PEOPLE IN THIS TOWN HAVE BEEN HOARDING SUPPLIES DUE TO THE HIGH VALUE OF COIN, YOU SEE.
MR. KIEMAN, I FULLY CONCUR WITH MR. LAWRENCE'S THOUGHTS.
GATA (RATTLE)
SHALL WE FORM A CONTRACT EMBODYING THIS IDEA?

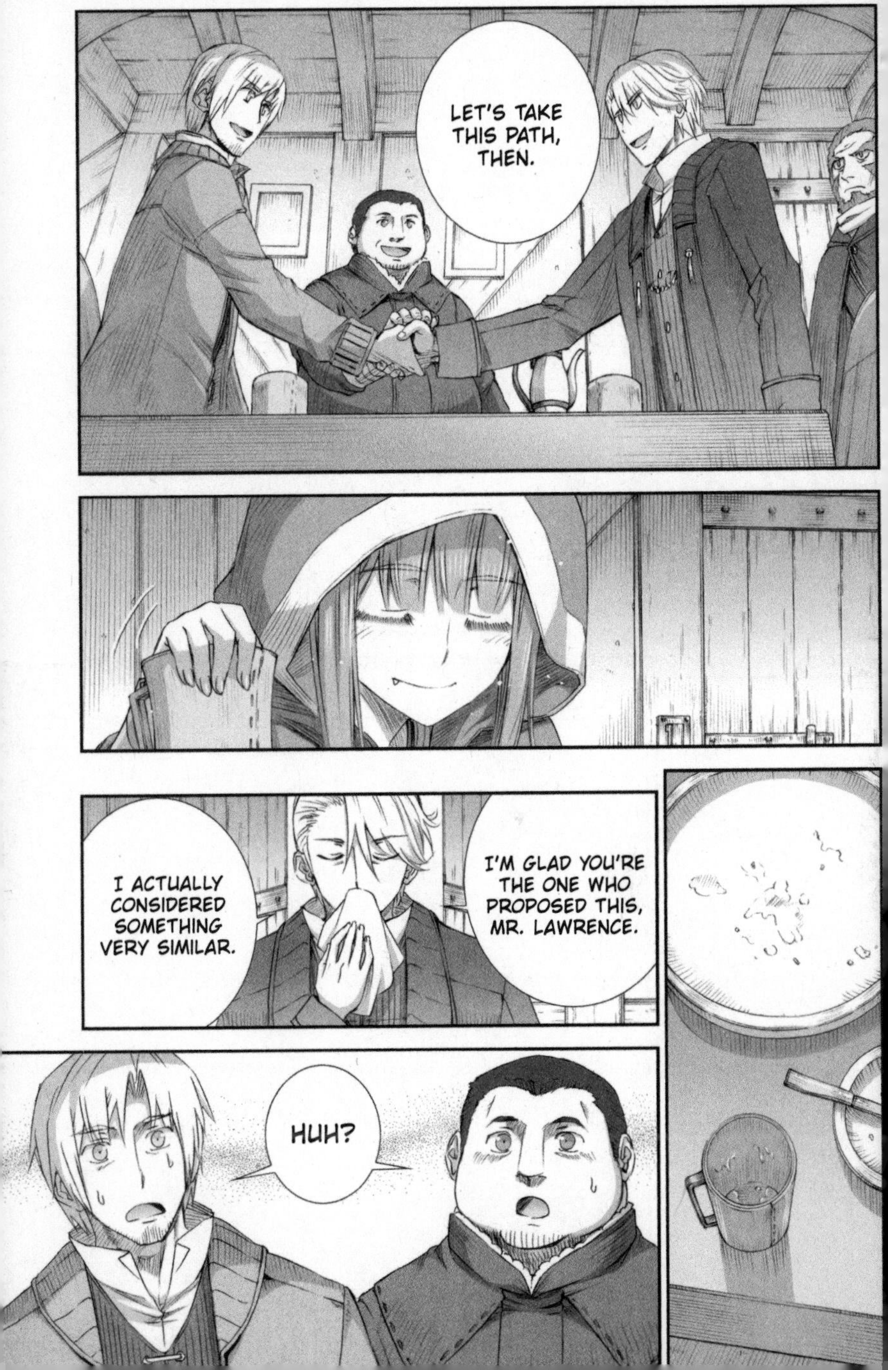
LET'S TAKE THIS PATH, THEN.
I'M GLAD YOU'RE THE ONE WHO PROPOSED THIS, MR. LAWRENCE.
I ACTUALLY CONSIDERED SOMETHING VERY SIMILAR.
HUH?

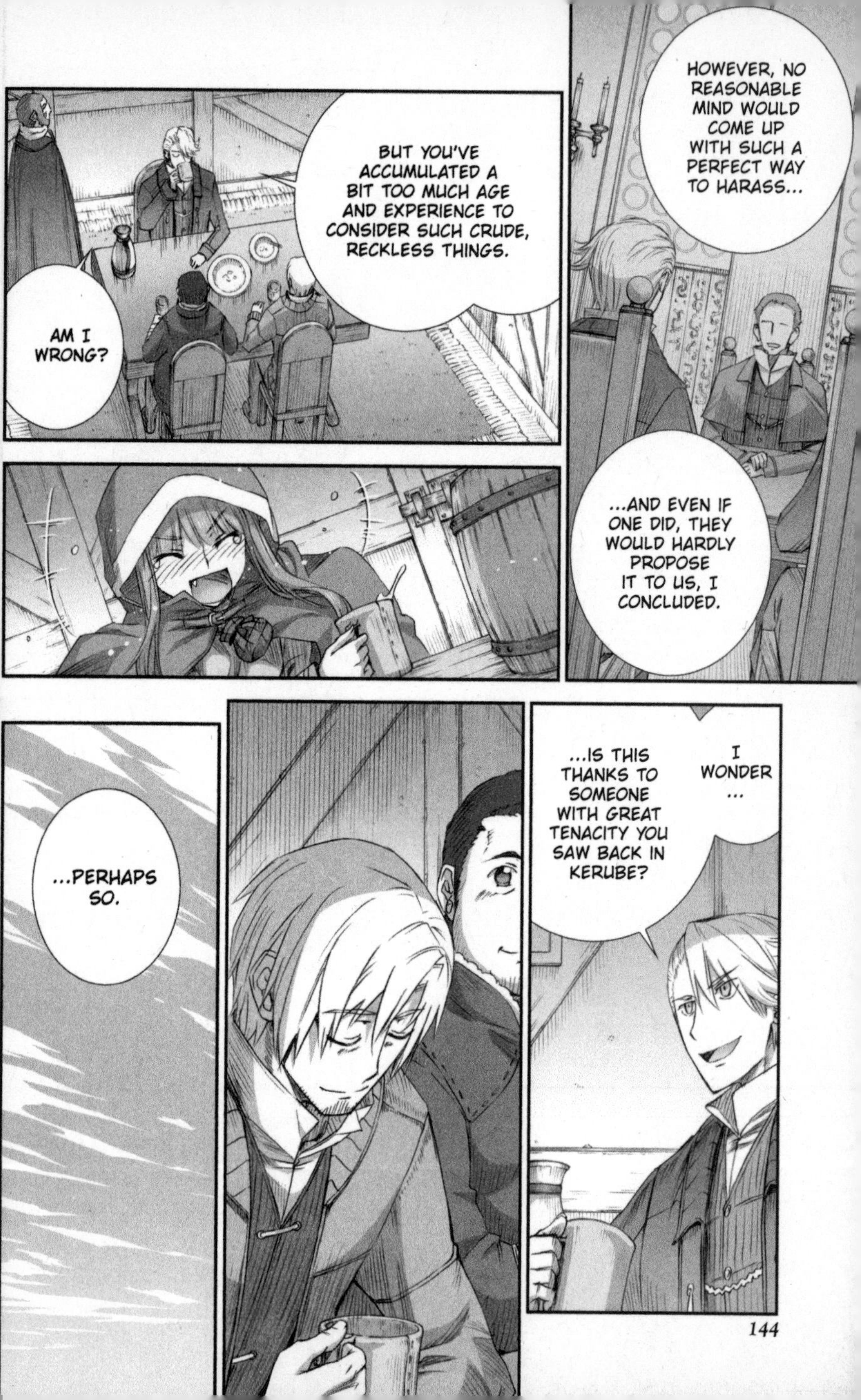
HOWEVER, NO REASONABLE MIND WOULD COME UP WITH SUCH A PERFECT WAY TO HARASS...
...AND EVEN IF ONE DID, THEY WOULD HARDLY PROPOSE IT TO US, I CONCLUDED.
BUT YOU'VE ACCUMULATED A BIT TOO MUCH AGE AND EXPERIENCE TO CONSIDER SUCH CRUDE, RECKLESS THINGS.
AM I WRONG?
I WONDER...
...IS THIS THANKS TO SOMEONE WITH GREAT TENACITY YOU SAW BACK IN KERUBE?
...PERHAPS SO.

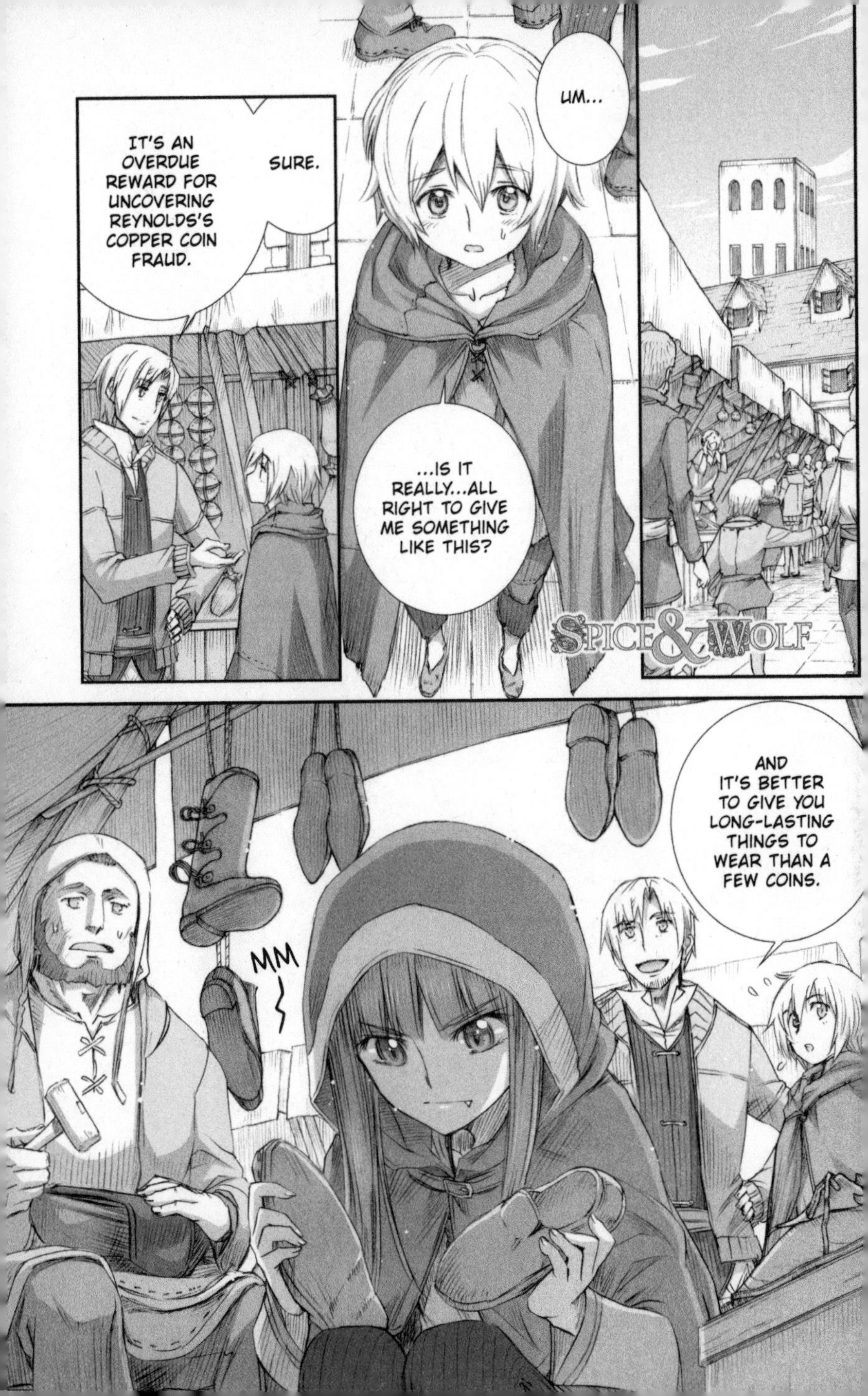
UM...
...IS IT REALLY...ALL RIGHT TO GIVE ME SOMETHING LIKE THIS?
SURE.
IT'S AN OVERDUE REWARD FOR UNCOVERING REYNOLDS'S COPPER COIN FRAUD.
AND IT'S BETTER TO GIVE YOU LONG-LASTING THINGS TO WEAR THAN A FEW COINS.
MM

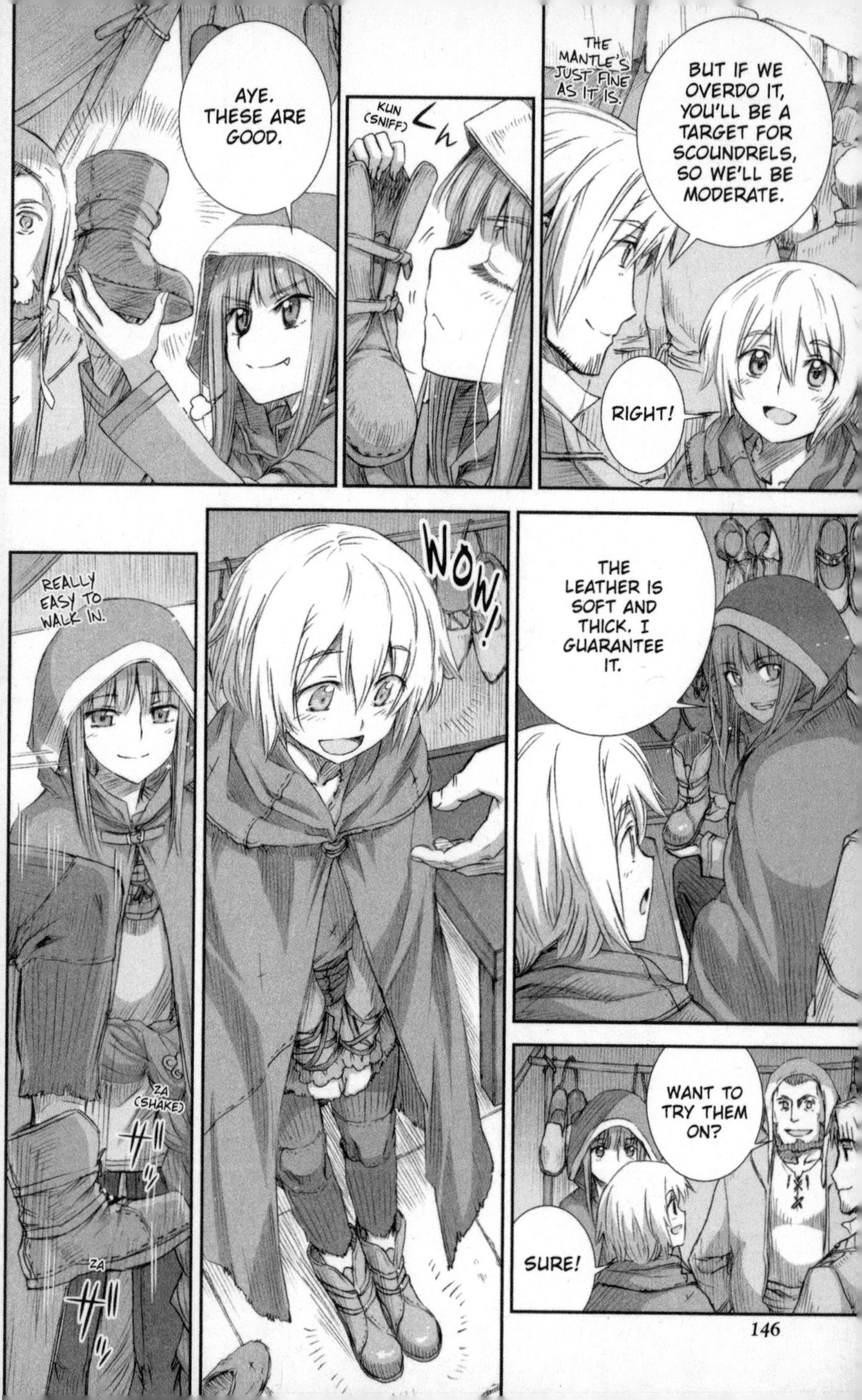
THE MANTLE'S JUST FINE AS IT IS.
BUT IF WE OVERDO IT, YOU'LL BE A TARGET FOR SCOUNDRELS, SO WE'LL BE MODERATE.
RIGHT!
KUN (SNIFF)
AYE. THESE ARE GOOD.
THE LEATHER IS SOFT AND THICK. I GUARANTEE IT.
WANT TO TRY THEM ON?
SURE!
WOW!
REALLY EASY TO WALK IN.
ZA (SHAKE)
ZA

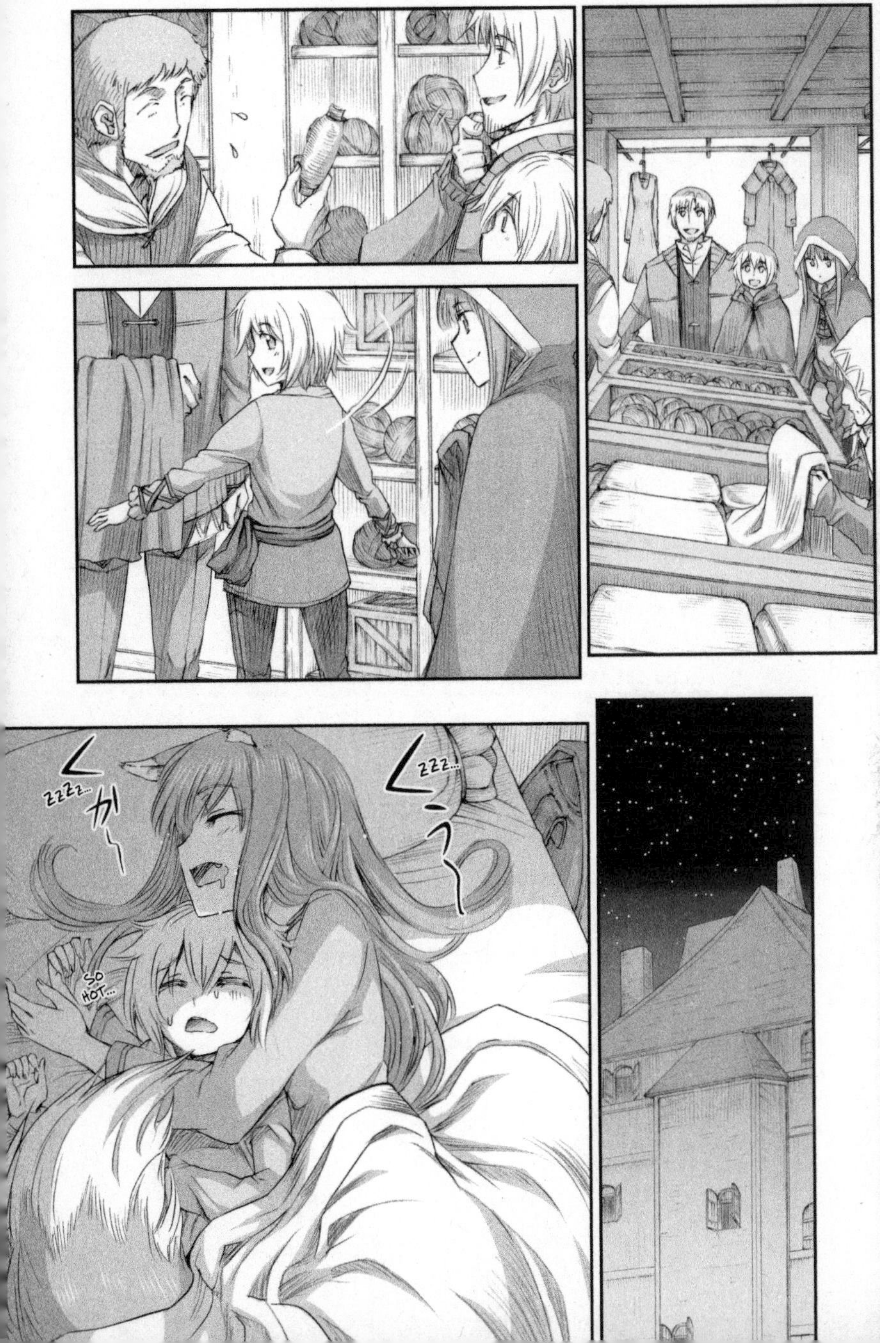
ZZZ...
ZZZZ...
SO HOT...

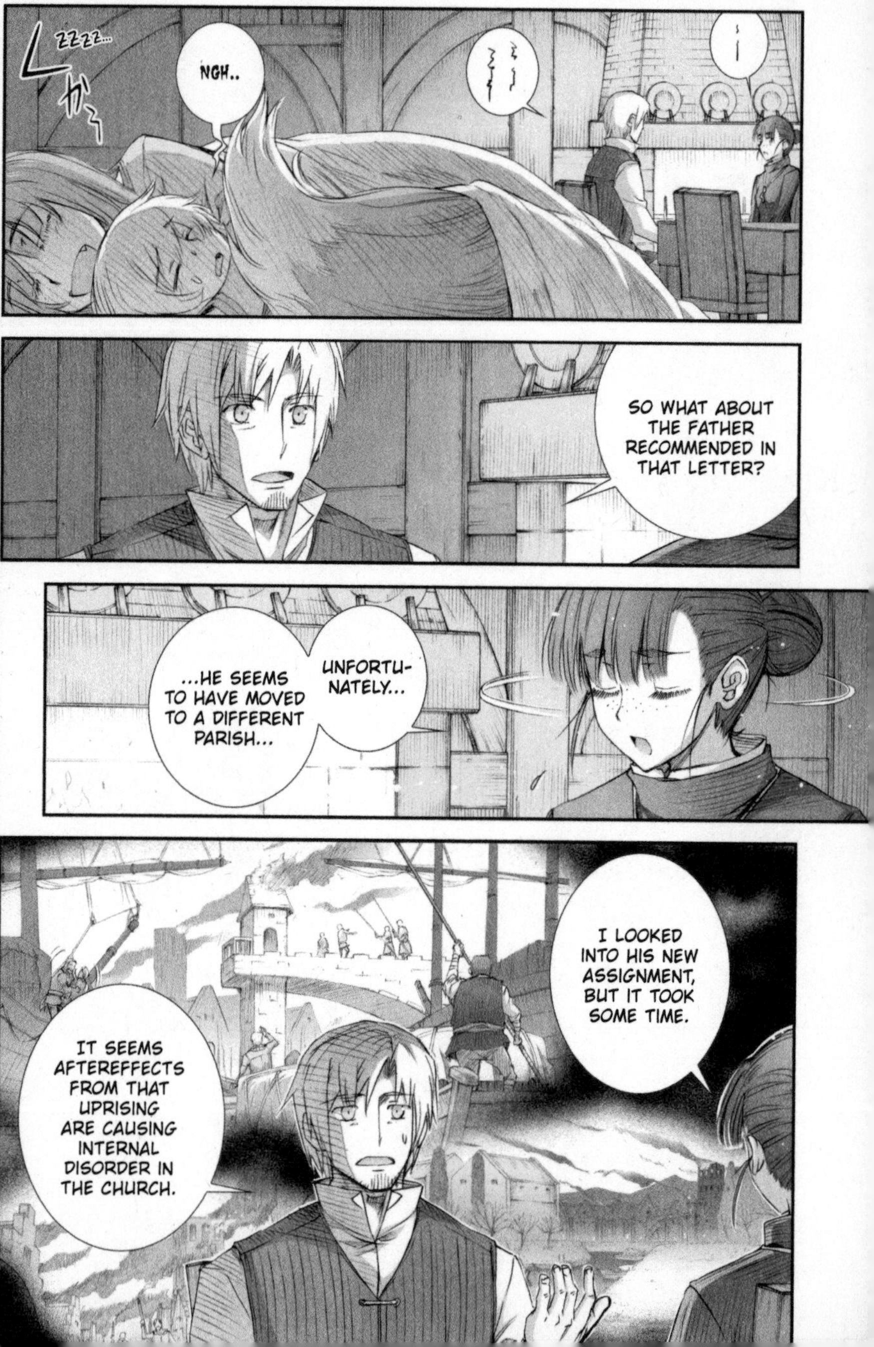
NGH..
ZZZZ...
SO WHAT ABOUT THE FATHER RECOMMENDED IN THAT LETTER?
UNFORTUNATELY...
...HE SEEMS TO HAVE MOVED TO A DIFFERENT PARISH...
I LOOKED INTO HIS NEW ASSIGNMENT, BUT IT TOOK SOME TIME.
IT SEEMS AFTEREFFECTS FROM THAT UPRISING ARE CAUSING INTERNAL DISORDER IN THE CHURCH.

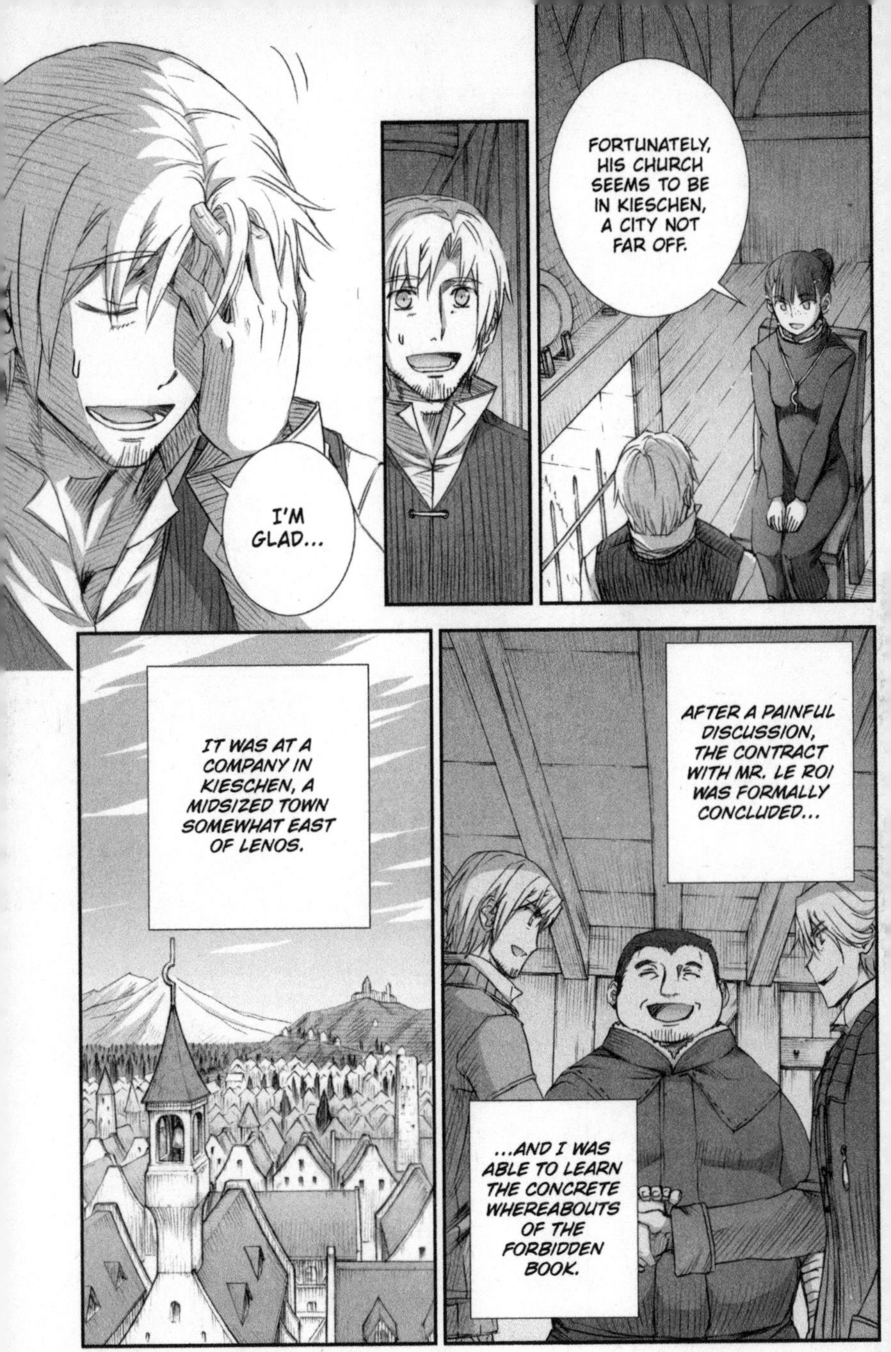
FORTUNATELY, HIS CHURCH SEEMS TO BE IN KIESCHEN, A CITY NOT FAR OFF.
I'M GLAD...
AFTER A PAINFUL DISCUSSION, THE CONTRACT WITH MR. LE ROI WAS FORMALLY CONCLUDED...
...AND I WAS ABLE TO LEARN THE CONCRETE WHEREABOUTS OF THE FORBIDDEN BOOK.
IT WAS AT A COMPANY IN KIESCHEN, A MIDSIZED TOWN SOMEWHAT EAST OF LENOS.

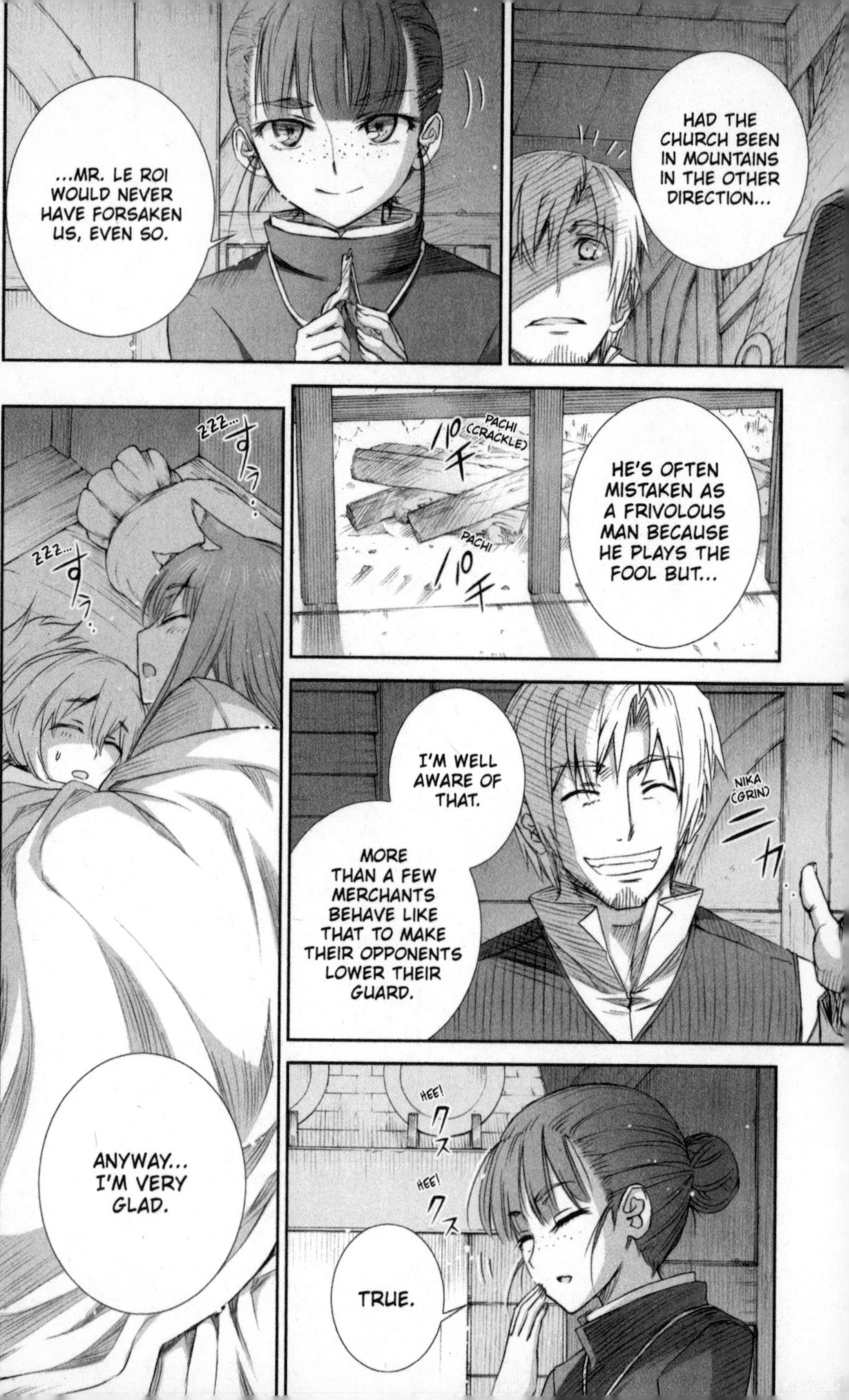
HAD THE CHURCH BEEN IN MOUNTAINS IN THE OTHER DIRECTION...
...MR. LE ROI WOULD NEVER HAVE FORSAKEN US, EVEN SO.
PACHI (CRACKLE)
PACHI
HE'S OFTEN MISTAKEN AS A FRIVOLOUS MAN BECAUSE HE PLAYS THE FOOL BUT...
NIKA (GRIN)
I'M WELL AWARE OF THAT.
MORE THAN A FEW MERCHANTS BEHAVE LIKE THAT TO MAKE THEIR OPPONENTS LOWER THEIR GUARD.
HEE!
HEE!
TRUE.
ZZZ...
ZZZ...
ANYWAY... I'M VERY GLAD.

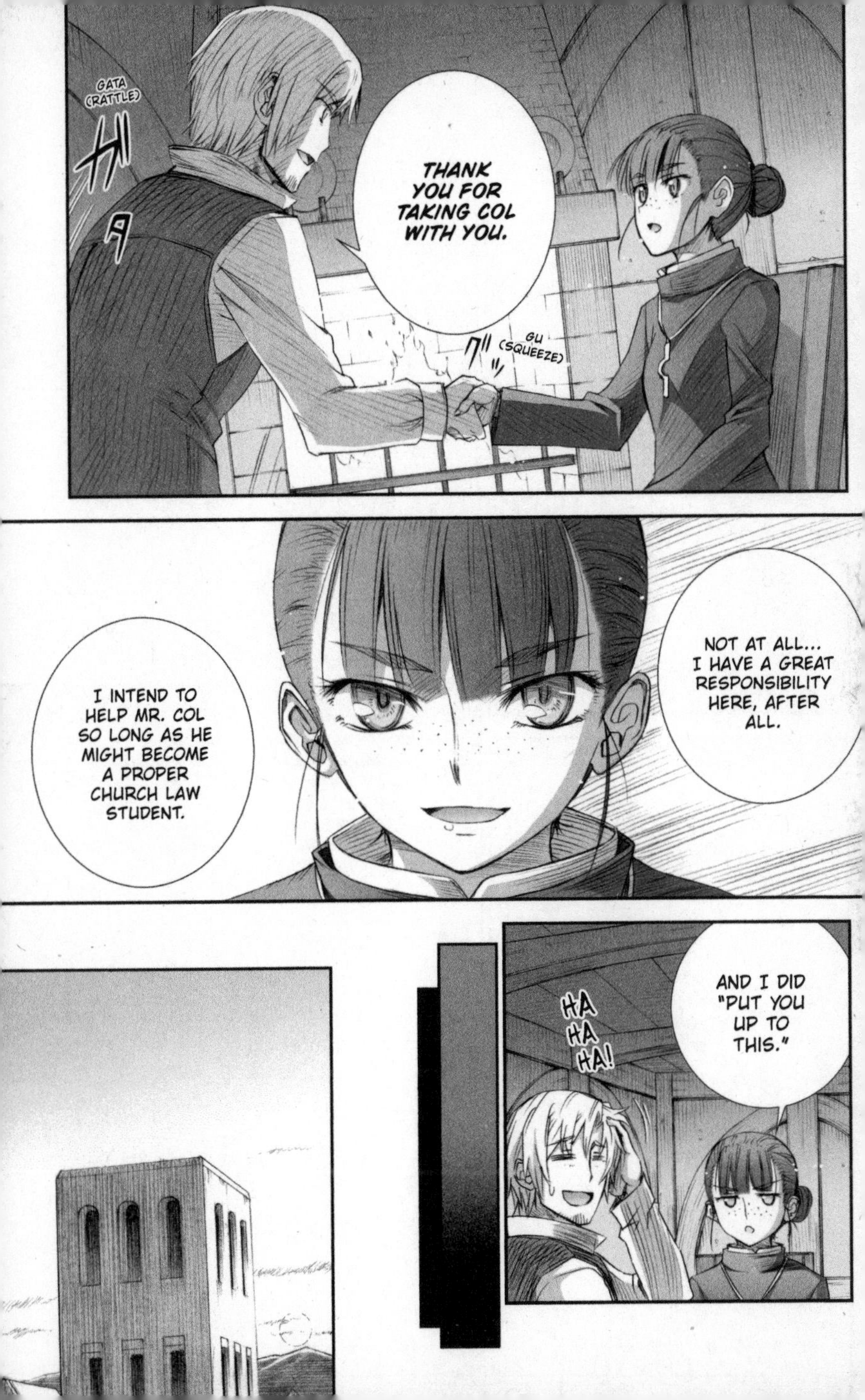
THANK YOU FOR TAKING COL WITH YOU.
GATA (RATTLE)
GU (SQUEEZE)
NOT AT ALL... I HAVE A GREAT RESPONSIBILITY HERE, AFTER ALL.
I INTEND TO HELP MR. COL SO LONG AS HE MIGHT BECOME A PROPER CHURCH LAW STUDENT.
AND I DID "PUT YOU UP TO THIS."
HA HA HA!

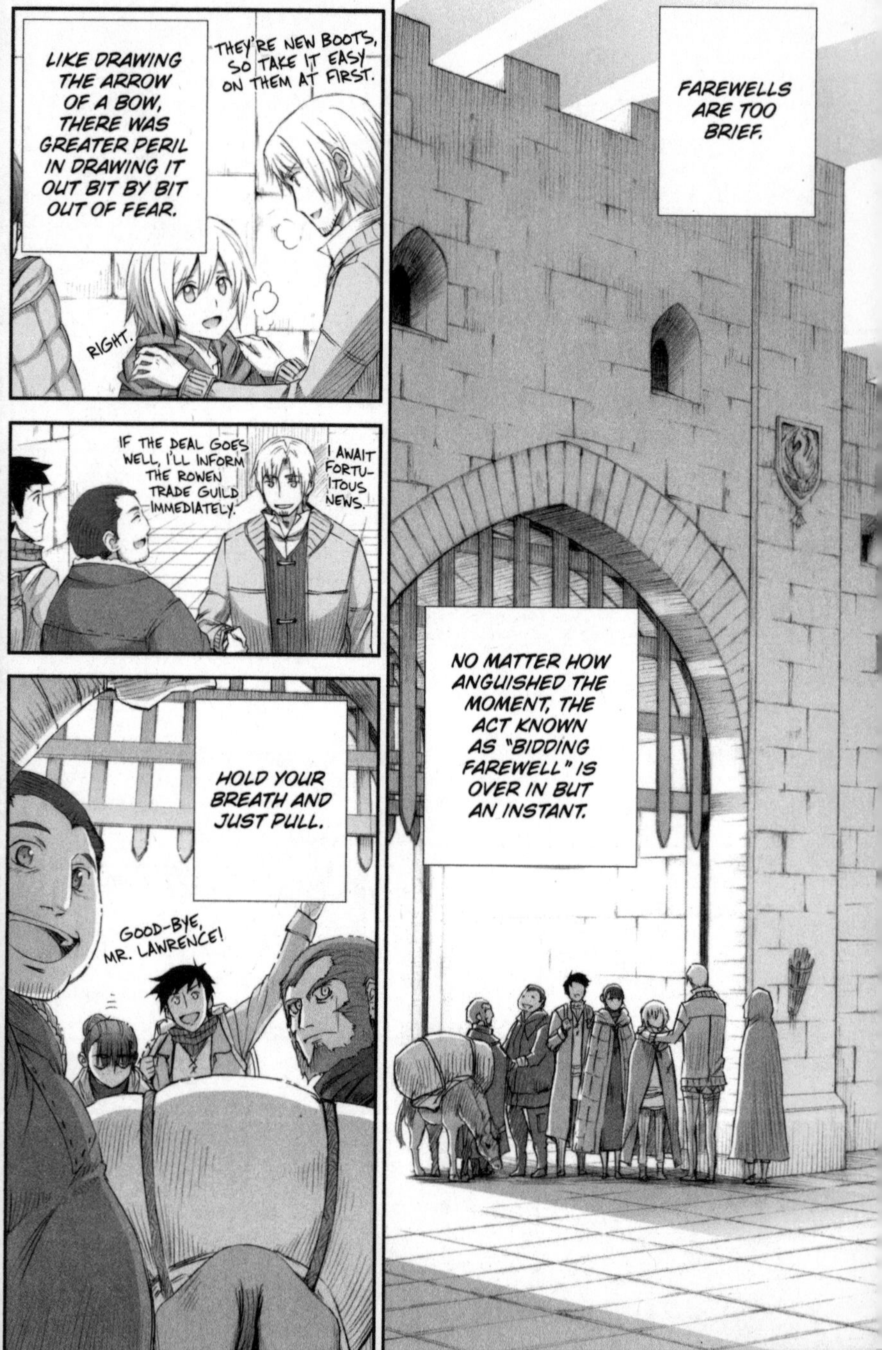
FAREWELLS ARE TOO BRIEF.
NO MATTER HOW ANGUISHED THE MOMENT, THE ACT KNOWN AS "BIDDING FAREWELL" IS OVER IN BUT AN INSTANT.
THEY'RE NEW BOOTS, SO TAKE IT EASY ON THEM AT FIRST.
LIKE DRAWING THE ARROW OF A BOW, THERE WAS GREATER PERIL IN DRAWING IT OUT BIT BY BIT OUT OF FEAR.
RIGHT.
I AWAIT FORTUITOUS NEWS.
IF THE DEAL GOES WELL, I'LL INFORM THE ROWEN TRADE GUILD IMMEDIATELY.
HOLD YOUR BREATH AND JUST PULL.
GOOD-BYE, MR. LAWRENCE!

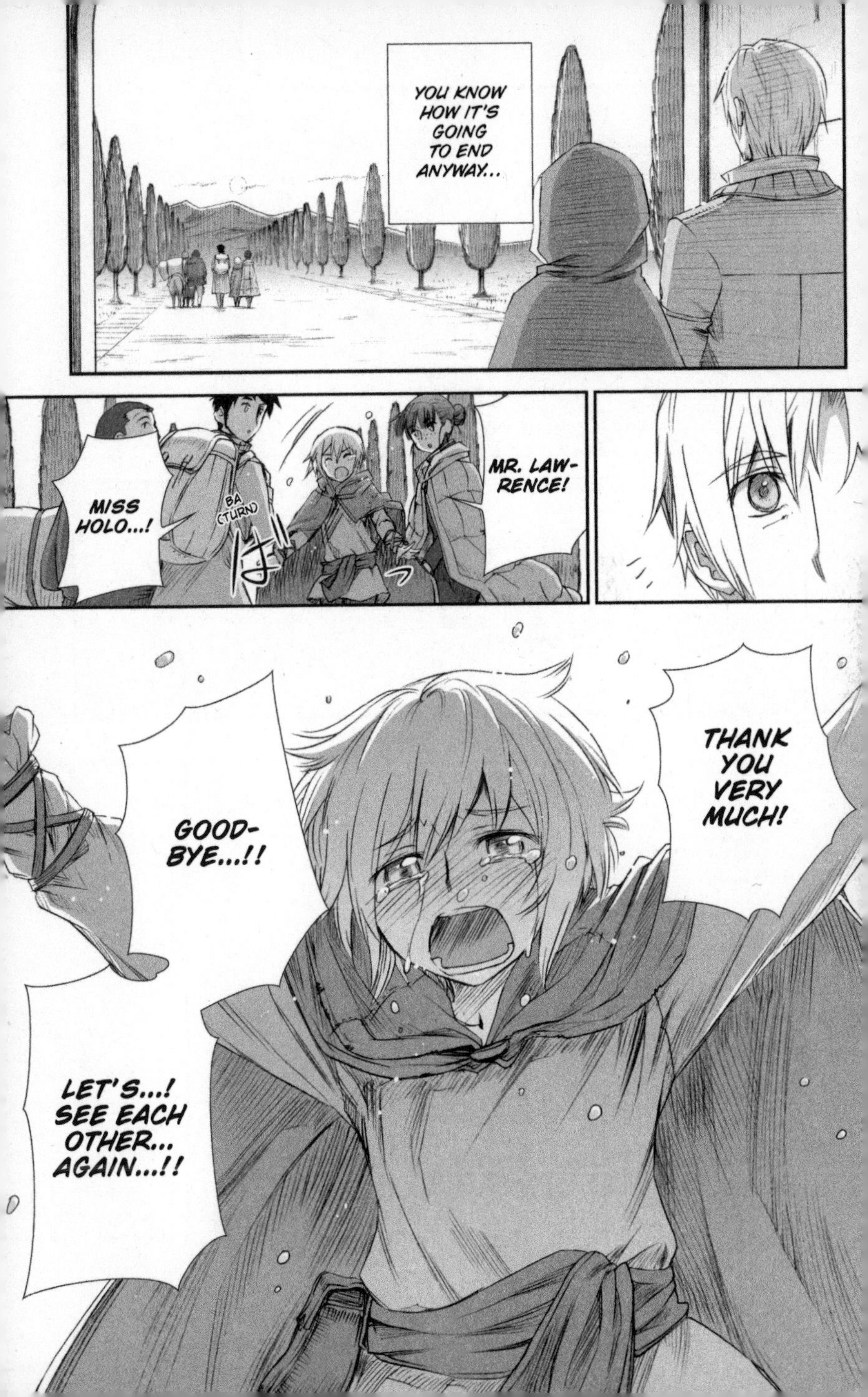
YOU KNOW HOW IT'S GOING TO END ANYWAY...
MR. LAW-RENCE!
BA (TURN)
MISS HOLO...!
THANK YOU VERY MUCH!
GOOD-BYE...!!
LET'S...! SEE EACH OTHER... AGAIN...!!

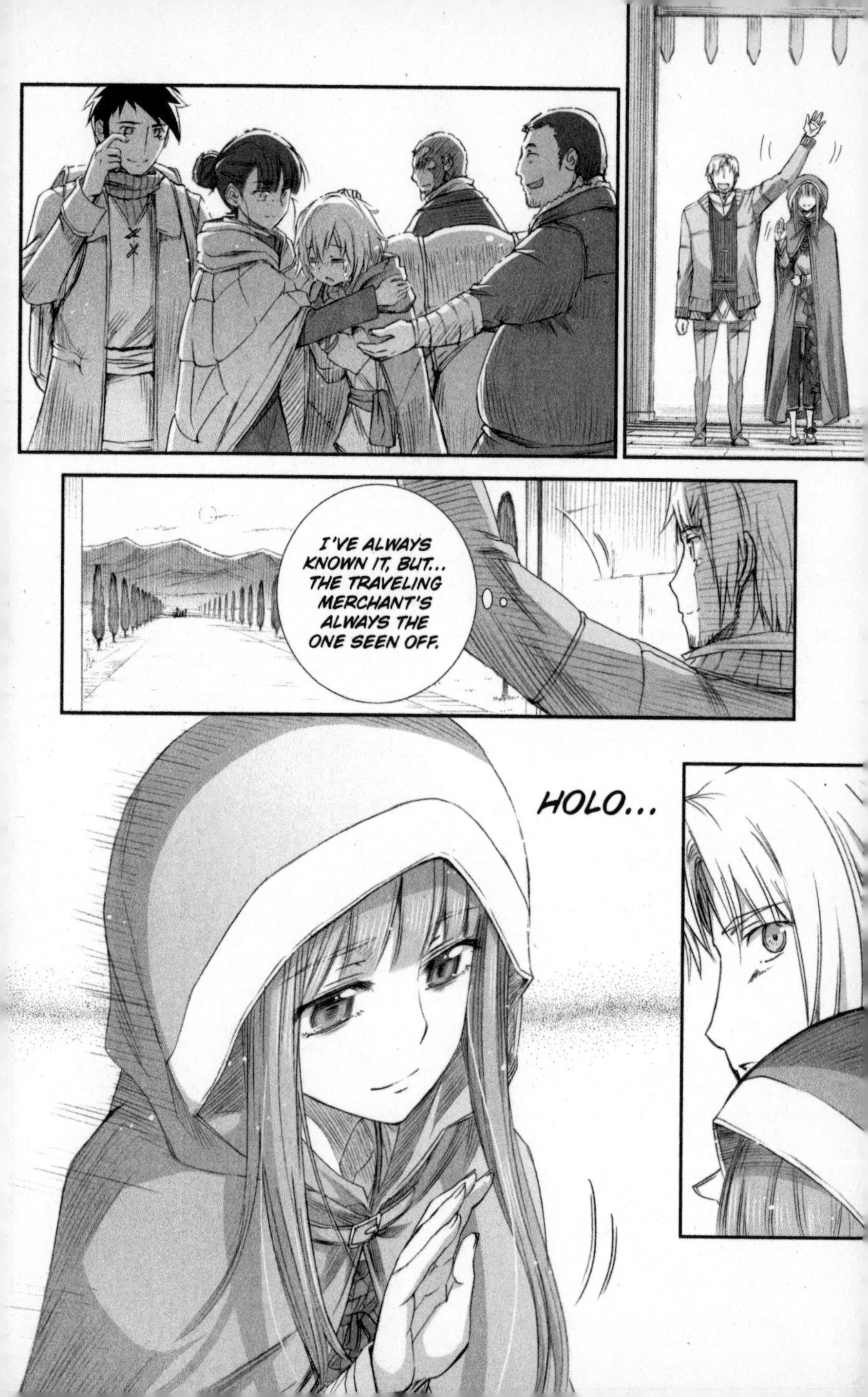
I'VE ALWAYS KNOWN IT, BUT... THE TRAVELING MERCHANT'S ALWAYS THE ONE SEEN OFF.
HOLO...

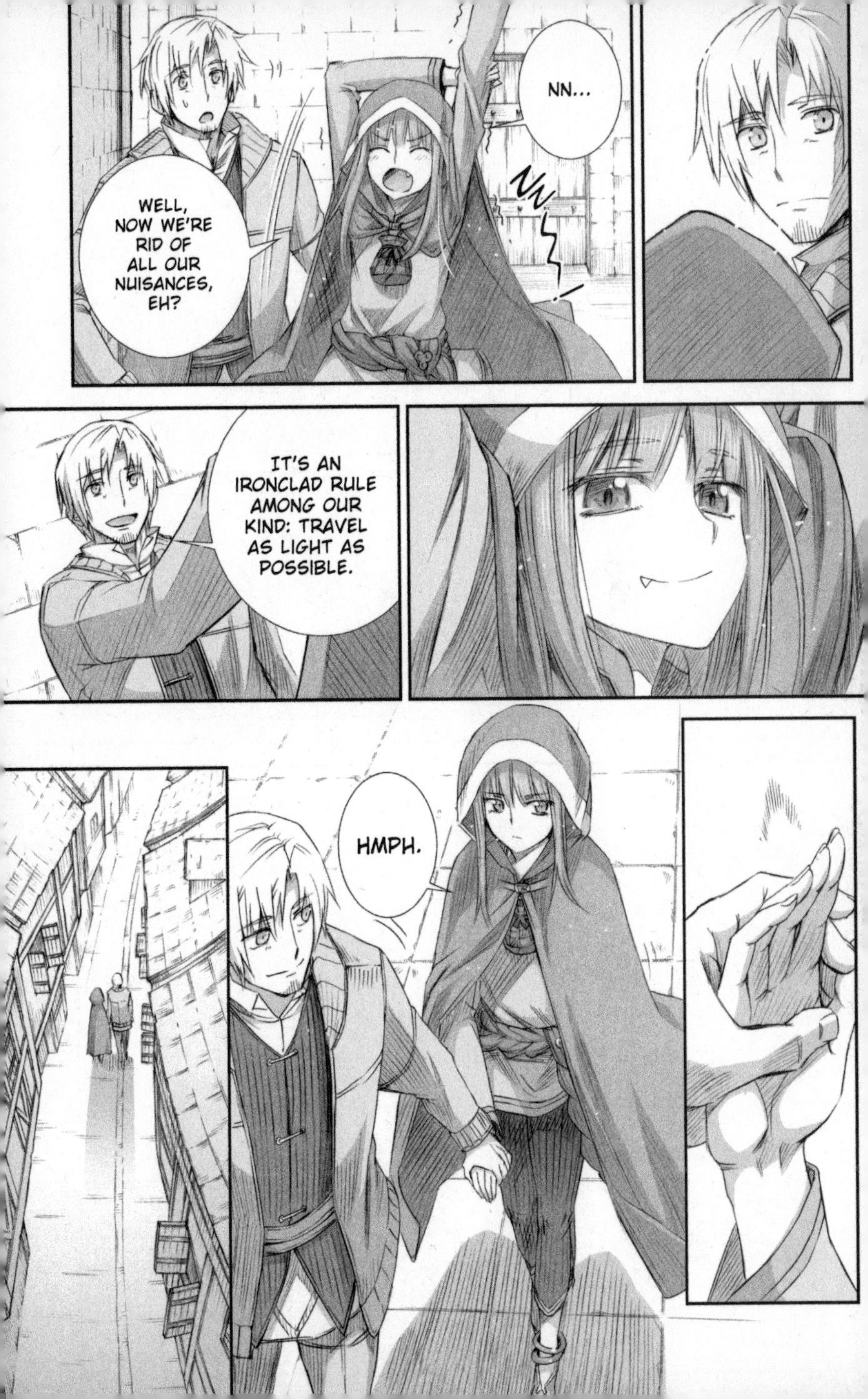
NN...
WELL, NOW WE'RE RID OF ALL OUR NUISANCES, EH?
IT'S AN IRONCLAD RULE AMONG OUR KIND: TRAVEL AS LIGHT AS POSSIBLE.
HMPH.

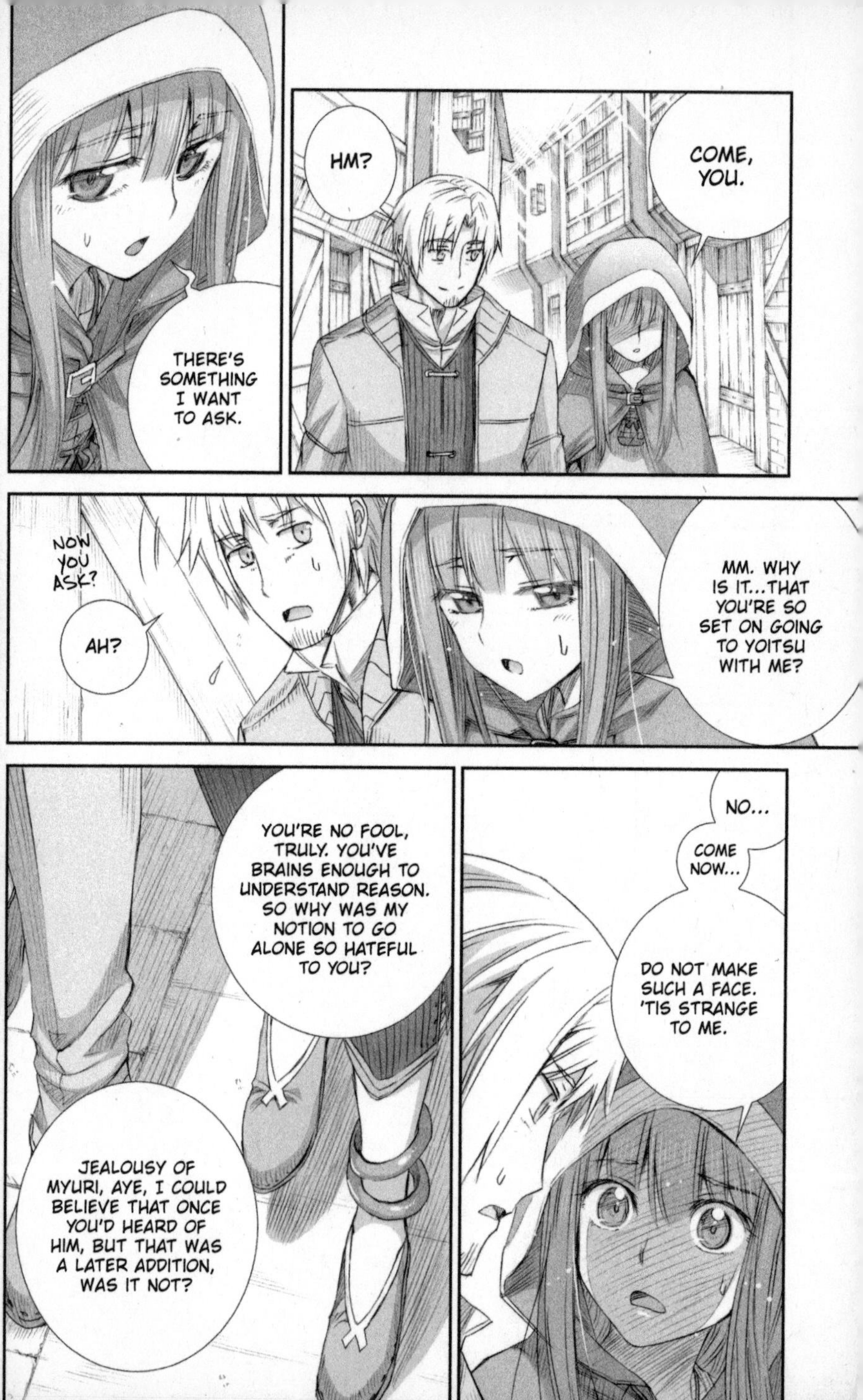
COME, YOU.
HM?
THERE'S SOMETHING I WANT TO ASK.
MM. WHY IS IT...THAT YOU'RE SO SET ON GOING TO YOITSU WITH ME?
NOW YOU ASK?
AH?
NO...
COME NOW...
DO NOT MAKE SUCH A FACE. 'TIS STRANGE TO ME.
YOU'RE NO FOOL, TRULY. YOU'VE BRAINS ENOUGH TO UNDERSTAND REASON. SO WHY WAS MY NOTION TO GO ALONE SO HATEFUL TO YOU?
JEALOUSY OF MYURI, AYE, I COULD BELIEVE THAT ONCE YOU'D HEARD OF HIM, BUT THAT WAS A LATER ADDITION, WAS IT NOT?

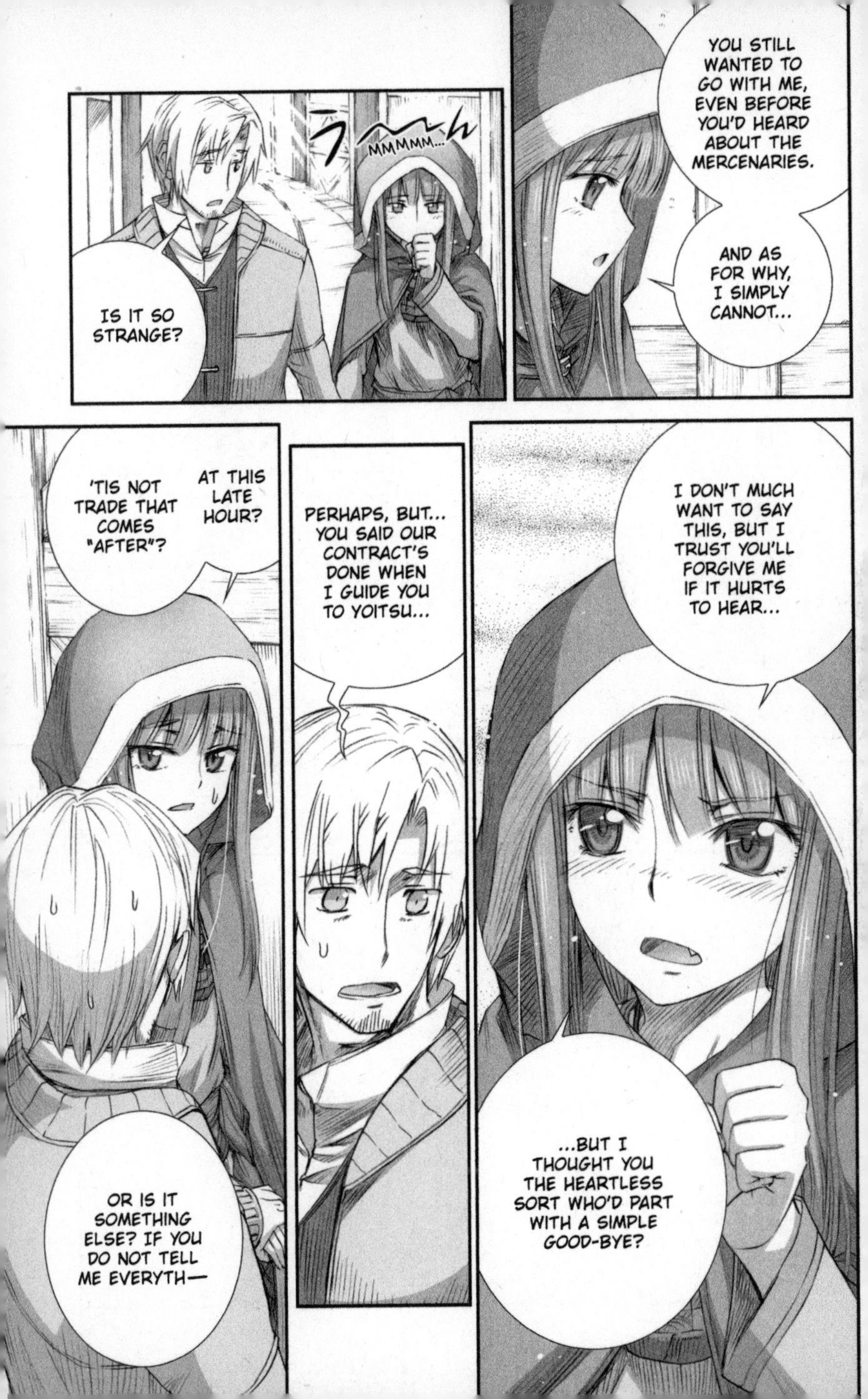
YOU STILL WANTED TO GO WITH ME, EVEN BEFORE YOU'D HEARD ABOUT THE MERCENARIES.
AND AS FOR WHY, I SIMPLY CANNOT...
うーん
MMMMM...
IS IT SO STRANGE?
I DON'T MUCH WANT TO SAY THIS, BUT I TRUST YOU'LL FORGIVE ME IF IT HURTS TO HEAR...
...BUT I THOUGHT YOU THE HEARTLESS SORT WHO'D PART WITH A SIMPLE GOOD-BYE?
PERHAPS, BUT... YOU SAID OUR CONTRACT'S DONE WHEN I GUIDE YOU TO YOITSU...
AT THIS LATE HOUR?
'TIS NOT TRADE THAT COMES "AFTER"?
OR IS IT SOMETHING ELSE? IF YOU DO NOT TELL ME EVERYTH—

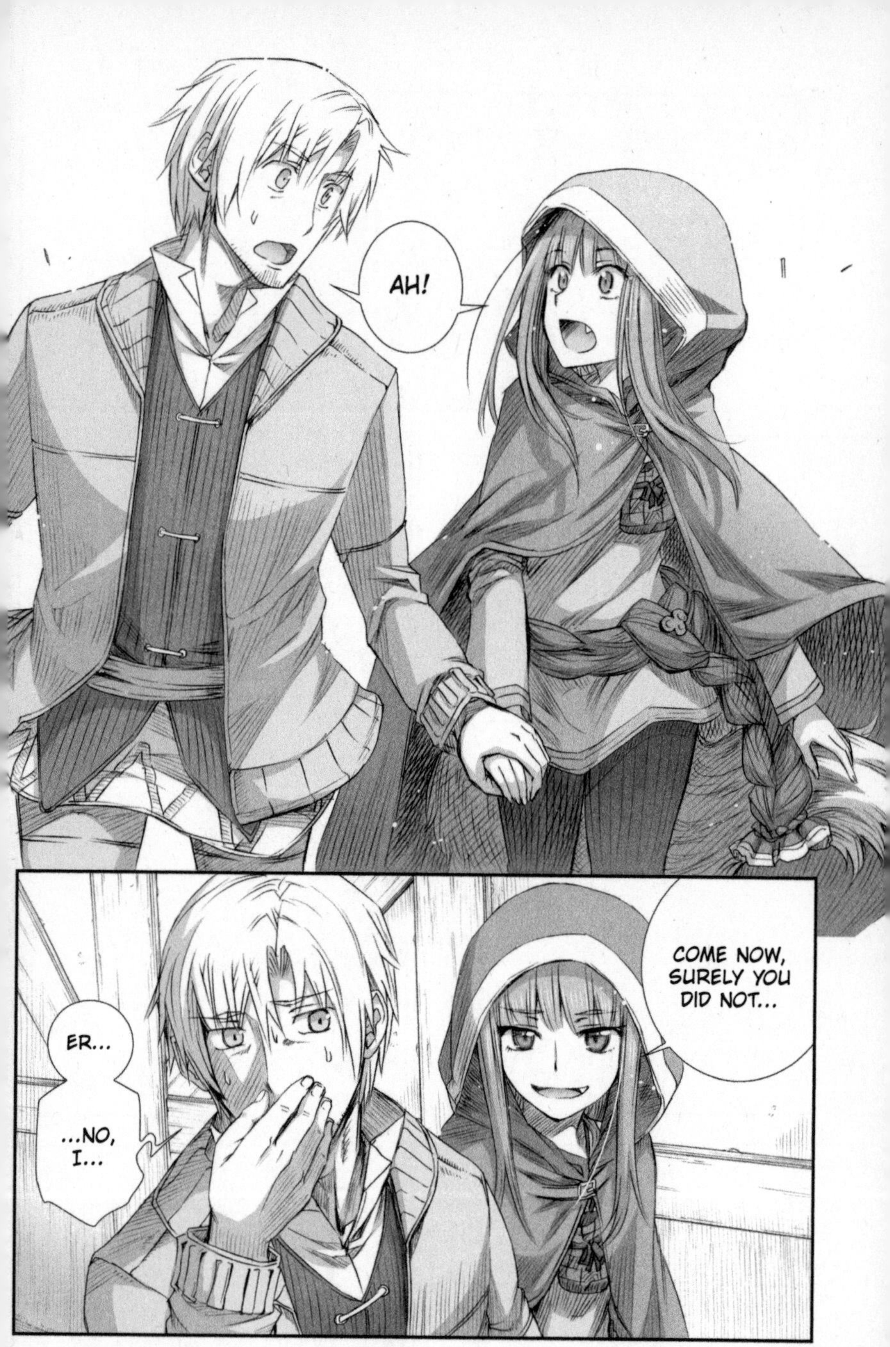
AH!
COME NOW, SURELY YOU DID NOT...
ER...
...NO, I...

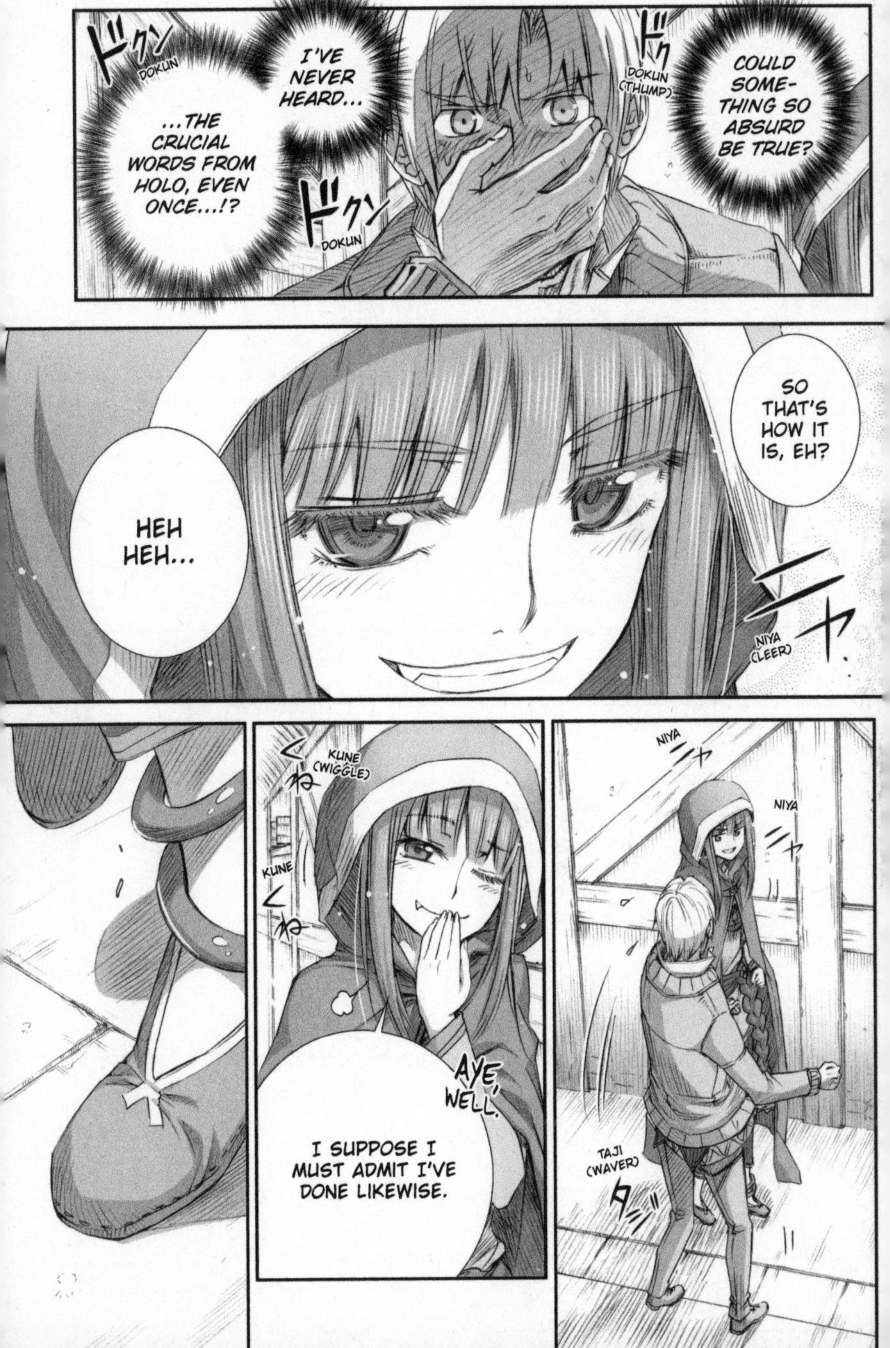
COULD SOMETHING SO ABSURD BE TRUE?
ドク DOKUN (THUMP)
I'VE NEVER HEARD...
ドクン DOKUN
...THE CRUCIAL WORDS FROM HOLO, EVEN ONCE...!?
ドクン DOKUN
SO THAT'S HOW IT IS, EH?
ニヤ NIYA (LEER)
HEH HEH...
ニヤ NIYA
ニヤ NIYA
タジ TAJI (WAVER)
くね KUNE (WIGGLE)
くね KUNE
AYE, WELL.
I SUPPOSE I MUST ADMIT I'VE DONE LIKEWISE.

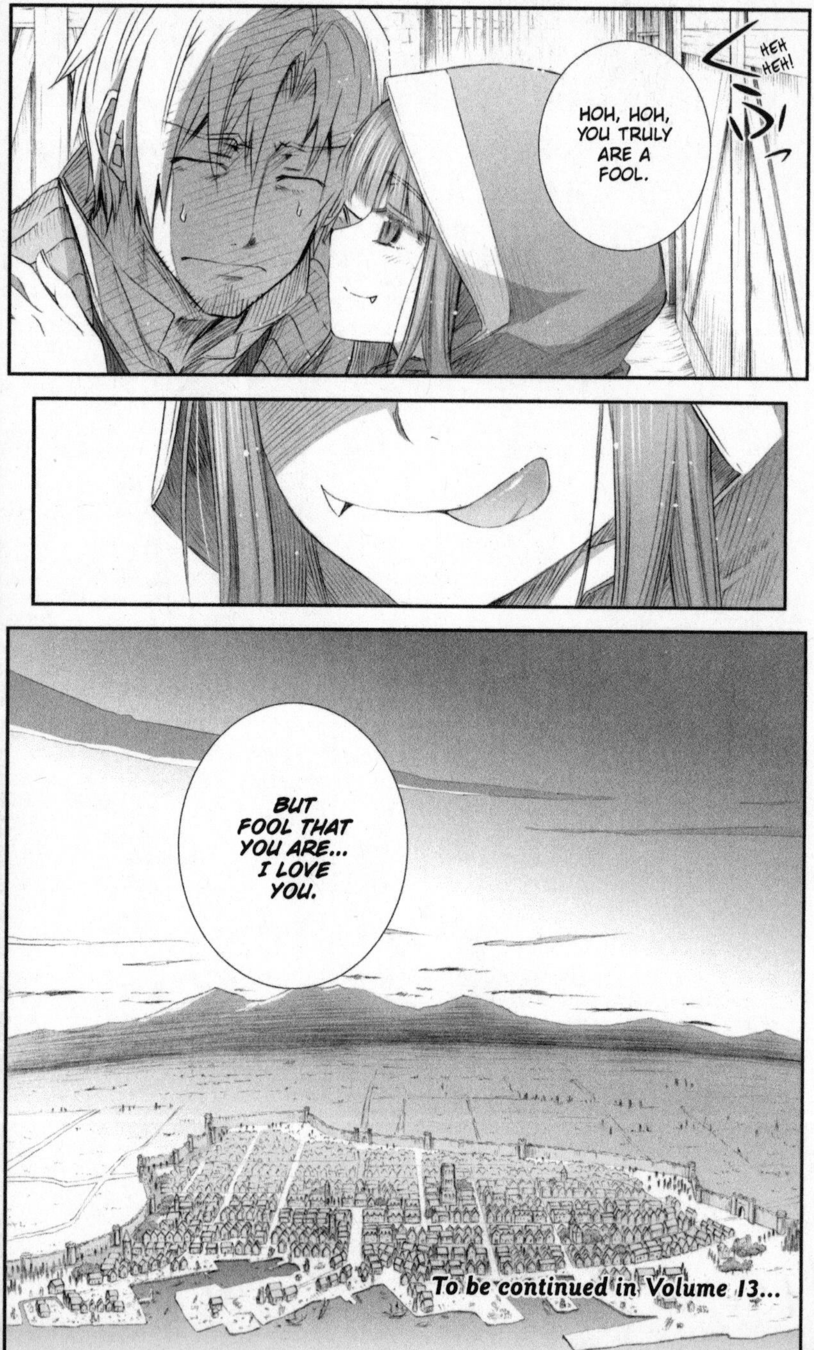
HEH HEH!
HOH, HOH, YOU TRULY ARE A FOOL.
BUT FOOL THAT YOU ARE... I LOVE YOU.
To be continued in Volume 13...

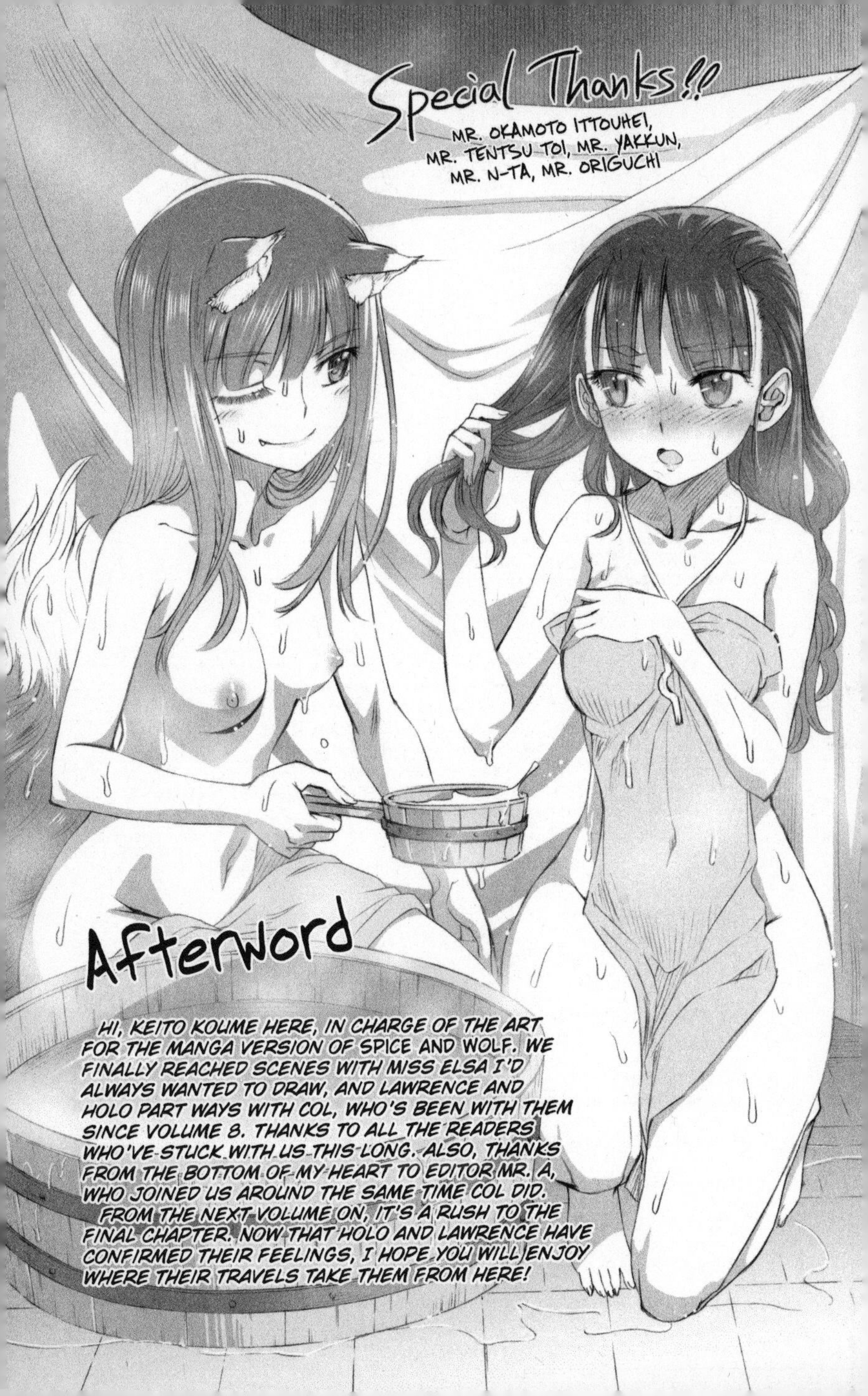

Special Thanks!!

MR. OKAMOTO ITTOUHEI,
MR. TENTSU TOI, MR. YAKKUN,
MR. N-TA, MR. ORIGUCHI

Afterword

HI, KEITO KOUME HERE, IN CHARGE OF THE ART FOR THE MANGA VERSION OF SPICE AND WOLF. WE FINALLY REACHED SCENES WITH MISS ELSA I'D ALWAYS WANTED TO DRAW, AND LAWRENCE AND HOLO PART WAYS WITH COL, WHO'S BEEN WITH THEM SINCE VOLUME 8. THANKS TO ALL THE READERS WHO'VE STUCK WITH US THIS LONG. ALSO, THANKS FROM THE BOTTOM OF MY HEART TO EDITOR MR. A, WHO JOINED US AROUND THE SAME TIME COL DID.

FROM THE NEXT VOLUME ON, IT'S A RUSH TO THE FINAL CHAPTER. NOW THAT HOLO AND LAWRENCE HAVE CONFIRMED THEIR FEELINGS, I HOPE YOU WILL ENJOY WHERE THEIR TRAVELS TAKE THEM FROM HERE!

SPICE & W

Keito Koume
Character design:
Jyuu Ayakura

Translation: Jeremiah Bourque

Lettering: Lys Blakeslee

This book is a work of fiction. Names, characters, places, and incidents are the product of the author's imagination or are used fictitiously. Any resemblance to actual events, locales, or persons, living or dead, is coincidental.

OOKAMI TO KOUSHINRYOU Vol. 12
©Isuna Hasekura/Keito Koume 2015
Edited by ASCII MEDIA WORKS
First published in Japan in 2015 by
KADOKAWA CORPORATION, Tokyo.
English translation rights arranged with
KADOKAWA CORPORATION, Tokyo,
through Tuttle-Mori Agency, Inc., Tokyo.

Translation © 2016 by Hachette Book Group

Yen Press
Hachette Book Group
1290 Avenue of the Americas
New York, NY 10104

www.HachetteBookGroup.com
www.YenPress.com

Yen Press is an imprint of Hachette Book Group, Inc. The Yen Press name and logo are trademarks of Hachette Book Group, Inc.

Library of Congress Control Number: 2015956856

First Yen Press Edition: March 2016

ISBN: 978-0-316-31476-3

10 9 8 7 6 5 4 3 2 1

BVG

Printed in the United States of America